CLIMATE CONSIDERATIONS IN BUILDING AND URBAN DESIGN

CLIMATE CONSIDERATIONS IN BUILDING AND URBAN DESIGN

Baruch Givoni

JOHN WILEY & SONS, INC.

New York • Chichester • Weinheim • Brisbane • Singapore • Toronto

Library of Congress Cataloging-in-Publication Data:

Givoni, Baruch.
    Climate considerations in building and urban design / Baruch Givoni.
      p.   cm.
    Includes bibliographical references.
    ISBN 0-471-29177-3
    1. Architecture and climate. 2. Urban climatology. I. Title.
NA2541.G56   1997
720'.47—dc21   97-22458

CONTENTS

Preface   ix

PART I: BUILDING CLIMATOLOGY   1

CHAPTER 1: COMFORT ISSUES AND CLIMATE ANALYSIS FOR BUILDING DESIGN   3

Introduction   3

Human Responses to the Thermal Environment   5

Effects of the Climate and Other Factors on Heat Discomfort   14

Comfort Indices and Bio-Climatic Charts   22

The Building Bio-Climatic Charts   36

References   46

CHAPTER 2: ARCHITECTURAL FEATURES AFFECTING THE INDOOR CLIMATE   49

Introduction   49

Impacts of Building's Layout on the Indoor Climate   50

Thermal Impacts of Windows' Orientation and Shading
   Conditions   53

Thermal Effect and Efficiency of Shading Devices   62

Thermal Effects of Walls' Orientation and Color   74

Natural Ventilation   87

Architectural Features Affecting Ventilation   92

Experimental Studies on Ventilation   96

References   105

CHAPTER 3: MATERIALS PROPERTIES AND THERMAL PERFORMANCE OF BUILDINGS   107

Introduction   107

Heat Exchange Between the Building and Its Environment   108

Modes of Heat Transfer in Buildings   109

Thermal Properties of Materials and Building Elements   114

Standard Procedures of Building Heat Loss/Gain Calculation   127

Quantifying the Interactions Between Heat Capacity and Thermal Resistance   133

References   148

CHAPTER 4: PASSIVE SOLAR HEATING SYSTEMS   149

Introduction   149

Direct Gain   150

Collecting Storage (Trombe) Walls   159

Convective Loops: The Steve Baer System   167

The Barra System: Insulated, Glazed, Solar Wall, and Storage in Concrete Ceiling   169

Sun Spaces   171

Applicability of the Various Passive Solar Systems   179

References   182

CHAPTER 5: PASSIVE COOLING OF BUILDINGS   185

Introduction   185

Comfort (Daytime) Ventilation   186

Nocturnal Ventilative Cooling   189

Radiant Cooling   191

Evaporative Cooling Towers   196

Indirect Evaporative Cooling   200

The Earth as a Cooling Source   207

References   212

CHAPTER 6: CLIMATIC CHARACTERISTICS OF HOUSING TYPES   213

    Introduction   213

    Single-Family Detached Houses   214

    Town Houses (Row Houses)   217

    Multistoried Apartment Buildings   220

    High-Rise Buildings   230

    Climatic Characteristics of Internal Courtyards and Attached
        Enclosed Open Spaces   232

PART II: URBAN CLIMATOLOGY   239

CHAPTER 7: GENERAL CHARACTERISTICS OF THE URBAN CLIMATE   241

    Introduction   241

    The Urban Temperature: The "Heat Island" Phenomenon   243

    Overall Spatial Pattern of the Urban Heat Island   244

    Heat Island Models   248

    Impact of the Nocturnal Urban Heat Island Phenomenon on
        Human Comfort, Health, and Energy Use in
        Different Climates   254

    The Urban Wind Field   256

    Urban Radiation and Sunshine   266

    References   273

CHAPTER 8: URBAN DESIGN EFFECTS ON THE URBAN CLIMATE   275

    Introduction   275

    Location of a Town within a Region   276

    Effect of Size of Cities on the Urban Heat Island   280

    Climatic Effects of Density of the Built-Up Area   281

    Climatic Impacts of Street Width and Orientation   286

    Impact of Urban Density on Energy Demand and Potential for Solar
        Energy Utilization   291

    Urban Density and the Urban Wind Field   293

    Pedestrian Reactions to Excessively Windy Environments   295

Special Design Details of Buildings Affecting
    the Outdoor Conditions   298
References   301

CHAPTER 9: IMPACT OF GREEN AREAS ON SITE AND URBAN CLIMATES   303

Introduction   303
Functions and Impacts of Urban Green Areas   304
Effect of Plants on the Environmental Conditions   306
Climatic Impact of Plants Around Buildings   308
Experimental Studies on the Thermal Effect of Planted Areas   309
Climatic Effects of Public Urban Parks and Playgrounds   318
Impact of Green Spaces on Air Pollution   320
Planted Areas as Noise Controls   322
Social Functions of Urban Parks   324
References   327

PART III: BUILDING AND URBAN DESIGN GUIDELINES   331

CHAPTER 10: BUILDING AND URBAN DESIGN FOR HOT-DRY REGIONS   333

Introduction   333
Characteristics of Hot-Dry Regions   333
Comfort and Energy Conservation Issues in Hot-Dry Regions   337
Architectural Guidelines for Hot-Dry Regions   340
Building Materials in Desert Regions   358
Building Types Considerations in Hot-Dry Climates   363
Urban Design in Hot-Dry Regions   366
References   376

CHAPTER 11: BUILDING AND URBAN DESIGN FOR HOT-HUMID REGIONS   379

Introduction   379
Climatic Considerations of Hot-Humid Regions Relevant to Building and
    Urban Design   380
Architectural Guidelines for Hot-Humid Regions   382

Structural Design and Choice of Materials in
   Hot-Humid Regions   397
Climatic Characteristics of Different Building Types in Hot-Humid
   Regions   404
Urban Design Guidelines for Hot-Humid Regions   407
References   414

**CHAPTER 12: BUILDING AND URBAN DESIGN
IN COLD CLIMATES**   417
Introduction   417
Building and Extended Site Design in Cold Climates   418
Urban Design in Cold Climates   422
References   429

**CHAPTER 13: REGIONS WITH COLD WINTERS
AND HOT-HUMID SUMMERS**   431
Introduction   431
Climatic Characteristics and Thermal Comfort Requirements   432
Building Design Considerations   434
Urban Configuration for Regions with Hot-Humid Summers and Cold
   Winters   437

Index   443

PREFACE

This book has three parts. Part I, **Building Climatology,** deals with human thermal comfort and with the effect of various architectural and structural design elements on the indoor climate. Special chapters deal with passive solar heating, especially in regions with hot summers, and with passive cooling of buildings.

Part II, **Urban Climatology,** deals with the specific features by which the climate in densely built urban areas differs from the surrounding regional climatic conditions, and with various urban design elements affecting the outdoor climatic conditions in cities, as well. It presents an analysis of the design factors which impact the urban climate, the energy demand of a town, and the potential for utilizing solar and other natural energies for heating and cooling of buildings.

Part III, **Building and Urban Design Guidelines,** applies the basic information contained in the previous parts to the design of buildings and cities in different climates. It provides recommendations with respect to specific design features, for buildings and for settlements, which can improve comfort and energy conservation in the particular climate.

THE INDOOR CLIMATE

The climatic conditions inside buildings (indoor climate) are different from the surrounding outdoor climate. Indoors, people are protected from the solar radiation to which people outdoors are exposed. Indoor temperatures are usually different from the outdoor temperature, even when the buildings are not mechanically heated or cooled. Indoor air in closed buildings is calm even when outdoor wind speeds are high. When buildings are naturally ventilated the indoor air speeds are related to, but different from, the wind speeds surrounding the buildings. The actual relationship between the indoor and the outdoor climates depends to a great extent on the architectural and structural design of the buildings and thus the indoor climate can be controlled by building design to accommodate human comfort needs.

THE OUTDOOR (URBAN) CLIMATE

The outdoor temperature and wind speed conditions to which an individual building is exposed may differ appreciably from those in the surrounding natural or rural environs (regional climate). Differences exist also in the humidity, wind conditions, solar radiation and long-wave nocturnal radiation, fog, and precipitation, as well as in the turbidity and chemical quality of the air.

The urban local microclimate is modified by the "structure" of the city, mainly of the neighborhood where a given building is located. The urban microclimatic conditions thus form the immediate environment of the individual buildings. This modified climate directly affects the indoor comfort conditions and the energy use of the inhabitants for heating and/or air conditioning.

INTERACTIONS BETWEEN THE URBAN CLIMATE AND BUILDINGS

The urban geometry and profile—shape, height, and size of the buildings, orientation of streets and of buildings, and nature of the surfaces of the urban open areas—all these factors have an impact on the urban climate. Thus each urban manmade element (buildings, roads, parking area, factories, etc.) creates around and above it a modified climate with which it interacts.

Complex interaction and feedback exists between the buildings and their outdoor environment. On one hand, the indoor climate and comfort conditions in any given building depend on the climatic conditions surrounding the building. But, on the other hand, the building itself, and especially groups of buildings, modifies the climatic conditions surrounding it.

A number of building design details have a marked influence on the climatic conditions affecting pedestrians walking outdoors, especially with regard to protection from rain, sun, and glare in the streets.

Protection from sun and rain for pedestrians on the sidewalks can be provided by buildings with overhanging roofs, or colonnades, in which the ground floor is set back from the edge of the road, with the upper stories jutting out, supported by pillars (or other means). Such protection can create more pleasant climatic conditions for the urban pedestrian. Planned use of such means can be very important with respect to lessening the thermal load on pedestrians in the city's streets.

The color of the building's walls affects not only the interior climate conditions, but also the light and glare in the streets. Light colors, especially white, reflect the solar radiation and thus reduce the heat gain of the building and its indoor temperatures. Thus, white buildings are preferable from the indoor climate aspect in hot climates but increase the glare in the streets. In this respect there may be, in some instances, a conflict between the requirements concerning indoor climate and those necessary to reduce the glare in the streets.

However, appropriate design details can resolve the conflict between these demands. For example, horizontal overhangs from buildings, which protect the windows from solar radiation, can be extended over the entire length of the wall. Thus they will also shade the wall below the projections from direct solar radiation while hiding part of the sunlit wall above them, and in this manner also reduce the glare at the street level.

Thus the urban climate and the building indoor climate are both parts of a climatological continuum, differing in scale, which starts with the regional natural climate and is modified at the urban scale by the structure of the town, and at the site scale by the individual buildings.

STATE OF KNOWLEDGE IN BUILDING AND IN URBAN CLIMATOLOGY

Research on building climatology has produced a comprehensive understanding of the effect of building design on the indoor climate and energy use of buildings. This subject is discussed in the first part of this book.

On the other hand, systematic research into the effect of town physical planning on urban climate has started only recently. Most previous studies were confined to registering climatic differences between the urban core and the surrounding country, without taking into account the various physical features of the towns in question and the effect of these features on the observed climatic differences. Recently, however, the effect of specific urban design details on various components of the urban climate has been studied by various investigators, either experimentally or by mathematical simulation. The information on this subject is summarized in the second part of the book.

Based on these studies, and on a general understanding of the factors affecting the relationship between the regional and the (modified) urban climates, it is possible to suggest guidelines for urban design in different climates, as discussed in the third part of this book. Such guidelines have to be different for each climate because the objectives and comfort requirements are different. For example, in cold regions the objectives may be to minimize the wind near the ground and to elevate the urban temperature, while in hot climates the objectives would be quite the opposite.

Emphasis is placed on problems arising in warm climates and in climates with cold winters but hot summers, in light of the personal experience of the author.

Two types of climates, namely hot-dry and hot-humid, are discussed in relatively greater detail than other types, because they have a dominant "problematic" summer season. Other regions, which have composite climates, cold winters and hot-humid summers, were discussed in less detail, because the problems encountered in each season were discussed in detail in the chapters dealing with the "single problem season" regions.

CLIMATE CONSIDERATIONS IN BUILDING AND URBAN DESIGN

Part I

Building Climatology

Chapter **1**: COMFORT ISSUES AND CLIMATE ANALYSIS FOR BUILDING DESIGN

INTRODUCTION

This chapter deals with issues of human thermal comfort and comfort standards, and their impact on climate analysis as a basis for formulating building design principles for different climates, especially hot climates. It also discusses the implications of comfort standards on evaluating the needs for mechanical cooling and on the energy use (and often waste) in air conditioned buildings.

Thermal comfort can be defined operationally as the range of climatic conditions considered comfortable and acceptable inside buildings. It implies an absence of any sensation of thermal (heat or cold) discomfort. In dealing with heat discomfort there are two distinct and independent sources of discomfort: the thermal sensation of heat and discomfort resulting from skin wetness (sensible perspiration). Therefore, in delimiting the climatic boundaries of the "comfort zone," it is useful to start with analysis of the nature of these two sources of thermal discomfort and their relationship to various climatic factors.

Analysis of the climatic conditions of a given place is the starting point in formulating building and urban design principles aimed at maximizing comfort and minimizing the use of energy for heating and cooling. The presentation of the climatic data is usually in graphic forms, enabling the reader to grasp the diurnal patterns in different seasons and the average annual interrelationship between several climatic elements. Often the climatic graphs contain the boundaries of human thermal comfort as the basis for evaluation of the severity of the outdoor climate, the needs for heating and/or for cooling, as well as the design options for improving the indoor conditions.

The first published graphic presentation of climatic data, designed specifically as a basis for evaluating human comfort needs and building design objectives, was by Olgyay (1963). His procedure of graphical presentation and interpretation of climatic data had profound impact, and many books and papers on the subject are still using his data.

The problematic of applying Olgyay's procedure and some other currently often used climate analysis tools and comfort standards (such as that of the American Society of Heating, Refrigeration and Air Conditioning [ASHRAE]) for un-air conditioned buildings, especially in developing hot countries, is reviewed in this chapter. (See Givoni 1976 *Man, Climate and Architecture*).

The chapter illustrates the use of the Building Bio-Climatic Charts in establishing the climatic boundaries of applicability of various passive and low-energy cooling systems in different climates. These boundaries are based on the expected indoor temperatures achievable with the different cooling systems. The cooling systems include daytime "comfort" ventilation, the utilization of the structural mass for thermal storage in conjunction with nocturnal ventilation for lowering indoor temperatures, and direct and indirect evaporative cooling. The physical characteristics and the performance of these cooling systems are discussed in Chapter 5 and in more detail in another book, *Passive and Low Energy Cooling of Buildings* (Givoni 1994).

Design and Economic Implications of the Comfort Standards

The issue of defining the boundaries of acceptable indoor comfort conditions in buildings may have significant implications for building design and also may have economic consequences. It affects evaluation of the usefulness of natural ventilation and decisions concerning the need for mechanical air conditioning, as well as the level of energy consumption for heating (and especially for cooling) in air conditioned buildings.

Setting upper limits of temperature and airspeed (often rather low speed) for the acceptable climate conditions in air conditioned buildings means that when the indoor temperature rises above that limit the mechanical cooling will be activated, although in many cases higher temperatures, with a higher airspeed, would be comfortable for the inhabitants. A higher indoor temperature would, of course, lower the heat gain of the buildings and thus lower the energy spent on the cooling.

The impact of the humidity comfort limits affects the energy use for dehumidifying the air, especially in a hot-humid climate. As the effect of humidity on comfort depends greatly on the airspeed (see following section) a low "permissible" indoor airspeed increases the energy (and money) spent on dehumidification.

In un-air conditioned buildings comfort standards affect the design strategies concerning choice of building materials and design for natural ventilation. Comfort boundaries are also the basis for Bio-Climatic Charts, which help in formulating appropriate design principles for different climates.

The opinion of the author is that different comfort standards are justified for countries with different climatic conditions and stages of economic development. Arguments and data supporting this view, and comfort boundaries suggested accordingly, are presented in this chapter.

HUMAN RESPONSES TO THE THERMAL ENVIRONMENT

The body produces heat by food metabolism and this heat is transferred to the environment by convection and radiation ("dry" heat loss). The dry heat exchange can be, of course, also positive (heat gain) when the air and/or temperatures of the surrounding surfaces are higher than that of the skin (about 34°C, 93°F). Some heat is lost by evaporation of water in the lungs, in proportion to the breathing rate which, in turn, is proportional to the metabolic rate. If the dry heat loss is not enough to balance the metabolic rate (and especially when the dry heat exchange is positive), sweat is produced at the skin glands and the evaporation of that sweat provides the additional required cooling.

The convection exchange depends on the ambient air temperature and the airspeed. The radiant exchange, in an indoor environment, depends on the average temperature of the surrounding surfaces (the mean radiant temperature). Outdoors, solar radiation is, of course, the major source of radiant heat gain. The rates of all the modes of heat exchange depend on the clothing properties.

The humidity does not play any role in the dry heat loss. It affects the rate of evaporation from the lungs but, contrary to common notions, ambient humidity does not affect the rate of sweat evaporation, except under extreme conditions. In fact, at higher humidity levels the sweat evaporation rate does not decrease, and may even *increase*. The reason is that in low humidity conditions the sweat evaporates within the skin pores, through a small fraction of the skin area. When the humidity is rising and the evaporative capacity of the environment decreases, the sweat is spread over a larger skin area. In this way the required evaporation rate can be maintained over a larger skin area at the higher humidity. Under certain conditions at high humidity the cooling efficiency of sweat evaporation decreases, when part of the latent heat of vaporization is taken from the ambient air instead of from the skin (Givoni 1976; Givoni and Belding 1962). In such cases the body produces, and evaporates, more sweat than in lower humidity in order to obtain the required physiological cooling.

The state of the body's heat exchange also affects the sensory responses to the environmental thermal conditions, producing sensations of either general comfort, cold discomfort, heat discomfort, and/or discomfort from wetted skin. However, the relationship between the body's heat exchange conditions and the sensory responses is complex and does not lend itself to straightforward correlation.

Two major approaches of research on human responses to the thermal environment can be applied. The first focuses on "thermal comfort," defined from subjective responses of subjects, while the second approach focuses on objective physiological responses to climatic factors and physical activity, aiming at evaluating the level of thermal stress. Comfort studies usually (but not always) deal with lightly clad subjects, at rest or while performing sedentary work. The main application of the results of this approach is in formulating quantitative indoor climate limits, the so-called "comfort standards," for air conditioned buildings, usually offices and public buildings.

The sensory responses to the thermal environment include the sensations of cold, general or localized, of heat, and (in hot, humid conditions), the discomfort from too-wet or too-dry skin (sensible perspiration). The sensations of heat discomfort and of wet skin may or may not be correlated, as discussed below.

People living in hot regions and acclimatized to the prevailing thermal environment would prefer higher temperatures and would suffer less in hot environments than people living in cold regions. This issue is discussed in more detail later in this chapter in the Effects of Heat Acclimatization section.

The physiological research dealing with human responses to the thermal environment has covered the whole range of climatic conditions encountered by humans, from extreme cold to extreme heat. The main physiological human responses to changes in the thermal environment are the sweat rate, heart rate, inner body temperature, and the skin temperature. The comfort range is viewed as a certain limited range within the total range of thermal responses.

Mathematical models predicting with reasonable accuracy these physiological responses—as functions of the climatic conditions, work (metabolic rate) and clothing properties, including acclimatization effect—have been developed and validated (Givoni 1963; Givoni 1976; Givoni and Belding 1962; Givoni and Goldman 1971, 1972, 1973a).

Under rest and sedentary activity conditions, and on the warm side of the comfort range, the most sensitive physiological response to climatic stress is the sweat rate, measured usually in terms of weight loss rate.

The human sensory and physiological responses to the thermal environment are, to some extent, interrelated. The sensation of cold is associated with lower skin temperature. The sensation of heat, for resting or sedentary persons, is correlated with higher skin temperature/higher sweat rate. Both responses reflect a higher thermal load on the body.

The sensory thermal responses are discussed in the following section. (The physiological responses are covered in more detail in Givoni 1976.)

The Thermal Sensation

As noted above, the main sensory thermal responses are the sensations of cold and heat and the discomfort from sensible perspiration.

The thermal sensation, over the whole range from very cold to very hot, is often graded (in comfort studies) along a seven-point numerical scale:

1 cold
2 cool
3 slightly cool
4 neutral (comfortable)
5 slightly warm
6 warm
7 hot

A scale from minus 3 (cold) to +3 (hot) is sometimes used to express the same thermal sensations, with 0 stating neutral sensation. The range from slightly cool to slightly warm can be considered as designating acceptable conditions.

Studies of sensory thermal responses by the author (Givoni 1963, 1976; Jennings and Givoni 1959) have demonstrated that a given individual, after acclimatization, is quite consistent in evaluations of his or her own state of comfort or level of discomfort. One can distinguish not only between the various levels of the preceding scale but also consistently determine intermediate levels. For example, a "vote" of 4.2 may state a feeling of being not entirely comfortable but definitely not slightly warm.

However, each individual has his or her own interpretation of the sensory meaning of the various levels. Consequently, there are significant differences among individuals in the values assigned to a given thermal environment. Therefore, in sensory studies, the *average response* of a group is more significant than the *individual response*, and the *relative response* to different environmental factors is more significant than the *absolute response* in a given climatic combination of these factors.

Cold Discomfort

In dealing with cold discomfort a distinction should be made between "general" sensation of cold discomfort and "localized" discomfort (at the feet, the fingers, and so on). Localized discomfort is mainly experienced outdoors, when the overall insulation of the clothing is adequate but at certain specific points it is insufficient or that part of the body is exposed. Localized discomfort may be also experienced indoors when, for example, cold air "sinking" down large glass doors or windows accumulates near the floor; while the air at higher levels is at a higher temperature, the feet may feel too cold, but without the general sensation of cold. Persons sitting close to the glazing may feel localized discomfort only on the body side facing the glazing.

A correlation exists between the subjective sensation of cold and the physiological response of the average skin temperature. The "general" thermal sensation of cold discomfort is experienced, under steady-state climatic conditions, when the average skin temperature is lowered below the lower level corresponding to the state of comfort, which under sedentary activity is about 32–33°C (90–92°F).

Thermal comfort in buildings in cold climates involves three aspects:

a. Providing comfortable indoor air and mean radiant temperatures of the interior surfaces of the external walls.
b. Prevention of directional radiative cooling, usually from large glazing areas.
c. Prevention of cold "drafts": discomfort resulting from localized cold air currents, usually from cracks between and around the sashes (wind penetration).

The actual level of the comfort zone, especially in winter, depends greatly on clothing. By wearing warmer clothing, it is possible to significantly lower the indoor temperatures and still remain comfortable. The acceptable indoor temperature at night, during the sleeping hours, is usually lower than during the daytime and evening hours.

Heat Discomfort

The thermal sensation of heat discomfort is experienced, under steady-state conditions, when average skin temperature is elevated above the upper level corresponding to the state of comfort which, under sedentary activity, is about

33–34°C (91.4–93.2°F). However, the rate of elevation of the skin temperature when the ambient temperature rises above the comfort zone is much smaller than the rate of drop when the temperature falls below the comfort zone. The reason is that sweat evaporation reduces the rate of skin temperature rise.

The comfort skin temperature, T_s, is *lowered* with increasing metabolic rate, M, (physical activity) as a result of a higher sweat-evaporation rate and a diversion of blood flow from the peripheral skin to the working muscles, a point discovered by Fanger (discussed later in this chapter in The Fanger Comfort Equation).

Sensible Perspiration

Thermal comfort is also associated with a neutral state of skin moisture (absence of discomfort from a wet skin). While thermal sensation exists in both cold and hot conditions the perception of sensible perspiration exists only on the warm side of the comfort zone, in specific combinations of temperature, humidity, air motion, clothing, and physical activity. It is of special significance in hot-humid climates.

This sensation has two distinct limits. The lower limit is when the skin is completely dry and the upper limit is when the whole body and clothing are soaked with sweat. Between these two limits there are intermediate levels which can be defined quite clearly.

When the evaporation rate is much faster than sweat secretion, the sweat evaporates as it emerges from the pores of the skin, without forming a liquid layer over the skin. The skin is then felt as "dry."

With increasing sweat rate, or decreased rate of evaporation, sweat spreads over the skin, increasing the effective area from which evaporation takes place. In this way the body can keep a rate of evaporation cooling sufficient to maintain thermal equilibrium over a wide range of the evaporative potential of the environment. However, *subjectively* the moist skin causes discomfort although it is an essential ingredient in the physiological thermo-regulation.

The rate of sweating is determined by the balance between metabolic heat production and the heat loss by convection and radiation. Under hot-humid conditions the cooling efficiency of sweating decreases, as part of the sweat evaporates over hair and the clothing and derives part of the energy from the ambient air instead of from the body. The sweat rate and evaporation then *exceed* the need for evaporation cooling to compensate for the reduced cooling efficiency.

Sensible-perspiration perception can be expressed by the following numerical scale:

0 Forehead and body completely dry
1 Skin clammy but moisture invisible
2 Moisture visible
3 Forehead or body wet (sweat covering the surface; formation of drops)
4 Clothing partially wet
5 Clothing almost completely wet
6 Clothing soaked
7 Sweat dripping off clothing

In several physiological studies (Givoni 1963; Jennings and Givoni 1959) the subjective sensation of sensible perspiration was recorded under controlled conditions over a wide range of climatic conditions.

The author has developed a mathematical model predicting the subjective response of sensible perspiration to the climatic conditions, clothing, and metabolic rate. It was found that the sensation of skin wetness (by the above scale) can be expressed as a function of the ratio E/E_{max}, where E is the required evaporative cooling, which equals to the physiological (total metabolic and environmental) heat stress, and E_{max} is the evaporative capacity of the air (Givoni 1963, 1976)

$$S.P. = -0.3 + 5 \ (E/E/E_{max})$$

where:

$E \quad = (M - W) + (C + R)$
$E_{max} = pV^{0.3} * (35 - HR_a)$
$M \quad =$ Metabolic rate
$W \quad =$ Mechanical work performed by the body
$C \quad =$ Convective heat exchange
$R \quad =$ Radiant heat exchange
$V \quad =$ Airspeed over the body (m/s)
$HR_a =$ Humidity ratio of air (gr/kg)
$p \quad =$ Coefficient depending on clothing type

All the energy units are in kilocalories per hour (Givoni 1976).

Relationship Between Heat Sensation and Sensible Perspiration

These two types of discomfort may be experienced simultaneously or one of them experienced without the other. They can be affected by air velocity in opposite ways. Therefore, in different climatic types one or the other discomfort source is predominant. The following examples will illustrate such cases.

In a desert the humidity is very low, and wind speed is high. Discomfort is due exclusively to a feeling of excessive heat. The skin is actually too dry, although sweating is high (about 250 gr/hr, 0.55 lb/hr for a resting person). Evaporative potential far exceeds the rate of sweat secretion, so that sweat evaporation takes place within the skin pores. The skin's excessive dryness itself may become a source of irritation. Alleviation can be achieved by lowering the wind speed at the skin (e.g., by closing the openings) and, mainly, by lowering the ambient temperature.

In contrast to the desert situation, discomfort in a warm-humid region, especially in still-air conditions, may be mainly due to excessive skin wetness. The air temperature in such regions is often below 26°C (79°F), and the rate of sweat secretion, at sedentary activity, is rather low (about 60 gr/hr, 0.13 lb/hr, per person). In spite of the low rate of sweating, the skin becomes wet because the evaporative potential of the still, humid air is very low. The physiological thermal balance is maintained, in spite of the lower evaporative potential, because the required evaporation rate is achieved over a larger wetted area of the skin. In practice, when the airspeed is suddenly increased, a sensation of chilliness may also accompany discomfort from the wet skin until the skin dries out sufficiently.

Alleviation of discomfort due to skin wetness is best achieved, in the absence of dehumidification, by maintaining a high-enough air velocity so that the required evaporation can be obtained with a smaller wetted area of the skin. Another option is to wear clothing of greater permeability (or to take off most clothes, as is common on a beach).

There are, of course, many climatic situations in which thermal discomfort results from the combined effects of heat sensation and sensible perspiration. Higher indoor air velocity can then be very effective in alleviating discomfort, especially when the air temperature is below about 33°C (91.5°F).

The boundaries of temperature and humidity within the acceptable comfort can be maintained by sedentary people under still-air conditions and with airspeed of 2 m/s (400 ft/min), as is discussed later in this chapter.

Relationship Between Physiological Heat Stress (Sweat Rate) and Thermal Sensation

On the hot side of the comfort range, both the sweat rate (expressing the physiological stress) and the thermal sensation of heat respond to changes in temperature, humidity, and airspeed. However, there is a basic difference in the pattern of the physiological and the sensory responses. The physiological response to higher temperature is almost linear up to the upper tolerance level, about 50°C, (122°F). On the other hand, the subjective ability to distinguish between the different "levels" of discomfort, as specified by the customary scales, is not linear.

This difference in the "scaling" of the responses is illustrated in Figure 1-1, which shows the correlation between measured weight loss (representing the sweat rate) and the subjective responses of thermal sensations and skin wetness of subjects at sedentary activity. The data are from extensive research on the physiological and sensory effects of the climatic conditions, metabolic rate, and clothing properties (Givoni 1963).

The subjects in these series of experiments were dressed in light summer clothing and engaged in sedentary activity for three hours. The temperature

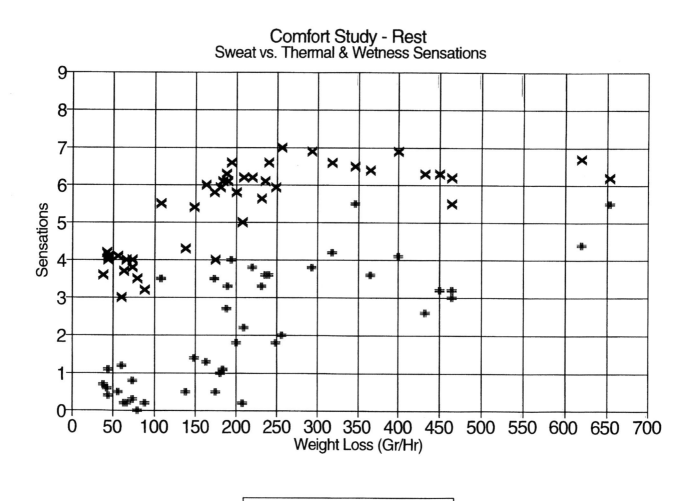

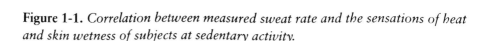

Figure 1-1. *Correlation between measured sweat rate and the sensations of heat and skin wetness of subjects at sedentary activity.*

range in the different series was from 20 to 45°C (68 to 113°F), the vapor content from 8 to about 28 gr/kg (0.008 to 0.028 lb/lb), and the airspeed from still to 4 m/s (800 ft/min).

The weight loss of sedentary subjects represents the overall physiological climatic stress. It can be seen from Figure 1-1 that, up to a sweat rate of about 250 gr/hr (0.55 lb/hr), there is linear relationship with the thermal sensation, from 4 (comfortable) to 6 (warm). However, the subjects could not clearly express the subjective heat sensation ("hot" and "very hot" or "unbearably hot"), or the sensation of skin wetness, at climatic stress levels expressed by a sweat rate above 250–300 gr/hr (0.55–0.65 lb/hr).

The relationship of the skin wetness to the sweat rate is rather poor. In the range of 150 to 250 gr/hr (0.33 to 0.55 lb/hr) of weight loss there is a wide spread of the skin wetness, from about 0.2 (dry skin) to 4 (clothing partially

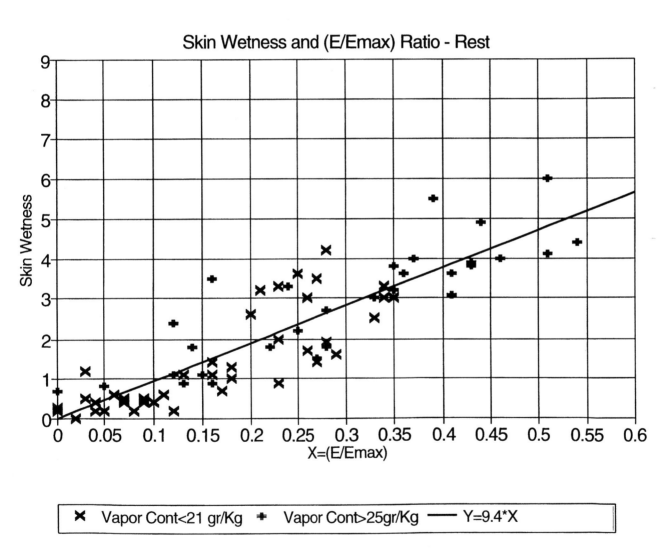

Figure 1-2. *Relationship between sensible perspiration (skin wetness) and the* E/E_{max} *ratio.*

wet). This variability of the response was caused by the different humidity and wind speed conditions.

Relationship Between Skin Wetness and the Ratio E/E_{max}

The lack of a clear relationship between the sweat rate and the skin wetness can be explained by the fact that a given level of physiological heat stress, manifested by a given sweat rate, can be caused by either high temperature at low humidity and high wind speed (in a desert) or by a medium temperature at high humidity and still air (in a hot-humid climate). In the first case the skin will be dry, as the high evaporative capacity of the air evaporates the sweat as it just emerges from the skin pores. In the second case discomfort can be caused by wet skin, as sweat has to spread out over most of the skin in order to enable the required evaporation to take place in spite of the low evaporative capacity of the air.

Givoni has found that the sensation of skin wetness is related linearly to the ratio of the required evaporative cooling (E = the physiological heat stress) to the evaporative capacity of the air (E_{max}). Both E and E_{max} are computable (Givoni 1963, 1976). Figure 1-2 on the preceding page shows the relationship between the sensible perspiration and the E/E_{max} ratio. Further discussion of the effect of the E/E_{max} ratio is presented later in this chapter.

EFFECTS OF THE CLIMATE AND OTHER FACTORS ON HEAT DISCOMFORT

Heat discomfort may involve, as mentioned previously, two separate sensations: sensible heat and sensible perspiration. These two sensations are affected differently by the temperature, humidity, and airspeed. The effect of these climatic elements depends greatly on the clothing and physical activity. The quantitative effect of each one of these factors depends on the levels of the other factors, so that there are strong interactions between the physiological and sensory effects.

The Environmental (Air and Radiant) Temperature

The air temperature determines the convective heat exchange between the skin and the ambient air. The average skin temperature, in indoor situations, is about 33–34°C (91–93°F). With lower air temperature the body loses heat; with higher temperatures it gains heat by convection. The rate of convective heat exchange depends on the airspeed (roughly proportional to the square root of the speed). It is greatly affected by the insulation value of the clothing (the CLO value).

The mean radiant temperature of the enclosure (in practice, the average temperature of the surrounding surfaces) determines the radiant heat exchange between the skin and the environment, similar to the effect of air temperature on the convective heat exchange.

Heat discomfort inside buildings is correlated mainly with the environmental temperature and the airspeed over the body. The environmental temperature expresses the combined effect of the air temperature and the mean radiant temperature of the enclosure. When air and mean radiant temperatures are not the same, the Globe Temperature, as measured by a Globe Thermometer, is a reasonable measure of the resulting environmental temperature.

The effect of the environmental temperature on comfort is straightforward: raising temperature always results in a correspondent change in the thermal sensation. The conditions of humidity and airspeed modify the magnitude of the temperature effect but do not change its direction.

Effect of Humidity on Comfort

The impact of humidity on human thermal balance and on comfort is complex. Humidity does not directly affect the heat balance and the sensory or physiological responses to the thermal environment, except for the evaporation within the lungs. The role of humidity is in its effect on the environmental potential for evaporation and the way by which the body adapts to changes in the evaporative potential. The evaporative capacity of the air (E_{max}) is a function of the air humidity (vapor pressure) and airspeed.

When the dry heat loss (plus evaporation within the lungs) is not sufficient to balance the metabolic heat production the body activates the sweat glands to get the required additional cooling by evaporation (E_{req}). As the dry heat exchange is a function of the air and radiant temperatures and the airspeed, any change in these climatic elements directly affects the required evaporative cooling—the human thermal sensation of heat and the physiological thermal control mechanisms.

Very low humidity may cause irritation: the skin becomes too dry and cracks may appear in some membranes (e.g., the lips). At higher humidity levels its effect on human comfort and physiology is indirect, through its effect on the evaporative capacity of the air. A higher humidity reduces the evaporative cooling potential from a given surface area of the skin, but the body can counter this reduction by spreading the sweat over the skin and thus increasing the fraction of the skin surface from which evaporation takes place. As a result of this physiological control mechanism the same amount of sweat evaporation, and of evaporative cooling, can be obtained over a wide range of humidity.

Up to a certain limit of the skin's "wetted" area, and the increase in humidity which causes it, a person does not have any change in his or her sensations, and within this range of humidity the changes in its level are imperceptible. Therefore, when lines of equal comfort sensations are plotted on a psychrometric chart, the lines should be vertical and not affected by the temperature. Beyond this range, however, the skin wetness becomes subjectively excessive and causes a distinct sense of discomfort, namely sensible perspiration.

It should be realized that the increased wetness of the skin is, physiologically, a positive adaptation to the lower evaporative potential or to a need for a higher evaporative cooling. However, subjectively, it causes discomfort. The level of this discomfort depends in part on the clothing: a person in a bathing suit on the beach would not feel discomfort at skin wetness levels which would be very uncomfortable when dressed in a business suit. It is also probable that acclimatization to hot-humid conditions affect the sensitivity to skin wetness. If so, it would have an impact on the range of acceptable humidity level as demarcated in comfort diagrams. No research on this subject is known to the author, and such research would be very useful.

The issue of the physiological and sensory effects of humidity was a subject of extensive research studies by the author (Givoni 1963; Jennings and Givoni 1959; Givoni and Belding 1962; Givoni and Goldman 1972, 1973a). The results of this research are summarized briefly in the following paragraphs.

The first research project dealing specifically with the effect of humidity in which the author was involved, in 1958–1959, was conducted at the Central Research Laboratory of ASHRAE, then located in Cleveland, with the lab's Director, Professor B.H. Jennings. The objective of this study was to examine the original Effective Temperature Index, which was developed at the same laboratory in 1923–1925.

This study has demonstrated that up to about 25°C (77°F), the (sedentary) subjects could not experience any difference between relative humidities of 30 and 80 percent, in their subjective sensations: thermal sensation and skin wetness (sensible perspiration). Also, no difference was found in their physiological responses: sweat rate, body temperature, and heart rate. Only above that temperature, near the upper humidity level, did the subjects sense a difference in the environment. Subsequent physiological studies, extended to higher temperatures and metabolic levels (Givoni 1963), have provided a better understanding of the dependence of the effect of humidity on the combination of temperature, airspeed, clothing properties, and metabolic rate, as discussed below.

The physiological effect of humidity, at still-higher levels of temperature and metabolic rates, was also studied by the author at the U.S. Army Institute of Environmental Medicine (USARIEM), in Natick, Massachusetts (Givoni and Goldman 1972, 1973, 1973b). In these studies a set of mathematical models was developed, predicting the physiological responses to the factors specified above. These models were validated by comparison with results from many extensive physiological studies in several countries and the comparison has yielded high correlations.

These physiological models, together with the studies of the subjective responses to changing humidity levels, summarize the effect (on noneffect) of humidity as follows: The factor which determines the limit of conditions in which the humidity level does not have any effect is the ratio of the evaporative cooling required for thermal balance (E_{req}) to the evaporative capacity of the air (E_{max}), i.e., the E_{req}/E_{max} ratio.

The importance of this ratio was first discussed by Belding and Hatch (1955), during the development of their "Heat Stress Index," which directly represents this ratio. However, Givoni 1963 demonstrated that this ratio only indirectly determines the physiological heat stress, through its effect on the cooling efficiency of the sweating (Givoni and Belding 1962).

It was found that as long as the ratio E_{req}/E_{max} is below about 0.2 the humidity does not have any observable effect, either physiological or sensory. Above an E_{req}/E_{max} ratio of about 0.3 there starts a drop in the cooling efficiency of sweat evaporation, which increases progressively with higher values of E_{req}/E_{max}, as part of the latent heat is taken from the ambient air instead of from the body. Thus, above this limit, humidity has progressively greater physiological and sensory effects, which can be calculated. Details about the calculations of E_{req} and E_{max}, as functions of all the above factors, are given in Givoni 1976.

Effect of Air Speed on Comfort

The criterion for defining an "acceptable" airspeed may be different in residential buildings and in office buildings. The *ASHRAE Guide* (1985) specifies an upper limit of 0.8 m/s (160 ft/min) for indoor airspeed, presumably to prevent papers flying around and/or feeling cold drafts from the cooled air flowing out of the ventilation system's diffusers. In naturally ventilated residential buildings, on the other hand, the airspeed limit can be based on its effect on comfort which, of course, depends on the temperature.

The effect of airspeed on comfort depends on the environmental temperature and humidity, as well as on the clothing. At temperatures below about 33°C (91.5°F), increasing air velocity reduces the heat sensation due to the higher convective heat loss from the body and the lowering of the skin temperature. At temperatures between about 33 and 37°C (91.5 and 98.5°F), air velocity does not affect significantly the thermal sensation, although it might have very significant effect on discomfort from excessive skin wetness, depending on the humidity level and the type of clothing. At temperatures above about 37°C (98.5°F), increased air velocity actually increases the thermal sensation of heat, although it still reduces skin wetness and so might be desirable.

Alleviation of discomfort due to skin wetness is best achieved, in the absence of dehumidification, by maintaining a high-enough airspeed over the body, so that the required evaporation can be obtained with a smaller wetted area of the skin. Another option is to wear clothing of greater permeability (or to take off most clothes as is common on a beach).

STUDY OF TANABE

Tanabe (1988) has studied the comfort reactions of Japanese subjects to various airspeeds, up to 1.6 m/s (320 ft/min) and at temperatures from about 27 to 31°C (80.6 to 87.8°F) with relative humidity of 50 percent. The *preferred* airspeed increased with higher temperatures, from 1 m/s (200 fpm) at 27°C (80.5°F) to 1.6 m/s (320 fpm) at 31°C (88°F) (all preferred airspeeds were above the upper limit recommended by ASHRAE—0.8 m/s (160 fpm). Figure 1-3 (after Tanabe 1988) shows the preferred airspeed of the subjects as a function of the temperature, together with the ASHRAE airspeed limit.

Tanabe also cites the study of McIntyre 1978, in which the subjects were allowed to regulate the speed of overhead ceiling fans. The subjects increased the airspeed up to 2 m/s (400 fpm) at a temperature of 30°C (86°F). In a comprehensive physiological research of the author the effect of airspeeds on comfort and general feeling of pleasantness was monitored, up to a speed of 4 m/s (800 fpm). At air temperature of 30°C (86°F) and airspeed of 2 m/s (400 fpm) the subjects were comfortable, without noticing excessive wind (Givoni 1963).

STUDY OF WU

Wu (1988) has studied the effect of airspeeds on comfort, at three "warm" temperatures having the same "Effective Temperature" of 31°C (88°F) at the Arizona State University. The three temperature/humidity combinations: Dry Bulb Temperature (DBT), (C)/Wet Bulb Temperature (WBT), and (C)/moisture content (gr/kg)* were: 31/23.3/14.5, 32/21.7/12, and 33/20.6/11. The airspeeds

---

* The moisture content was derived from the DBT and WBT data as plotted on a standard psychrometric chart, thus not taking into effect the higher elevation of Phoenix, Arizona.

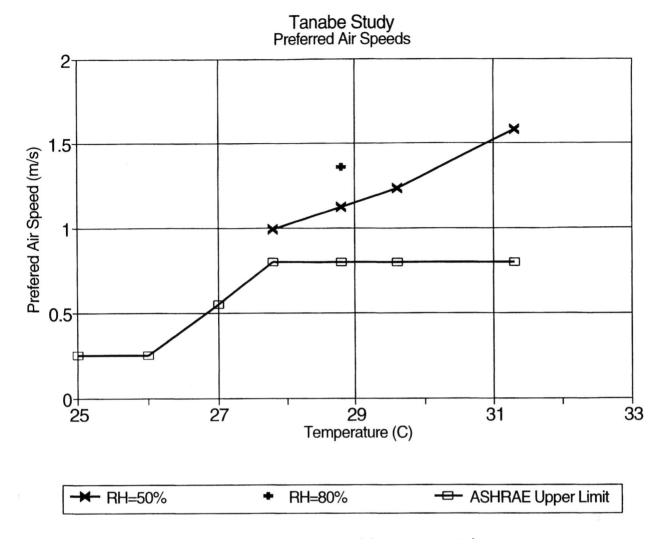

Figure 1-3. *Preferred airspeed of the subjects as a function of the temperature (after Tanabe 1988).*

were produced by oscillating fans, so that at different distances from the fans different speeds were generated, with maximum speeds of 0.25, 0.5, 1.0, and 1.5 m/s (50, 100, 200, and 300 fpm). Still air of about 0.1 m/s (20 fpm), without operation of the fans, has served as a control.

Ninety-three subjects in light summer clothing, all acclimatized to Arizona's hot-arid summer climate, took part in this study and all subjects were required to participate in tests with the four airspeeds. Thermal sensations were recorded on a 1–9 scale (1 = very cold, 5 = comfortable, 9 = very hot). The range between votes of 4 (slightly cool) and 6 (slightly warm) may be considered as designating acceptable conditions in naturally ventilated (un-air conditioned) buildings. Table 1-1 (adapted from Wu 1988) summarizes the mean thermal sensation votes at the different test conditions.

Figure 1-4 illustrates the comfort data of Wu as a function of the airspeed, showing the effect of higher airspeeds in reducing discomfort. It also throws

TABLE 1-1. MEAN THERMAL SENSATION VOTES (5=COMFORTABLE)

Speed	DBT/WBT/H.R. (gr/kg)		
	31/23.3/14/5	32/21.7/12	33/20.6/11
0.1 (m/s)	7.2±0.61	7.1±1.10	6.6±2.20
0.25	6.4±0.97	6.1±1.10	6.2±1.00
0.5	6.4±0.91	5.8±1.00	6.0±0.84
1.0	5.9±0.84	5.7±1.10	5.7±1.00
1.5	5.8±0.87	5.5±0.98	5.6±0.96

(adapted from Wu 1988)

some light on the relative effects of temperature and absolute humidity on comfort, at this range of climatic conditions. Consistently, at 31°C (88°F) and humidity ratio of 14.5 gr/kg (0.0145 lb/lb), the subjects felt less comfortable than at higher temperatures 32 and 33°C (89.5 and 91.4°F) but with lower humidity. At very still air (0.1 m/s) (20 fpm) humidity had more of an effect than tempera-

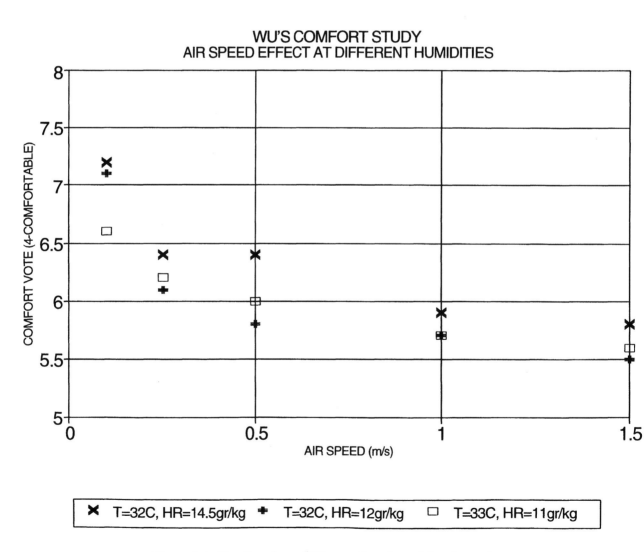

Figure 1-4. *Comfort data of Wu as a function of the airspeed.*

ture, but at airspeeds higher than 0.25 m/s (50 fpm), lower discomfort was experienced at 32°C (89.6°F) and 12 gr/hr (0.012 lb/lb) than at 33°C (91.4°F) and 11 gr/hr (0.011 lb/lb).

At all three combinations of temperature and humidity increasing the airspeed reduced systematically the thermal sensation.

It is notable that even a temperature of 33°C (92°F) with WBT of 20.6°C (69°F) with an airspeed of 1.5 m/s (300 fpm) was considered comfortable by 68 percent of the subjects.

In residential buildings, where distraction from loose papers caused by air motion is generally not a problem as in offices, an airspeed of about 2 m/s (400 fpm) may be quite acceptable. It is therefore suggested that with indoor airspeed of 2 m/s (400 fpm) the comfort zone could be extended to about 30°C (86°F) in the developed countries. For people acclimatized to hot climates in developing countries the suggested upper temperature limit with an airspeed of 2 m/s (400 fpm) would be higher, at about 32°C (89.5°F).

Effects of Heat Acclimatization

Heat acclimatization, namely physiological adaptation to a hot climate or to "artificially" induced heat stress, has an important role in the susceptibility to the physiologically harmful effects of heat and to the sensory discomfort caused by hot environments. Newcomers to a hot region, who previously have lived in cooler regions, are likely to suffer more from the heat than persons already living in these places.

Weihe (1986) cites several studies dealing with this issue: Shattuck and Hilferty (1936) reported on mortality from heat stress in various countries. In comparing soldiers from the British Isles and natives in India, they have found much higher death rates for the British soldiers.

Givoni and Goldman (1973b) have studied the quantitative physiological mechanism of heat adaptation. The main physiological manifestations of improved heat tolerance are a higher sweat rate (providing more evaporative cooling), and lower inner body temperature and heart rate, indicating lowering of the physiological strain imposed by a given heat stress.

It was shown in Givoni and Goldman 1973b that a suitable procedure of "artificial" acclimatization, comprised of daily sessions of controlled work under heat, produces a very significant, almost complete, physiological adaptation which can be achieved within about two weeks.

EFFECTS OF HEAT ACCLIMATIZATION ON THERMAL DISCOMFORT

Numerous studies have indicated that persons living in hot countries prefer higher temperatures than the temperatures recommended by American and European "comfort standards," such as the ASHRAE comfort nomogram and the comfort equation developed by Fanger (1972). This subject is discussed in detail later in this chapter.

Comfort Consideration for Daytime and Nighttime

In many regions there is some conflict, from the building design aspect, between the provision of comfort during the daytime or during the nighttime. For instance, by providing high mass inside an insulated "envelope" of the external surface, the daytime temperature is lowered but the same design solution elevates the nighttime indoor temperature. When such conflicts exist, it is worthwhile to know the physiological consequences of thermal discomfort during daytime and during the night hours. In this way, the most critical period can be determined. It should be stressed, however, that in many cases it is possible to satisfy the conflicting requirements by suitable design solutions, which will be discussed in later chapters of this book.

From the physiological viewpoint, comfort at night is more important than during the daytime. If a person can have good, restful sleep, then high heat stress during the daytime can be tolerated, because at night one can recuperate, so that fatigue is not accumulated.

On the other hand, if the nights are so uncomfortable as to prevent restful sleep, then fatigue accumulates. Over the long period of the summer, such accumulated fatigue can cause more severe consequences than daytime discomfort from which one recovers every night.

COMFORT INDICES AND BIO-CLIMATIC CHARTS

Climate data analysis, aimed at formulating building design guidelines, often involves presentation of the annual patterns of the main climatic factors affecting human comfort and the thermal performance of buildings in various forms, such as graphical monthly patterns of the local temperatures, humidity, wind speed, cloudiness, and so forth, as well as in Bio-Climatic Charts (Olgyay 1963, Givoni 1976).

Bio-Climatic Charts facilitate the analysis of the climatic characteristics of a given location from the viewpoint of human comfort, as they present, on a psychrometric chart, the concurrent combination of temperature and humidity at any given time. They can also specify building design guidelines to maximize indoor comfort conditions when the building's interior is not mechanically air conditioned. All such charts are structured around, and refer to, the "Comfort Zone."

Comfort standards define the acceptable temperature, humidity, and airspeed conditions, usually inside buildings, and thus delineate the comfort zone, defined as the range of climatic conditions within which the majority of persons would not feel thermal discomfort, either of heat or cold.

A number of graphic "Comfort Indices," evaluating the combined effect on comfort of several climatic factors, and demarcating comfort zones, have been developed by various investigators. A detailed review and evaluation of different comfort indices is presented in Givoni 1976.

The ASHRAE Effective Temperature and Comfort Zone

ASHRAE developed in 1923–1925 the Effective Temperature index, (ET), which expresses in one number the combined effect on comfort of air temperature, humidity, and airspeed. The original index underwent several examinations (among them Jennings and Givoni 1959) and modifications. A graph (ASHRAE 1985) enables graphical determination of the ET for any combination of the above climatic factors. In addition the *ASHRAE Handbook* specifies the comfort zone.

The ASHRAE comfort zone is drawn on a conventional psychrometric chart. It specifies boundaries, of air temperature and humidity for sedentary people, within which the mechanical system has to maintain the indoor climate. It was constructed mainly for use in air conditioned office buildings but is also used in evaluating the indoor climate in residential buildings. This comfort zone is also used extensively as the basis for structuring bio-climatic charts.

It extends between two fixed levels of vapor content, namely between 4 and 12 gr/kg (0.004 and 0.012 lb/lb). Different temperature ranges are given in the latest version for the summer, when the buildings are mechanically cooled, and for the winter, when the buildings are heated, to take into account changes in "seasonal clothing habits" and to enhance energy conservation. The upper temperature limit slightly decreases linearly with higher humidity (between the above humidity boundaries) and increases with higher airspeed.

For still-air conditions—0.15 m/s (30 fpm) in winter and 0.25 m/s (50 fpm) in summer—the ASHRAE upper limit of acceptable temperature in summer extends from 26°C (78.8°F) at moisture content of 12 g/kg (0.012 lb/lb) to 27°C (80.6°F) at 4 gr/kg (0.004 lb/lb). The new ET chart (ASHRAE 1985) shows a shift of the upper limit of comfort sensation, from 27 (80.6°F) to 29.7°C (85.5°F), when the airspeed is increased from 0.1 (20 fpm) to 1.5 m/s (300 fpm). The complete boundaries of the comfort zones, for summer and for winter, are given in the chapter on comfort in the 1985 *ASHRAE Fundamentals Handbook* [ASHRAE 1985]. With higher airspeed the upper temperature limit is elevated by 1°C (1.8°F) for an increase of 0.275 m/s (55 fpm), up to a temperature of 28°C (82.4°F) at an airspeed of 0.8 m/s (160 fpm), *which is the highest indoor airspeed allowed*. The acceptable upper humidity limit is not affected at all by the higher airspeed in the *ASHRAE Standard*.

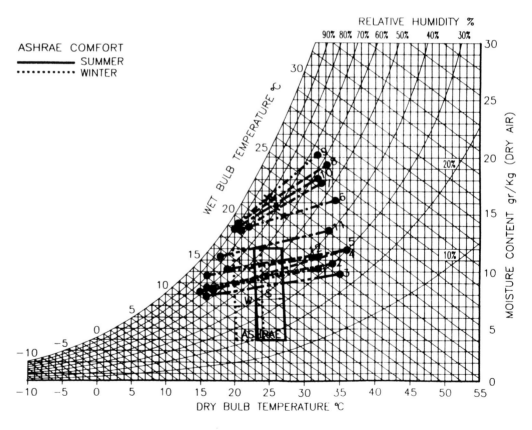

Figure 1-5. *Climatic data of Colima, Mexico, together with the ASHRAE comfort zone.*

APPLICABILITY OF THE ASHRAE COMFORT STANDARDS IN HOT CLIMATES

It is reasonable to assume that people in developing hot countries, living mostly in un-air conditioned buildings, are acclimatized to, and would tolerate, higher temperature and/or humidity (Humphreys 1975; Nicol 1974; Tanabe 1988). The problem associated with the application of the ASHRAE comfort standards in hot-humid places can be illustrated by plotting on a psychrometric chart the climatic conditions of a not-so-severe warm-humid town (Colima, Mexico) together with the ASHRAE comfort zone, as is shown in Figure 1-5 on the preceding page.

It can be seen from Figure 1-5 that from June through October (the rainy season in Colima) even the minimum temperatures would be considered as uncomfortable by the ASHRAE comfort zone, suggesting that air conditioning is needed continuously, day and night, throughout the summer. While visiting the University of Colima and talking with faculty members it was mentioned that almost all of the residential buildings in the city are not air conditioned and that the late hours of the nights and the early mornings are experienced as comfortable, both outdoors and indoors, or even as chilly, apparently reflecting their acclimatization to the local climate.

The Bio-Climatic Charts of Olgyay

Olgyay (1963) was the first to develop a bio-climatic diagram, the "Bio-Climatic Chart" (Figure 1-6 a). The chart has relative humidity as the abscissa and temperature as the ordinate. The comfort range is plotted on the chart. It is bounded by a fixed lower temperature (21°C/70°F) and by a humidity-dependent upper temperature limit. At relative humidities below 50 percent the upper comfort limit is 27.8°C (82°F). At relative humidities above 50 percent the upper temperature limit drops down gradually, until it intersects with the lower limit at 90 percent relative humidity.

For underheated conditions, the chart specifies the amount of desirable long-wave radiation from interior surfaces to elevate the Mean Radiant Temperature of the environment. Solar radiation is then needed indoors. In the absence of solar energy, conventional heating would then be needed.

Any hour when the temperature is above the upper limit of the comfort zone is defined as "overheated." The ability to extend the summer comfort range to higher temperatures and humidities with increasing wind speeds, and the ability to lower the air temperature by water evaporation, are also plotted on the chart. Monthly hourly diurnal "loops" of temperature and humidity conditions for

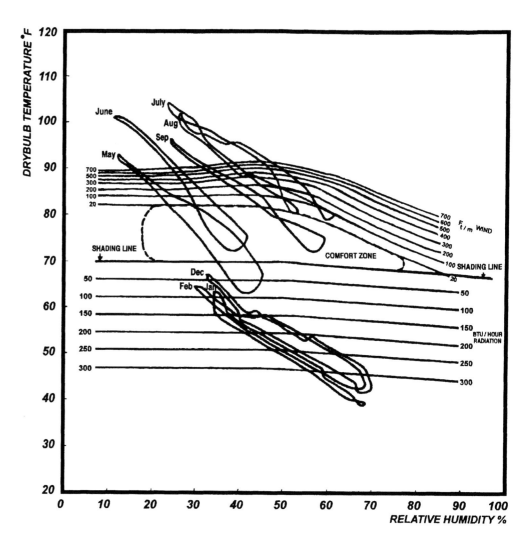

Figure 1-6a. *Olgyay's (1963) Bio-Climatic Chart.*

each month, in any given location, can be plotted on the Bio-Climatic Chart, thus providing a "diagnosis" of the extension of underheated, comfortable, and overheated conditions in that place. In the overheated range the chart specifies the airspeed of evaporation rate which may restore comfort.

Another comfort chart which was developed by Olgyay is the Timetable of Climatic Needs (Figure 1-6b). In this chart the abscissa marks the months of the year and the ordinate marks the hours of the day. The sunrise and sunset hours for each month are also plotted on this chart. For any given location the under-heated, comfortable, and overheated periods, as determined from the plots of the annual climatic conditions on the Bio-Climatic Chart, can be marked on the Timetable. For the underheated periods the amount of long-wave radiation which can restore the feeling of comfort can be transferred from the Bio-Cli-matic Chart into the Timetable. For the overheated period, the months and hours when shading is needed, or when wind or evaporation is needed to restore

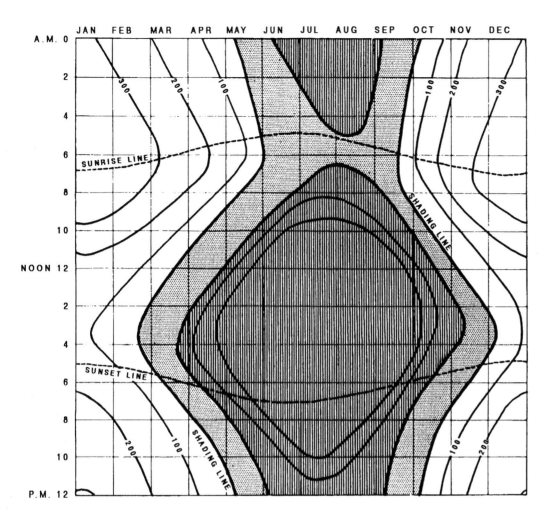

Figure 1-6b. *Olgyay's Timetable of Climatic Needs.*

comfort, can also be plotted (Figures 1-6a and 1-6b, for Phoenix, Arizona. Adapted from Olgyay 1963).

COMMENTS ON THE OLGYAY'S CHARTS

The climatic conditions specified in the Bio-Climatic Chart and the Timetable are the outdoor conditions. However, Olgyay has made the comment (in conversation with the author) that, in his experience, indoor temperatures are very close to the outdoor level. Therefore he has suggested that these charts could be used also as guidelines for buildings (e.g., for the advisability of ventilation). This can be a reasonable approximation in lightweight buildings in humid regions, like the eastern United States, where Olgyay has lived and where residential buildings are usually ventilated naturally during the summer through open, although usually screened, windows. But even in this case indoor night temperatures, also in winter, are significantly higher than the outdoors even in unheated buildings, leading to overestimation of the need for heating.

The problems with the Olgyay charts may be more severe in the summer. Indoor daytime temperature in un-air conditioned buildings, especially in high-mass buildings in hot-arid regions, can be very different from the outdoor's ambient conditions. The indoor daytime maximum temperature can be significantly lower (by up to about 7–8°K) than the outdoor maximum, especially if the building is ventilated during the night hours and closed and shaded during the daytime. Guidelines based on the outdoor conditions may not be the right ones when the actual indoor temperature is considered.

The following discussion illustrates the likelihood of inappropriate guidelines which may result from the use of Olgyay's Timetable in hot-arid regions. Concerning the need for heating during hours which fall in the "underheated" zone, it should be noted that in almost any type of building, even low-mass ones, indoor night temperatures in unheated buildings are above the outdoor temperatures. In uninsulated sheet metal structures, however, the indoor night temperature may be the same as outdoors. In high-mass buildings indoor night temperatures, even in unheated buildings, may be about 5°C (9°F) or more above the outdoor temperatures. Thus, using the Olgyay charts to define the times when heating is needed leads to significant overestimation of the heating needs in all types of buildings, and in certain months in all types of climate.

Concerning the cooling needs in the "overheated" hours the situation is more complicated. Indoor daytime temperatures may be below or above the outdoor temperatures, depending on the solar gain of the building. In high-mass buildings, with shaded windows, white walls, and roof, indoor daytime temperatures are significantly below those outdoors. For example, in a region with maximum temperature of about 35°C (95°F) low humidity and minimum temperature of about 17°C (62.5°F) (typical of many arid regions), the guidelines derived from the Chart and the Timetable would be to heat the building during the late night hours and to ventilate the building during the daytime. In reality, under the above climatic conditions, especially in a high-mass building well designed for an arid region, the indoor temperature in an un-ventilated building would be well below the outdoors.

Concerning the recommendation of Olgyay for daytime comfort, it should be taken into account that during the time of the outdoor's maximum 35°C (95°F) temperature, the indoor temperature may only be about 27°C (80.5°F) (see Chapter 2), within the summer comfort zone in arid regions for persons acclimatized to a hot climate. The indoor night temperatures may be about 22°C (71.5°F), so that no extra heating would be required. Ventilation during the daytime, as is suggested by Olgyay's charts, would elevate the indoor temperature and result in heat storage within the building's mass. This stored heat will be released back into the indoor space during the evening and night hours, when the wind usually subsides, thereby increasing the likelihood of thermal discomfort.

A better alternative to daytime ventilation in this climate would be to close the building during the daytime and to ventilate it only during the night hours (when the Bio-Climatic Charts actually would suggest the need for heating), thus ensuring comfortable indoor temperatures, both day and night.

Alternative Bio-Climatic Charts, delineating the possibilities of providing indoor thermal comfort by architectural means and utilization of "natural" energies, are described below.

The Fanger Comfort Equation

A comprehensive research on the effect of the climatic factors on thermal sensation was done by Fanger (1972). His assumption was that comfort can be derived from a human heat balance equation that he formulated, and that ". . . a condition for thermal comfort, for a given person at a given activity level, is that his mean skin temperature (t_s) and his sweat secretion (E_{sw}) must have values inside narrow limits." Skin temperatures and evaporative heat losses, obtained in climatic chamber experiments, were expressed, respectively, by statistical regression analysis, as two functions of the metabolic rate. These statistical formulae were inserted into a general human heat balance equation. In this way the climatic conditions for comfort, under a given metabolic rate and clothing thermal resistance (CLO values), were derived analytically.

Fanger defines *comfort* as the conditions under which the subjective thermal comfort votes are between "slightly cool" and "slightly warm" on a seven-point scale. The mathematical model that he derived ("Comfort Equation") is used widely in defining the limits of the "comfort zone." This equation, however, is too complex to be described in this book and an interested reader is referred to Fanger's book, *Thermal Comfort.* (See Fanger 1972.)

Fanger also derived from the comfort equation the "Predicted Mean Vote" (PMV) on the seven-point comfort scale. The equation is rather complex and Fanger provides tables and graphs of the PMV for a wide range of metabolic rates, climatic conditions, and clothing (CLO) values (Fanger 1972).

By comparing the computed PMV with climatic chamber votes in studies in Denmark and the United States, Fanger has derived the Predicted Percentage of Dissatisfied (persons) (PPD).

Fanger has also studied the quantitative relationship between the skin temperature, when people experience thermal comfort, and the metabolic rate. The equation he has derived is:

$$T_s = 35.7 - 0.032 \, (M/A_s)$$

when A_s is the skin's surface area.

Fanger's formulae have been used in many studies (often without direct observations of human responses) for evaluating comfort conditions in buildings. These formulae served also as a basis for a procedure for determination of the optimum "design" temperature in buildings by the International Standard Organization (ISO) (ISO 1984). Because of its wide use it deserves an extended evaluation.

COMPARISON OF FANGER'S PMV WITH FIELD STUDIES

Fanger's studies were conducted in climatic chambers with subjects from the United States and Denmark. Fanger maintains that his formulae are applicable in all types of buildings and in all climatic regions. However, this is in disagreement with a number of recent studies of the thermal sensations of persons in their homes or offices, especially in hot climates. Some of these studies are discussed below.

THE RESEARCH OF TANABE

Tanabe (1988) has monitored thermal sensations of Japanese subjects in four conditions (combinations of temperature and humidity ratio). Temperature range was from 26 to 31°C (78.8 to 87.8°F), with six airspeeds ranging from 0.13 to 1.63 m/s (25 to 325 fpm). Tanabe also calculated the PMV for each climatic condition.

Figure 1-7 (prepared from Tanabe data) shows the mean thermal sensation votes (on the Fanger scale, 0 = comfortable) as function of the PMV. It can be seen that practically all the votes were below the predicted PMV line. This means that conditions that the PMV perceives as too warm (above 0.5) were felt by Tanabe's subjects as acceptable (–0.5 to 0.5). The discrepancy increases sharply with the airspeed. This result indicates that the PMV does not take into account properly the cooling effect of airspeed at medium-high temperatures.

REVIEW OF HUMPHREYS

Humphreys (1992) has summarized five field comfort studies (Baillie et al. 1987; Busch 1990; Dedear and Auliciems 1985; Griffiths 1990; and Schiller 1990). All were sufficiently detailed for PMV calculation, and Humphreys compared the observed comfort votes with the predictions by the Fanger formula. He presented a table comparing the PMV calculations and the actual mean comfort votes, the differences between them, and the average temperature prevailing in the respective locations during the periods when these studies were conducted. Figures 1-8 and 1-9 (on pages 32 and 33 respectively) have been prepared by me from Humphreys' table.

Figure 1-8 shows the observed Mean Votes in these field studies as a function of the calculated PMV (by Humphreys). A zero vote signifies comfortable

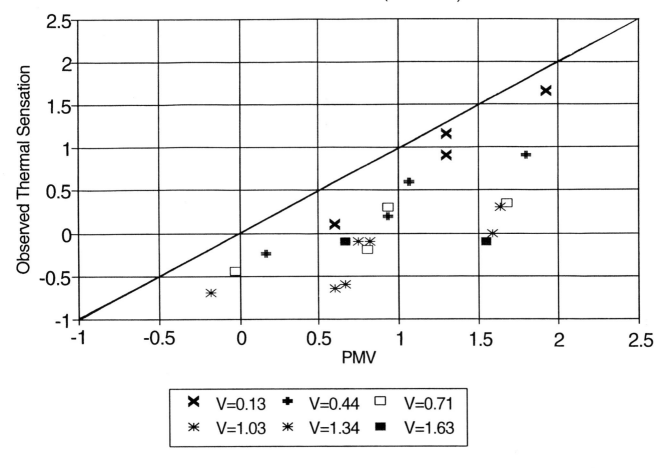

Figure 1-7. *Mean thermal sensation votes (on the Fanger scale) as a function of the Predicted Mean Vote (PMV) (prepared from Tanabe data).*

conditions. It can be seen that over a wide range of the PMV the actual Mean Votes were above the PMV predictions. At negative values of the PMV (uncomfortable cool) the subjects were actually comfortable to warm.

Figure 1-9 shows the difference between the observed Mean Vote and the PMV as a function of the mean temperature in each study. It can be seen that the difference increases as the ambient temperature was lowered.

RESEARCH OF OSELAND IN THE UNITED KINGDOM

Oseland (1994), at the British Research Establishment (BRE), conducted surveys in new homes during summer and winter to examine heating and ventilating behavior. The questionnaire also included questions concerning the comfort. The occupants were asked, "How would you rate the temperature in this room at the moment, using the seven-point comfort scale?" The interviewers

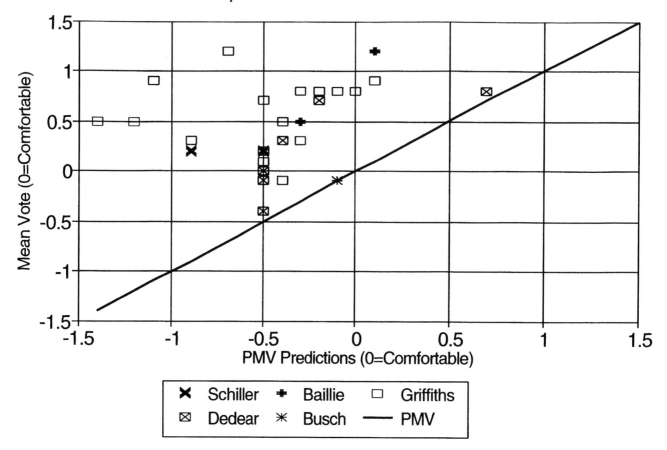

Figure 1-8. *Observed Mean Votes in the field studies summarized by Humphreys as a function of the calculated PMV.*

then measured the indoor air temperature, Globe temperature, and the WBT. Indoor air velocity was estimated by an equation taking into account the outdoor Beaufort scale. The data for analysis was provided by 515 interviews.

The recorded thermal sensations were compared with Fanger's PMV. On page 34 figure 1-10 (slightly modified, from Oseland 1994) shows the reported thermal sensations, for the summer and the winter seasons, as functions of the PMV. The figure shows also the 1:1 line (the PMV). In the case of the winter observations the regression line is almost parallel to the PMV line, but with a difference of about one unit on the comfort scale. It means that in winter the people in the United Kingdom feel comfortable at lower temperatures than considered as required by the PMV model.

The regression line for the summer is less steep than the PMV line, suggesting the comfort range of the U.K. population extends to temperatures considered too warm by the PMV model.

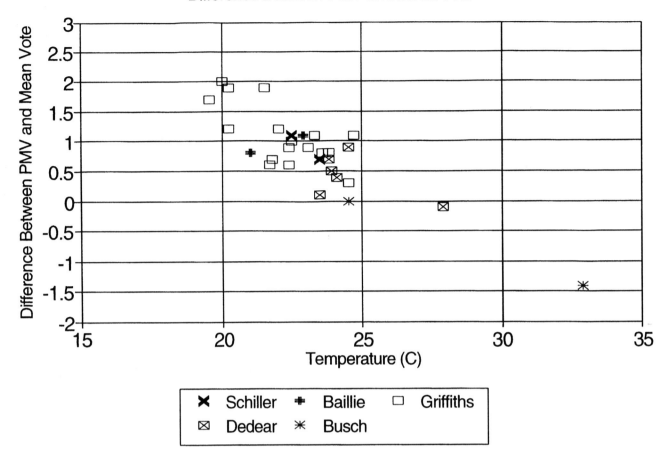

Figure 1-9. *Difference between the observed Mean Vote and the PMV as a function of the mean temperature in each study.*

DISCUSSION OF THE FANGER'S FORMULAE

It seems to the author that one of the "problems" with Fanger's heat balance equation is that the effect of airspeed is taken into account only with respect to the convective heat exchange, while its effect on sweat evaporation is not included in the heat balance formula. Consequently, at a given warm temperature and humidity, when the convective heat exchange is rather small, the PMV will have almost the same value at different wind speeds. This point limits greatly the ability of the Fanger formulae to evaluate the physiological and sensory effects of airspeed, which is a very significant factor in hot-humid climates. It may be one of the reasons for the disagreement among the prediction of the formulae, the field studies summarized by Humphreys, and the research of Tanabe.

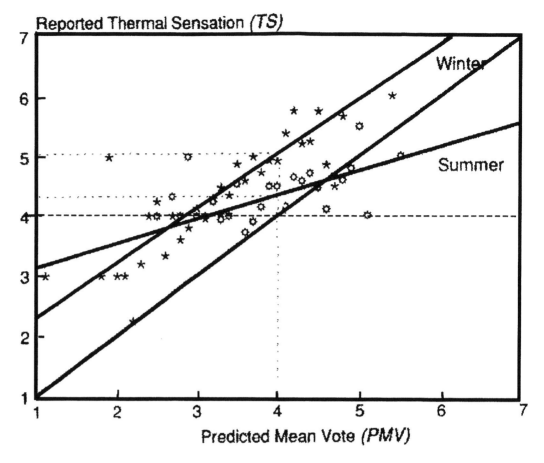

Figure 1-10. *Reported thermal sensations, for the summer and the winter seasons, as functions of the PMV.*

Effect of Acclimatization and Economic Conditions on Comfort Expectations

Research on the effect of acclimatization and standard of living on comfort sensations and expectations in residential buildings in hot developing countries is limited, although some studies were mentioned previously. These studies suggest that there is a real rise in the temperature that people consider acceptable as the local average annual temperature of the place is higher. Humphreys (1975), in summarizing previous studies on comfort in different countries, derived a formula correlating the "neutral" temperatures observed in the different studies (T_n) with the mean air temperature of the location during the experimental period of each study (T_m):

$$T_n = 2.6 + 0.831 * T_m; (^\circ C)$$

$$T_n = 36.7 + 1.496 * T_m (^\circ F)$$

No studies are known to the author that deal with the relationship between acclimatization to a hot-humid climate and the subjective response to high humidity, especially the discomfort from wetness of the skin.

In addition to the humidity issue, the subject of acceptable indoor airspeed in un-air conditioned buildings deserves special attention. A higher airspeed is the most common "remedy" to high temperature, and especially to high humidity. The ASHRAE limit of 0.8 m/s (160 fpm) seems therefore to be far too restrictive when dealing with providing comfort in un-air conditioned residential buildings in countries with hot summers.

The effects of acclimatization and comfort expectations should be taken into account, especially when comfort diagrams and building design guidelines are constructed for and applied in warm/hot developing countries.

Conclusions Concerning the Application of Existing Comfort Indices and Standards in Un-air conditioned Buildings

Application of any given comfort standards, based on a given comfort index, may lead to the use of energy-consuming air conditioning even in cases where it is, physiologically speaking, not really needed. Even in mechanically conditioned buildings, the use of a universal comfort standard can cause a waste of energy by heating or cooling buildings to temperatures and humidity levels not justified by the actual comfort needs of the local population.

APPLICABILITY OF THE ASHRAE COMFORT STANDARDS AND FANGER FORMULA IN UN-AIR CONDITIONED BUILDINGS

In the opinion of the author, some problems exist when either the ASHRAE comfort standards or the Fanger comfort formula are used to evaluate the conditions in un-air conditioned buildings. One issue concerns the boundaries of acceptable climatic conditions in buildings which are not air conditioned. Another problem concerns the application of the ASHRAE and Fanger humidity and airspeed limits in hot-humid locations, taking into account the actual acclimatization and comfort expectations of the inhabitants in such places and the role of higher airspeeds in enhancing comfort at high humidity.

Indoor climate in un-air conditioned buildings responds to the variations in outdoor climate and the inhabitants usually experience a wider diurnal climatic range than in air conditioned buildings. For example, indoor temperatures ranging from 20°C (68°F) in the morning to 26°C (78.8°F) in the afternoon on summer days are common in non-air conditioned buildings. The indoor airspeed in cross-ventilated buildings is often around 2 m/s (400 fpm). Persons living in buildings which are un-air conditioned and naturally ventilated usually accept such a wider range of temperatures and of airspeeds as a normal one.

The conventional comfort indices assume fixed conditions in a given situation in terms of the clothing and activity. However, persons living in un-air conditioned (free-running) buildings can adjust to diurnal and seasonal changes in the indoor climate by several modes of adaptation; opening and closing windows, clothing modifications, posture and subtle activity modifications, and so forth.

Baker and Standeven (1993, 1994) have summarized several observational studies in un-air conditioned buildings that were performed in the framework of the European PASCOOL project. In these studies the occupants of the buildings were observed during the day while the indoor temperatures and airspeed were monitored. The observations included any adjustments in the clothing and several such changes were observed in six out of seven studies. They have concluded that by "adaptive behavior" (e.g., clothing modification aimed at lowering the clothing insulation), 70 percent of the occupants in one study were satisfied at temperatures as high as 27.8°C (82°F) and in another study 89 percent were satisfied at 30.5°C (87°F). These temperatures are much higher than recommendations based on conventional comfort theory.

The difference between the acceptable indoor conditions in air conditioned and un-air conditioned buildings should be reflected in the charts specifying boundaries of acceptable indoor climate for un-air conditioned buildings and in the boundaries of applicability of various building design strategies and "passive" cooling systems. The narrow temperature range specified in the *ASHRAE Handbook* suggests the need for cooling in situations where natural ventilation may provide acceptable indoor conditions.

It seems to the author that it is basically impossible to have "universal" comfort indices and standards. Countries, or even regions with different climates within a given country, may have to develop comfort indices and standards taking into account specifically the acclimatization of the population, as well as its standard of living and experiences.

THE BUILDING BIO-CLIMATIC CHARTS

The Building Bio-Climatic Chart (BBCC) was developed by Givoni (1976) to address the problems associated with the Olgyay's charts discussed previously. It is based on the *indoor temperatures* in buildings (expected on the basis of experience or calculations) instead on the *outdoor temperatures*. Recent research has provided more information and a better scientific basis for demarcation of the climatic conditions under which different design strategies for summer comfort can be applied. Revised Building Bio-Climatic Charts are presented below, and in Chapter 5, Passive Cooling of Buildings.

Graphically, the BBCC differs from Olgyay's chart as it is drawn on a conventional psychrometric chart, like the ASHRAE chart. The BBCC suggests boundaries of the climatic conditions within which various building design strategies, as well as passive and low-energy cooling systems, can provide indoor comfort in hot climates without air conditioning.

These cooling options include:

- Daytime ventilation
- High mass, with or without and nocturnal ventilation
- Direct evaporative cooling
- Indirect evaporative cooling by roof ponds.

Discussion of the physical processes, design details, and expected performance of the various natural cooling systems is presented in Chapter 5. More detailed discussion of the subject is in Givoni 1994.

Considerations of Acclimatization and Standard of Living

The boundaries of the comfort zone and the different design strategies for ensuring indoor comfort, demarcated on the BBCC charts, are based on the expected indoor temperatures in buildings without mechanical air conditioning, properly designed for the location where they are built. The original boundaries of comfort in the BBCC were based on research conducted in the United States, Europe, and Israel. It can be assumed that the upper limits of accepted temperature and humidity would be higher for persons living in developing countries and acclimatized to hot-humid conditions. Extension of these limits for application in hot developing countries is suggested in the present version of the charts, *based on the personal evaluation by the author,* taking into account data obtained in studies mentioned previously, which were conducted in hot countries.

Acceptable Conditions Under Still Air

Figure 1-11 shows the boundaries of the range of acceptable conditions for still air, suggested by the author, as demarcated in the BBCC. Different boundaries are marked for temperate climate (developed countries) and for hot climate (developing countries).

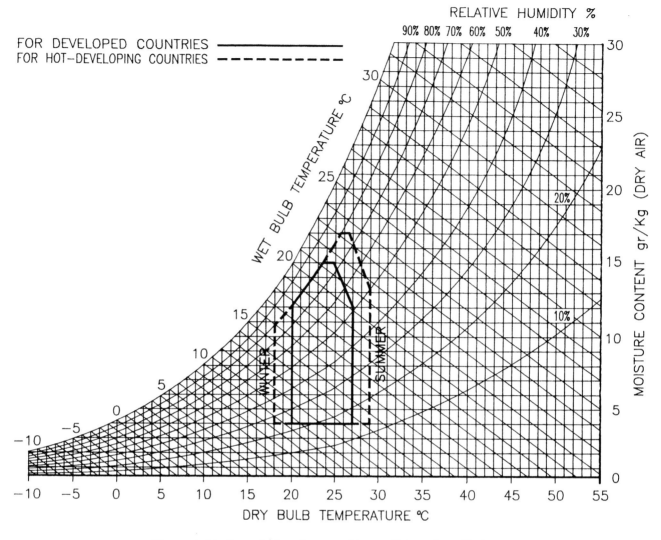

Figure 1-11. *Boundaries of acceptable conditions for still air.*

The temperature boundaries at low and medium humidities are independent of the humidity level, because in this range of humidity it does not affect the comfort of sedentary persons with ordinary clothing. At higher humidities the effects of temperature and humidity are interrelated and the upper temperature limit decreases with higher humidity.

The suggested temperature limits of acceptable conditions at still air, for people living in developed countries, are from 18 to 25°C (64.4 to 77°F) in winter and from 20 to 27°C (68 to 80.6°F) in summer. This upper temperature limit is applicable at low humidity levels, below a vapor content of 10 and 12 gr/kg (0.01 to 0.012 lb/lb), for people living in developed and in hot developing countries, respectively. At higher humidities the upper temperature limit decreases progressively. The upper limit of humidity, in terms of absolute humidity, is 15 gr/kg (0.015 lb/lb).

For persons living in hot developing countries the author suggests elevations of about 2°C (3.6°F) in the upper temperature limit and 2 gr/kg (0.002 lb/lb) in the upper vapor content, taking into account the acclimatization resulting from living in un-air conditioned buildings in a hot climate.

Providing Comfort by Ventilation

There are two ways in which ventilation can improve comfort. One is by a direct effect, providing a higher indoor airspeed by opening the windows to let the wind in, thus enhancing the cooling sensation of the inhabitants. This strategy is termed *comfort ventilation*. The other way is an indirect one—to ventilate the building only at night and thus cool the interior mass of the building. During the following day the cooled mass reduces the rate of indoor temperature rise. This strategy is termed *nocturnal ventilative cooling*. (See Chapter 4 for further discussion of both methods.) From the building design viewpoint these two options call for different details (Givoni 1994).

Enhanced Comfort by Daytime Ventilation

The simplest strategy for improving comfort when the indoor temperature (under still-air conditions) is felt as too warm is by daytime ventilation: providing comfort through higher indoor airspeeds. The flow of outdoor air through a building extends the upper limits of acceptable temperature and humidity. However, when a building is cross-ventilated during the daytime hours the temperature of the indoor air and surfaces follow closely the ambient temperature. Therefore there is a point in applying daytime ventilation only when indoor comfort can be experienced at the outdoor temperature, with acceptable indoor airspeed.

Figure 1-12 shows the boundaries of the outdoor temperature and humidity within which indoor comfort can be provided by natural ventilation during the day and with indoor airspeed about 2 m/s (400 fpm) (a very light breeze). These boundaries are based on the information and arguments presented above.

Building design guidelines for comfort ventilation are discussed in Chapter 2 and in more details in Givoni 1976.

Comfort Strategy of Nocturnal Ventilative Cooling

The term Nocturnal Ventilative Cooling refers to the case when a high-mass building is ventilated only during the evening and night hours and the openings

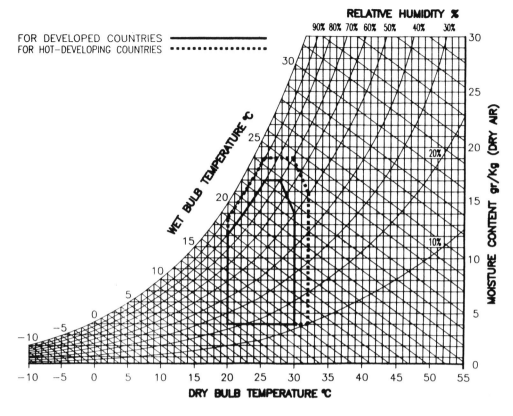

Figure 1-12. *Boundaries of outdoor temperature and humidity within which indoor comfort can be provided by natural ventilation during the day, with indoor airspeed about 2 m/s (400 fpm).*

are closed during the daytime. In this way the structural mass of the building is cooled by convection during the night and is able to absorb the heat penetrating into the building during the day with only a small elevation of the indoor temperature. Under these conditions it is possible to lower the average indoor daytime temperatures below the outdoor's average.

CLIMATIC APPLICABILITY OF NOCTURNAL VENTILATIVE COOLING

The potential for lowering the indoor daytime temperature below the outdoor level is proportional to the outdoor's diurnal temperature range. The outdoor range, in turn, increases as the humidity is lower. Significant reduction of the indoor daytime temperature below the outdoor's maximum can be obtained only in high-mass buildings with effective solar control. For a high-mass, well-insulated and shaded building, closed during the daytime and ventilated only during the night, a drop of the indoor maximum below the outdoor maximum of about 45 to 55 percent of the outdoor range is possible. At night the indoor temperatures are higher than outdoors.

Figure 1-13 shows the climatic boundaries, in terms of the outdoor *maxi-*

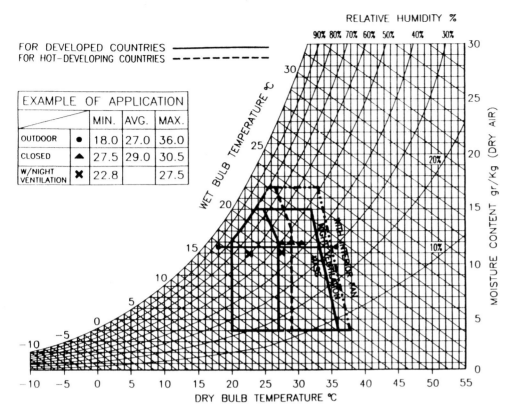

Figure 1-13. *Climatic boundaries, in terms of the outdoor* maximum *daily temperatures, under which nocturnal convective cooling is applicable.*

mum daily temperatures, under which nocturnal ventilative cooling is applicable. The temperature limit is reduced with higher humidity, reflecting the corresponding decrease of the outdoor range with higher humidity. Increasing the indoor airspeed by internal fans (not by ventilation) can extend the indoor comfort range, without elevating the indoor temperature. A simple procedure for estimating the expected indoor maximum and minimum temperatures in high-mass buildings, either closed all the time or ventilated during the evening and night hours, is presented in Chapter 3. Figure 1-13 also contains a tabulated numerical example of the application of this procedure.

Convective cooling is applicable mainly in arid and desert regions where the maximum temperature is below about 36°C (96.8°F). In desert regions with daytime temperatures above 36°C (96.8°F), night ventilation alone would not maintain the indoor daytime temperature at an acceptable level, and other passive cooling systems, such as evaporative cooling (as discussed on the next page) or compression or absorption air conditioning, should be applied during the hot hours. Even in this case, however, the application of nocturnal convective cooling can significantly reduce the length of the periods and duration of the time when the additional cooling systems will be needed.

As a rule of thumb it can be estimated that in arid and desert regions, with a summer diurnal temperature range of 15–20°K, the expected reduction of the indoor maximum temperature can be about 6–8°K below the outdoor maximum. On very hot days, which usually have a larger diurnal range, the drop of the indoor temperature, during the time of the outdoor maximum, may be up to about 10°K.

Evaporative Cooling

The energy consumed in the process of water evaporation can be utilized in two different ways to cool buildings. One is by direct evaporative cooling of the outdoor air, which then is introduced into the building. The temperature of the air is lowered and its water vapor content is elevated, following a constant Wet Bulb Temperature (WBT).

The second way is an indirect one—for instance, the roof of the building can be cooled evaporatively by having a shaded pond on the roof, and the ceiling then acts as a passive, very effective, cooling element for the space below.

DIRECT EVAPORATIVE COOLING

Direct evaporative cooling of air can be done either by mechanical systems (swamp coolers or desert coolers) or by passive means, such as by cooling towers. In direct evaporative cooling, either passive or mechanical, the air temperature is reduced by about 70 to 80 percent of the WBT depression, namely the difference between the Dry Bulb Temperature (DBT) and the WBT. Therefore the climatic criterion for the applicability of evaporative cooling is the ambient WBT and a large WBT depression, a characteristic of hot-dry climate.

Direct evaporative cooling involves high rates of outdoor airflow, because of the high humidity of the cooled air. As a result of the high airflow rate, the indoor air and surface temperatures are governed mainly by the temperature of the cooled air. Typical indoor average air temperatures in a well-insulated building are only about 1–2°C (2–4°F) above the temperature of the air exiting from the evaporative cooler.

Taking into account the opposite effects on comfort of the higher indoor humidity and the higher airspeeds associated with direct evaporative cooling, it is suggested by the author that direct evaporative cooling is advisable, in developed countries, only where and when the WBT maximum in summer is about 22°C (71.6°F) and the DBT maximum is about 42°C (107.6°F). Under these conditions the temperature of the air exiting from the evaporative system would be about 26–27°C (78.8–80.6°F) and the average indoor air temperature would be about 27–29°C (80.6–84.2°F). In hot, dry developing countries, taking into account acclimatization, the suggested limits are 24°C (75.2°F) (WBT) and 44°C (111.2°F) (DBT). These boundaries are demarcated in Figure 1-14.

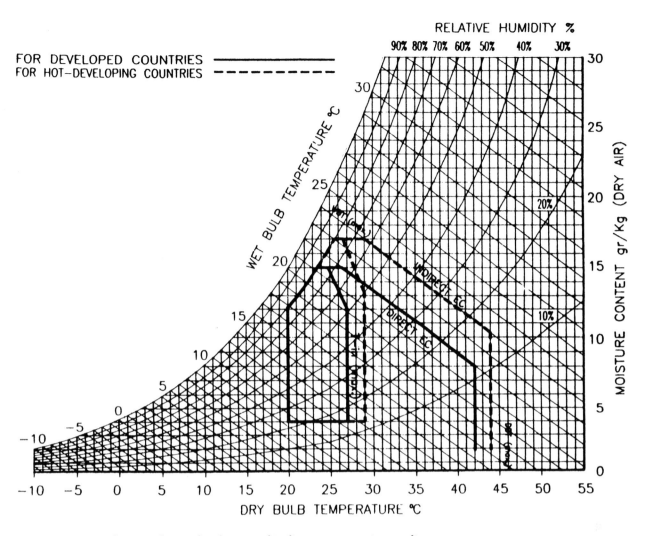

Figure 1-14. *Application limits for direct and indirect evaporative cooling.*

INDIRECT EVAPORATIVE COOLING BY ROOF PONDS

Evaporative cooling can also be passive and indirect, for example, by providing a shaded water pond over an uninsulated roof. The roof should be, of course, insulated during the winter. Details about possible design solutions for the insulation of roof ponds are given in Givoni 1994, including a mathematical model for calculating the indoor temperatures of a building cooled by a roof pond.

The pond's water temperature follows closely the ambient *average* WBT, with some elevation and swing that depends on the depth of the water in the pond. The ceiling, cooled by heat conduction to the water, acts as a radiant/convective cooling panel for the space under it. Thus, the indoor air and radiant temperatures can be lowered without elevating the indoor humidity level. With a pond over a conductive roof, the heat exchange between the cooled ceiling and the indoor space below is maximized, enabling satisfactory cooling even

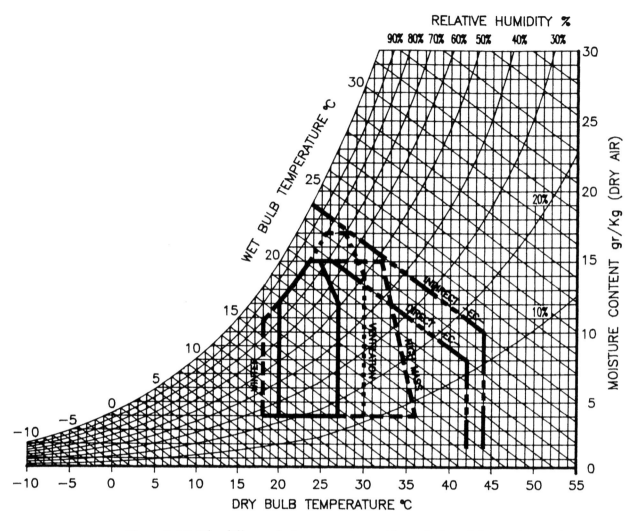

Figure 1-15. *The different design strategies and boundaries of the passive cooling approaches, for developed countries.*

with a small difference of about 2–3°K between the indoor air and the ceiling temperatures (Givoni 1994).

In arid regions the diurnal range of the WBT in summer is about 5–6°K. As both the pond's water temperature and the ceiling's temperature of a conductive roof follow the average diurnal WBT, they are often below the maximum WBT. As the indoor humidity is not elevated by indirect evaporative cooling and indoor airspeed can be augmented by internal fans, it is possible to apply roof pond cooling in places where the maximum WBT is higher, by about 2°C (3.6°F) than the applicability limits for direct evaporative cooling, namely, in developed countries, a WBT of 24°C (75.2°F) and DBT of 44°C (111.2°F).

In the case of cooling by roof ponds the suggested upper temperature (DBT) limit for acclimatized people in developing countries is the same as those for the developed countries. The reason is that a higher heat gain through less-insulated walls can be assumed in the developing countries, counteracting the effect of acclimatization. Consequently, the climatic applicability limits of indirect evaporative cooling, for hot, developing countries, as marked in Figure 1-14, are also maximum WBT of 24°C (75.2°F) and maximum DBT of 44°C (111.2°F).

The Complete Forms of the Building Bio-Climatic Charts

Figure 1-15 on the preceding page shows the different design strategies and boundaries of the passive cooling approaches, suggested for developed countries. Figure 1-16 shows the boundaries of the suggested strategies for hot, developing countries. These figures show also the climatic conditions under which more than one strategy can be applied.

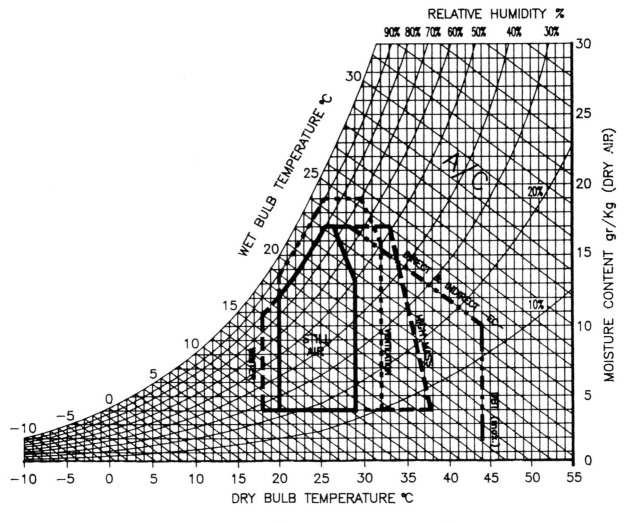

Figure 1-16. *The different design strategies and boundaries of the passive cooling approaches for hot, developing countries.*

REFERENCES

American Society of Heating, Refrigerating, and Air Conditioning Engineers (ASHRAE). 1985. Physiological principles for comfort and health. In *ASHRAE Fundamental Handbook*. New York: ASHRAE, 1985.

Baillie, A.P., I.D. Griffiths, and J.W. Huber. 1987. Thermal Comfort Assessment. Report ETSU-S-1177, Department of Psychology, University of Surrey, U.K.

Baker, N., and M. Standeven. 1993. Comfort Criteria for Passively Cooled Buildings—A PASCOOL Task. Proc. Conference Solar Energy in Architecture and Planning, Florence. H.S. Stefens & Assoc. The Martin Center for Architectural and Urban Studies. Department of Architecture, University of Cambridge, U.K.

Baker, N., and M. Standeven. 1994. Thermal Comfort in Free-Running Buildings. Proc., The Dead Sea, Israel. 25–32. Passive and Low Energy Architecture (PLEA '94) Eleventh International Conference.

Busch, J.F. 1990. Thermal Response to the Thai Office Environment. *ASHRAE Trans* 96 (1):859–872.

Dedear, R.J., and A. Auliciems. 1985. Validation of the Predicted Mean Vote Model of Thermal Comfort in Six Australian Field Studies. *ASHRAE Transactions* 91 (2):452–468.

Fanger, P.O. 1972. *Thermal Comfort*. New York: McGraw-Hill Book Co.

Givoni, B. 1963. Evaluation of the Effect of Climate on Man: Development of a New Thermal Index. Ph.D. diss., School of Medicine, Hebrew University of Jerusalem, Israel.

Givoni, B. 1976. *Man, Climate and Architecture*. 2d ed. London: Applied Science Publishers.

Givoni, B. 1994. *Passive and Low Energy Cooling of Buildings*. New York: Van Nostrand Reinhold.

Givoni, B., and H.S. Belding. 1962. The Cooling Efficiency of Sweat Evaporation. Proc., First International Congress of Bio-Meteorology. London: Pergamon Press. 304–314.

Givoni, B., and R.F. Goldman. 1971. Predicting Metabolic Energy Cost. *Journal of Applied Physiology* 30 (3):429–433.

Givoni, B., and R.F. Goldman. 1972. Predicting Rectal Temperature Response to Work, Environment and Clothing. *Journal of Applied Physiology* 32(x): 312–332.

Givoni, B., and R.F. Goldman. 1973a. Predicting Heart Rate Response to Work, Environment and Clothing. *Journal of Applied Physiology* 34(x): 201–204.

Givoni, B., and R.F. Goldman. 1973b. Predicting Effect of Heat Acclimatization on Heart Rate and Rectal Temperature. *Journal of Applied Physiology* 35(x): 875–879.

Griffiths, I.D. 1990. Thermal Comfort in Buildings with Passive Solar Features. Report ENS-090-uk, Department of Psychology, University of Surrey, U.K.

Humphreys, M.A. 1975. Field Studies of Thermal Comfort Compared and Applied. Building Research Establishment, Current Paper. CP 76/75, Garston, Watford, UK.

Humphreys, M.A. 1992. Thermal Comfort Requirements, Climate and Energy. Proc. of the Second World Renewable Energy Congress. Reading, U.K. 1725–1734.

International Standard Organization (ISO). 1984. International Standard 7730, moderate thermal environment - determination of the PMV and PPD indices and specification of the conditions for thermal comfort. Geneva, Switzerland.

Jennings, B.H., and B. Givoni. 1959. Environmental reactions in the 80°–105°F Zone. *ASHRAE Transactions.*

McIntyre, D.A. 1978. Preferred Air Speeds for Comfort in Warm Conditions. *ASHRAE Transactions* V-84:264–277.

Nicol, F., G.N. Jamy, O. Sykes, M.A. Humphreys, S. Roaf, and M. Hancock. 1994. *Thermal Comfort in Pakistan.* U.K.: Oxford Brookes University, School of Architecture.

Olgyay, V. 1963. *Design With Climate.* New Jersey: Princeton University Press.

Oseland, N.A. 1994. A Comparison of the Predicted and Reported Thermal Sensation Vote in Homes During Winter and Summer. *Energy and Buildings* 21 (1):45–54.

Schiller, G.E. 1990. A Comparison of Measured and Predicted Comfort in Office Buildings. *ASHRAE Transactions* 96 (1).

Tanabe, S.I. 1988. Thermal Comfort Requirement in Japan. Waseda University, Tokyo, Japan.

Weihe, W.E. 1986. Life Expectancy in Tropical Climates and Urbanization. World Meteorological Organization. 313–353.

Wu, H. 1988. The Potential Use & Application of Oscillating Fans in Extending the Summer Comfort Envelope. Research Report. Environmental Testing Laboratory. Arizona State University, Tempe, Arizona.

Chapter **2:** ARCHITECTURAL FEATURES AFFECTING THE INDOOR CLIMATE

INTRODUCTION

Many architectural design features of a building affect the indoor climate. They do this by modifying four forms of interaction between the building and its environment:

a. The *effective solar exposure* of the glazed and opaque elements of the building's envelope (its walls and roof);

b. The *effective solar heat gain* of the building;

c. The rate of *conductive and convective* heat gain from, or loss to, the ambient air; and

d. The *potential* for natural ventilation and passive cooling of the building.

The main relevant design features which affect some or all of the above-mentioned interactions of the building with the environment, discussed in this chapter, are:

• The building's layout (shape)
• Orientation and shading conditions of the windows
• Orientation and colors of the walls
• The size and location of the windows from the ventilation aspect
• The effect of the ventilation conditions of a building on its indoor temperatures

The effect of the *building materials* on the building's heat gain and loss, and the resulting indoor temperatures, is discussed in Chapter 4. The effect of *site landscaping* on indoor climate is discussed in Chapter 9.

In dealing with the subject of the building's orientation there are two separate effects of orientation: on the solar exposure of the building (orientation with respect to the sun) and on the ventilation potential (orientation with respect to the wind direction).

There are significant interactions between the effects of these design features, so that the quantitative effect of one feature (e.g., orientation) may greatly depend on the design details of other features (in this case the shading of the windows and the color of the walls and the roof). Therefore, in discussing the effect of a given design feature, frequent back-and-forth references are made to this dependence on specific conditions of other features.

The subjects of human comfort and building climatology are discussed in Chapter 1 and in more details in (Givoni 1976).

IMPACTS OF BUILDING'S LAYOUT ON THE INDOOR CLIMATE

The term *layout* in the context of this chapter refers to the compactness of the house plan. Other terms describing this feature are the shape, or configuration, of the building.

The main impact of layout, from the indoor climate point of view, is its effect on the envelope's surface area, relative to the floor's area or the space volume, and consequently on the rate of heat exchange of the building with the outdoors. It also has an effect on the building's potential for natural ventilation and for natural illumination.

The ratio of the building envelope's surface area to its volume or floor area determines, on the one hand, the relative exposure of the building to solar radiation and, on the other hand, its exposure to the ambient air.

A spacial case of building's layout is that of a patio, or a courtyard, surrounded by walls and thus partially isolated from the full impact of the outdoor air. This configuration is very common in regions with hot-dry climate. The climatic conditions within the patio, and their effect on the indoor climate of the surrounding building, may vary greatly, depending on the design details of the patio. This subject is discussed in detail in Chapter 10, dealing with design guidelines for hot-dry regions.

Heat Gain and Loss

The more compact the building's plan, the smaller the exposed surface area of the walls or the roof, for a given volume or floor area of the building. As a result, the heat exchange by conduction between the building and the ambient air is decreased. In seasons and hours when the house is either heated or air conditioned, a smaller surface area reduces the energy demand of the house. In contrast, when the plan of the house is spread out, the larger surface area of the walls causes a greater heat gain or loss and a greater energy expenditure of the air conditioning equipment.

Ventilation Potential

Generally speaking, the more spread out the building is, and the more irregular its shape, the better is the potential for cross-ventilation. As the area of the external walls for a given floor area is larger, there are more opportunities to provide openings which will catch the wind from different directions. A spread-out building also provides more opportunities for direct and independent ventilation to the various rooms of the building.

A spread-out plan may offer better opportunities not only for natural ventilation but also for natural daylighting, and more freedom and flexibility in the design of the space. It may also enable faster cooling in seasons and hours when comfort can be provided by natural ventilation, and thereby reduce the duration of the time when air conditioning is needed.

The issue of daylighting, and its relation to the building's configuration, is of special interest in large office buildings, where electrical lighting constitutes a major expense, in addition to its contribution to the air conditioning load. Only the peripheral strip of a large compact building, along the external walls, can have windows and daylighting. The "core" area of the building has to rely only on electrical lighting and needs cooling year-round because, even in winter in cold regions, it cannot lose, by any natural heat-loss mechanism, the internal heat produced by the lighting, equipment, and people. One of the design approaches to reduce the lighting and air conditioning energy consumption and expenses is to introduce into the plan of the building projections and indentations (recesses), thus increasing the length of the external walls relative to the floor area.

Changeable Configuration of Residential Buildings

There are often conflicts of objectives between design for enhancing natural ventilation, calling for a spread-out building, and design for energy conservation when the building is either heated or air conditioned, when a compact configuration is more desirable. An interesting solution, especially in the case of residential buildings in regions with hot-humid summers and cold winters, would be the ability to change the building's configuration: having it compact in winter and spread out in summer, when ample ventilation is desirable most of the time.

It is possible to design a building with special details which will enable it to be compact when it is heated or air conditioned, and to be widespread and irregular in shape when it is naturally ventilated. For instance, one could design a building with porches, recessed inward and flanked by the adjoining rooms, which should be equipped with operable large windows and/or insulated shutters, as is illustrated in Figure 2-1.

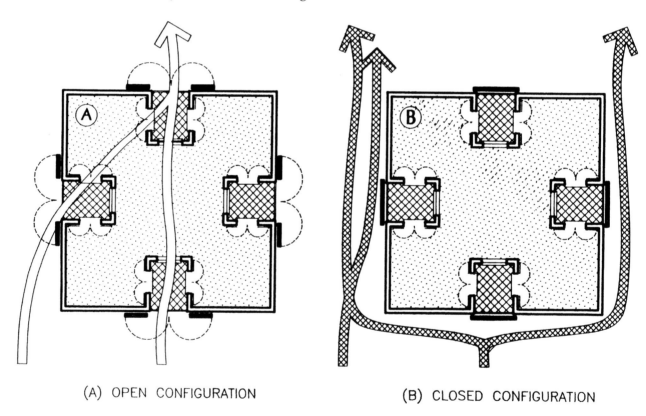

(A) OPEN CONFIGURATION   (B) CLOSED CONFIGURATION

A BUILDING WITH INDENTED PORCHES

Figure 2-1. *Scheme of a building with porches recessed inward, equipped with operable insulated shutters.*

When windows and shutters are open, the porch is a semi-open space, providing ventilation option for the adjoining rooms through windows or doors open to it. On the other hand, when the windows and/or shutters of the porch are closed, the facade becomes smooth, reducing the area of heat loss, while the porch becomes part of the interior space.

The subject of changeable configuration is further elaborated on in Chapter 10, dealing with hot-dry regions, where such a configuration can be most effective.

THERMAL IMPACTS OF WINDOWS' ORIENTATION AND SHADING CONDITIONS

Windows fulfill many functions in buildings, such as providing visual and auditory contact with the outdoors, views to attractive scenery (when available), natural ventilation, and daylighting. In addition they can serve as elements in passive solar heating and cooling systems.

There is a common psychological need to be aware of what is going on outdoors: changes in weather, sunlight, and passing clouds; variability and changes in surrounding vegetation; foliage and flowers; "information" on activities of people outside the building, and so on.

When the location of the building provides views to attractive sceneries, either natural, such as mountains; valleys; or sea fronts; or urban scenery, such as attractive buildings and streets, the windows provide the ability to view these scenes. Sometimes, of course, there is also the need to shut out the outdoor environment: to avoid noise and exclude daylight. Thus windows, especially when openable, are the "natural" building element which provides the contact with the outdoors and its control.

Consequently, the energy considerations should not be the only factor which determine the size and orientation of the windows in a given climate. In fact, as will be discussed later, it is possible to minimize the undesirable effects of windows in a given orientation (e.g., western windows—excessive solar gain in summer) and to secure their beneficial effect (e.g., utilizing the western wind for ventilation) by appropriate design details.

Windows, and often skylights in upper stories, are the source for daylighting of the interior. Such daylight is desired not only for energy conservation but is usually considered superior (psychologically) to electrical lighting. The location, size, and shading details of the windows determine the quality and quantity of the interior lighting.

Glazed openings in walls have traditionally been among the primary means for articulating and defining the architectural character of a building. The overall fraction of the wall given up to windows, as well as the shape and distribution of the windows throughout the wall, are among the main elements of the architectural articulation of the facades of the building. This chapter deals with the impact of windows' design, including their shading, on the indoor climate. The impact of windows' design on ventilation and passive cooling is discussed in Chapter 4.

Sun Motion and Solar Radiation

The position of the sun determines the intensity of solar radiation striking the various surfaces of a building, such as walls and windows with different orientations and roofs of different slopes. The sun follows accurately predictable diurnal and annual patterns, so the radiation intensity striking a given area of the buildings at different hours and seasons is also predictable, and its impact can be controlled by design. The relevant design details concern the shape of the building, orientation of its main facades, shading of windows, and colors of the walls and the roof, as well as other design details specific for different orientations, aimed at maximizing or minimizing the solar impact, depending on the climate and the related design objectives.

INTENSITY OF SOLAR RADIATION STRIKING A SURFACE

The amount of solar radiation striking a given surface of a building, wall, or roof changes constantly as a result from the changing position of the sun in the sky. The diurnal and annual patterns of the sun's motion in the sky depend on the latitude of the location in question (distance, north or south, from the equator). For a given latitude these patterns are symmetrical about the Equator.

The position of the sun at any time (date and hour) can be described mathematically by two angles: its altitude (A) and its azimuth (Z). The altitude is the vertical angle of the sun above the horizon. The azimuth is the angle of the sun's position east or west from true north.

A site in the Northern Hemisphere is assumed in the following descriptions of the sun's motion. (However, because of the symmetry, the sun's position in the Southern Hemisphere is repeated six months later, with the north substituted for the south.)

The intensity of the direct solar beam reaching the earth's surface, measured normal to the beam, I_{DN}, depends on the solar altitude, A, and the extinction coefficient of the atmosphere, E. It is calculated by the formula:

$$I_{DN} = I° / \exp (E/\sin A)$$

where I° is the "solar constant," namely the radiation at the top of the atmosphere: 1550 W/m², (492 Btu/h/ft²).

The extinction coefficient of the atmosphere, E, depends on the climate (sky clearance) and the level of air pollution at the location in question. Under a clear sky in winter in an arid area, its value is about 0.07. In a humid area in summer it is about 0.2. In a polluted urban area in a humid climate it may be above 0.3, even with cloudless sky.

For a vertical wall or a window with a given orientation (angle between the Normal to the wall and the South, Z_W) the "bearing angle" of the sun, b, would simply be:

$$b = Z - Z_B$$

With a given altitude of the sun, *A,* and its bearing angle to the wall, b, it is possible to calculate the incidence angle of the sun with respect to the wall O:

$$O = \cos A * \cos b$$

The total solar radiation striking a given surface is the sum of three components: the Direct, Diffused, and Reflected Radiations.

THE DIRECT SOLAR RADIATION

The direct solar radiation, I_{DV}, falling on a vertical surface with an incidence angle O, is given by the formula:

$$I_{DV} = I_{DN}\cos O$$

The incidence angle of the sun on a horizontal surface (e.g., a roof), O_h, is 90° – A. The direct radiation striking a horizontal roof, I_{DH}, is then:

$$I_{DH} = I_{DN}\sin A$$

DIFFUSED SOLAR RADIATION

Diffused solar radiation reaching a horizontal area, I_{dH}, comes from the whole sky vault. The amount of diffused radiation is very variable, depending on the atmospheric haziness and cloudiness. It may range from about 5 percent of the total radiation, on a clear day in an arid region, to above 80 percent on an overcast day.

Under clear-sky conditions I_{dH} is proportional to the direct normal radiation, I_{DN}, with proportional constant, k, of about 0.75 of the atmospheric extinction coefficient, E, which is used in calculating I_{DN} in the first place. Consequently it can be estimated by the formula:

$$I_{dH} = k * I_{DN} \text{ or } I_{dH} = 0.75E * I_{DN}$$

A value of k = 0.12 can be used as a good approximation for estimating the diffused radiation during clear days.

Diffused sky radiation reaching a wall in an open field, I_{dV}, comes from only one-half of the sky vault. Therefore:

$$I_{dV} = 0.5 * I_{dH} = 0.5 * k * I_{dN}$$

In a built-up urban area a large part of the sky vault may be obscured, of course, by nearby buildings.

TOTAL HORIZONTAL SOLAR RADIATION

The total amount of solar radiation on an unobstructed horizontal surface (unobstructed ground or a horizontal roof), I_{TH}, is the sum to the direct and the diffused radiation. Namely:

$$I_{TH} = I_{DH} + I_{dH}$$

REFLECTED SOLAR RADIATION

Solar radiation is reflected from nonshining surfaces in all directions (diffused reflection). The radiation reflected from the surrounding ground and walls is a function of the colors of those surfaces, as the color determines their reflectivity (or albedo) for solar (short-wave) radiation. The reflectivity of bare ground depends on the type of the soil, ranging from about 70 percent for sand dunes to about 20 percent for dark loam soil. Reflectivity of concrete and asphalt surfaces varies with the "age" of the surfaces, as they become lighter with time. Plant leaves' reflectivity depends on the type of the plants, and changes with the seasons. Taking all this variability into account, any numbers used in calculations of the intensity of reflective solar radiation should be considered only as estimates.

Reflected solar radiation concerns mainly walls and windows, as the roofs "see" mainly the sky. Solar radiation striking the ground is reflected in all directions and only one half of the radiation reflected from an unlimited ground area reaches a given wall. Therefore, for a given average reflectivity of the surrounding, r, the reflected radiation reaching a vertical wall in open field, I_{RV}, can be calculated by the formula:

$$I_{RV} = (r * I_{TH}) / 2$$

In a built-up urban area the reflected radiation field is much more complex. The radiation reflected from a wall with a given reflectivity of its surface is proportional to the solar radiation striking that wall, which changes during the day.

In each specific situation the radiation pattern on the surrounding surfaces, and their reflectivity, have to be taken into account when it is desired to calculate the reflected radiation accurately.

TOTAL RADIATION IMPINGING ON A VERTICAL WALL

The total solar radiation reaching a wall, I_V, is the sum of the direct, diffused, and reflected radiations. Namely:

$$I_V = I_{DV} + I_{dV} + I_{RV}$$

Figure 2-2, from Givoni 1976, shows diurnal patterns of solar radiation striking walls (and windows) at different orientations during the year.

Optical Properties of Windows

A unique property of glass is its selective transparency to short-wave (solar) and long-wave (thermal) radiation. Different types of glass transmit different fractions of the solar radiation spectrum, in the range of 0.4 to 2.5 microns. At the same time all glasses are opaque to the long-wave radiation emitted from indoor surfaces. Thus the "greenhouse effect" is created—namely transmission of solar radiation into the building while blocking and trapping indoors the long-wave radiation. The result of the greenhouse effect is an elevation of the indoor temperature, beyond the level which would result from penetration of solar radiation through open windows. This effect is, of course, in addition to the blocking of the convection heat exchange (cooling) by the glazing.

The solar spectrum itself can be divided into three main ranges: the ultraviolet (wavelength below 0.4 microns), the visible spectrum (0.4–0.7 microns), and

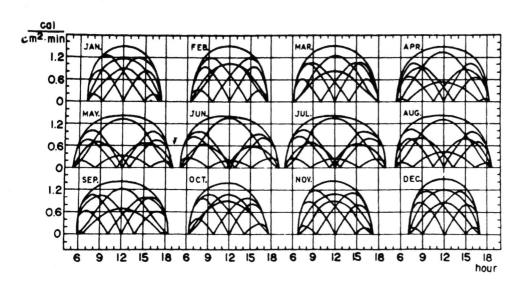

Figure 2-2. *Diurnal patterns of solar radiation striking walls (and windows) at different orientations, for a latitude of 32°N.*

the infrared (above 0.7, up to about 2.5 microns). Different glasses transmit different fractions of each one of these ranges.

When solar radiation impinges on a window glass, it is divided into three fractions. One part is reflected outward without any effect on the building's temperature. The second part is absorbed within the glass, raising its temperature, and the rest is transmitted through the glazing into the building. The relative proportions of these three parts depend on the type of the glass, as well as on the angle of incidence of the radiation. Details on the effect of incidence angle are given later in this chapter. The different fractions of solar transmissivity are determined by the composition and/or treatment of the glass, and can be chosen to fulfill a wide range of ratios of light-to-heat transmission.

SHADING COEFFICIENT AND THE *KE* FACTOR OF GLAZING

The ratio of the total solar transmittance of a given glazing type to that of a single pane of clear glass is defined as the shading coefficient, SC, of that glazing.

While the function of all windows is to admit daylight into the building, any light inherently heats up the interior because all the transmitted solar energy is ultimately transformed inside the building into heat. The different ratios of light-to-heat transmission characterizing different types of glazing are achieved by modifying the amounts of different ranges of the solar spectrum, which are either reflected, absorbed, or transmitted by the glass. New types of glazing with "dynamic" optical properties are in the research and development stages.

Sweitzer et al. (1986) from Lawrence Berkeley Laboratory (LBL) have suggested to use the ratio of visible transmittance to shading coefficient, which they termed the Ke factor, as one of the criteria for evaluating windows' performance.

Thus, glass can be classified into several types, according to their selective transmission, reflection, and absorption of different wavelengths of radiation, such as: Clear glass, Heat-absorbing glass, Heat-reflecting glass, Gray glass, Low-emissivity (Low-E) glass, and Super-insulating. Each one of them can be characterized by its U or R values and its shading coefficient and Ke factor. The R, SC, and Ke values for different glazing types are shown in Table 2-1 on page 60 (from Sweitzer et al. 1986).

Heat Transfer—the Thermal Resistance of Windows

The term *U factor* refers to the amount of heat transfer through a window due to the temperature difference between the indoor space and the outdoors. The thermal resistance (R value) of the glazing is the reciprocal of its U value. These properties depend on four independent factors of the windows' system:

- The existence and number of airspaces between glazing layers.
- The properties and/or treatments of the glazing material and surfaces.
- The gas which fills the airspaces.
- The materials and detailing of the window's frames.

EFFECTS OF AIRSPACES IN THE WINDOWS

Windows are available with a single pane of glass or with multiple panes, usually two, and in cold countries three panes, with an airspace (or spaces) between them. The airspaces add to the thermal resistance of the window, thus reducing its overall heat transfer coefficient (U value). The heat flow across the airspace is by convection and radiation. The convection component depends to some extent on the width of the space. The radiation component can be reduced by special treatments (for heat reflection) of the glass.

The thermal conductivity of the gas which fills the window's airspace has a significant effect on its overall U value. The spaces can be filled by argon or krypton, which have lower conductivity than air. Consequently, the overall U value of windows can vary substantially, by a factor of between single-glazed windows and those with special gas-filled two- and three-pane windows.

Glazing Types

According to the specific treatments of the glass, different types of glazing are manufactured. The main common types are the following:

CLEAR GLASS

Clear glass transmits the highest amounts of all the wavelengths of the solar spectrum. Consequently, it transmits the highest amount of daylight but also causes the highest solar heat gain into the building, a property which in summer increases the cooling load on the building. In winter, however, such glass may be the best for passive solar of the buildings by direct solar gain.

HEAT-ABSORBING GLASS

Heat-absorbing glass selectively absorbs a higher fraction of the infrared (heat) part of the solar spectrum, compared with its absorption of visible light. Consequently the light-to-heat-radiation ratio of such glasses is higher than for clear glasses.

The temperature of the glass itself rises as a result of the absorbed infrared radiation. This may lead to increased convection and long-wave radiation heat flow into the building. Thus, the "apparent" advantage of such glasses from the heat gain viewpoint may be reduced.

A solution to this problem is to place a heat-absorbing glass as the external layer in a double-glazed window. In this arrangement most of the absorbed energy flows outward and only a small part of it is transferred to the indoors.

HEAT-REFLECTING GLASS

Heat-reflecting glass is produced by deposition of a very fine semitransparent metallic coating on the glass surface, which selectively reflects a larger part of the solar infrared radiation. Thus the total solar heat gain is reduced, although often with a reduction of the light transmission, as well.

LOW-EMISSIVITY GLASS

Low-emissivity glass is produced by coating the glass with a layer of selective low-emissivity long-wave radiation. This coating reduces the radiant heat loss from the glazing, which is in the long-wave part of the radiation spectrum.

SUPER-INSULATING GLASS

Super-insulating glass has often three glazing layers, the interior layer with Low-E coating, and the spaces between the layers filled with a gas of lower conductivity than air, such as Argon.

GRAY AND COLORED GLASS

Gray and colored glass absorb more visible than infrared radiation. They are used mainly to reduce glare and excessive sunlight from large windows and glazed walls. The absorbed light elevates the glass temperature, or course, as well as the heat flow inward due to convection and long-wave radiation.

Table 2-1 shows the R values in (m^2C/W), Shading coefficient (SC), Solar transmittance (Ts), Visible transmittance (Tv), and the Ke factors (Tv/SC) of several double pane windows, from Sullivan and Selkowitz 1986.

Table 2-2 shows the U values for winter (U-W) and summer (U-S) (W/m^2C), Shading coefficient (SC), Solar transmittance (Ts), Visible transmittance (Tv), and the Ke factors of several glazing types, some with higher insulating values, as given in Sullivan and Selkowitz (1986). It shows the effects of Low-E treat-

TABLE 2-1. R VALUES, SC, VT, AND KE FACTORS OF SELECTED GLAZING

WINDOW	R	SC	Tv	Ke
Reflective—bronze	0.44	0.20	0.10	0.5
Tinted—bronze	0.35	0.57	0.47	0.8
Clear	0.35	0.82	0.80	1.0
Low-E—bronze	0.53	0.42	0.41	1.0
Low-E—clear	0.53	0.66	0.72	1.1
Tinted—green	0.35	0.56	0.67	1.2
Low-E—green	0.53	0.41	0.61	1.5

WINDOW	GAS	U-W	U-S	SC	Ts	Tv	Ke
G-G*	Air	2.85	3.16	0.88	0.71	0.82	1.15
G-G-G	Air	1.86	2.20	0.79	0.61	0.74	0.94
G-EpG	Air	2.34	2.63	0.86	0.64	0.73	0.85
G-EsG*	Air	1.94	2.00	0.73	0.58	0.74	1.01
G-EpG	Argon	2.09	2.38	0.86	0.64	0.73	0.85
G-EsG	Argon	1.62	1.68	0.73	0.58	0.74	1.01
G-EsG-G	Air	1.32	1.53	0.71	0.52	0.71	1.00
G-Esg-G	Argon	1.11	1.30	0.72	0.52	0.71	0.99
GEp*		5.05	4.54	0.92	0.75	0.80	0.87

Notes:

G = glazing layer;

Ep = Low-E of 0.35 and Es = Low-E of 0.15 on one side of glazing;

(*) indicates windows examined in warm locations.

ments and argon filling on the insulation values and optical properties of the windows.

Effect of Orientation of Unshaded Windows

When a window is unshaded its quantitative effect on the indoor temperature depends on its orientation, in relation to the diurnal and annual patterns of solar radiation intensity on vertical surfaces. The differential radiation patterns on different orientations depends on the latitude of the location of the building. In particular, a distinction should be made between near-equatorial latitudes (e.g., within about 15 degrees of the equator) and higher latitudes.

Within the equatorial zone, solar radiation on northern and southern walls is much less year-round than on eastern and western walls. In this zone the year-round air temperature is rather high so that summer *overheating* is much more important than winter heating needs (except for locations with high elevation above sea level). Therefore, unshaded windows should be avoided as much as possible in eastern and western walls because they are sources of significant overheating of the interior. It should be pointed out, however, that the equatorial zone is within the Trade Winds belt, where wind direction is mainly from the East. Eastern windows are therefore very desirable in this zone for natural ventilation, which is essential for comfort in this high-humidity zone. The solution, of course, is in providing eastern windows with effective shading, as will be discussed later. At higher latitudes the annual pattern of solar radiation of windows with different orientation is very different, especially when a southern window (in the Northern Hemisphere) is concerned. With higher latitude the

South receives more and more radiation in winter, when heating is needed, while a northern window does not receive any radiation in winter, while getting an insignificant amount in summer. The eastern and western windows receive much more radiation in summer than in winter.

THERMAL EFFECT AND EFFICIENCY OF SHADING DEVICES

Shading devices can be divided broadly into two types: fixed and operable.

Fixed Shading

There are two basic types of fixed shading devices: horizontal (overhangs) and vertical (fins). They can also be combined in different combinations (egg crates). Each one of the basic types casts a distinctive shade pattern, which can be plotted easily as a "shading mask." A shading mask shows the angles between the bottom center of the glass area (the reference point) and the edges of the shading device. In this way the horizontal projection of the sky segment, which is not blocked from the viewpoint of the reference point by the shading device, is plotted. Whenever the sun is in that sky segment some solar radiation reaches the reference point. Examples of shading masks of a horizontal overhang and a vertical fin are shown in Figure 2-3 (Givoni 1976).

Horizontal overhangs are most effective for southern windows. In summer they can block the rays of the sun and in winter they can admit radiation from the sun's lower position. There are, however, some problems during the spring and fall seasons. While the sun is the same on February 21st as on October 21st, February is still cold and solar heating is usually welcomed while October may be still a warm month and sun penetration may cause overheating. Contrary to common beliefs, horizontal overhangs are more effective in summer than fixed vertical fins even for eastern and western windows.

Fixed shading is usually an integral part of the building's structure. Once built, fixed shading's diurnal and annual patterns depend only on the incident angle of the sun's rays. These shading devices cannot ensure complete adjustment of the shade to changing shading needs, although with proper design the overall performance can be reasonably good, especially with respect to southern windows.

An obvious advantage of fixed shading is that it needs no handling by the occupants and is also maintenance free.

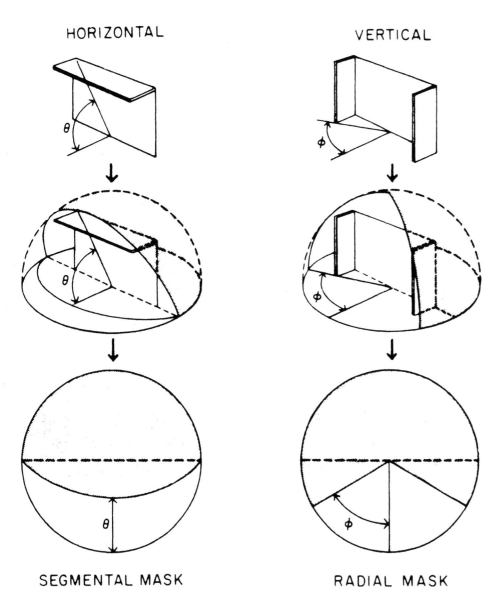

HORIZONTAL   VERTICAL

SEGMENTAL MASK   RADIAL MASK

Figure 2-3. *Examples of shading masks of a horizontal overhang and a vertical fin.*

Operable Shading

The configuration of operable shading devices can be changed, and therefore their performance can be much better than that of fixed devices. However, their position has to be adjusted, daily or seasonally, to the changing patterns of the sun's motion and the shading needs. They also usually need maintenance to keep them in good condition.

Operable shading can be external or internal to the glazing. From the thermal viewpoint there is a very significant difference in the performance of these two types and therefore they will be discussed separately.

Thermal Effect of Shading
in Different Orientations

The effect of window orientation on the indoor temperatures is largely determined by the ventilation conditions and the window's shading conditions. When windows are not shaded, or when the shading is not effective, solar radiation enters through the windows and directly heats the building interior. The amount and diurnal pattern of the penetrating radiation depends on the window's orientation. The effect of the penetrating radiation on the indoor temperatures depends, in turn, on the ventilation conditions. Thus, there are strong interactions between the effect of a window's orientation and the shading conditions and the ventilation of the space in question. Some experimental studies of the subject are discussed below.

An extensive investigation of the effect of a window's orientation under various conditions of shading and ventilation was conducted by the author at the Building Research Station of the Technion, in Haifa, Israel (Givoni 1976). The experimental setup was comprised of four identical rotatable models of 1 x 1 x 1, with walls 15 cm thick made of Ytong (a lightweight concrete). One wall of the model had a window and the rear wall had a smaller opening with an insulated shutter-board. When this small opening was open and the windows remained closed the models could have one-sided low-rate ventilation. The windows could be partially opened, so that cross-ventilation could be provided with the rear openings open also.

The windows were equipped with shading devices (venetian blinds) either white or dark green in color. The four models were oriented with the window of each facing one of the four cardinal directions. Indoor air temperatures, with the windows facing the four orientations, were measured with different shading and ventilation conditions.

The area of the windows, relative to the models' volume, was rather large, to maximize the effects of the windows' orientation and its interaction with their shading and ventilation conditions.

The results of the following test conditions are shown below.

- Closed unshaded windows. Models unventilated.
- Closed models. Windows with internal dark shades.
- Models ventilated only by the rear opening (low-ventilation rate). Windows with internal dark shades.
- Models cross-ventilated. Windows unshaded (Givoni 1976).

Figure 2-4a on page 66 shows air temperatures within unventilated models with unshaded windows. Before sunrise the thermal conditions in all the models were approximately the same, but during the day the differently oriented windows had distinctly different temperature patterns. Immediately after sunrise the model with the eastern window, as expected, showed a steep rise temperature. The indoor maximum in the model with the eastern window was about 6°C (11°F) above the outdoor's maximum. In the western window model the temperature rise was moderate until noon, but due to exposure to direct radiation in the afternoon this rise accelerated and reached a maximum of about 11°C (20°F) above the outdoor maximum temperature.

The models with the unshaded southern and northern windows had roughly similar patterns, with much lower elevation of their indoor maximum above that of the outdoor. The temperature rise of the north-facing model was caused in part by the early-morning and late-afternoon solar radiation striking the glazing.

Figure 2-4b shows the same models when the windows were shaded by dark venetian blinds. It can be seen that the relationship between the indoor and outdoor temperature patterns are similar to those in Figure 2-4a, although the indoor temperature elevation is less, indicating the low efficiency of internal dark shading.

These results, although exaggerated by the relative large area of the windows, demonstrate the sensitivity of unventilated buildings with unshaded windows, or with windows shaded by inefficient interior devices, to the effect of orientation.

Figure 2-4c shows the indoor temperature of the models when the windows were closed and shaded by dark external blinds and the rear small opening was open (low-ventilation rate). It can be seen that with effective shading, and with even low-ventilation rate, the effect of the orientations of the windows almost disappeared. The temperature patterns are similar in all the models.

Figure 2-4d shows the indoor temperature of the models when the windows were without any shading and were partly open, with the rear openings open, to produce cross-ventilation. It can be seen that with cross-ventilation, even when the windows are not shaded, the effect of the orientations of the windows disappeared. The temperature patterns in this configuration were similar in all the models.

COMMENT: EVALUATING THE QUANTITATIVE TEMPERATURE ELEVATIONS IN THE MODELS

In evaluating the actual temperature elevations of the models with the different orientations it should be taken into account that the windows' sizes were very large relative to the volume of the models, in order to accentuate the effect of orientation. In real buildings the actual differences will be smaller but the relative temperature elevations obtained in the different orientations under the

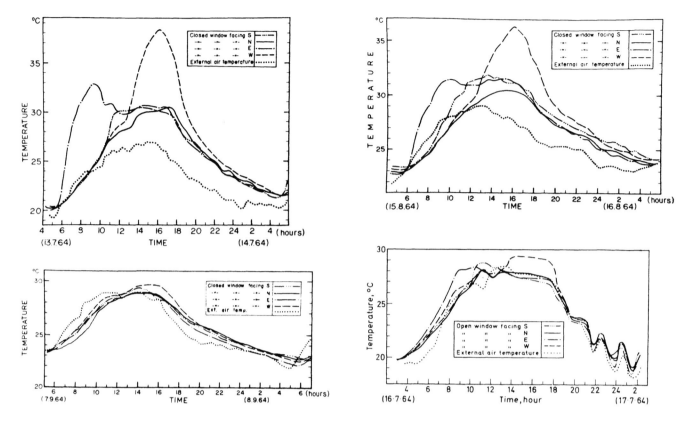

Figure 2-4. *Indoor air temperatures in thermal models with different shading and ventilation conditions.*

  a. closed and unshaded windows;
  b. closed with internal dark blinds;
  c. external dark blinds and low-ventilation rate;
  d. cross-ventilation without shading.

various shading and ventilation conditions would be similar to those obtained in this study.

Ventilation, Thermal Mass, and Indoor Temperatures

Ventilation will have quite different effects on the indoor temperatures, depending on the daily pattern of the ventilation: whether it takes place during the daytime or continuously day and night, or if the building is ventilated *only* during the nighttime and is closed during the daytime hours. Daytime ventilation has relatively small effect on the indoor temperature of buildings protected from solar radiation and its main function is to enhance directly the comfort of the occupants and is termed "comfort ventilation." On the other hand, nighttime ventilation, when the building is kept closed and unventilated during the daytime hours, can significantly lower the indoor temperatures in high-mass buildings, and is termed "nocturnal ventilative cooling."

The effect of nocturnal ventilative cooling on the indoor temperatures of low-mass and high-mass buildings, monitored in California, is covered in detail in Chapter 3. In this chapter, the effect of daytime ventilation, as interacting with the effect of thermal mass, is discussed.

Two buildings, very similar in their thermal resistance but with different levels of mass in their walls, were used in this study. They had identical design: an area of 23 m² (245 sq ft), divided into two equally-sized (south and north) rooms, with ceiling height of 2.4 m (8'). The ceilings of all buildings were identical: insulated low-mass. The first building is a low-mass and the second one is a high-mass.

The low-mass building has stud-wall construction: all external walls are fiberglass insulated to a resistance of R-11 (1.94 m²C/W) (sq ft hr E/Btu). The ceiling is insulated with fiberglass in the attic to an R-19 (3.35 m²C/W) level. The high-mass building has solid concrete walls, 10 cm thick (0.33 ft), insulated externally with rigid foam to the same level as the low-mass building. The partition wall between the two rooms is also of solid concrete. These two buildings offered a unique opportunity to observe the effect of ventilation in buildings with very different levels of thermal mass.

In September–November 1993 the buildings were shaded and ventilated day and night. Figure 2-5 shows outdoor and indoor temperatures of the low-mass and the high-mass buildings during the period from October 31 through November 5, 1993. It can be seen that the daily temperatures of the low-mass building, and most importantly the maximum temperatures, follow closely the outdoor temperature pattern. On the other hand, the maximum temperatures of the high-mass building were lower than the outdoor's maxima. The maximum temperature reduction was larger as the outdoor maximum was higher and daily swings larger. Similar effects were obtained throughout the whole period of continuous ventilation.

The observation that continuously ventilated, high-mass buildings have lower indoor maximum temperature than low-mass buildings with the same thermal insulation has practical significance for building design in hot-humid climates.

Interaction Between Orientation, Solar Control, and Ventilation

As demonstrated in the experimental studies discussed previously, the effect of window's orientation on the energy gain and the indoor temperatures of

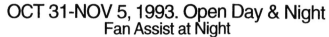
OCT 31-NOV 5, 1993. Open Day & Night
Fan Assist at Night

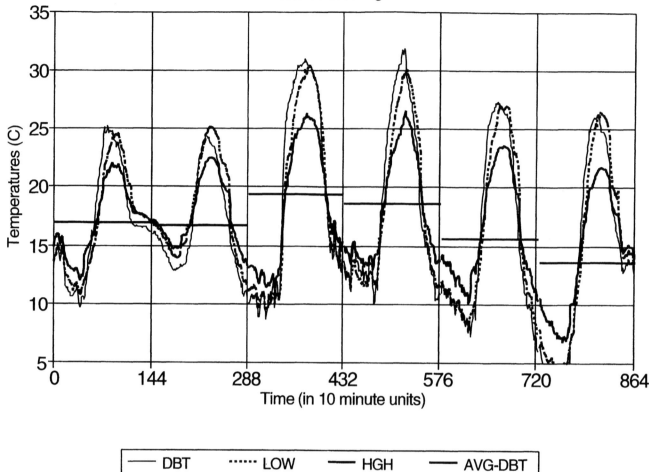

| DBT | ...... LOW | HGH | AVG-DBT |

Figure 2-5. *Indoor and outdoor temperatures of test buildings in Pala, California. The buildings were shaded and ventilated day and night.*

buildings can vary greatly, depending on the shading conditions of the windows and the ventilation of the space in question. The following discussion centers on the impact of a window's orientation in summer (as in winter there is a clear advantage to windows facing the equator—south in the Northern Hemisphere).

UNVENTILATED BUILDING WITH UNSHADED WINDOWS

When windows are not effectively shaded and the space is not ventilated different orientations of windows result in significant variations in the solar heat gain. If the buildings are air conditioned these variations affect the cooling load and the energy demand of the building. In the case of un-air conditioned buildings the result is very significant differences in the indoor temperatures and the comfort conditions of the occupants.

The "worst" orientation from this aspect is the west, as the time of the maximum solar energy striking the window in summer in this orientation coincides with the time of the peak outdoor temperature and close to the peak of the indoor temperature even without solar gain.

On clear days eastern windows receive the same amount or solar radiation as western windows, but the impact of the radiation in this case is somewhat different. The radiation strikes an eastern window when the building is not yet heated. In the early morning the radiation is welcome in most cases, even in hot regions, as some sun penetration into the space is considered desirable from the aspects of hygiene and health.

In many regions (e.g., California) the morning sky is often partly cloudy so that the actual solar gain from an eastern window is less than from a western one. Furthermore, the temperature elevation in the morning, when the building is still cool, causes less discomfort than when it occurs at a time when the building has already reached a temperature near its maximum.

Southern and northern windows have much lower solar gain in summer, when unshaded, than western and eastern windows, and their impact on the indoor temperatures in summer is quite similar. In winter, however, southern windows (in the Northern Hemisphere) have the best solar exposure and are very useful in providing passive solar heating. Northern windows in winter are a liability from the thermal aspect but still are very useful for natural lighting and view.

UNVENTILATED BUILDING WITH EFFECTIVELY SHADED WINDOWS

This study has demonstrated clearly that when windows are effectively shaded, namely by shading devices exterior to the glazing, their orientation has very little effect on the heat gain of the building and its indoor temperatures. This conclusion has far-reaching implications for the evaluation of climatic impacts of western and eastern windows. In many regions of the world the main wind direction is from the west (the Westerlies belt) or from the east (the trade winds belt). To the extent that effective shading is provided, eastern and western windows are very useful in providing natural ventilation.

VENTILATED BUILDING WITH UNSHADED WINDOWS

The experimental studies have demonstrated that when buildings are effectively ventilated during the daytime, the orientation of the windows, and the differences in the solar gain associated with it, have minor effect on the indoor temperatures. With ventilated buildings there is, of course, no energy used for cooling so that the window's orientation has no effect at all on the energy use for cooling.

Effectiveness of Fixed Shading Devices in Different Orientations

As the sun is much higher in summer than in winter, and always reaches the highest altitude at noon, horizontal overhangs above the glazing are most effective for solar control when applied to glazing facing the equator (south in the Northern Hemisphere). In low latitudes in particular, between 20 degrees north and south of the equator, southern and northern overhangs can provide effective protection from the *direct* sun rays, as the sun is at very high altitude when its light strikes these building elevations.

In a study of conditions in Israel (latitude about 32°) the shading efficiency of various shading devices under different orientations was computed in Givoni 1976.

The shading conditions include:

a. No shading
b. Horizontal overhang, only above the window   (H)
c. Horizontal overhang extending sideways infinitely   (Hoo)
d. Vertical fin on both sides, extending only to the window's height   (V)
e. Vertical fins extending infinitely upward   (Voo)
f. Horizontal overhang plus a vertical element oblique at 45 degrees toward the south   (H + V$_{45°}$)

Some results from this study are shown graphically in Figures 2-6 and 2-7. Figure 2-6 shows diurnal patterns of impinging solar radiation on a 1 x 1 m (10.7 sq ft) square eastern window with different fixed shading devices projecting over the window one-third of its dimension, in June and December. Figure 2-7 on page 72 shows the effect of the projection depth of the various shading devices on the total impinging radiation in eastern and western orientations.

As can be seen from these figures the vertical fins exhibited the worst performance in summer as well as in winter. In summer, when the sun is normally at the eastern wall most of the morning hours and at the western wall in the afternoon, the fixed fins, normal to the wall, provide very little protection even at great depth. The horizontal overheads provided better, although insufficient, protection. In winter, on the other hand, the fins cast more shade on the window than the horizontal overhangs.

The best annual performance was exhibited by the frame with vertical fins oblique towards the south. On southern windows the best shading is provided by a horizontal overhead extending well beyond the sides of the window.

Vertical fins are useful when applied to northern windows (in the Northern Hemisphere) especially at latitudes of 30 to 50 degrees, mainly because they can

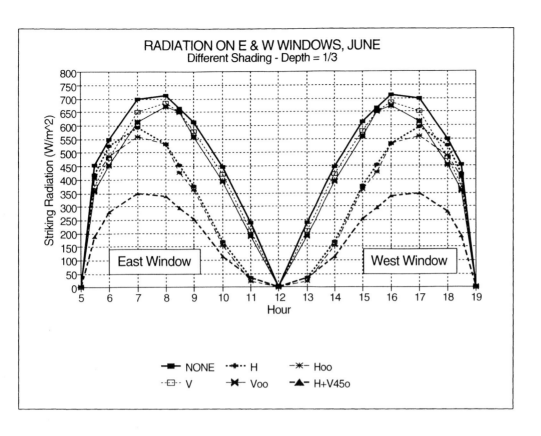

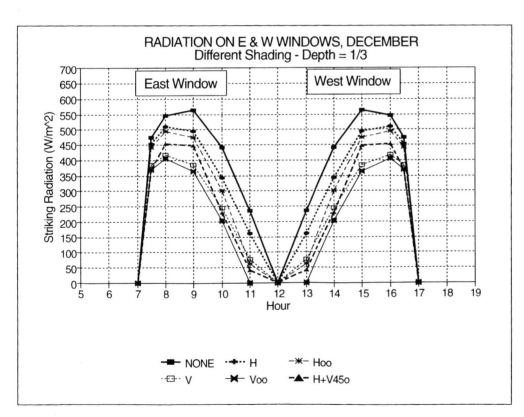

Figure 2-6. *Daily pattern of direct solar radiation striking eastern and western square windows, with various fixed shading devices, in June (a) and in December (b).*

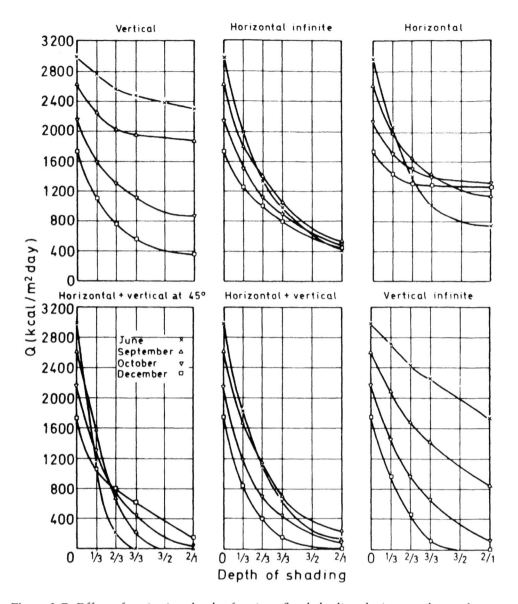

Figure 2-7. *Effect of projection depth of various fixed shading devices on the total impinging radiation in eastern and western orientations.*

block the low sun from the northwest in the afternoon. As the morning sun is often desired even in summer, a single fin on the west side of the window may be better than two symmetrical fins.

The situation is more complex with regard to the relative efficiency of the various types of fixed shadings in eastern and western orientations. Contrary to the conception commonly found in many publications, horizontal overhangs of a given depth are more effective than vertical fins, not only for south-facing glazing but also for glazing facing east or west, especially if the windows are in the form of elongated horizontal strips. This point can be seen in Figures 2-6 and 2-7.

Comparing the horizontal and vertical shadings from the aspect of sun penetration, the horizontal devices let less radiation into the building in June while enabling more sun penetration in December. The best balance between summer minimizing and winter maximizing solar impingement on eastern and western windows is provided by the horizontal overhang, plus a vertical element oblique at 45 degrees toward the south.

Elongated horizontal windows are the easiest to shade by overhangs. Also, with sill height of about 80 cm (2.6 ft), they are also more effective in providing wind-induced ventilation in the "occupied" space of a room than vertical windows with the same open area.

The actual radiation impinging on a window also includes both the diffused and reflected radiation, so that the actual amount of solar radiation striking a window will be larger than the values shown in the figures. The diffused and reflected radiation often are not very different in the different orientations and this factor will reduce the relative differences between the various orientations. Still, Figures 2-6 and 2-7 illustrate the significant differences in the effectiveness of the different fixed shading types, and especially that horizontal shades are superior to vertical types even for eastern and western windows.

The following statements summarize the interactions between the effects of the location and color of shading devices:

a. External shading is much more effective than internal shading.
b. The difference between external and internal shading increases as the color of the shade material is made darker.
c. For external shading the efficiency increases as the color is made darker.
d. For internal shading the efficiency increases as the color is made lighter.
e. Efficient external shading can eliminate about 90 percent of the striking solar radiation.
f. With inefficient shading, such as dark internal devices, the solar gain may amount to about 70–80 percent of the striking radiation.

The high efficiency of external dark shading exists only when the windows are closed, so that the glass can intercept the long-wave radiation emitted from the dark shades. With windows open for cross-ventilation the effect of shading is much smaller.

THERMAL EFFECTS OF WALLS' ORIENTATION AND COLOR

The amount of solar radiation striking a given surface of a building, wall, or roof changes constantly with the seasons of the year as a result of the changing position of the sun in the sky. The diurnal and annual patterns of the sun's motion in the sky depend on the latitude of the location in question (distance, north or south, from the equator). For a given latitude these patterns are symmetrical about the equator. Consequently, surfaces with different orientations, vertical walls as well as horizontal or inclined roofs, will have different exposure to the sun in summer and in winter.

In most regions the objective of orientation with respect to the sun is to maximize solar exposure in winter and to minimize it in summer. This is possible because of the seasonal changes in the altitude and azimuth of the sun.

Eastern and western walls (as well as the roof) are exposed to a high intensity of solar radiation in summer and to much lower radiation in winter. The walls facing the equator (the southern walls in the Northern Hemisphere) are exposed to the highest solar intensity in winter and to relatively low solar radiation in summer.

This pattern of solar impingement on the different walls results in a clear preference, from the solar exposure aspect, for north-south orientations for the main facades of a building, and especially for the windows. Such orientation also enables easy and inexpensive shading in summer on the southern windows, and the southern wall in general, by horizontal overhangs. Such overhangs effectively block the rays of the midsummer sun. In winter, the rays of the lower sun can penetrate below the overhang and be used for heating.

Effect of Colors of the Walls and Roof

The colors of the building's external envelope determine the impact of solar radiation on the building—in effect, what fraction of the solar energy striking the building is actually absorbed at the building's envelope, affecting its heat gain and indoor temperatures, and what fraction is reflected away, without any effect on the building's thermal conditions.

RADIANT PROPERTIES OF SURFACES OF DIFFERENT COLORS

Three physical properties determine the radiant exchange of a surface with its environment: the absorptivity, a, reflectivity, r, and emissivity, E, of the surface in question.

The absorptivity and reflectivity of a surface determine its response to solar (short-wave) radiation striking it. The radiation is partly absorbed at the surface and partly reflected. Only the absorbed fraction of the striking radiation has any effect on the temperature of the surface in question and, consequently, also on the heat gain and the indoor temperature of the building.

The absorbed radiation is proportional to the short-wave (solar) absorptivity, a, of the surface which, practically, depends on its color. The reflected radiation is proportional to the reflectivity, r, of the surface. Solar absorptivity and reflectivity are related by the formulae:

$$r = 1 - a \text{ or } a = 1 - r$$

Any surface also emits and absorbs long-wave radiant energy in proportion to its emissivity, E. This property is independent of the color and for almost all nonmetallic surfaces the emissivity is about 0.9, regardless of their solar absorptivities. In any specific wavelength, such as the long-wave radiation, the emissivity equals the absorptivity, so that with respect to long-wave radiation:

$$E = a$$

Metallic surfaces, and especially polished metals, on the other hand, have very low emissivity and consequently absorb and emit very little long-wave radiation.

Table 2-3 gives the absorptivity, reflectivity, and long-wave emissivity of different surfaces.

The amount of solar radiation striking the different walls of a building varies greatly with the walls' orientation. Therefore, in practice, the colors of the walls determine the quantitative effect of their orientation. In the case of white walls the effect of orientation is very small as most of the impinging radiation is reflected away. In contrast, when the walls have dark colors, the effect

TABLE 2-3. ABSORPTIVITY AND EMISSIVITY OF SURFACES

MATERIAL OR COLOR	ABSORPTIVITY	EMISSIVITY
Whitewash, new	0.15–0.2	0.9
White, "dirty"	0.3–0.35	0.9
White paint	0.2–0.3	0.9
Gray, green, brown, light colors	0.4–0.5	0.9
Gray, green, brown, dark	0.7–0.8	0.9
Ordinary black paint	0.85–0.9	0.9
Aluminum foil, polished	0.05	0.05
Aluminum foil, oxidized	0.15	0.12
Galvanized still, bright	0.25	0.25
Aluminum paint	0.5	0.5

of orientation on their external and internal temperatures is very significant, as is discussed in detail in Chapter 3.

As a result from the effect of the envelope color on the temperatures of its sunlit elements the colors of the walls and the roof affect greatly cooling load of the building and the need for thermal insulation in summer in hot regions.

The Sol-Air Temperature

The surface temperature of a wall or a roof exposed to solar radiation and the resulting heat flow into the building, and the indoor temperatures and cooling needs, depend on the combined effect of several factors: the striking radiation, the surface absorptivity, the ambient air temperature, and the wind speed next to the surface in question. This combined effect is expressed quantitatively by the "sol-air temperature."

The sol-air temperature, for the surface of a given envelope element, is a theoretical external air temperature which produces the same thermal effects on that element as the existing combination of incident radiation and ambient air conditions. That is, it would produce the same external surface temperature, heat flow into and across the element, and internal temperatures.

The general formula of the sol-air temperature is:

$$T_{sa} = T_a + a * I / h_o - LWR$$

where:

T_{sa} = Sol-air temperature

T_a = Outdoor air temperature

a = Absorptivity of the external surface, which depends on its color

I = Intensity of incident solar radiation on the surface

h_o = Overall external surface coefficient, which depends on the wind speed

LWR = Temperature drop due to long-wave radiation to the sky (For a roof: about 6°C (11°F) in an arid climate with a clear sky; 4°C (7°F) in a humid climate with a clear sky. For one-third of the above values. Zero under cloudy sky conditions).

The external surface coefficient, h_o, represents the combined effect of the long-wave radiation and the convective heat loss from the surface to the environment. The magnitude of h_o depends on the wind speed near the surface. A value of 20 W/m²C (6.0 Btu/h.ft²F), with an assumed wind speed of 3.5 m/s

(700 fpm), is suggested for design purposes. However, with a given regional wind speed the actual speed next to a wall is affected to a significant extent by the site design details.

For example, when "specified" wind speed is 3.5 m/s (700 fpm) the actual speed in a densely built urban area, or in a courtyard, would be much smaller (e.g., about one-half of that speed, namely about 1.8 m/s (360 fpm), or even less. The surface coefficient of the same wall, exposed to a wind speed of 1.8 m/s (360 fpm) would be about 13 instead of 20. Thus a wall exposed to a low wind speed, having a given color and exposed to a given intensity of solar radiation, will have a much higher surface temperature, resulting in a higher heat gain, than a wall facing the external environment.

As an example, let us consider a dark wall with absorptivity a = 0.70, exposed to solar radiation I = 600 W/m² (190 Btu/hr. sq ft), an outdoor air temperature T_a = 30°C (86°F), and wind speed of 3.5 m/s (700 fpm) under a clear sky in an arid region (LWR = 2°C (3.6°F).

$$T_{sa} = 30 + 0.7 * 600 / 20 - 2 = 49°C$$

$$T_{sa} = 86 + 0.7 \times 190 / 3.5 - 3.6 = 120°F$$

The sol-air temperature of the dark wall, with wind speed of 1.8 m/s, will be:

$$T_{sa} = 30 + 0.7 * 600 / 13 - 2 = 60°C (140°F)$$

The sol-air temperature of a white wall (a = 0.25) under the same ambient temperature and solar radiation conditions, and with wind speed of 3.5 m/s, will be:

$$T_{sa} = 30 + 0.25 * 600 / 20 - 2 = 35.5°C (96°F)$$

The sol-air temperature of the same white wall, with wind speed of 1.8 m/s, will be:

$$T_{sa} = 30 + 0.25 * 600 / 13 - 2 = 39.5°C (103°F)$$

The above calculations demonstrate how color affects the sensitivity of the thermal response of a building to solar radiation and orientation, especially in summer in hot regions. They also demonstrate that the wind speed mainly affects the sol-air temperature (and the external surface temperature) of dark walls (or roofs) while the wind speed effect in case of light-colored walls is much smaller.

Experimental Data on the Effect of Colors on Exterior and Interior Surface Temperatures of Walls and Roofs

This section presents some results of experimental studies by the author on the effect of the colors of walls and roofs, made of different materials, on external and internal surface temperatures. The quantitative effect of the envelope color on the indoor air temperature, and on the energy demand of a building, depends on the thermal properties of the walls and the roof, as well as on the ventilation conditions. That subject is discussed in more detail in Chapter 3. In this chapter the effect of external color on indoor conditions will be briefly illustrated.

Figure 2-8 shows side-by-side the external and internal surface temperatures

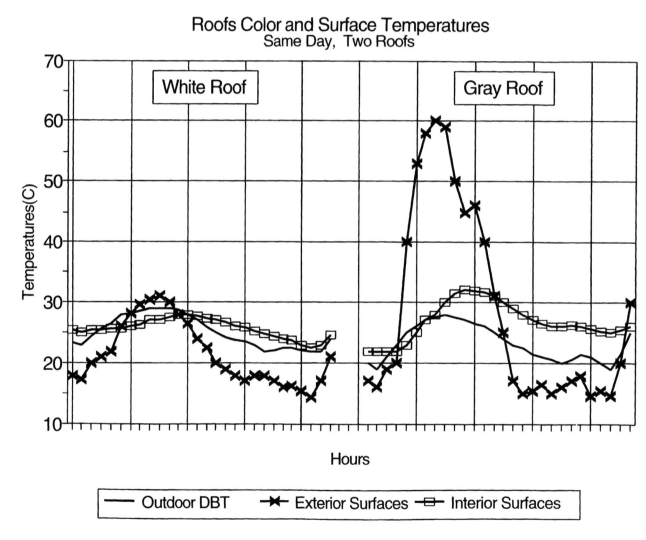

Figure 2-8. *External and internal surface temperatures of a horizontal roof, with white and gray colors.*

of a horizontal roof, together with the ambient air temperature during two days, measured during two experimental series. The roof in this study was a sandwich made of two layers of asbestos-cement with an insulation of 3-cm (1.2") expanded polystyrene in between. During the series of the first day shown in the figure, the roof was white, and during the series of the second day its color was gray. This study was conducted in midsummer in Haifa, Israel.

It can be seen from Figure 2-8 that during the first series, with an outdoor air maximum of about 29°C (84.2°F), the surface temperature maximum of the white roof was about 31°C (87.8°F), about two degrees above the outdoor maximum. The interior surface's maximum temperature was about 28°C (82.4°F), namely about one degree below the outdoor's maximum.

In the day when the color of the same roof was gray the outdoor maximum was about 27.5°C (81.5°F), the roof's exterior surface maximum was about 60°C (140°F), about 32 degrees C (57.6°F) above the outdoor's maximum. The interior surface's maximum of the insulated roof was about 32°C (89.6°F), about 4.5 degrees above the outdoor's maximum.

Figures 2-9 and 2-10 on pages 80 and 81 show indoor temperatures of thermal models (1 x 1 x 0.8 m) (2.6') with walls built of different materials and thicknesses. The walls shown are concrete and Ytong, 12 and 22 cm (4.8 and 8.8") thick. In Figure 2-9 the exterior color of the walls was white and in Figure 2-10 it was gray. The roofs of all models were identical (insulated lightweight panels) and painted white. The values shown are the averages of the temperatures measured during the experimental series, each lasting several weeks.

It can be seen from Figure 2-9 that with the white wall the maximum temperatures of all the models were close to the outdoor's maximum; the models with the thick walls (22 cm) (8.8") below the outdoor's maximum; and the models with the thin walls (12 cm) (4.8") a little above the outdoor's maximum. With the gray walls, as shown in Figure 2-10, all the indoor maxima were appreciably above the outdoor's maximum. The effect of the walls' thickness is manifested mainly in the smaller temperature swing: the maxima were lower and the minima were higher in the models with the thicker walls. The effect of walls' thickness on the maxima was larger than on the minima.

Visual Attributes of Colors

The exterior colors of the building's envelope chosen by the architect, in most cases those of the walls but, in the case of a sloped roof, also the roof's color, are among the very distinctive features of the building. Although from the thermal aspect the main parameter of interest is the solar absorptivity of the surface, the actual decision of the building's designer is between various colors.

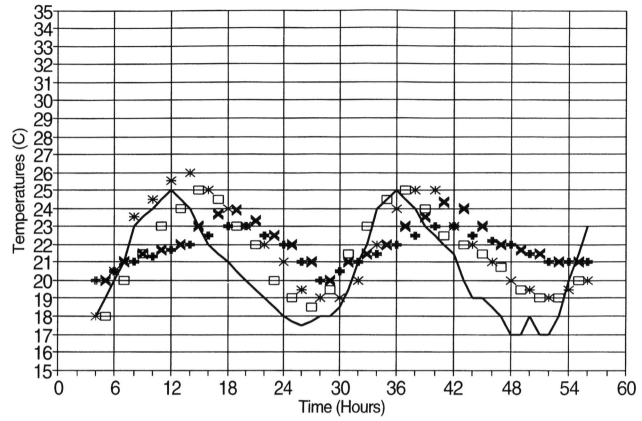

Models of different materials-White

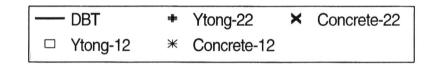

—— DBT	✳ Ytong-22	✕ Concrete-22
☐ Ytong-12	✻ Concrete-12	

Figure 2-9. *Indoor air temperatures of thermal models with walls built of different materials and thicknesses. White exterior color.*

From the visual aspect colors are defined by three attributes: hue, lightness, and saturation (Jones 1968), and each of them has some impact on the thermal effect of the building element in question. *Hue* is the attribute which defines the principal color: red, yellow, green-blue, and purple, and their adjacent hues. In the Munsell System of Colors (Munsell Color Company, Inc. 1950) there are ten hues. Each hue has a distinctive wavelength, and thus can be measured physically.

Lightness is the attribute which corresponds to the physical property of reflectivity, but evaluated visually via a scale which locates the position of the color between black and white. The scale is from nine (near-black) to one (near-white).

Saturation is the attribute of color which describes the visual brightness-

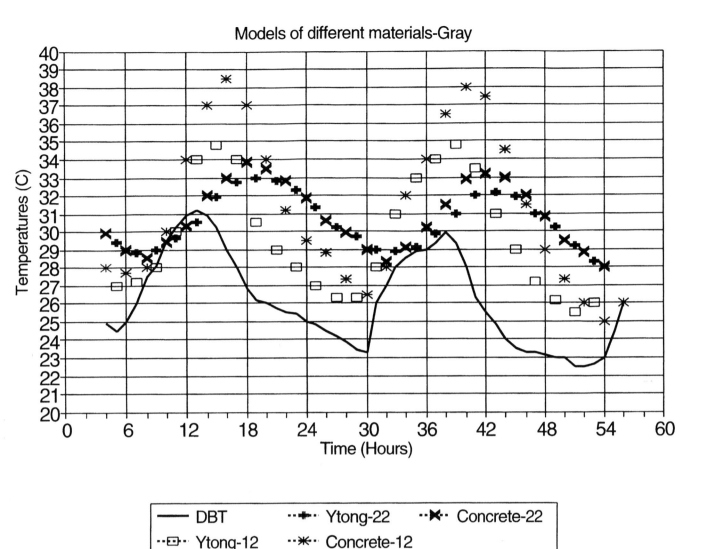

Figure 2-10. *Indoor air temperatures of thermal models with walls built of different materials and thicknesses. Gray exterior color.*

grayness ratio. Jones (1968) gives the example of the saturation graduation of the blue color: bluish gray (near-gray), grayish blue, moderate blue, strong blue, and vivid blue. He notes that in the case of red, yellow, and purple the eye can detect more different degrees of saturation than can be discriminated in such colors as blue and green.

In the Munsell System each color is denoted by a letter for its hue, and two numbers separated by a slash, specifying its lightness and saturation, respectively. For example, R 4/2 would designate dark reddish-gray, R 4/8 a moderate red, R 7/2 a pinkish-gray, and a YR 7/2 would designate a brownish-pink.

Jones measured the temperatures of metal plates painted with colors of different hues, lightness, and saturation (all with designations of 6/6), exposed to the midday sun. He found that, for colors with the same visual brightness and saturation, the hues in the middle wavelength, such as green and yellow and colors having enough green to carry green in their hue name, such as blue-green, absorb more heat, resulting in higher temperatures—about 70°C (159°F), with ambient temperature of about 38°C (100°F). Colors with longer or shorter wavelengths, such as red and yellow-red on one hand, and blue and purple on the other hand, had equally lower temperatures—about 60°C (141°F). This finding is of significance to architects considering a choice of an external color in a hot climate.

Effect of Orientation on External Surface Temperatures

The quantitative effect of solar radiation depends primarily on the external color, and to a lesser extent on the airspeed close to the surface. The temperature elevation of a surface, caused by a given amount of solar radiation striking it, varies inversely with the lightness of the surface color and with the wind speed next to the surface.

The actual external surface temperature of a wall at a given orientation depends both on the ambient air temperature and on the solar radiation absorbed at the surface. The former is almost independent of orientation, and the variations in the wind speed over the different walls and the roof, except under special situations, are not very great. Therefore, for general surface temperature estimations, an average (default) value of the wind speed is adequate. The latter is more dependent on orientation, as discussed earlier in this chapter.

In the absence of solar radiation, for example on a cloudy day, the temperature patterns of wall surfaces in any orientation are more or less close to that of the outdoor air diurnal pattern. But on exposure to solar radiation, whether direct, diffused, or reflected, the external wall's temperature rises above the ambient air level, in proportion to the *absorbed* radiation. When the color of the surface is light, and correspondingly its absorptivity is low, the ambient air temperature has a greater thermal effect than the incident radiation, whereas with dark external colors the influence of solar radiation may be the dominant factor.

The effects of color and orientation on the surface temperatures of walls and roofs were also part of the author's experimental study at the Building Research Station of the Technion University in Haifa, Israel (Givoni 1976).

Figure 2-11 (Givoni 1976) on page 84 shows external surface temperatures of gray walls (Figure 2-11a) and of white-painted walls (Figure 2-11b), respectively. The walls faced the four cardinal directions. Comparison of the two parts of this figure indicates that there was considerable interaction between the effects of orientation and of color. Differences of up to (23°C) (73.4°F) were observed in the temperatures of gray walls in different orientations, while for whitewashed walls deviations were all less than (3°C) (5.4°F).

These results demonstrate that discussion of the thermal effect the orientation of walls is meaningless unless reference is made to the external color (absorptivity) of the walls in question. It is also clear that considerable control on the effect of solar radiation is possible through choice of color. The interaction between the effects of the walls' orientation and their color can thus be evaluated by calculating the sol-air temperature of walls facing different orientations.

Figure 2-12 (Givoni 1976) on page 85 shows the external surface temperatures, in January and in July (Figures 2-12a and 2-12b, respectively), calculated for the climatic conditions of the arid region of the Negev in Israel. Three levels of absorptivity (0.8, 0.5, and 0.2) are assumed, representing dark, medium, and white colors of the walls.

Effect of Wall Orientation on Indoor Temperatures

The magnitude of the thermal effect of wall orientation on the indoor temperatures depends, in addition to the wall's color, on its material and thickness, which determines its thermal resistance and heat capacity, as will be discussed in Chapter 3.

To provide a starting point, one may consider a building with rooms facing several directions, with white external walls, the thermal resistance is medium-to-high, and the windows are effectively shaded. Because of the low absorptivity of all the surfaces, the external temperatures of the different walls will closely follow the outdoor air pattern, showing little variation of the external surfaces with orientation. Differences which still do exist in the external temperatures of the walls with the different orientations are further diminished by the insulation properties of the walls. As a result, the internal surface temperatures of the walls will be very close, regardless of their different orientations. The shaded windows prevent direct penetration of solar energy into the building but allow the rooms to be ventilated by a flow of external air, having the same temperature irrespective of the rooms' orientation. Thus, under these conditions, the indoor air temperatures of all the rooms will follow a pattern determined by that of the outdoor air and modified by the structural heat capacity and the thermal resistance of the building materials (see Chapter 3).

If, instead of white, the exterior of the walls is dark, the external temperature pattern would vary according to the radiation striking the different surfaces, as determined by their orientation. The magnitude of the temperature elevation above the ambient level also depends on the wind direction. For instance, in an area where the prevailing winds are westerly, the elevation above

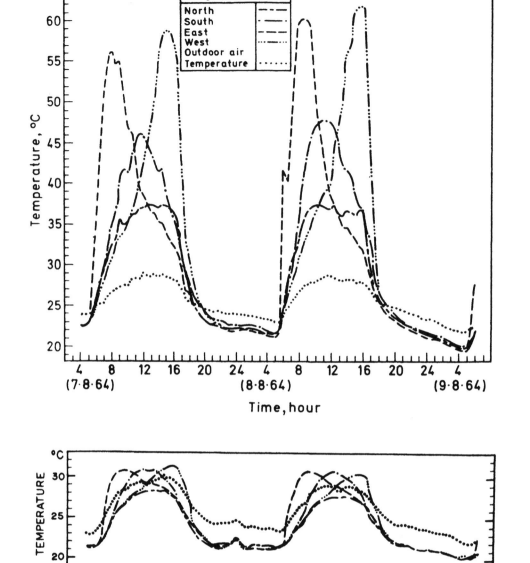

Figure 2-11. *External surface temperatures of gray- and of white-painted walls, facing the four cardinal directions.*

the outdoor level of the surface temperature of an east-facing wall in the morning will be above that of a west-facing wall in the afternoon, although the intensity of irradiation is almost the same in both cases.

The influence of orientation on the external temperatures, in turn, affects the heat flow through the wall and the resulting internal surface temperatures. Quantitatively, the pattern and amount of the temperature elevation depends on the heat capacity and thermal resistance of the walls. The internal temperatures follow the external patterns more closely as the heat capacity and the thermal

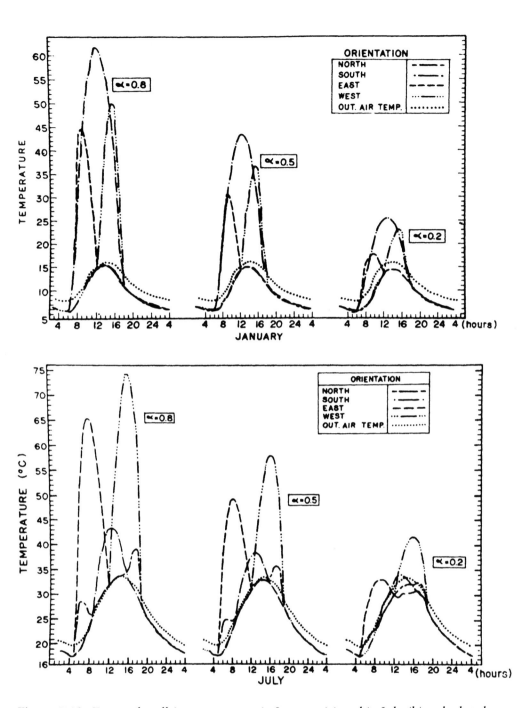

Figure 2-12. *External walls' temperatures, in January (a) and in July (b), calculated with dark, medium, and white colors.*

resistance are reduced, and are less influenced by orientation when these properties, particularly the thermal resistance, are high.

To illustrate the interdependence of the effects of orientation, external color, and wall thickness, Figure 2-13 (Givoni 1976) shows internal surface temperature patterns measured on lightweight concrete walls facing the four cardinal directions; the walls were Ytong, of two thicknesses—10 cm (4") and 20 cm

(8")—externally painted gray and white, measured in two experimental series, respectively.

It can be seen from Figure 2-13 that with a white exterior color the internal temperatures fluctuated above the average outdoor level, but the extent of the fluctuation was greater with the thinner walls. Only slight differences in the

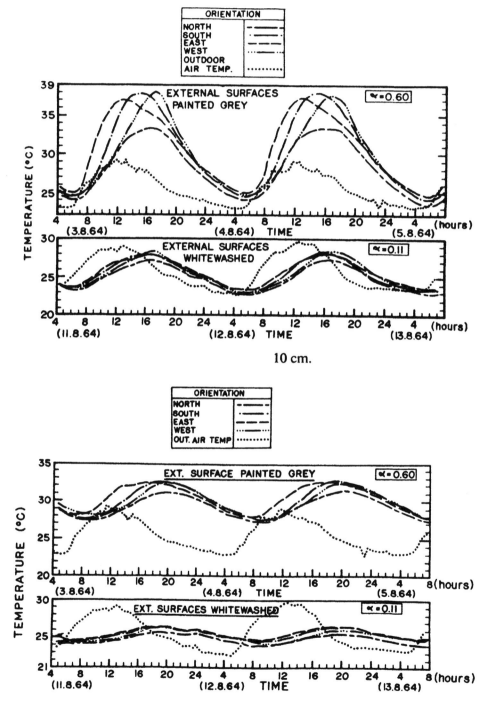

Figure 2-13. *Measured internal surface temperature of lightweight gray and white concrete walls, 10 cm and 20 cm (4" and 8") thick.*

temperature pattern were observed between the walls with the different orientations. The maximum differences between the warmest (east or west) and the coolest (north) walls were larger for the thinner than for the thicker walls: less than 1°C (2°F) as compared with 1.5°C (3°F).

When the external color was gray, however, the temperature differences between walls with different orientations and thicknesses were much more marked. For the 10-cm (4") walls the minima were all somewhat below the average outdoor temperature, while the range of maxima was about 4.5°C (8°F). The largest difference at any instant was about 7°C (13°F).

Increasing the thickness to 20 cm (8") effectively moderated these variations. The range of minimum temperatures was about 2.5°C (4.5°F), the range of maxima about 1.3°C (2°F), and the greatest difference observed was about 2.7°C (5°F).

Comparing the Effects of Color and Thermal Insulation and Mass

Although there is a similarity between the effect of whitewashing and of increasing the thermal resistance and capacity, in that both reduce the differential effects of orientation, a basic difference exists in mechanism and a practical qualitative difference in effect between the two methods. Whitewashing, by reducing the absorptivity of the wall surfaces, minimizes the quantity of solar radiation effective in heating the building, and thus reduces both the maximum and minimum temperatures. In contrast, increasing the resistance and heat capacity of the structure moderated the internal heating effect of the elevated external surface temperature and, while the internal maxima are lowered, the minima are raised. For this reason whitewashing is more important for un-air conditioned buildings in hot countries. High levels of insulation are needed in hot regions primarily for air conditioned buildings and, for all buildings, in regions with cold winters.

NATURAL VENTILATION

In all climatic regions of the world there are times when the outdoor temperature is pleasant and natural ventilation can be the simplest and most effective way to provide indoor comfort. Even in most hot regions there are months and times of the day when ventilation can provide comfort and, even in houses equipped with air conditioning, reduce the use for mechanical cooling. In warm-humid regions ventilation is an effective cooling strategy year-round. The role of ventilation in maintaining adequate indoor air quality and thermal comfort was discussed in Chapter 1.

Ventilating the building only at night can cool the interior mass of the building. By closing the windows during the daytime hours, the cooled mass reduces the rate of indoor temperature rise and thus may keep the indoor temperature significantly below the outdoor level. This strategy is termed nocturnal ventilative cooling. The effectiveness of nocturnal ventilation in lowering the indoor daytime temperature depends on the properties of the building materials, the shading conditions of the windows, and the external color of the building's envelope. This subject is discussed in detail in Chapter 4.

Natural ventilation takes place mostly through windows, so that building design for ventilation means, to a great extent, decisions by the designer concerning the location, number, size, orientation, and design details of the windows.

The ventilation potential of a building depends on the wind speed around the building—at the building's site. The site's wind conditions, in turn, depend on two factors: the urban wind approaching the site and the design details of the site's landscaping. The effect of urban design on the urban wind conditions is discussed in Chapter 8. The effect of site landscaping on the wind conditions around a building is discussed in Chapter 9.

Ventilation Requirements

Ventilation has three functions, which require different levels of airflow through the building:

1. Maintaining acceptable indoor air quality by replacing indoor air, vitiated in the processes of living and occupancy, with fresh outdoor air. This function of ventilation is needed in all climates but is of interest mainly in cold climates, and also in air conditioned buildings in all climate types.

2. Providing thermal comfort in a warm environment by increasing convective heat loss from the body and preventing discomfort from excessively moist skin through a higher airspeed over the body (comfort ventilation). Comfort ventilation was discussed in more detail in Chapter 1.

3. Cooling the structural mass of the building during the night and utilizing the cooled mass as a "heat sink" during the following daytime hours in order to maintain the indoor temperature well below the outdoor level (nocturnal ventilative cooling). This subject is discussed in further detail in Chapter 3.

The relative importance of each of these functions depends on climatic conditions prevailing in a given region during different seasons.

VENTILATION FOR MAINTAINING AIR QUALITY

In occupied buildings the composition and quality of the indoor air are affected by living processes and occupancy activities. Oxygen is consumed by breathing. Carbon dioxide (CO_2) and water vapor, as well as bacteria, are discharged from the lungs. Odor-producing organic materials are given off by the body, depending greatly upon the hygienic habits and diet of the building's occupants. Smoking pollutes the air for both health and odor aspects. Some building, furniture, and flooring/carpeting materials also give off objectionable gasses.

The ventilation rate to maintain air quality depends on the number of persons per unit volume of the habitable space, and their lifestyle and sensitivity. A ventilation rate of about 0.5 air changes per hour (ACH) can be suggested as the minimum health ventilation rate in residential buildings with low-occupancy density for maintaining adequate indoor air quality in all climatic conditions.

COMFORT (DAYTIME) VENTILATION

The need for comfort ventilation exists only when the indoor environment is felt as too warm or stuffy under still-air conditions. From the comfort aspect, the relevant ventilation parameter is the airspeed *over the body* and not necessarily the rate of airflow through the building. Natural ventilation is desirable when the outdoor air is at a lower temperature than the indoor air or when it can prevent elevation of the indoor temperature above the outdoor's level, caused by direct solar energy penetration through unshaded windows or by indirect solar heating caused by dark colors of the building's walls and roof. In particular, natural ventilation is desirable when it minimizes discomfort resulting from wet skin, a situation common in hot-humid regions.

On the other hand, in hot-dry regions the indoor temperature during the daytime can be kept, by appropriate building design (effective shading, light colors of the building's envelope, and suitable choice of materials; see Chapter 3), at significantly lower levels than the outdoor's maximum temperature. The humidity level in such regions is rather low, so that indoor vapor generation does not raise it to levels producing discomfort due to sensible perspiration. In this case, when a higher indoor airspeed is desired, it may be preferable to provide it by fans rather than to ventilate the building by opening the windows, bringing in warmer outdoor air.

The delineation of the boundaries of the climatic conditions under which ventilation can be applied is discussed in Chapter 1.

The Physical Forces Generating Ventilation

Ventilation, namely the flow of outdoor air through a building, occurs when openings are available at points exposed to different levels of air pressure. Such pressure gradients (or pressure heads) can be generated by two forces:

a. Temperature difference between the indoors and the outdoors (thermal, or thermosyphonic, force)
b. Wind flow against the building (wind pressure force)

Regardless of the source of the pressure gradient the airflow rate generated is proportional to the square root by the pressure head.

Ventilation by Thermal Force

Air density and pressure are reduced with height. The rate of this pressure drop depends on the air temperature: the higher the temperature, the smaller the drop in air pressure with height. When the average indoor air temperature is higher than the temperature outdoors at the same height, the pressure gradient indoors, where the air is less dense, is smaller than outdoors. As a result, if openings are available at different heights, the indoor air pressure is higher at the upper opening and lower at the lower opening, as compared with the outdoor air pressure at the same levels. These pressure differences are called pressure heads. The pressure head generates an inward airflow at the lower opening and an outward airflow at the upper one (thermosyphonic flow).

If the indoor temperature is lower than the outdoor temperature, the thermosyphonic-flow pattern is reversed: outdoor air then enters at the upper opening and flows out through the lower opening.

The flow rate, Q, can be expressed directly in terms of height and temperature differences. It is calculated by the formula:

$$Q = K * A * (h * dt)^{0.5}$$

where:

> Q = Airflow rate, $m^3 / (min.m^2)$, or $ft^3 / (min.ft^2)$
> A = Net effective area of the opening, m^2 or ft^2
> h = Vertical distance between the centers of the upper and lower openings, m or ft
> dt = Difference between indoor and outdoor average temperatures, °C or °F

K = proportionality constant (It depends on the units used, on the flow resistance of the openings and the interior obstructions. ASHRAE gives a value of 9.4 for K with assumed 65 percent opening effectiveness. (The value of K in metric units is 6.96.)

Assuming a space with top and bottom openings of 1 m² (10.8 sq ft) each, at a vertical distance between their centers of 1 meter (3.3 ft)—a practical value in single-story apartments—an indoor temperature of 25°C (77°F) and an outdoor temperature of 20°C (68°F)—a very large temperature difference for ventilated buildings—the expected thermosyphonic flow rate would be:

$$Q = 9.4 * 10.76 * (3.28 * 9)^{0.5} = 550 \text{ ft}^{3/min}$$

In the metric system, with the same details (area of 10.76 ft², height of 3.28 ft, and temperature difference of 9°F) the airflow will be:

$$Q = 6.96 * 1 * (1 * 5)^{0.5} = 15.6 \text{ m}^3/min \text{ or } 934 \text{ m}^3/h$$

As will be seen later on, this flow rate is rather small under summer conditions, in comparison with the flow which can be induced in a cross-ventilated building even by a very light wind. Consequently, design for summer ventilation by wind force should be applied when summer ventilation is being considered.

In multistoried dwelling units (e.g., a two- or three-story townhouse or a single-family house), the effective vertical distance between inlets and outlets would be about five to seven meters, 16.5 to 23 ft or even nine meters (30 ft) when roof openings are provided. The flow rate would then be doubled or tripled. Although still a weak airflow in terms of summer comfort ventilation, it might be important for ventilation during windless night hours.

The situation is different in winter in cold regions, when much greater temperature differences exist between the indoors and the outdoors, especially at night, often 20–30°K or even more.

Ventilation Due to Wind Force

When wind blows against a building, it is deflected around the walls and above the roof. The air in front of the walls facing the wind is compressed, creating a *pressure zone,* and the air next to the leeward walls and above the roof expands, and the pressure is reduced, thus creating a *suction zone.* In this way pressure differences are created between different areas of the building envelope.

The pressure differences between any two points on the building's envelope determine the potential for ventilation when openings are provided at these points (driving force) and if air can flow inside the building from openings with the higher pressure to openings exposed to a zone with lower pressure.

Wind-induced airflow rate inside a building is proportional to the outdoor wind speed in front of the inlet window. The windows themselves, as well as obstructions within the ventilated space, present resistance to airflow. The effect of this resistance is to reduce the airflow rate. It is taken into account by a factor K, the permeability factor.

The flow rate, Q, through a building exposed to a perpendicular wind of V m/s, with an effective opening area of A_{eff}, and an overall permeability factor of K, would be

$$Q = K * A_{eff} * V$$

The value of the effective area A_{eff} is the area of the inlets when the outlets have the same area. If the inlets and the outlets are not of the same area, the smaller value should be taken into account, with some increase due to the larger openings, up to a value of 1.4 * A, when the outlet area is 5 times the inlet area (or vice versa).

The value of K for a space with direct cross-ventilation and without internal obstructions to the airflow is about 0.7. Internal obstructions, such as doors between two connected rooms when the air enters in one room and leaves through the other room, reduce the value of K and the resulting airflow rate.

Thus, for a space with an area of 30 m² (323 sq ft) and a volume of 75 m³ (2648 ft³), with inlet and outlet openings of 1.0 m² (10.7 sq ft) each and without any internal obstructions, exposed to a very mild wind of 2.0 m/s (400 fpm), the flow rate, Q, would be:

$$Q = 0.7 * 1 * 2 = 1.4 \text{ m}^3/\text{s, or } 5040 \text{ m}^3/\text{h (2966 cfm)}.$$

This is about 5.4 times the thermosyphonic flow induced by temperature difference of 5°K (9°F) computed above.

The ACH would be:

$$ACH = 5040 / 75 = 67 \text{ air changes per hour.}$$

ARCHITECTURAL FEATURES AFFECTING VENTILATION

The main design features which affect the indoor ventilation conditions are:

- Type of building.
- Orientation of the building, especially the openings, with respect to wind direction.

- Total area of openings in the pressure and suction regions of the building's envelope.
- Type of windows and details of their opening.
- Vertical location of openings.
- Interior obstructions to airflow from the inlet to the outlet openings.
- Presence or absence of fly screens in the openings.
- Specialized details which direct the air into the building.

The effect of the windows' size and orientation with respect to the wind direction was investigated extensively. These studies are summarized in the following section.

The major impact of the above-mentioned design details is in the extent to which they enable or inhibit cross-ventilation of the building as a whole and of its individual rooms. Cross-ventilation is defined as the situation in which outdoor air can flow from openings on one side of the building (the inlet) located in the pressure zones, through the building, and out via the outlet openings located in the suction sections of the building.

Type of the Building

The type of a building, especially housing (whether a detached house, a town house, a high-rise apartment building with single-loaded or double-loaded corridors, or a square building with four units), determines, in practice, the options of providing effective cross-ventilation. The main issue to consider is the possibility of providing, in the same residential unit, openings both on the windward and leeward sides of the unit.

This subject is discussed in Chapter 6.

Orientation of Buildings and Openings, with Respect to Wind Direction

To provide good potential for natural ventilation at least one of the walls of any dwelling unit should face the wind. It is *not* necessary to face the wind directly. Even with winds oblique to a wall by up to about 60 degrees from the perpendicular (normal) it is possible to use windows in the wall as inlets for the wind. This fact gives planners a great deal of freedom (over a range of 120 degrees with respect to the windward facade) in choosing adequate orientation from the ventilation aspect. The openings in the walls which are in the "shadow" of the wind can then serve as outlets for the wind, thus enabling cross-ventilation of the whole building.

In many regions the wind direction changes between day and night, and sometimes also between different seasons. In such cases the best orientation, from the aspect of ventilation, would be with respect to the wind direction during the periods with the lowest wind speeds, very often during the night hours.

It should be taken into account that from the design aspect it is easier to provide indoor protection from the wind in winter than to ensure cross-ventilation. Therefore the summer ventilation considerations may often be the more important.

It is a common belief that for obtaining good ventilation in elongated buildings the main walls should be perpendicular to the prevailing wind direction, as this orientation produces the largest pressure differential between the windward and leeward walls. In fact, such orientation may be the "best" only for an isolated elongated building located in an open field.

In reality, the situation in urban areas is often different. Rows of buildings oriented perpendicularly to the wind produce the largest resistance to the wind flow near the ground level. Most of the buildings (except for the first building in line) are exposed to suction zones on all sides, resulting in very poor ventilation potential.

On the other hand, groups of buildings which have an oblique orientation to winds, with angles of 30 to 60 degrees away from the normal, can provide better access to the wind at ground level into the depth of the "neighborhood," and thus better ventilation conditions for individual rooms and for the building as a whole. When the wind is oblique to a building, the two upwind walls are at pressure zones and the two downwind walls at suction zones, thus providing more options for placing of inlets openings.

Furthermore, in many situations rooms have only one external wall. If two windows are provided in that wall, and the wind is perpendicular to the wall, the two openings are exposed to about the same pressure, and this configuration reduces the ventilation potential of the room. When the wind is oblique to the building a pressure gradient is created along the windward walls and the upwind window is at a higher pressure than the downwind one. Thus, air enters the room through the upwind window and leaves through the downwind aperture, creating better ventilation even in rooms which have only one external wall (see discussion on wing-walls below).

The effect of windows' location (orientation with respect to the wind), is relevant mainly to the placement of the *inlet openings*. The location of the outlet openings has no significant effect on the indoor airflow.

Vertical Location of Windows

The height of the inlet opening may determine the level of the main indoor airflow. At levels below the sill of the inlet there is usually a sharp drop in airspeed unless this is prevented by special design features.

In some cases, architectural, functional, or privacy requirements call for placing openings near the ceiling, with their sills high above the level of occupancy. In this case, poor ventilation conditions may exist in the occupied zone of the room unless the flow is directed downward.

It is possible to direct the airflow in any desired direction by the opening details of the inlet. If the inlet window is hinged at the top and is opened inward and upward, it forces the flow downward when the sash is opened to an inclined position. The actual angle of the sash then determines the direction of the airflow (in the vertical plane). This point is of special importance in the case of earth-covered buildings, with walls bermed up the sill of high clerestories, which otherwise may suffer from poor ventilation conditions when comfort ventilation is desired.

Window Types and Ways of Opening

Different types of windows, when serving as inlets, produce different patterns of indoor airflow and provide different options for controlling the direction and level of the flow.

Double-hung windows, by their height, determine the vertical level of airflow but not its direction and pattern. The maximum openable area is less than one-half of the total area of the sashes, a factor which limits the effective ventilation rate.

Horizontally sliding windows also provide less than half of the free-opening area. They enable less control of the indoor flow pattern than double-hung windows because horizontal variations in the flow direction are much greater than in the vertical plane as a result of changes in wind direction.

Casement windows opened to the outside can serve as wing-walls, creating an elevated pressure when the downwind sash is opened, or creating a suction zone when the upwind sash is opened. However, when both sashes are opened, they may provide a smaller airflow compared with opening only the downwind sash owing to interference in the flow.

Horizontal center-pivot-hung windows enable control of the vertical pattern of airflow, either upward or downward, if the sashes can be made to open downward on the room side, 10 degrees below the horizontal. Experiments by the author (Givoni 1976) have demonstrated that by altering the angle to which the sash is opened it is possible to modify and alter airflow patterns and distribution of velocities throughout the indoor space.

In some cases, it is desirable to have a sharp drop in indoor airspeed at some level (e.g., at table level in offices and classrooms). This also can be accomplished by the detailing of the inlet windows.

Subdivision of the Interior Space

Whenever the air has to pass through more than one room on its way from the inlet opening to the outlet, it encounters additional resistance. Actual resistance depends on the size of interior openings (doorways or pass-throughs) through which the air flows. In addition, changes in the flow direction along the way, as well as contraction and expansion of the airstream while passing through interior passages, create turbulence, increase flow resistance, and reduce the flow rate. Therefore, if internal subdivision of the building enables independent cross-ventilation of individual rooms, better overall ventilation of the building is produced.

It should be noted that if the aperture connecting two rooms, through which the air flows, is smaller than either the inlet or the outlet, the smallest aperture will determine the actual flow rate. Thus, in many designs of apartment buildings, two bedrooms are located on opposite sides of the building with a corridor separating them. The planned ventilation path is from the inlet in the room on the windward side of the building, through shutters in the doors leading to the corridor from both rooms (because the doors may be closed for privacy), through the room on the leeward side of the building, and out through the outlet opening. The bottlenecks in this path are the door shutters in or above the doors. The flow resistance provided by these shutters is the limiting factor for the whole airflow.

EXPERIMENTAL STUDIES ON VENTILATION

The effect of building design features on the indoor ventilation conditions was investigated extensively in several experimental studies. Three of them, Givoni 1962, 1968, Sobin 1983, and Ernest 1991, were conducted in wind tunnels. One study was conducted in a full-scale building, at the Florida Solar Energy Center. They are all summarized next.

PRELIMINARY COMMENT ON THE COMPARABILITY
OF INDOOR AIRSPEEDS MEASURED IN DIFFERENT STUDIES

The quantitative results of different wind tunnel studies in which indoor air-speeds are measured and expressed as percentage of the outdoor wind speed are not directly comparable. Any relative values of the indoor airspeed depend on the reference outdoor wind speed which has served as the basis for calculating it.

The reference outdoor wind speeds which were used as the basis for calculating the relative indoor airspeed in different studies were measured at different points in the tunnels; the vertical airspeed distributions in the tunnels were different; and the shapes and sizes of the openings were also different in each one of these investigations. Furthermore, the wind tunnels themselves, and the models used, were of different designs.

In the study of Ernest 1991, the reference wind speed was 75 percent of the wind speed measured in front and well above the model. Givoni 1962, 1968 and Sobin (1983) have measured the reference wind in front of the building, at the same height above the ground as that of the windows, where the airspeed is much lower (about 60 percent) in comparison with the undisturbed airstream above the level of the model. Consequently the reported indoor relative airspeeds in the Givoni and Sobin studies are higher (by about 1.8) in comparison with the results of the Ernest study.

Although the numerical indoor airspeeds from different studies are not directly comparable, they can be compared if the difference in the reference wind speed is taken into account. The general relative quantitative effects of various design features can be generalized directly, and this is what matters from the building design aspect.

Studies on the Effect of Window Size

The author (see Givoni 1962, 1968) has studied in a wind tunnel the indoor airspeeds in a square model. The distribution of speeds at different points in the model was measured under different combinations of inlet and outlet openings. These combinations included, inter alia, one-sided single window and windows in opposite and in adjacent walls, under two wind directions: normal (perpendicular) to the inlet windows and oblique, at 45 degrees. The average indoor speed was calculated, and the maximum speed, obtained with every combination, was noted. In particular, the ventilation conditions were compared under conditions with the same overall area of the openings, with and without cross-ventilation.

With two openings, the location of the outlet was either in the wall opposite to the inlet wall or in an adjacent wall. In the second case, when the wind was oblique to the wall, the outlet was in a suction zone of the model. In this investigation it has been found that the indoor airspeeds are not proportional to the size of the windows: the effect of increasing the window's size is strong when the window is small but it decreases with increasing size, suggesting that the effect of window's size is approximately proportional to the square root of the opening size.

THE RESEARCH OF ERNEST

In the research of Ernest the effect of window size was tested with ten relative sizes (termed "wall's porosity"), from 6 to 25 percent of the walls' area, under seven wind angles, between Normal (zero degrees) and Parallel (90 degrees) to the wall. Ernest in his report also cited the experimental data of Chand and Krishak 1969. Analysis of the experimental data of Ernest has demonstrated that the effect of increasing size depends on the wind incidence angle. With decreasing angle (from Parallel to Perpendicular) the effect of increasing opening size also increases.

Analysis of the data of Ernest, done by the author, enabled the development of a formula expressing the indoor average airspeed, (V), as a function of the opening size, (P for porosity), and the wind incidence angle, (A):

$$V = [2.4 + 0.5 \times (90 - A)^{0.5}] \times (P)^{0.5}$$

Figure 2-14 shows the correlation between the combined measured data of Ernest and of Chand and Krishak, and the values calculated by the above formula for conditions corresponding to those of the tests. The R^2 is 0.98 and the Standard Deviation 1.1. For the data of Figure 11 (of Ernest only), from which the formula has been derived, the R^2 is 0.99 and the S.D. is 0.85 (Ernest 1991).

THE EFFECT OF SIZE AND SHAPE OF THE WINDOWS

Sobin (1983) measured the effect of increasing the window size (percentage of the wall's area) with three shapes of windows: square, horizontal strips, and vertical strips. He has found that the indoor average speeds (averages of the data with perpendicular and with oblique wind directions), measured at the "occupation zone" with three types of windows: square, horizontal strips, and vertical strips, while keeping the inlet and outlet at the same size, as a function of the windows' size. While the differences were relatively small, the lowest average speeds in a plan at the height of the occupation zone are with vertical windows, and the highest were obtained with horizontal windows.

The expected indoor airspeed was calculated by the formula described above, when the formula includes a factor of 1.8, to take into account the dif-

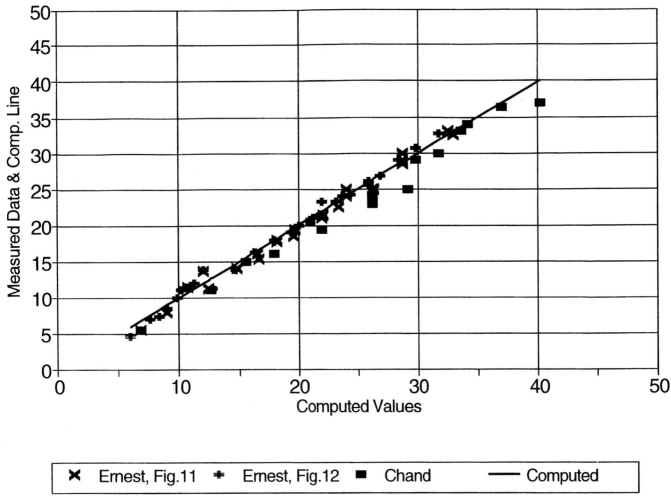

Figure 2-14. *Correlation between computed and measured data of Ernest and Chand & Krishak.*

ference in the reference wind speed, as discussed previously. With this correction the formula also represents rather well the data of Sobin.

RELATIVE SIZE OF INLETS AND OUTLETS (WHEN NOT EQUAL)

Generally, when inlets and outlets are not of equal area, the smaller one will have the main role in determining the ventilation conditions, regardless of whether the inlet or the outlet opening is the smaller one. This was a conclusion from two wind tunnel investigations by the author (Givoni 1962, 1968). Even an increase of about threefold in size of the inlet or the outlet alone had relatively small effect on the indoor average speed. Thus, the size of the smaller openings, either inlets or outlets, practically determines the ventilation conditions.

AVERAGE AND MAXIMUM AIRSPEED

While the differences in the indoor *average* airspeeds with a given wind direction, when the same combination of window sizes was kept in the experimental studies, but with changing inlets and outlets, were quite small, there were very significant differences in the measured *maximum* indoor speed. Systematically, with a smaller inlet and a larger outlet the indoor maximum speed was much higher, as compared with the cases when, with the same combination of sizes, the larger opening served as an inlet. In many cases the indoor maximum speed was even higher than the outdoor airspeed in front of the model (see Table 2-4).

Taking into account these characteristics, it can be suggested that small inlets may be suitable in rooms where the place of occupancy is defined and is close to the inlet—for example, in a bedroom with the bed next to the window. In this case, even a small horizontal inlet, if placed slightly over the bed, can provide a good airflow over it. It should be possible, by the design details of the window, to direct the flow away from the bed (upward) when high speed is not desirable. On the other hand, in a living room in which any spot may be occupied—at a level of 0.5 to 1.0 meter (1.65 to 3.3 ft) above the floor—a large inlet would be most suitable even if the outlet is a small one.

TABLE 2-4. EFFECT OF CROSS-VENTILATION AND INLET/OUTLET SIZES
(% OF APPROACHING OUTDOOR WIND SPEED)

	NUMBER & LOCATION OF OPENINGS	WIND DIRECTION	TOTAL WIDTH OF OPENINGS			
			2/3 WALL AVG.	MAX.	3/3 WALL AVG.	MAX.
CROSS-VENTIL-ATION	1, in pressure zone	Normal	13	18	16	20
		Oblique	15	33	23	36
NONE	1, in suction	Oblique	17	44	17	39
NONE	2, in suction	Oblique	22	56	23	50
WITH CROSS-VENTIL-ATION	2 in adjacent walls	Normal	45	68	51	103
		Oblique	37	118	40	110
	2 in opposite walls	Normal	35	65	37	102
		Oblique	42	83	42	94

| WIND DIRECTION | OUTLET SIZE | INLET SIZE | | | | | |
| | | 1/3 | | 2/3 | | 3/3 | |
		AVG.	MAX.	AVG.	MAX.	AVG.	MAX.
NORMAL	1/3	36	65	34	74	32	49
	2/3	39	131	37	79	36	72
	3/3	44	137	35	72	47	86
OBLIQUE 45°	1/3	42	83	43	96	42	62
	2/3	40	92	57	133	62	131
	3/3	44	152	59	137	65	115

Induced Cross-Ventilation in Rooms with an External Projection (Wing-Walls)

A room with windows in one wall only has usually poor ventilation because the indoor-outdoor pressure gradient across the opening is very small. When the wind is oblique to the wall it flows along, and parallel to, the wall and a small pressure gradient is established along the wall.

It is possible to utilize this pressure gradient by providing two lateral windows in the same wall. A pressure gradient would then exist between the two openings, and air could enter through the upwind opening and leave the room through the downwind opening. But, as the usual pressure gradient along the wall is rather small, the resulting improvement in the ventilation is also only moderate.

However, experiments by the author (see Givoni 1968) have demonstrated that by some window design modification it is possible to create strong pressure gradients between the two openings and thus to achieve ventilation conditions comparable to those existing in conventionally cross-ventilated buildings. The modification consists of adding to each opening a single vertical projection, a downwind projection to the upwind opening, and an upwind projection to the downwind opening.

A projection placed downwind of the window creates a high pressure in front of it. A projection upwind of a window creates a strong suction behind it. Thus a high-pressure gradient is established between the two windows, increasing the airflow in the space in which the two windows are located.

The idea of using such projections for enhancing ventilation in buildings with a single external wall was first developed, and its effect on the ventilation

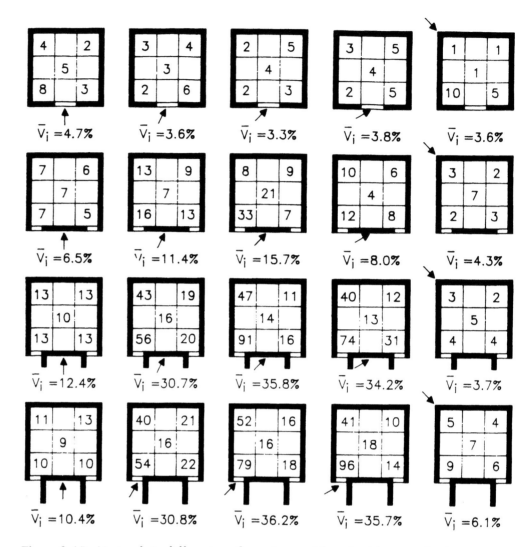

Figure 2-15. *Airspeeds in different configurations, with and without projections, at different wind directions.*

tested, by the author in a wind tunnel (Givoni 1962, 1968, 1976). The airspeed distribution was measured in models—65 x 65 cm (26 x 26") and 50 cm (20") high—with only one "external" wall, with one or two windows in that wall. It was then expressed as a percent of the wind speed in front of the model, at the same height above the ground. The height of all windows was one-third of the room's height while their width was a variable in the experiments. These measurements were taken in models with a single window or with two windows of the same total area, which was different in different test series. The external wall was at different orientations with respect to the wind direction.

With a window's area one-ninth of the wall's area, the effect of the depth of the projections, and of their location with respect of the windows was tested with the following configurations:

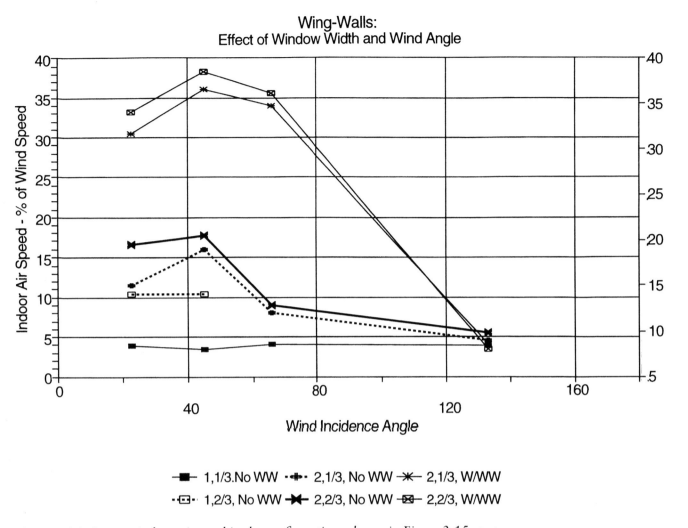

Figure 2-16. *Average indoor airspeed in the configurations shown in Figure 2-15, as a function of the wind angle.*

- Two ordinary lateral openings with the same total area as the Control.
- Two lateral openings, with vertical projections of depth equal to the opening width.
- Two lateral openings, with vertical projections of depth double the opening width.
- Two lateral openings within a projecting balcony.

The distribution of the airspeeds in the different configurations, with and without the projections, under the different orientations, are reproduced in Figure 2-15 on the preceding page (Givoni 1968). Figure 2-16 shows the average indoor airspeed in the different configurations as a function of the wind angle of incidence.

Strong pressure differences can be created not only by simple projections but

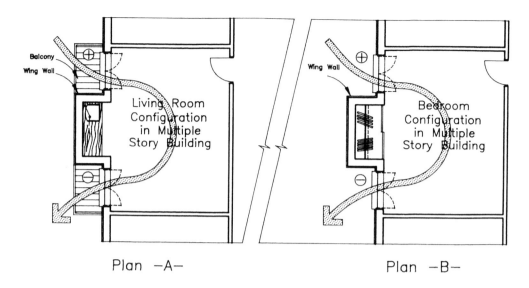

Figure 2-17. *Architectural functional elements as alcoves projecting slightly from the room, recessed or projecting porches.*

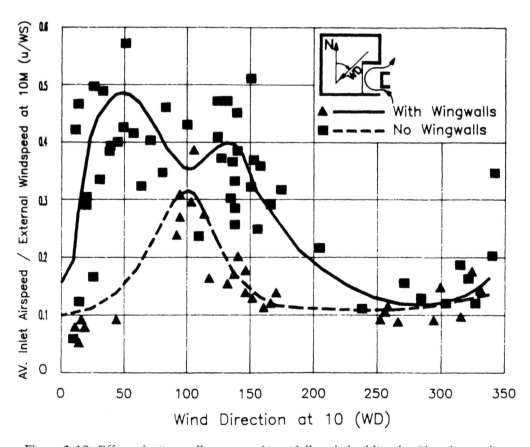

Figure 2-18. *Effect of wing-walls measured in a full-scale building by Chandra et al.*

also by such architectural functional elements as alcoves projecting slightly from the room, recessed or projecting porches, etc., as is illustrated in Figure 2-17.

The application of such projections for enhancing ventilation was discussed by the author during a visit at the Florida Solar Energy Center (FSEC) with the scientists working on natural ventilation. Later, the performance of these projections was studied extensively by Chandra et al. (1983) at FSEC in a full-scale experimental building. They have coined the term "wing-walls" for such projections and have publicized the concept in several publications (e.g., Chandra et al. 1983). Their results of the tests in the full-scale building are reproduced in Figure 2-18 on page 104.

REFERENCES

Chand, I., and N.L.V. Krishak. 1969. Effect of Window Size, Location and Orientation on Indoor Air Motion. *Journal of the Institution of Engineers (India)* vol. 49 (X):375–378.

Chandra, S., P. Fairy, and M. Houston. 1983. *A Handbook for Designing Ventilated Buildings.* Cape Canaveral, Florida: Florida Solar Energy Center.

Ernest, D.R. 1991. Predicting Wind-Induced Indoor Air Motion, Occupant Comfort, and Cooling Loads in Naturally Ventilated Buildings. Ph.D. diss., University of California, Berkeley.

Givoni, B. 1962. *Basic Study of Ventilation Problems in Housing in Hot Countries.* Research Report to the Ford Foundation. Technion, Haifa, Israel: Building Research Station.

Givoni, B. 1968. *Ventilation Problems in Hot Countries.* Research Report to the Ford Foundation. Technion, Haifa, Israel: Building Research Station.

Givoni, B. 1976. Man, Climate and Architecture. 2d ed. New York: Van Nostrand Reinhold.

Jones. 1968. The Influence of Color on Heat Absorption. Report No. 246. Agricultural Experimental Station, The University of Arizona, Tucson.

Munsell Color Company, Inc. 1950. Munsell Book of Colors. Baltimore, Maryland: John Wiley and Sons.

Sobin, H. 1983. Analysis of Wind Tunnel Data on Naturally Ventilated Models. Tucson, Arizona: Harris Sobin & Assoc.

Sullivan, R., and S. Selkovitz. 1986. Residential Heating and Cooling Energy Cost Implications Associated with Window Type. Report LBL-21578. Lawrence Berkeley Laboratory, Berkeley, California.

Sweitzer, G., D. Arasteh, and S. Selkowitz. 1986. Effects of Low-Emissivity Glazing on Energy Use Patterns in Nonresidential Daylighted Buildings. Report LBL-21577. Lawrence Berkeley Laboratory, Berkeley, California.

Chapter **3**: MATERIALS PROPERTIES AND THERMAL PERFORMANCE OF BUILDINGS

INTRODUCTION

The materials of which a building (and especially its envelope) is constructed determine the relationship between the outdoor temperature and solar radiation conditions, and the indoor temperatures in non-air conditioned buildings. In the case of buildings heated or cooled by a mechanical system the envelope's materials determine the energy consumed by the system to maintain the indoor temperatures within the comfort limits, as specified by the thermostat setting.

Outdoor temperature and solar radiation follow diurnal cyclic patterns. The outdoor temperature has its minimum about sunrise, rises and reaches its maximum at an early afternoon hour, and then drops down. Quantitatively it is characterized by an average (the range between the maximum and the minimum) and a given swing around that average. Solar energy, striking and absorbed at the walls and roof surfaces during the daytime hours, causes an elevation of the indoor average temperature above the outdoor's average.

While both the outdoor temperature and the solar radiation patterns are climatological factors beyond the control of the architect, there is a major difference between them from the aspect of the controllability of their effect on the indoor temperature and the energy consumption by mechanical thermal control systems. Using design details, it is much easier to control the effect of solar radiation than that of the outdoor temperature conditions.

The indoor temperatures in buildings not controlled by a mechanical system follow the outdoor air pattern with a modified cycle: an average that is usually above the outdoor's average, with elevation depending on the solar control of the building (sol-air temperature elevation); a diurnal swing that is usually smaller but may also be higher than the outdoor's swing; and a delay in the time of the indoor maximum behind the hour of the outdoor's maximum (time lag).

The properties of the building's materials govern the relationship between the indoor average temperature and swing and the corresponding outdoor air temperature pattern. Three properties of the building's envelope govern this relationship: its heat conductance of, or resistance to, heat flow across the envelope; the temperature change of the building's mass with absorption and release of energy heat capacity, and the absorption (or reflection) of solar energy striking the envelope.

Conduction and resistance are determined by more basic properties: thermal conductivity, specific heat and density of the materials, and by the thickness of the building elements made of them. The response to striking solar radiation is determined by a basic property of the surface: its absorptivity, which depends mainly on the external color of the building and its shading conditions.

HEAT EXCHANGE BETWEEN THE BUILDING AND ITS ENVIRONMENT

The modifying effect of the envelope materials on the indoor temperature and energy consumption for heating and cooling results from its effect on the heat exchange between the building and its environment. This heat exchange (both gain and loss) takes place through the envelope by different physical modes (discussed below). Its rate depends on the thermal properties of the envelope materials, mainly their thermal transmission. Different standard procedures are applied in calculating the heat loss than in calculating the heat gain of a building because of the different effects of orientation, windows' shading, and the color of the various surfaces on the calculations of heat loss and of heat gain.

In calculating heat loss for the purpose of sizing heating equipment the extreme conditions are taken into account, namely without any "mitigation" by solar heat gain. The reason is that the "worst case," from the heat loss aspect, occurs at night. Therefore the orientation of the different envelope elements, and their colors, do not affect the standard procedures of calculating the heat loss. The heat loss from a building, and its standard calculation, can therefore be determined without a basic distinction between different orientations, and without distinction between the opaque parts (walls and the roof) and the transparent parts (windows) of the envelope (although their different thermal properties—U values—are taken into account).

The standard heat loss calculation also assumes "steady state" conditions—approximately constant indoor temperature (maintained by a given heating system) and a large difference between the indoor and outdoor average temperatures. In this situation the effect of the thermal mass (heat capacity) of the building can be disregarded without introducing too large an error in the estimation of the heat loss, and especially in the calculation of the *peak* heat loss, and the corresponding size of the heating plant. The procedure of heat loss calculation is discussed later.

On the other hand, the heat gain of a building involves two major factors which are not involved in the standard procedure of heat loss calculation, namely solar heat gain and the impact of the thermal mass of a building on its thermal performance. The main interest in heat gain concerns the worst case, which is the summer daytime hours. Solar energy that is absorbed at the external surfaces of the opaque parts of the envelope and that penetrates through the windows may constitute a major part in the overall heat gain and cannot be disregarded even in simplified standard procedures, as is the case in heat loss calculation. The heat gain is greatly affected by the orientation of the windows and their shading conditions, as well as by the colors of the walls and the roof.

Furthermore, the *average* outdoor temperature in summer in most regions is much closer to the human comfort zone than in winter. The outdoor daily maximum is often above the comfort range while the minimum is below it. In this situation the building's heat capacity has significant effect on the indoor temperature and the cooling needs. Therefore the effect of the mass of the building has to be taken into account in calculating the diurnal pattern of the heat gain and the cooling needs.

MODES OF HEAT TRANSFER IN BUILDINGS

The heat flow between a building and its environment takes place in several physical modes—conduction, convection, and radiation—and through different paths and elements of the building's envelope—the roof, the opaque elements of the walls, and the windows, as well as by air infiltration.

When the addition or loss of heat causes a temperature change, it is referred to as *sensible heat*. When it is accompanied by a change in the state of water from liquid to vapor (evaporation), or vice versa (condensation), it is termed *latent heat*. In some specific cases latent heat transfer in the form of evaporative cooling and/or condensation (heat release) should also be considered in buildings. Evaporative heat loss takes place when the building walls and roof are wet, such as, after rains. Condensation also occurs over internal surfaces, or within the wall's materials, mainly when the indoor humidity level rises above the dew point of the internal surfaces. Latent heat transfer, which is mainly important in cooling load calculations in air conditioned buildings, is discussed in detail in Chapter 5.

Conduction

Conduction is the process of heat transfer from warmer to cooler molecules within a solid material. Molecules of any substance vibrate, and this vibration becomes more vigorous as the temperature of the substance rises. Conductive heat flow is caused by the transfer of energy from the faster-vibrating warmer molecules to the cooler molecules. In this way the transfer of the kinetic energy of the vibration is converted into heat transfer. *Thermal conduction* in buildings is thus the process of heat transfer through solid materials (a wall or a roof) from the hotter side to the cooler side of the building element. Its rate depends on the *conductivity* of the material and the thickness of the envelope element in question. Conductive heat flow is discussed in detail later in this chapter.

Convection

Convection is heat transfer by a fluid motion (in most cases air). Convective heat exchange occurs in several situations, when heat is transferred from a solid surface to the adjacent air, and vice versa, or heat transfer between two surfaces at different temperatures by means of airflow. Convection can be of two types, caused by two forces: by temperature differences (natural, or thermosyphonic, convection) and forced air motion generated by wind or fans.

Natural thermosyphonic convection occurs when air is heated by contact with a hotter surface, for example, expands, becomes lighter, and rises. It then flows toward a cooler surface, is cooled by transferring heat to that surface, becomes more dense, and finally, sinks down. In this way heat is transferred by airflow from the hotter surface to the cooler one. The rate of natural convective heat transfer depends not only on the temperature difference but also on the position of the hot surface. It is maximized when the floor is the warmest surface and is minimized when the ceiling is the warmest surface.

Natural convection tends to create temperature stratification in the space where it takes place. Warmer air accumulates near the ceiling and cooler air near the floor, forming layers of rising temperatures as one moves upward. This stratification pattern is maximized when the ceiling is the warmest surface in a room, which is often the case in summer daytime hours.

Forced convective heat transfer is commonly generated by wind flow around the building (at the external surfaces of the building's envelope) or by wind flow through the interior space (in the case of natural cross-ventilation). Its rate depends mainly on the airspeed next to the surface in question.

Convective heat transfer can occur in buildings in several situations:

a. The internal surfaces of the walls exchange heat by convection with the indoor air. The indoor air is usually assumed to be almost "still" and the convection coefficient usually assumes a low, fixed value. It should be realized that when a building is ventilated the indoor air is not still. However, no accepted formula is available at present to determine its value in this case, so the value for still air is usually applied to interior surfaces even when the building is ventilated.

b. The ceiling also exchanges heat with the indoor air underneath it by convection, as well as with the attic space (when the roof contains an attic). The value of the convection coefficient is different in winter—the heated building is warmer than the outdoor air and heat flows upward. In summer, the roof, exposed to the sun, is hotter than the indoor air, and the heat flows downward. Convective heat flow upward is much higher than downward.

c. The external surfaces, exposed to the wind, exchange heat by convection with the ambient air. The wind speed greatly increases the convective coefficient. Although the wind speed changes constantly and is different along the various walls of the same building, a fixed wind speed is assumed in standard calculations, leading to an assumed fixed external convective coefficient.

d. In walls with an embedded internal airspace, heat flows by convection from the warmer side to the cooler side of the airspace. Air next to a warmer surface of the space heats, rises, and flows toward the cooler surface where it sinks, thus carrying heat from the warmer to the cooler side of the airspace. This internal convective heat flow is produced only by temperature differences (natural convection). In the case of an airspace in a roof structure, convection is enhanced in winter, when the indoor space is warmer than the outdoors, and is suppressed in summer, when the roof is warmer than the indoor space.

e. Convective heat transfer takes place also when the building is ventilated, when outdoor air flows through the interior space. If the ambient temperature is different from the temperature of any element of the interior space convective heat transfer takes place. For instance, when a building is ventilated at night its mass is cooled by convective heat transfer from the warmer walls and ceiling to the cooler flowing air. Conversely, when a building, especially a high-mass one, is ventilated during the hot hours of the day its mass is usually heated convectively by the hotter outdoor air.

f. *Infiltration* is unintended leakage of outdoor air through cracks around windows or doors. In winter it may be a significant source of heat *loss*, and during hot summer hours a source of heat *gain*, especially in the case of well-insulated buildings.

Radiant Heat Exchange

Radiant heat transfer in buildings is energy exchanged between surfaces by electromagnetic waves across a space. Any surface emits radiant energy which can be described either by discrete "quanta" (photons) or by waves with certain wavelengths. In the context of radiant heat transfer in buildings, the wave description is the applicable one. The origin of the emitted radiant energy is the vibration of the surface molecules; it is proportional to the fourth power of the surface absolute temperature (273+°C or 492+°F). Due to the loss of energy by the emitted radiation the temperature of the emitting element is lowered. The radiation wave is transmitted through space till it strikes an opaque surface, where it is partly absorbed (and partly reflected). The absorbed radiation increases the vibration of the surface molecules and thus raises the temperature of the material where the absorption took place. A surface warmer than its surroundings emits (radiates) more energy than the radiation it gets from the cooler surfaces around it. In this way heat is transferred by radiation from warmer to cooler surfaces.

The wavelength of radiant energy is measured in microns (one millionth of a meter) or in nanometers (one billionth of a meter, abbreviated nm). The smaller the wavelength the higher the energy level of the radiation. A basic distinction should be made, from the aspect of the properties of building materials and the role of radiation in buildings' energy balance, between solar short-wave radiation (discussed in Chapter 2) and thermal long-wave radiation (discussed in this chapter). Solar radiation itself is broadly subdivided into three wavelength bands: the ultraviolet (below 400 nm), which has biological effects; the visible (light) radiation (400–760 nm); and the infrared radiation (760–3000 nm), which is not visible by the human eye but has a heating effect. The thermal (long-wave) radiation, which is emitted by surfaces at temperatures common on earth, has a wavelength range of 3000 to 20,000 nm.

Surfaces of *opaque* materials have three properties which determine their behavior with respect to radiation—emissivity, absorptivity, and reflectivity—which may vary with the radiation-specific wavelength. The emissivity concerns emission and absorption of long-wave radiation, while the absorptivity and reflectivity of the surface concern its responses to solar radiation.

The emissivity of a surface, E, is its capacity to emit long-wave radiation, relative to a "perfect" black body. ("Black body" is a body, or a surface, which absorbs all the impinging radiation.) The long-wave radiation, Rad, emitted from a surface having a given emissivity E, in Watts/mC² (Btu/hr ft².F) is given by:

$$Rad = \sigma E \, (T / 100)^4$$

where T is the Absolute Temperature (C+273.15) or (F+459.67) and σ is the Stefen-Boltzmann constant, having a value of 5.67 in the metric system and 0.1713 in the British system.

The emissivity of a "perfect" black surface is 1. The emissivity of most common surfaces (except metals), regardless of their color, is about 0.9. The emissivity of polished metals (e.g., aluminum foil) is about 0.05.

The absorptivity for solar radiation, a, of a surface depends on its color. It determines the fraction of the striking solar radiation which is absorbed at the surface and converted into heat energy. The reflectivity, r, is the fraction of the striking solar radiation which is reflected away, without affecting the surface temperature. Thus:

$$r = 1 - a$$

With respect to long-wave radiation the values of the emissivity and absorptivity of a given surface are the same, namely:

$$E = a$$

However, with respect to solar radiation, the values of the absorptivity and emissivity of a given surface can be very different. The visible color of a surface is a good indicator of its absorptivity but not of its emissivity.

The emissivity of all ordinary surfaces, except metals, is about the same regardless of their color—namely about 0.9. Their absorptivities, on the other hand, vary greatly, depending on the color of the surface. Thus, for example, an ordinary white surface has very low absorptivity (about 0.2–0.3) and a dark surface may have an absorptivity of about 0.8, but the emissivity of both is about 0.9.

THE ALBEDO OF SURFACES

The overall response of a surface to the radiation over the whole solar spectrum including the invisible-to-the-human-eye infrared—its effective reflectivity—is defined as its *albedo*. Surfaces with colors which seem to be of similar darkness (or brightness) can have different albedo and will have different temperatures under exposure to given conditions of air temperature and solar radiation. However, from the practical aspect, the color of a surface is a good indication of its reflectivity.

When solar radiation strikes a transparent or translucent glazing element another property has to be taken into account—the material's transmissivity. Part of the radiation is transmitted to the interior, part is reflected back, and part is absorbed within the glazing material. Different glazing materials have very different reflectivities and absorptivities, as was discussed in Chapter 2.

CHANGES IN THE MODES OF HEAT TRANSFER

During the process of flow through a wall or a roof the heat may change its mode of transfer. Thus, solar energy reaches a wall in the form of short-wave radiation, is absorbed in the external surface, and flows across the wall material by conduction. The external surface may be heated to a temperature above the ambient environment and lose part of the absorbed energy by convection and long-wave radiation to the outdoor environment. If the wall contains an airspace, the heat flows across the space by a combination of convection and long-wave radiation, and continues to flow through the inner layer by conduction. Finally, heat is transferred from the interior surface to the indoor air and interior surfaces by convection and long-wave radiation, respectively.

THERMAL PROPERTIES OF MATERIALS AND BUILDING ELEMENTS

Materials are organized in buildings to form *elements* with a certain thickness: the envelope of the building (exterior walls and the roof) and interior elements (internal partitions and floors). Each element may be composed of several layers of different materials. The composition of the different layers in the envelope and, to some extent, in the interior layers as well, determine the thermal performance of the building. Thus the effect of the building elements on thermal performance depends on the physical properties, thickness, and location (within the element) of the layers of which the elements are composed.

This section discusses the thermal properties of building materials which affect the indoor temperatures in un-air conditioned buildings and in passive solar buildings, and energy consumption in mechanically heated and cooled buildings. Properties of glazing materials with respect to radiation were discussed in Chapter 2.

The two basic thermal properties of building elements, which control the heat flow and determine their impact on the thermal performance of buildings, are their *thermal resistance, R* (or its reciprocal, the U value), and their *heat capacity*. These element properties are a function of the properties of the materials and the thickness of the layers of which they are composed. The basic properties of the materials are the *density* (ø), *conductivity* (k), and *specific heat* (c).

The interaction between the thermal resistance (or U value) and the heat capacity of the building elements and the sequence (order) of the layers of which they are composed creates specific composite thermal properties of the elements: the *Thermal Time Constant* (TTC) and the *Diurnal Heat Capacity* (DHC). The physical meaning and impact of these composite properties are defined below.

In addition to the thermal properties of the material, the surfaces of building elements absorb and reflect solar radiation striking the surface, and emit and absorb long-wave radiation. Transparent and translucent elements (glazing) transmit part of the striking radiation. Thus, the material's properties related to radiation are: *absorptivity* (a), *reflectivity* (r), *transmittance* (t), and *emissivity* (E). These terms are also defined in the following section.

Properties Definitions and Units (British Units in Parentheses)

- **Thermal conductivity (k):** The rate of heat flow through unit surface area of a building element of unit thickness, per unit temperature difference. Its unit is W/m.C (Btu/h.ft.F or Btu.in/ft^2.F).
- **Density (ρ):** Mass per unit volume, kg/m^3 (lb/ft^3)
- **Specific heat (c):** The energy required to raise the temperature of a unit mass by one degree Celsius. Its units are Wh/kg.C (Btu/lb.F).
- **Volumetric heat capacity (c_v):** Specific heat multiplied by density. The energy required to raise the temperature of a unit volume of a material by one degree. Its units are Wh/m^3.C (Btu/ft^3.F). Thus:

$$c_v = \rho * c$$

- **Thermal diffusivity (a):** conductivity (k), divided by the specific heat capacity, namely; a = (k/ρ.c). (Its unit is m^2/h). See comment b on page 118.

PROPERTIES OF BUILDING ELEMENTS

- **Surface conductances (h_o and h_i):** The coefficients of heat exchange between the surfaces of the wall (or the roof) and the outdoor and indoor air, respectively. Its unit is W/m^2.C (Btu/h.ft^2.F).
- **Surface resistances (r_o and r_i):** The reciprocals of the surface conductances: $r_o = 1/h_o$ and $r_i = 1/h_i$, respectively.

- **Thermal resistance (r_j):** Of a given layer within a building element is the ratio of *thickness* (l) of a given layer to the conductivity of the material of that layer, namely: $r_j = l_j/k_j$. The total thermal resistance of an element composed of the various layers, R, is the sum of the resistances of the individual layers, including the surface resistances, regardless of the order of the layers within the element: $R = (r_j)$.

    The resistances of the surface's air films (the air attached to surfaces) depend on the airspeed next to it. The indoor surface is usually exposed to still air and its resistance, R_{in}, is commonly assumed as 0.12 in the metric system and 0.68 in the British system. The outdoor surface is usually exposed to the wind (assumed in standard calculations to be about 7 m/s, 15 mph). Its film resistance is commonly assumed as 0.03 in the metric system and 0.17 in the British system.

- **Thermal transmittance (U value):** The thermal transmission through a unit area of the element, in unit time (hour), per unit temperature difference between the indoor and outdoor air temperatures. Its unit is $W/m^2.C$ ($Btu/h.ft^2.F$).

- **Heat capacity (Q):** Energy required to raise the temperature of a unit area of a building element by one degree. Its units are $Wh/m^2.C$ ($Btu/ft^2.F$). See Comment a. on page 118.

- **Thermal time constant (TTC):** The TTC is the *effective* product of the thermal resistance and heat capacity of an envelope element. Its unit is time (hours). The TTC is the sum of the products of heat capacity, Q, and the resistance, R, values of the different layers, when the resistance of each layer is calculated from the external surface. The procedure for calculating the TTC is described later in this chapter. See also Comment c. on page 118.

- **Unit area diurnal heat capacity (dhc); $W/m^2.C$ ($Btu/h.ft^2.F$):** Penetrating solar energy that is stored during the daytime in a unit area of a thermal mass element and released back to the indoor space during the night, per degree temperature swing. See Comment d. on page 118.

- **Element's diurnal heat capacity (DHC); W/C ($Btu/h.F$):** Solar energy that is stored during the daytime in an element and released back to the indoor space during the night, per degree of temperature swing. See Comment d. on page 118.

Properties of Whole Buildings

- **Building's heat-loss coefficients (UA and BLC):** *UA* expresses the total *hourly* heat loss or gain of the whole building, per degree difference between the indoor and outdoor temperatures. It is the sum of the U values of the different envelope elements (including windows), multiplied by their respective areas. Its unit is: W/C ($Btu/h.F$).

BLC is the *daily* heat-loss coefficient of the whole building, per degree difference between the *daily averages* of the indoor and outdoor temperatures. Its unit is Wh/C.Day (Btu/F.Day).

- **Building's total diurnal heat capacity (BLC$_B$):** Solar energy that is stored during the daytime in all of the thermal mass elements and released back to the indoor space during the night, per degree of temperature swing. Its unit is Wh/C.Day (Btu/F.Day).

- For discussion of the differences in the impacts of the UA, TTC, and BLC on the thermal performance of buildings, see page 119.

RADIANT PROPERTIES OF SURFACES AND GLAZING

- **Emissivity (E):** The capacity of a surface to emit long-wave radiation, relative to the radiation emitted by a "black body."

- **Absorptivity (a):** The fraction of the striking radiation absorbed at the surface. For long-wave radiation: E = a. For solar radiation, E is often not equal to a.

- **Reflectivity (r):** The fraction of the striking radiation which is reflected away. For opaque surfaces r = 1 – a.

- **Solar transmittance of glazing (t$_g$):** The fraction of the striking solar energy which is transmitted indoors through the glazing element.

Comments on Impact of Materials Properties

a. **Relationship between density and heat capacity.** Of the two components of the volumetric heat capacity—specific heat and density—the range of the first is very small. Among building materials the highest specific heats are those of wood and plastics (0.4–0.5, according to their water content) and the lowest is that of steel (0.11), so that the entire range is about 1–4.5. In contrast, the density range of building materials is very wide. The density of air (which can be considered as a "building material" in the form of airspaces) is about 1.15, while that of dense concrete is 2400—a range about 1 to 2000. Even if the density of light expanded polystyrene (20) is taken as the lowest among the materials in use, the range is 1 to 120. As a result, the heat capacity of a wall, or of the structure as a whole, is closely related to its weight.

   Since the specific heat of almost all masonry materials (concrete, brick, stone, or adobe) is similar (about 0.2–0.24 Whr/kg.C) or (Btu/lb.F), the nominal heat capacity is essentially proportional to the total volume and density of the material.

b. **Role of diffusivity in thermal performance of buildings.** A higher diffusivity results in faster diffusion of heat through the mass of the material. In most building materials commonly in use, the conductivity and the heat capacity both increase with the density of the material, so that there is no clear and simple relationship between density and diffusivity.

For most building materials the heat capacity is proportional to density, while the conductivity increases disproportionately faster than with increased density. Thus, for example, cast concrete with density of 2200 kg/m³ (137 lb/ft³) has conductivity of about 1.3 (W/C.m) (0.75 Btu/hr.F.ft) while the conductivity of lightweight concrete with 600 kg/m³ (37.5 lb/ft³) is only about 0.2 (0.012). As a result, the diffusivity of dense concrete is about 1.8 times that of lightweight concrete.

The role of diffusivity with respect to the thermal performance of buildings is mainly theoretical, as it enters into many analytical solutions of non-steady heat transfer problems.

c. **Thermal Time Constant (TTC).** The Thermal Time Constant (TTC) of an envelope element is the main property, in un-air conditioned buildings, which determines the effect of this element on the damping of the indoor temperature swing, relative to the outdoor swing. It is the sum of the products of heat capacity, Q, and resistance, R, of the different layers in the elements—namely, the sum of the Q x R values. It depends on the organization (sequence) of the layers of which the element is composed. For example, the QR value of the third layer (counted from the external surface) is calculated by the formula:

$$QR_3 = [l/h_o + (l/k)_1 + (l/k)_2 + ((l/2)/k)_3] * (l * \rho * c)_3$$

which is equivalent to:

$$QR_3 = [r_o + r_1 + r_2 + 0.5 * r_3] * (l * \rho * c)_3 \text{ (Givoni 1979)}$$

A more detailed discussion of the TTC and the procedure for calculating it, including two numerical examples, are presented later in this chapter.

d. **Diurnal Heat Capacity (DHC).** The Diurnal Heat Capacity (DHC) of the building determines its capacity of the interior thermal mass to absorb solar energy penetrating through the windows, thus bypassing the modifying effect of the walls and the roof, and to release the absorbed heat back in to interior air during the night hours. The DHC also determines the effective capacity of a building ventilated at night and closed during the daytime hours to store nocturnal "cold energy." These effects depend mainly on the properties of the layer *directly exposed* to the interior air and expresses the effective product of heat capacity of that layer and the conductivity of its material. The layers in a given building element that are further away from the interior space have rather small effect on the capacity of the element to store and release solar energy, or nocturnal "cold" energy, during diurnal cycles. The DHC is thus of particular importance in direct-gain passive solar heating and in night ventilative cooling of buildings. Its units are Wh/C or Btu/F.

The *whole building diurnal heat capacity,* (DHC), is the sum of the diurnal heat capacities of all the mass elements surrounding the interior space of a building and located within it (internal partitions), which effectively participate in the diurnal thermal storage process of heat bypassing the building's envelope:

$$DHC = \sum A_i x (dhc)_i$$

The concept of the diurnal heat capacity has been developed by Balcomb (Balcomb et al. 1982, Balcomb 1983). A mathematical model predicting the quantitative effect of the DHC on the performance of direct-gain passive solar buildings was developed by the author (see Givoni 1987) and is described in Chapter 4.

Thermal Conductivity of Common Building Materials

For masonry materials (concrete, bricks, etc.), the conductivity increases with the density of the material: a dense concrete (density of about 2,300 kg/m^3 or 144 lb/ft^3) has much higher conductivity than structural, autoclaved, lightweight concrete (density of about 700 kg/m^3 or 44 lb/ft^3).

Figure 3-1 shows the relationship between density (in kg/m^3) and conductivity for solid masonry materials: different stones, different types of concrete with a wide range of density or bricks. The data were collected from several different sources, mainly from Szokolay (1991) and the *ASHRAE Handbook* (1981). A formula which describes this relationship in masonry materials is:

$$\text{Conductivity} = 0.072 * \exp(1.35 * (\text{Density}/1000))$$

This formula can be used for estimating the conductivity of masonry materials when the density is known.

Insulating materials, like plastic foams and fiberglass, are very lightweight. The conductivity of insulating plastic foams, such as polystyrene or polyurethan, is not related clearly to the density of the foam, and is ranged between 0.025 and 0.035 W/m^2.C (0.17 and 0.24 Btu.in/h.ft^2.F).

Table 3-1 on page 121 shows conductivities of different building materials. The actual conductivity value of a given building material varies also with its moisture content (which, in turn, varies under different exposure conditions).

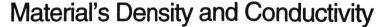

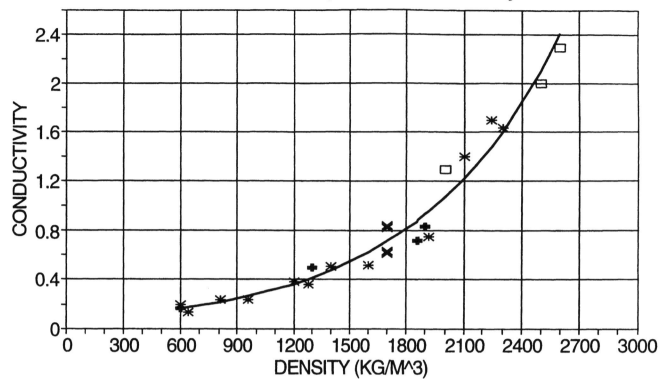

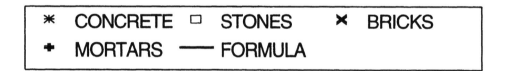

Figure 3-1. *Relationship between density (in kg/m³) and conductivity for solid masonry materials. Different sources.*

Therefore any published value can be considered only as an approximation of the actual value to be found in field exposure.

Conductance and Resistance of Fabricated Building Components

Many building components, such as bricks, concrete blocks, gypsum boards, and batt insulation, are manufactured at standard thicknesses and then assembled as parts of the envelope elements' cross-section. It is useful to know the conductance and resistance of such components for these standard thicknesses, to facilitate the calculations of the U value of the assembled elements.

The conductances and resistances of a number of manufactured products are shown in Table 3-2. The conductance of such fabricated standard products is designated as C, and their resistance as R = 1/C. The resistances of a given layer can be added to the resistances of the other layers, to yield the *overall* resistance of the building element. A number of books (e.g., *ASHRAE Handbook* 1981; Stein et al. 1986) contain detailed tables of the conductance and resistance of many such standardized building components.

Table 3-3 provides the conductances of various window types, including recently developed high-resistance (low-conductance) glazing, utilizing low-emissivity coatings (Low-E glass).

TABLE 3-1. THERMAL CONDUCTIVITIES OF SOME BUILDING MATERIALS

MATERIAL	METRIC (W/m.C)	BRITISH UNITS (Btu.in/ft^2.hr.F)
Dense (vibrated) concrete	1.7	12
Cast concrete w/o vibration	1.5	10.5
Solid concrete blocks	1.3	9
Face bricks	1.3	9
Common bricks	0.7	5.0
Cement mortar	0.8	5.5
Stucco/interior plaster	0.7	5
Light concrete, 600 kg/m^3	0.25	1.8
Gypsum/plaster boards	0.16	1.1
Hardwood (oak, redwood)	0.16	1.1
Softwood (fir, pine)	0.12	0.8
Plywood	0.12	0.8
Fiberglass (resin binder)	0.05	0.35
Expanded polystyrene	0.035	0.25
Cellular polyurethane	0.025	0.16

TABLE 3-2. THERMAL CONDUCTANCES AND RESISTANCES OF SOME FABRICATED MANUFACTURED PRODUCTS

	METRIC COND.	RESIST.	BRITISH COND.	RESIST.
Gypsum or plaster board, 15 mm	10.0	0.10	1.78	0.56
Plywood (Douglas fir), 12 mm	9.0	0.11	1.60	0.62
Mineral fiber batts, 9 cm	0.5	2.0	0.09	11
Mineral fiber batts, 15 cm	0.30	3.3	0.05	19
Hollow concrete blocks, 20 cm	5.6	0.18	0.96	1.04
Hollow clay tiles, 10 cm	5.0	0.20	0.90	1.11
Hollow clay tiles, 15 cm	3.7	0.27	0.66	1.52
Hollow clay tiles, 20 cm	3.0	0.33	0.54	1.85

TABLE 3-3. THERMAL CONDUCTANCES (U VALUES) OF SOME WINDOW TYPES

WINDOW TYPE	METRIC	BRITISH UNITS
Single clear glass	6.0	1.1
Double clear glass	3.0	0.55
Triple glass	2.0	0.35
Low-E double glass	2.3	0.4
Double skin plastic glazing	2.8	0.5

Resistances of Airspaces

Airspaces in buildings can be vertical, in walls, and horizontal or inclined, in roofs. The total conductance of an enclosed airspace is the sum of two components: convective and radiative heat transfers. The convective component depends on the position of the airspace (vertical or horizontal). In the case of a horizontal airspace it depends on the direction of the heat flow, up or down, which is reversed between summer and winter. The radiative component depends on the emissivity of the surfaces bounding the airspace.

In winter, when the building is heated and the lower side of a roof's airspace (an attic) is warmer than the upper side, natural convection is enhanced. In summer, when the roof is usually hotter than the interior space and the upper side of the airspace is hotter than the lower side, convection is suppressed. The differences due to the heat flow direction in horizontal and inclined airspaces are maximized when the space is lined with a reflective layer because the radiant exchange is suppressed and the main heat flow is then by convection. In the case of vertical airspaces in walls, the warmed air next to the warmer surface expands and rises while cooled air next to the colder surface sinks down. The heat flow direction is horizontal and the convection coefficient assumes an intermediate value between the two cases of the roof airspace.

The radiant component is unaffected by the orientation of the airspace and by the heat flow direction but can vary greatly with the emissivity, E, of the surfaces bounding the airspace. The emissivity of ordinary surfaces is about 0.9; that of polished metals, such as aluminum foil, is about 0.05, reducing the radiant heat transfer by a factor of almost 20. When the two surfaces of the airspace are bounded by reflective materials, with emissivities of E_1 and E_2, respectively, the effective emissivity, $E_{eff.}$, is calculated by the formula:

$$E_{eff.} = 1 / (1 / E_1 + 1 / E_2 - 1)$$

The radiative component of the total conductance, h_r, is then:

$$h_r = 5.67 * E_{eff} * (T / 100)^4 \text{ (metric) or}$$

$$h_r = 0.1713 * E_{eff} * (T / 100)^4 \text{ (British)}$$

when T is the absolute temperature.

The conductance of airspaces increases at higher temperatures (effect on convection) and with greater temperature differences across the two sides of the space (affecting both convection and radiation). The resistances of the spaces (the numbers used in calculations of the overall resistance and U value) are correspondingly smaller with higher temperatures and temperature differences.

Table 3-4 presents thermal resistances of airspaces, with ordinary surfaces and with one reflective surface, at different positions and different heat flow directions. Mean temperature inside the airspace is assumed as 30°C (86°F) in summer and as 0°C (32°F) in winter. The assumed temperature difference is 10°K (18°F). The suggested values for lined airspaces are somewhat lower than published data, taking into account the common deterioration in the reflectivity due to dust settlement, oxidation, and so on.

It can be seen in Table 3-4 that reflective lining of one surface increases its thermal resistance by two- to threefold. This is particularly useful when placed at the upper surface of horizontal airspaces where dust accumulation is minimal. Lining the lower surface is much less effective because, in time, the reflective power can be greatly reduced by dust.

For vertical airspaces, higher resistance can be obtained by flexing the reflective layer in the middle of the space. In this case two additional surfaces, both reflective, are provided and, in addition, the air attached to them adds to the overall thermal resistance of the airspace. Such application, however, may be more labor intensive.

TABLE 3-4. RESISTANCES OF AIRSPACES
(DELT = 10° C, BRITISH UNITS IN PARENTHESES)

POSITION OF SPACE	HEAT FLOW DIRECTION			SURFACES: MEAN REFLECTIVE TEMP.		NON-REFLECT.	
Horizontal	Up	(Sumr)	30	0.39	(2.2)	0.15	(0.80)
		(Wntr)	0	0.35	(2.0)	0.18	(1.0)
	Down	(Sumr)	30	0.93	(5.3)	0.18	(1.0)
		(Wntr)	0	1.1	(6.2)	0.23	(1.3)
Vertical	Horiz.	(Sumr)	30	0.65	(3.7)	0.15	(0.8)
		(Wntr)	10	0.58	(3.3)	0.18	(1.05)

Reflective Insulation (Radiant Barriers)

Reflective insulation consists of aluminum foil-faced sheets installed in walls and/or attics, with an adjacent air gap. The insulation effect is achieved through two physical processes: reflection of long-wave radiation emitted toward the barrier from a warmer surface and/or greatly suppressed emission of long-wave radiation toward colder surfaces. Radiant barriers can be installed both in walls (vertical position) and in a roof's attic (horizontal or inclined position).

In the wall/vertical position there is no basic difference in the seasonal performance (summer versus winter) of radiant barriers. Also, no major difference is expected in the performance of a wall with a radiant barrier as compared with a wall with conventional insulation having the same thermal resistance.

On the other hand, horizontal radiant barriers in an attic are more effective in summer, in reducing heat gain, than in winter, in reducing heat loss. The reason is that in winter convective heat flow upward comprises more than one-half of the total heat flow and it is not reduced by the radiant barrier. In summer, however, when heat in the attic flows downward, convection is naturally greatly suppressed and the impact of the radiant barrier, in suppressing the radiant component of the heat gain, is maximized.

Very extensive experimental research and simulations, on the effect of radiant barriers on thermal performance of buildings, both in summer and in winter, was conducted by Chandra et al. (1986) at the Florida Solar Energy Center (FSEC) in Cape Canaveral, Florida.

Chandra et al. compared the effects of enhancing the thermal resistance of a "base case" attic (R-19), on cooling energy consumption in summer and on heating energy in winter, in several cities in the United States by adding either R-11 ceiling fiberglass batt insulation or a radiant barrier with R-11.

Table 3-5 is an abbreviated version of the results of Chandra et al., showing energy savings (in KWh) resulting from the enhanced attic insulation by the two techniques, for cooling with an air conditioner with a rated SEER (Seasonal Energy Efficiency Rating, Whr/Btu) of 8.0, and heating with a system having COP (Coefficient of Performance: delivered cooling/energy consumed) of 2 (presumably a heat pump).

Chandra et al. noted that the added radiant barrier outperformed the equivalent conventional (conductance resistance) insulation, on an annual basis, in all analyzed climates, except in Chicago. In the more southern cities, where cooling is a major energy load, the savings with the radiant barrier were about twice the savings with improved conventional insulation.

Radiant barriers are often added to conventional insulation (e.g., fiberglass batts), in order to upgrade it. In this case their intrinsic resistance is added to

CITY	COOLING		HEATING		ANNUAL	
	R-11	RB	R-11	RB	R-11	RB
Jacksonville, FL	217	427	100	100	317	526
Houston, TX	202	389	122	95	324	484
Atlanta, GA	155	342	224	163	380	504
Baltimore, MD	125	283	372	249	497	532
Chicago, IL	94	211	475	278	569	490

that of the "standard" insulation, to yield the total resistance of the composite element. Radiant barriers are best applied to roofs of skin-load-dominated homes in regions with a major solar component of the cooling load. Their larger impact would be in single-story buildings in hot-sunny regions.

Chandra et al. 1986 contains detailed construction techniques for the application of radiant barriers in various types of roofs and walls.

Sample Calculations of U Values of Composite Walls

As examples of the procedure for calculating the U values of envelope components, the conductance of two composite walls are calculated below—the first one *without* and the second one *with* an internal airspace.

The first wall consists of (from the outside):

- a layer of cement plaster 2 cm (0.8") thick,
- expanded polystyrene 2.5 cm (1"),
- dense concrete 10 cm (4"), and
- interior plaster of 1 cm (0.4").

The second wall (brick veneer, stud-wall type) consists of:

- a layer of face bricks 10 cm (4") thick,
- airspace 3 cm (1.2") wide with reflective lining on its inner side,
- common bricks 5 cm (2"), and
- interior plaster of 1 cm (0.4").

The calculations of the overall resistances of the two walls are illustrated in Table 3-6a in the metric system and in Table 3-6b in the British system.

Once the U value of an envelope element, a wall or a roof, is calculated, the heat flow rate per hour, per unit area (m² or ft²), can be calculated. The heat flow, Q_i, (in Watts or Btu/h) is the U value of that element multiplied by the difference between the indoor (T_{in}) and outdoor (T_{out}) air temperatures, namely:

$$Q_i = U_i * (T_{in} - T_{out})$$

This formula does not take into account the thermal mass of the building and is valid, strictly speaking, only under steady-state conditions, when the indoor and outdoor temperatures are fixed at a certain level throughout the day. However, it is also useful when the indoor-outdoor average temperature difference is large in comparison with the diurnal temperature swing, such as the case of heated buildings in winter in cold regions.

TABLE 3-6A. CALCULATION OF THE OVERALL THERMAL RESISTANCE OF TWO WALLS (METRIC)

Wall # 1

LAYER	THICKNESS (METERS)	CONDUCTIVITY	RESISTANCE	
External surface resistance				0.03
Exterior plaster	0.02	0.8	0.020/.8	= 0.025
Polystyrene	0.025	0.035	0.025/.035	= 0.71
Concrete	0.10	1.7	0.10/1.7	= 0.06
Interior plaster	0.01	0.7	0.01/7	= 0.014
Internal surface resistance				0.12
Overall Thermal Resistance, R			R =	0.959
U Value (1/R)			U =	1.043

Wall # 2

LAYER	THICKNESS (METERS)	CONDUCTIVITY	RESISTANCE	
External surface resistance				0.03
Exterior plaster	0.02	0.8	0.020/.8	= 0.025
Concrete	0.10	1.7	0.10/1.7	= 0.06
Airspace (reflective)				0.6
Bricks	0.05	0.7	0.05/.7	= 0.07
Interior plaster	0.01	0.7	0.01/.7	= 0.014
Internal surface resistance				0.12
Overall Thermal Resistance, R			R =	0.92
U Value (1/R)			U =	1.09

Wall #1

LAYER	THICKNESS (INCHES)	CONDUCTIVITY	RESISTANCE	
External surface resistance				0.17
Exterior plaster	0.8	5.5	0.8/5.5	= 0.15
Polystyrene	1.0	0.25	1.0/.25	= 4.0
Concrete	4.0	12	4.0/12	= 0.33
Interior plaster	0.4	5.0	0.4/5.0	= 0.08
Internal surface resistance				0.68
Overall Thermal Resistance, R				R = 5.41
U Value (1/R)				U = 0.185

Wall # 2

LAYER	THICKNESS (INCHES)	CONDUCTIVITY	RESISTANCE	
External surface resistance				0.17
Exterior plaster	0.8	5.5	0.8/5.5	= 0.15
Concrete	4.0	12	4.0/12	= 0.33
Airspace (reflective)				= 3.3
Bricks	2.0	5.0	2/5	= 0.4
Interior plaster	0.4	5.0	0.4/5.0	= 0.08
Internal surface resistance				0.68
Overall Thermal Resistance, R				R = 5.11
U Value (1/R)				U = 0.195

STANDARD PROCEDURES OF BUILDING HEAT LOSS/GAIN CALCULATION

The total heat loss of a building is the product of the heat loss coefficient, UA, and the temperature difference between the assumed indoor temperature (T_{in}) and a "design" outdoor temperature (T_o), namely:

$$\text{Heat Loss, } Q = UA * (T_{in} - T_o)$$

The heat loss coefficient of a building (for winter conditions) consists of two components: the conductive heat loss, Q_c, and the infiltration heat loss, Q_v.

To the extent that there are "reliable" internal heat sources, such as lighting and electrical equipment (refrigerator, stove, computers, and so on), operating during the hours when operation of the heating system is needed, the heat produced by these sources, Q_i, is taken into account as *heat gain*, reducing the computed needed capacity of the heating plant. Thus, the "net" needed heat, Q_{net}, is:

$$Q_{net} = UA(T_{in} - T_o) - Q_i$$

Heat loss calculations are used primarily to determine the size of the heating plant and take into account the worst conditions. Therefore "credit" for solar heat gain, which is absent on cloudy days, is not considered in standard calculation of heat loss and heating plant sizing.

The situation is different in passive solar buildings, which are designed specifically to utilize solar energy as a major heat source. This subject is discussed in Chapter 4.

CONDUCTIVE HEAT LOSS

The conductive heat loss of a building, Q_c, is the sum of the heat losses through the various elements of its envelope, opaque elements (walls and the roof) as well as windows and other glazed elements, taking into account their respective areas, A_i, U_i values, and the indoor-outdoor air temperature difference $(T_{in} - T_o)$:

$$Q_c = (A_i * U_i) * (T_{in} - T_o)$$

A special case is a building with a concrete slab floor on the ground (at grade). The heat loss through the floor is commonly assumed to be only from the perimeter of the floor. This component of heat loss is calculated per length of the perimeter (m or ft), usually taking into account a (linear) conductance value of 1.1 W/m.C (0.64 Btu/h.ft.F).

INFILTRATION HEAT LOSS

The infiltration airflow can be expressed in two forms:

a. Airflow rates, V, in m³/hr or ft³/hr.
b. Air change rates, *ach,* specifying how many times the whole air volume of the space, *Vol,* changes in an hour:

The two expressions are related by the formula:

$$V = Vol * ach$$

Both the airflow and the air change rates depend on the air *tightness* of the building. A very tight building may have an ach rate of about 0.5 or even lower. In standard calculations of heat loss a value of 1 ach is often assumed.

Infiltration heat loss, Q_v, is proportional to the difference between the indoor air temperature, T_{in}, and the outdoor temperature, T_o, and can be expressed in two forms:

a. In terms of airflow rate:

$$Q_v = V * (ø * c)_a * (T_{in} - T_o)$$

b. In terms of air change rates:

$$Q_v = ach * (ø * c)_a * (T_{in} - T_o),$$

where $(ø * c)_a$ is the heat capacity of air. Its value changes with temperature, which determines the density of the air. In standard calculations the value of $(ø * c)_a$ is taken as 0.33 (Wh/m^{3}C) in the metric system, as 1200 (J/m^{3}C) in the SI system, and as 0.018 (Btu/ft^{3}F) in the British system.

Overall Heat Loss Coefficient, UA, and Heat Loss from a Building

The information needed for calculating the overall heat loss coefficient of a building, UA (conduction + infiltration), is commonly organized in a table, as is illustrated in Table 3-7a in metric units. Table 3-7b presents the same procedure in British units (the two sets differ slightly due to rounding of figures).

The example assumes a single-story building with (gross) floor area of 100m^2 (1080 ft^2), with southern and northern walls each 12 m long (40 ft) and the eastern and western walls each 8.3 m (27 ft) thick, with ceiling height of 2.5 m (8 ft). The south and east walls are like type 1 in Table 3-7, with U values of 1.043 W/m^2.C (0.185 Btu/h.ft^2.F). The north and west walls are like type 2 in Table 3-7, with U values of 1.09 W/m^2.C (0.195 Btu/h.ft^2.F). Each of the long walls has three windows and each of the short walls has two windows, all single-glazed with U values of 6 W/m^2.C (1.06 Btu/h ft^2.F). The area of each windows is 1 m^2 (10.76 ft^2). The (flat) roof is similar in construction to the wall type 1, but instead of the external plaster it has a lightweight concrete and waterproofing layers, yielding a U value of 0.95 W/m^2.C (0.167 Btu/h.ft^2.F). The floor is a concrete slab on grade. The volume of the building is 240 m^3 (8475 ft^3).

Total internal heat source is assumed as 1 KW (3.41 KBtu). The indoor temperature is assumed as 20°C (68°F) and the "design" outdoor temperature is 0°C (32°F).

Monthly Heat Loss Calculations by the Degree-Day Method

The Degree-Day (DD) of a given day is the difference between the diurnal average outdoor temperature and a "base" temperature which varies with the

TABLE 3-7A. HEAT LOSS COEFFICIENT (UA) OF A BUILDING (METRIC)

COMPONENT	AREA (A)	U_i VALUE	$A \times U_i$ (W/C)
South wall	27	1.043	28.2
North wall	27	1.09	29.4
East wall	18.7	1.043	19.5
West wall	18.7	1.09	20.4
10 windows @ 1 m² each	10	6.0	60.0
Roof	100	0.95	95.0
Floor (perimeter length)	40.6 m.	1.1	44.7
Total conductive heat loss			297 (W/C)
Infiltration heat loss (1 ach): 240x1x0.33			79
Total heat loss coefficient (UA)			376 (W/C)
Total instantaneous heat loss: 376*(20-0)-1000			6.52 KW

TABLE 3-7B. HEAT LOSS COEFFICIENT (UA) OF A BUILDING (BRITISH-ROUNDED)

COMPONENT	AREA (A)	U_i VALUE	$A \times U_i$ (Btu/h.F)
South wall	290	0.18	54
North wall	290	0.19	56
East wall	201	0.18	37
West wall	201	0.19	39
10 windows @ 10.7 ft²	107	1.06	114
Roof	1076	0.17	180
Floor (length)	133 ft.	0.64	85
Total conductive heat loss			565 (Btu/h.F)
Infiltration (1 ach): 8475x1x0.018			150
Total heat loss coefficient (UA)			715 (Btu/h.F)
Total instantaneous heat loss: 715* (68-32)-3410			22.33 KBtu/h

internal heat generation. The monthly degree-day is the sum of degree-days for the whole month. Often 18.3°C (65°F) is used as the basis for calculating the degree-day in residential buildings, with the assumption that only when the average outdoor temperature in a given day is below this level heating will be required.

The total monthly heating needs of a building can be estimated by the product of the building's heat loss coefficient (UA) and the monthly degree-days (DD_{mon}):

$$\text{Monthly Heating Need} = (UA) * (DD_{mon})$$

Tables of monthly degree-days are available for many cities. For the United States such information can be found in Balcomb et al. (1980) for each month and in Stein et al. (1986) for January and July only.

"Standard" Heat Gain Calculations (Summer Conditions)

The main difference between standard heat loss and heat gain calculations is that in the case of heat gain the effects of the direct (penetrating through windows) and indirect (absorbed at the building's envelope) solar gains, as well as the effect of heat capacity on the heat gain pattern (damping of the amplitude and time lag of the maximum and minimum), *have* to be taken into account. Therefore, the procedures of calculating heat gain through opaque envelope elements (walls and the roof) and heat gain through windows are different, and more complex, than in the case of heat loss calculations.

In dealing with the impacts of heat capacity on the thermal performance (indoor temperatures) of buildings there are other considerations to be considered, besides the heat gain and its impact on the cooling loads. Such considerations include comfort issues in un-air conditioned buildings, where no energy is used, as will be discussed later in this chapter.

Heat Gain Through Windows

The heat gain through windows has two components: conductive gain and solar gain. The conductive gain through a unit area of the glazing depends on the U value of the glazing (U_{gl}) in the same way as in the case of heat loss, and it is calculated by the same formula:

$$q = U_{gl}(T_o - T_{in})$$

(assuming outdoor temperature higher than indoor temperature).

Solar heat gain through glazing occurs only when the sun actually irradiates the window in question. The solar heat gain component depends on the intensity of solar radiation striking the glazing, which changes during the daytime and is also different for different orientations of the window. It also depends on the solar transmission of the glazing. The solar transmission, in turn, depends on the type (and treatment) of the glazing, including the shading. Generally, the solar energy penetrating through windows may comprise a very significant fraction of the total heat gain.

Permanent reduction of the window's solar gain can be provided by specialized treatments of the glazing. For example, a reflective glass, by increasing the fraction of the impinging solar radiation which is reflected away, reduces the solar heat gain of the building, and thus provides an inherent shading effect without interfering with the ability to view the outdoors. However, such glass often causes glare problems for pedestrians and drivers.

The *shading coefficient* of glazing, SC, is defined as the total energy transmission, relative to that of single-clear glass. Single-clear glass transmits nearly the same fractions of visible light and total solar energy: about 87 percent and 84 percent for perpendicular radiation, respectively. For double-clear glazing the corresponding transmissions are 80 percent and 72 percent. With double glazing having light-gold coating on the inner side of the outer pane, light transmission is about 58 percent while total solar transmission is only 35 percent.

It should be realized, however, that such glazing also reduces the solar gain in winter, when it is desirable.

Heat Gain Through Opaque Building Elements

Heat gain through walls and the roof is affected by solar energy absorbed at the external surface, as is represented by the sol-air temperature (see Chapter 2). It is an equivalent outdoor air temperature which would produce the same heat gain through the element in question, with no solar energy, as would exist with the actual air temperature and incidence of radiation. The formula of the sol-air temperature, T_{sa}, is:

$$T_{sa} = T_a + (a * I / h_0) - LWR$$

where:

T_a = outdoor air temperature
a = surface absorptivity
I = striking solar radiation
h_0 = external surface heat transfer coefficient (20 in metric units, 3.5 in British units)
LWR = temperature drop due to long-wave radiating to the sky.

For a roof under a clear sky LWR is about 5°C (9°F), and for a wall facing an open field about 2°C (9°F). Under a cloudy sky, and for walls facing other walls in an urban built-up area, LWR can be assumed as zero (Givoni 1979).

APPROXIMATE METHOD FOR CALCULATING COOLING LOADS THROUGH OPAQUE ELEMENTS

ASHRAE (1981) has developed a simplified method for calculating design heat gain (cooling loads for the mechanical cooling system) for residential buildings by using "Design Equivalent Temperature Differences" (DETD). The indoor temperature commonly is assumed to be 28.3 °C (75°F) for the calculation based on the DETD.

The *ASHRAE Handbook* contains a table of DETD values for lightweight and high-mass walls, and for several (essentially lightweight) roofs. Values are given for different outdoor design temperatures and three levels of outdoor temperature range (L, M, and H). The DETD assumes dark walls and dark- or light-colored roofs. The heat gain through an element, with area A and conductance U, is calculated by the formula:

$$Gain = U * A * DETD$$

QUANTIFYING THE INTERACTIONS BETWEEN HEAT CAPACITY AND THERMAL RESISTANCE

The quantitative effect of the mass on the thermal performance of buildings depends on the interaction between the mass and the thermal conductivity of the material forming the mass elements, as well as on the relative position of different layers with different mass and thermal resistance. Many walls and roof types are composed of layers of materials with different thermal properties, such as high-mass (concrete or bricks) and insulating materials. The effect of the mass of such building elements on the indoor temperature average, swing, and time lag of a closed un-air conditioned building, relative to the pattern of the ambient air temperature, depends on the order of the layers of mass and insulation.

The effective mass (heat capacity) of a building is expressed in two "composite" properties: the Thermal Time Constant (TTC) and the Diurnal Heat Capacity (DHC).

The Thermal Time Constant (TTC)

The TTC is the *effective* product of the thermal resistance and heat capacity of a unit area of an envelope element. It is defined as the equivalent QR product of a multilayered structure, where Q is the heat stored in the material and R is its resistance to heat transmission through it.

Mathematically, the TTC is defined as the sum of the individual products of resistance times heat capacity, QR_i, of the various layers of the element, when the resistance for each layer is calculated from the external surface up to the center of the layer in question, including the external surface resistance, r_o, (0.03

in the metric system and 0.17 in the British system). The TTC has the dimension of time (hours).

Thus, for the first, external, layer the QR value is:

$$(QR)_1 = [r_o + (.5 * l_1 k_1)] * (l * \rho * c)_1$$

which is equivalent to:

$$(QR)_1 = [r_o + 0.5 * r_1] * (l * \rho * c)_1$$

The calculation sequence of TTC, for an element with n layers, is:

$$(QR)_1 = [r_o + 0.5 * r_1 * (l * \rho * c)_1$$
$$(QR)_2 = [r_o + (r_1 + _{0.5} * r_2] * (l * \rho * c)_2$$
$$(QR)_3 = [r_o + r_1 + r_2 + 0.5 * r_3] * (l * \rho * c)_3$$
$$(QR)_n = [r_o + r_1 + r_2 + \ldots + 0.5 * r_n] * (l * \rho * c)_n$$
$$\text{and } TTC = QR_1 + QR_2 + QR_3 + \ldots + QR_n$$

The TTC of an envelope element m, (TTC_m) is its area (A_m) multiplied by its TTC value:

$$TTC_m = A_m * TTC$$

The total TTC of the building, TTC_{Tot} is the sum of the TTC of the "opaque" envelope elements areas, excluding the windows. The average TTC is the total TTC divided by the total envelope area, including the glazing areas:

$$TTC_{Tot} = \Sigma TTC_m / \Sigma A$$

Thus, the effect of the mass does not depend only on the thickness and weight of its walls and roof but also on the amount and location of the envelope's insulation. In fact, a building with 20 cm (8") walls insulated externally by 5 cm (2") polystyrene is effectively much more "high-mass," from the thermal effect aspect than a building with 40 cm (16") concrete without insulation, although it has only one-half of the nominal mass. The derivation of the effective thermal mass of a building from its TTC is presented below.

A high TTC increases the thermal inertia of the building and results in strong suppression of the interior indoor temperature swing, thus stabilizing the indoor temperature around its diurnal average when the windows are closed (and shaded) so that the building is not ventilated.

The TTC does not have direct effect in situations when "diurnal energy waves" affect the internal air and surface temperatures directly, without the modification of the envelope. Such cases include, for example, solar radiation penetrating through the windows in direct gain passive solar buildings. The physical property which affects the response of the indoor temperature in these cases is the Diurnal Heat Capacity, discussed on page 136.

Table 3-8 gives an example of TTC calculations for two insulated concrete walls composed of the same layers, but in different orders. In the first wall the insulation is external to the concrete while in the second wall the insulation is internal.

It can be seen from Table 3-8 that the relative locations of the insulation and the mass layers had very significant effect on the effective heat capacity of the walls. The TTC of the wall with the external insulation is 43.8 hours and for the wall with the internal insulation it is only 8.8 hours. In effect, external insulation enhances the capability of the thermal mass to suppress the interior temperature swing under given outdoor swing, while internal insulation neutralizes the stabilizing effect of the mass in the concrete layer. The impact of the relative location of mass and insulation layers is discussed on page 137.

The addition of an extra *internal* insulation layer to a wall with external insulation wall will *slightly* increase its TTC value. But internal insulation, even in thin layers (e.g., 1 cm or 0.5 in of polystyrene) separates the mass from the indoor air and thus neutralizes its effect when the building is ventilated in summer or heated in winter by direct solar gain. This point is of particular practical importance in regions where it is desired to have a building which heats up very slowly during the daytime, when it is closed, but cools down rapidly in the evenings, when it is ventilated. A building with an envelope consisting of a high-mass core insulated externally, with a thinner internal insulating layer, will have a high TTC and therefore heats up very slowly in the daytime hours but, if ventilated in the evening, its interior air cools down rapidly.

THE EFFECTIVE THERMAL MASS OF A COMPOSITE LAYER IN AN UNVENTILATED BUILDING

The effective thermal mass of an unventilated building constructed of composite elements thus depends on the presence and location of insulation. External insulation augments significantly the effect of a given amount of mass in suppressing the indoor swing of a closed building while internal insulation will add only slightly to this effect.

As explained, the TTC represents the sum of the products of heat capacity and thermal resistance. Recalling that the TTC of an envelope element m, (TTC_m) is its area (A_m) multiplied by its TTC value:

$$TTC_m = A_m * TTC = QR \text{ (hrs)}$$

The effective heat capacity (or thermal mass), Q_m, of the building's envelope element can be derived from the formula:

$$Q_m = A_m * TTC / R_m; \text{ (Wh/C), Btu/F}$$

TABLE 3-8. CALCULATION OF THE THERMAL TIME CONSTANT OF 2 WALLS (METRIC)

Wall #1

LAYER	THICK $l_i(m)$	DENSITY $\rho_i(Kg/m^3)$	RESIST. r_i	CUMULAT. RESIST.	HC $\rho*c$	QR$_i$ Hr
Ext. surface						0.03
Ext. plaster	0.02	1800	0.025	0.0425	414	0.35
Polystyrene	0.025	30	0.71	0.41	12	0.12
Concrete	0.10	2200	0.06	0.795	506	40.2
Int. plaster	0.01	1600	0.014	0.832	368	3.1
Wall's TTC						43.8

Wall #2

LAYER	THICK $l_i(m)$	DENSITY $\rho_i(Kg/m^3)$	RESIST. r_i	CUMULAT. RESIST.	HC $\rho*c$	QR$_i$ Hr
Ext. surface						0.03
Ext. plaster	0.02	1800	0.025	0.0425	414	0.35
Concrete	0.10	2200	0.06	0.085	506	4.3
Polystyrene	0.025	30	0.71	0.47	12	0.14
Int. plaster	0.01	1600	0.014	0.832	368	3.1
Wall's TTC						7.8

The TTC of the whole building's envelope, Q_{env}, is:

$$Q_{env} = TTC_{env} * (UA)$$

where UA is the heat loss coefficient of the building.

The total thermal mass of the building also includes the mass of the internal elements: partitions, intermediate floors, etc. Assuming that these internal elements are not insulated from, and directly interact with, the interior space, their total mass, M_{int}, multiplied by their specific heat, c, (0.23 Wh/kg.C or Btu/lb.F for masonry materials), can be added to the envelope effective mass. Thus the total effective thermal mass of a building is given by:

$$Q_{total} = TTC_{env} * (UA) + (M \rho c)_{int} \text{ (Wh/C), Btu/F}$$

The Diurnal Heat Capacity (DHC)

The concept of the diurnal heat capacity was developed by Balcomb et al., (1982), to evaluate the potential of heat capacity in storing solar energy in direct-gain passive solar buildings. It is defined as the amount of stored heat per degree of temperature swing. The term *dhc* refers to an *element* (W/m²C or Btu/h.ft²F) and DHC for the *whole building* (W/C or Btu/h.F). The author (see

Givoni 1987) developed a simple mathematical model for calculating the DHC and its effect on the performance of direct-gain solar buildings.

The DHC of the building determines its capacity to absorb heat from the interior space (e.g., solar energy penetrating through the windows thus bypassing the modifying effect of the walls and the roof), and to release the absorbed heat back to interior air during the night hours. It depends mainly on the properties of the layer *directly exposed* to the interior air and expresses the effective product of heat capacity of the layer and the conductivity of the material.

The diurnal heat capacity of a building element, (dhc_i), with an area of A_i, refers to the amount of solar heat which can be stored during the day and released back to the interior space during the night hours, for one degree change in the indoor air (environmental) temperature. It is of particular importance in direct-gain passive solar heating of buildings. Its units are Wh/C or Btu/h.F.

The whole building diurnal heat capacity, (DHC), is the sum of the diurnal heat capacities of all the mass elements surrounding the interior space of a building, as well as elements located within the space (internal partitions), which effectively participate in the diurnal thermal storage process of heat inputs bypassing the building's envelope.

The DHC of various materials, shown as a function of thickness of the element, is presented in Figure 3-2 (Givoni 1987).

Impact on Performance of the Order of Mass and Insulation Layers in Multilayered Envelope Elements

The discussion of the TTC and the DHC has shown that different arrangements of mass and insulation layers in composite building elements have different effects in buildings, depending on the path of the thermal excitations, whether they affect the building through its envelope or bypassing it. When a building is affected mostly by heat flow *across the opaque parts of the envelope* (when it is not ventilated and when solar gain through windows is small relative to heat gain/loss through the envelope), its performance is determined mainly by the TTC.

Whenever the main interest is in the potential of minimizing the indoor temperature swing and/or in lowering the indoor daytime temperature below the outdoor maximum by means of the thermal mass, the building should be closed during the day. In this case the TTC represents the effective heat capacity of the building. The TTC also enables evaluation of the effective thermal mass of a building built of envelope elements containing several layers of different materials.

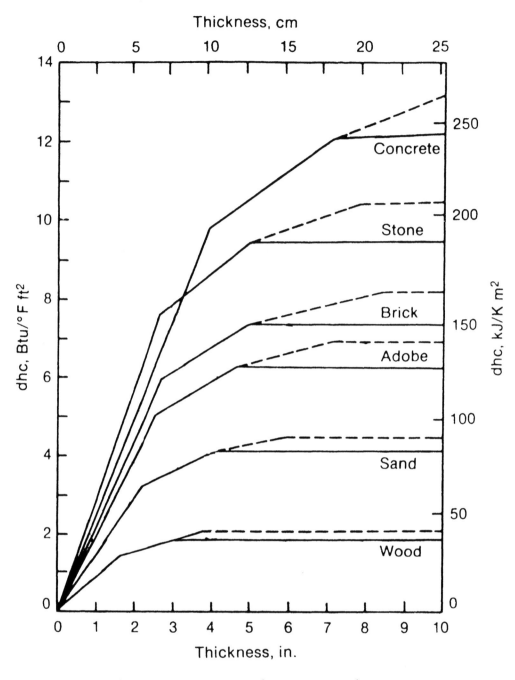

Figure 3-2. *Diurnal Heat Capacity (DHC) of various materials.*

The DHC expresses the effective mass when a large amount of solar energy penetrates through the windows, bypassing the modifying effect of the envelope. A similar situation exists when a building is ventilated at night, with the objective of storing the cooling effect and lowering the indoor temperature during the next day. In the two last examples the main heat gain or loss have bypassed the envelope.

In multilayered walls and roofs, composed of lightweight insulation and heavy conductive materials, the order of the different layers, from the external toward the internal surfaces, can modify radically the thermal characteristics of the building. Different orders of the same layers result in a different relationship between the indoor temperature and the ambient air temperature, which are different in ventilated and in unventilated buildings.

The order of the mass and insulation layers greatly modifies the temperature swing and the time lag of the indoor temperature. These modifications of the thermal characteristics make it possible to adjust the construction details to specific climatic conditions, particularly when the "common" building type appropriate to the climate present risks with respect to nonthermal factors, such as in the case of lightweight, low-mass buildings in regions experiencing tropical storms. This particular safety and comfort issue is relevant to many hot-humid regions, such as the Southeast of the United States and Southeast Asia. It is discussed in more detail in Chapter 11.

EXTERNAL INSULATION AND INTERNAL MASS LAYERS

The combination of external insulation and internal mass produces both a high TTC and a high DHC. When the building is without ventilation day and night its indoor temperature swing is suppressed and its maximum is delayed substantially behind that of the outdoor's.

In summer, and in regions with an outdoor temperature swing, when such a building is ventilated at night and is closed during the daytime it can effectively store "cold energy" during the night and absorb, during the daytime hours, solar radiation penetrating through windows as well as heat generated within the building, with relatively small elevation of the indoor temperature. Thus this construction type would be suitable especially in hot-dry regions.

However, the internal surface temperatures of the high-mass elements can remain, at night, significantly above the ambient air temperature, especially when the wind speed is low. In hot-humid regions with a small outdoor temperature swing and where the night temperatures are relatively high, such construction type may cause night discomfort.

In winter such a building can effectively be heated by solar energy admitted directly through windows. It can store the solar heat with relatively small elevation of the indoor temperature, thus minimizing the risk of overheating. During the night hours the stored heat flows mainly back to the indoor space, thus reducing the rate of cooling.

EXTERNAL MASS AND INTERNAL INSULATION

An internal insulation layer minimizes the effect of the mass on the indoor temperatures. It contributes only slightly to the TTC, relative to the case of the mass layer alone without the insulation, and minimizes the DHC. The indoor temperature swing and time lag in a closed, unventilated building will be determined mainly by the thickness of the mass layer. However, when the building is ventilated, its response is very close to that of a lightweight building.

This combination, of a high-mass building with thermal characteristics of a low-mass building, is of particular interest in humid regions which are subjected to strong storms, hurricanes, and typhoons. In a ventilated building the heavy external layer provides protection from the strong winds and the internal insulation enhances the cooling rate at night.

HIGH-MASS CORE COVERED BY EXTERNAL AND INTERNAL INSULATION

Some modern building systems are comprised of prefabricated, specialized, hollow building blocks of insulating material (e.g., polystyrene), typically of 25 cm (10") overall thickness and 16 cm (6.4") interior hollow core. After construction of the insulating wall, concrete is cast into the interlocking spaces of the blocks. Thus a composite wall is created with high-mass core, 16 cm (6.4") thick, insulated externally and internally by 4.5 cm (1.8") polystyrene layers. External and internal plaster layers are applied to the insulation. Such construction has a high TTC, resulting from the external insulation and the mass core, but negligible DHC, as the internal insulation separates the mass from the interior space.

When such a building is closed and penetration of solar radiation is prevented, it behaves like a typical high-mass building, with small indoor temperature swing and large time lag. On the other hand, when the building is ventilated, the building's response is similar to that of a lightweight building. When a large amount of solar energy penetrates through the windows the indoor temperature will rise sharply, because the internal insulation prevents absorption of the energy in the mass.

CORE INSULATION COVERED BY EXTERNAL AND INTERNAL CONCRETE LAYERS

Some modern building systems (e.g., Insteel 3-D in the United States) consist of a wire space frame integrated with a polystyrene insulation core, of a thickness which can be specified. Concrete is sprayed in situ to form exterior and interior finishing layers, with a minimum thickness of about 3.7 cm (1.5"), which can be increased as desired. The TTC of this type depends on the thicknesses of the polystyrene and internal concrete layers. A higher thickness of either layer increases the TTC. The DHC depends essentially on the specified thickness of the internal concrete layer.

With this system a low heat loss coefficient can be obtained using a large thickness of the insulation core.

Comparing Impacts of Heat Loss Coefficient and Heat Capacity

The UA (or the BLC) value of a building determines the daily average heating and cooling loads of mechanically conditioned buildings (strictly speaking, under steady-state conditions), regardless of the heat capacity of the building. Having a high mass flattens the "curves" of the heating and cooling loads and reduces the peak loads, but may not affect the average load. Therefore, when reducing overall energy consumption is of interest, requirements concerning the U value, especially in very cold or very hot regions, can be formulated without considering the heat capacity of the building, either directly or as expressed in the TTC and/or DHC.

The heat capacity of the building, as expressed by the TTC, strongly affects thermal performance and the indoor temperature diurnal pattern in un-air conditioned buildings. A building with a high-enough TTC can have a small diurnal temperature swing even in regions with very large swings (e.g., 15–35°C, 59–95°F). In such a case a high TTC can maintain comfortable indoor temperatures while the outdoor temperature is too high from the comfort aspect.

BUILDINGS WITH THE SAME UA VALUE BUT DIFFERENT TTC AND DHC

As the TTC is the product of (external) resistance and (internal) heat capacity, a given TTC can be obtained with quite different levels of insulation, and a given UA value with very different levels of mass. For example, if we compare a building built of 10 cm (4") stud-wall filled with polystyrene, and a building with a similar wall, but with additional internal layer of 10 cm (4") concrete, the two buildings have about the same UA value. When mechanically heated or air conditioned, both would have practically the same heating or cooling loads.

However, a building built with the first type of walls, especially if it has normal-size windows, would have a very low TTC and, in the climate mentioned above, a very large diurnal swing. It will be too hot during the day and too cool during the night, and may need both heating and cooling during the same day. A similar building built with the second wall type, on the other hand, has a very high TTC and may be comfortable throughout the whole day without heating or cooling.

Note that reversing the location of the two layers will result in a rather low TTC without changing the nominal mass level. The thermal performance of a building with this third wall type will not be very different from that of the building in the first example.

The main difference between the three building types is, however, in their

DHC, which determines their response to penetrating solar radiation, especially in winter. The building with the second wall type would have a very large DHC. It could absorb a large quantity of solar heat without too large a swing of the indoor temperature. During the day it could have an indoor temperature well above the outdoor level. At night it will release most of the stored heat back to the interior space and prevent too-low temperatures.

The buildings of the first and third type both have very low DHC because the internal layer of the walls is comprised of insulating material. With significant penetration of solar radiation they would overheat during the day. At night their temperatures will drop rather fast, especially in the first building.

Specific Impacts of Heat Capacity in Different Situations

The heat capacity of materials is significant mainly when the thermal conditions are fluctuating: large swings of the outdoor temperature with daily averages close to the human comfort zone; direct-gain passive solar buildings; intermittent heating or cooling; buildings occupied and conditioned only part of the day, etc. In each one of these situations the effect of heat capacity may depend on a different type of interaction with the thermal conductivity of the materials and the resistance of the envelope elements.

In conditioned (heated and/or cooled) buildings, under conditions approaching a steady state, as when there is a great difference between the outdoor temperature and the indoor (kept nearly constant by heating or air conditioning), the heat capacity has little effect on internal thermal conditions. The heat flow and temperature distribution depend, in this case, mainly on the thermal transmittance of the building envelope and on the amount of heating or cooling. But under strongly fluctuating conditions, even in air conditioned buildings, when the structure is heated and cooled periodically as a result of variations in outdoor temperature and solar radiation, or heated only intermittently, the heat capacity has a significant effect in determining indoor thermal conditions.

Thermal mass, provided by high-mass building elements in the envelope and/or in the internal partitions of a building, interacts with the thermal resistance of the envelope, and plays different roles in affecting the performance of the building. In different situations, with regard to the control of the indoor temperatures and/or with respect to the use pattern of the building, different design solutions concerning the building's mass may affect its thermal performance differently. For example, the following cases can be mentioned:

a. When the building's temperature is not controlled ("floating" conditions) the heat capacity determines the swing (maximum and minimum) of the indoor temperature around the daily average, with direct effect on the comfort of the occupants and the needs for cooling or for heating.

b. When a building is heated in winter by direct solar gain through large south-facing windows its heat capacity determines its ability to store excess solar heat from the daytime and utilize it during the night, thus minimizing the likelihood of overheating during the daytime and of the need to use conventional heating energy during the cooler nights.

c. When a building is cooled in summer by some passive systems (e.g., ventilating it during the nights in order to reduce the indoor temperatures during the following daytime hours), its heat capacity determines the extent to which the indoor maximum temperature can be lowered. This specific subject is discussed in more detail in Chapter 5.

d. When a building relies on daytime natural ventilation for providing comfort, especially in places with low wind speed or even still air at night, a high-mass building may cool down too slowly during the evening. Heat stored in the mass during the daytime hours will be released to the interior space during the windless night hours. This may cause sleep disturbances and accumulated fatigue. This subject is also discussed in more detail in Chapter 5.

e. When a building is heated and/or cooled by a mechanical system and is in use only part of the day—for example, a school or an office building—a high heat capacity causes slow response to the activation or stopping of the mechanical system. In this case the heating or cooling may have to start before the beginning of the building's occupation. At the end of the day's work, when the operation of the system stops, heat or cold energy is still stored in the building's mass, without actually being utilized. In such cases a high heat capacity may be a liability.

In the following sections the impact of heat capacity on the thermal performance of buildings is discussed with reference to different temperature control situations and building's use patterns.

Un-Air Conditioned Buildings in Regions with Large Diurnal Temperature Swings

The capacity of the building's materials to store heat during diurnal temperature cycles in un-air conditioned buildings has a profound effect on the comfort of the inhabitants and the indoor temperature swing in regions with large diurnal temperature swings. Buildings with high TTC are characterized by a stabilized indoor temperature even under large swings of the outdoor temperature. Thus, a building built of high-mass materials, such as dense concrete, and insulated externally, has a much smaller indoor diurnal temperature swing than an insulated building built of lightweight materials, like one with stud-wall wood construction, or even in comparison with a building built of heavy materials (bricks, stones, or adobe), but uninsulated.

In climates and seasons with large diurnal temperature swings (e.g., about 18°K) and where the *average* outdoor temperature is within the human comfort range, about 20–25°C (68–77°F), a high TTC building can maintain indoor comfortable temperatures even when the outdoor maximum temperature is up to about 36°C (97°F), provided that it is ventilated in the evening and night hours. A lightweight building, or an uninsulated high-mass building, will have, under the same conditions, too-high daytime temperatures from the human comfort aspect.

Thus, to maximize the effect of the mass, it is best to have an envelope with composite structure: high-mass materials insulated externally by a layer of high thermal resistance. The resistance layer insulating the mass can be composed of lightweight materials such as expanded polystyrene or provided by an airspace bounded by a reflective surface (e.g., aluminum foil), on the exterior side of a high-mass layer. Such a construction provides walls with a high TTC, maximizing the suppression of the indoor temperature maximum below the outdoor temperature maximum and the delay in the time of its occurrence.

In cases where the envelope is constructed of insulating low-mass elements it is still possible to have indoor air temperatures similar to those of a building with a high-mass envelope, if the interior elements (partition walls and floors), are built of high-mass materials and have a large area. However, the internal surface temperatures of the external walls will undergo a larger swing than the indoor air, thus producing higher daytime radiant temperatures than in buildings with a high-mass envelope. The "ideal" solution would be to have both the interior layers of the envelope and the internal elements, built of high-mass materials.

To get effective temperature suppression in a high-mass building its windows should be closed during the daytime, to minimize heating of the internal air by the hotter outdoor air. In such a high-mass building the temperature peak may be delayed till the outdoor temperature drops sufficiently so that the windows can be opened to allow natural ventilation to provide the indoor comfort.

AIR-CONDITIONED BUILDINGS (IMPACT ON COOLING IN SUMMER)

In air conditioned buildings, both residential and commercial (e.g., office buildings), the indoor temperature is controlled within a relatively narrow range by the mechanical system. However, there is a difference in the impact of thermal mass on the cooling energy consumption in these two building types.

Residential buildings are usually "skin dominated" and the internal heat generation, from kitchen appliances, and so on, is usually small in comparison with the cooling load resulting from heat gain through the envelope. In commercial buildings, on the other hand, internal heat generation by lighting, computers, and other office equipment, is very significant. Furthermore, commercial buildings often have a very large floor area relative to envelope area, and thus are "core dominated."

RESIDENTIAL BUILDINGS

The hourly cooling load in residential buildings is generated mainly by heat flow through the envelope, which the mechanical system has to accommodate, and to a smaller extent also by the solar gain through windows. The hourly pattern of the cooling load can significantly be affected by the thermal mass of the building, especially in residential buildings with small internal heat generation.

The hourly heat flow rates through walls of different orientations have very different patterns in low-mass and in high-mass buildings. In a low-mass building the heat flow from the internal surfaces of the envelope elements to the indoor air, which generates the "external" cooling load, closely follow the sol-air temperature patterns at the external surfaces. The direct solar gain through the windows also follows a similar pattern. Generally, in a building with a low-mass envelope, the resulting diurnal cooling load will have a large amplitude, meaning a high-peak cooling load and high-peak energy consumption by the mechanical system. The peak in such buildings usually occurs in the early afternoon hours.

A building with a high TTC, on the other hand, can suppress significantly the amplitude of the cooling load and delay the peak for several hours, till the evening. The suppression of the peak can result in a significant reduction in the size of the cooling system. Furthermore, the peak may be delayed till the outdoor temperature drops sufficiently so that natural ventilation could replace the mechanical cooling.

COMMERCIAL (OFFICE) BUILDINGS

Most commercial buildings are not in use during the night hours. The internal heat generation is usually larger than the heat flow through the envelope and is also mostly concentrated during the daytime hours. Commercial buildings often have relatively large windows to provide daylight, but such windows also serve to increase the internal heat generation. Consequently, the total cooling load, per unit floor area, is much higher than in air conditioned residential buildings.

The potential of thermal mass in such buildings to lower the cooling load or to modify its pattern (lowering the peak) is usually rather small, although obtaining such effect is not impossible. In order to achieve it there is a need to apply very specific design details, which will enable the building to store a large quantity of heat within the mass during the daytime hours, with a very small temperature swing, and to get rid of that heat during the night by nocturnal ventilation.

The required high mass in commercial buildings can be provided by reinforced concrete floors, where most of the mass would be concentrated. If the ceilings are exposed to the interior space they can absorb heat generated within the space. At night the stored heat can be "flushed" out by mechanically ventilating the space and thereby cooling the mass.

To enable passive flow of the heat in and out of the mass, "false/dropped ceilings" have to be avoided. However, such false ceilings are often applied to provide space for ducts, pipes, wires, etc., as well as for noise reduction in the use of acoustic ceilings. A design solution is to provide the service space *above the concrete floors,* by "false" floors raised about 0.5 meters (1.64') above the structural floors. Such a design was actually applied successfully in two large office buildings in Johannesburg, South Africa.

CONVENTIONALLY HEATED BUILDINGS (IN WINTER)

The impact of heat capacity on the energy use for heating in buildings heated with conventional systems is much smaller than its effect on the cooling energy use in air conditioned buildings. To some extent it depends on the temperature range and the duration of the heating needs during the winter.

Where the winter is cold, heating is needed almost continually and the heat capacity does not have a significant effect on the energy usage. On the other hand, where the winter is mild and heating is needed mostly during the nights only, a high heat capacity can reduce the heating energy use, and in particular reduce the peak heating load and the size of the heating system.

BUILDINGS HEATED BY DIRECT-GAIN SOLAR ENERGY OR COOLED BY NOCTURNAL VENTILATION

When solar energy penetrating through windows is a significant heating source (passive direct-gain solar buildings) high heat capacity is essential for effective utilization of the solar energy. A building without adequate amount of mass, and *effective* distribution of that mass around the heated space, may often overheat in the midday hours, making it necessary to ventilate the building or shade the windows, thus reducing the utilization of the available solar energy. Such a building may also cool down too fast in the evenings and thus need heating during nights when a high-mass building may be kept at comfortable temperatures throughout the night.

The quantitative effect of the mass in direct-gain solar buildings is expressed by the Diurnal Heat Capacity (DHC), as defined earlier in this chapter. The required effective heat capacity is proportional to the size of the "solar glazing":

the windows and other glazed areas facing the equator (south in the Northern Hemisphere). In a direct-gain building with high DHC the walls can absorb the penetrating solar energy more quickly and with a lower temperature elevation. On the other hand, when the value of the DHC is low (meaning a small amount of mass or small exposed surface area) the surfaces and the interior air are heated quickly even with a small amount of penetrating solar radiation.

The DHC value of the thermal mass depends almost entirely on the properties and thickness of the layer directly surrounding the space where the sun penetrates. The properties of layers further away from the interior surface have very little effect on the DHC. This is the main difference between the DHC and the TTC, which is affected by the properties of all the envelope layers.

The difference between the DHC and the TTC can be illustrated by the following example: A concrete layer of a wall insulated externally by a polystyrene layer will have both a high TTC and a high DHC. Adding a layer of insulation on the interior side of the concrete will increase, albeit slightly, the TTC of the wall. The effectiveness of the modified wall to suppress the indoor swing in unventilated buildings is not reduced at all.

However, such addition of internal insulation will reduce the DHC of that wall to an insignificant value, because the DHC is determined almost completely by the properties of the layer exposed to the interior space. The interior insulation will prevent absorption of solar energy in the mass layer behind it; such a wall is therefore inappropriate for solar energy storage. (The subject of passive solar buildings is discussed in much more detail in Chapter 4.)

A similar situation, with respect to cold energy collection and storage during the night hours and utilization of the stored cold energy during the following daytime, exists in nocturnally ventilated buildings. Also, in this case, a high DHC is essential for effective storage of the nocturnal cold energy and its release during the following daytime hours. This subject is discussed in detail in Chapter 5.

AIR CONDITIONED BUILDINGS OCCUPIED ONLY PART OF THE DAY

In air conditioned and/or conventionally heated buildings which are occupied only part of the day, such as schools and various offices, high heat capacity may be a liability and actually increase the energy use.

In summer, part of the cooling energy is used to cool the mass in the building. At the end of the building's occupation hours the mass is still cool, but without beneficial effect, so that the energy which was expended in cooling was practically "wasted." In winter a similar pattern of energy waste occurs in heating the mass. In the mornings of the spring season the mass may be too cool and a high-mass building may consume more heating energy than what would be needed for heating a lightweight building.

REFERENCES

American Society of Heating, Refrigerating and Air-Conditioning Engineers (ASHRAE). 1981. *ASHRAE Handbook of Fundamentals.* Atlanta, Georgia.

Balcomb, J.D. 1983. *Heat Storage and Distribution Inside Passive Solar Buildings.* Report LA9694. Los Alamos National Laboratory, New Mexico: Los Alamos.

Chandra, S., P.W. Fairey, and M.M. Houston. 1986. *Cooling with Ventilation.* Solar Energy Research Institute, Golden, Colorado.

Givoni, B. 1979. *Man, Climate and Architecture.* New York: Van Nostrand Reinhold.

Givoni, B. 1987. The Effect of Heat Capacity in Direct Gain Buildings. *Passive Solar Journal* 4 (1):25–40.

Stein, B., J.S. Reynolds, and W.J. McGuinness. 1986. *Mechanical and Electrical Equipment for Buildings.* New York: John Wiley & Sons.

Szokolay, S.V. 1991. Heating and Cooling of Buildings. In *Handbook of Architectural Technology.* New York: Van Nostrand Reinhold.

Chapter **4**: PASSIVE SOLAR HEATING SYSTEMS

INTRODUCTION

This chapter reviews the performance characteristics of various passive solar heating systems for buildings, the main design factors affecting their performance, their relative advantages and main problems associated with them, and their applicability to different building types and climatic regions. Emphasis is placed on the architectural design issues associated with the different passive solar heating systems and on the problems which may be encountered when passive solar heating is applied in regions with hot summers.

The solar passive heating systems discussed in the chapter are:

- Direct Gain
- Collecting Storage (Trombe) Walls
- Wall Convective Loops
- The Barra System
- Various Types of Sun Spaces

More information on the performance of passive solar buildings can be found in publications by researchers of the Los Alamos National Laboratory: Balcomb et al. 1980, 1982; Balcomb 1983, as well as in the book of Mazria 1979.

DIRECT GAIN

In Direct Gain buildings the sun is admitted directly into the inhabited spaces through conventional windows, skylights, etc. Rooms on the north side of the building can get the sun through clerestories placed above the roof level of the rooms to the south. The mass of the building fabric itself (in the floor, internal layers of external walls, internal partitions, the roof, and in the furniture) acts as the necessary thermal storage material, storing excess solar energy during the sunny hours and releasing it back during the night. The radiation may strike the mass elements directly or after reflection from other surfaces irradiated directly (Figure 4-1).

In many buildings not all the rooms have direct exposure to the sun through windows or clerestories. In such buildings, effective air circulation between "solar" rooms and "nonsolar" spaces is essential for achieving a high solar fraction by direct gain. In some circumstances, fan-assisted circulation, through openings in walls between rooms, ducts, or false ceilings, may be necessary to ensure adequate heat distribution, although the relatively small temperature differences of the indoor air limits the efficiency of such convective heat transfer.

The main factors affecting the performance of direct gain buildings are:

- Orientation and location of the solar glazing.
- Size and type of the solar glazing.
- The amount and design details of the mass available for thermal storage.
- Heat loss coefficient of the building as a whole.
- Arrangement of the furniture in the "solar" rooms.
- Thermal coupling between "solar" and "nonsolar" rooms.
- Control options of heat gain and loss through the glazing.

SIZE AND TYPE OF THE SOLAR GLAZING

Increasing the area of the solar glazing in Direct Gain buildings increases proportionately the solar gain during the daytime but it also increases the heat loss through the glazed area during the winter nights, as well as the (undesirable) heat gain during the summer. The ratio between these different thermal effects depends on the relative severity of the winter and the summer seasons in a given region, as well as on the properties and details of the solar glazing: the solar transmission and thermal conductance of the glazing itself, the availability of night insulation during the winter, the solar exposure and the availability of daytime insulation (in addition to shading) during the summer. Thermal properties of various glazing types were discussed in Chapter 2.

When the indoor temperature exceeds the upper limit of comfort, or when

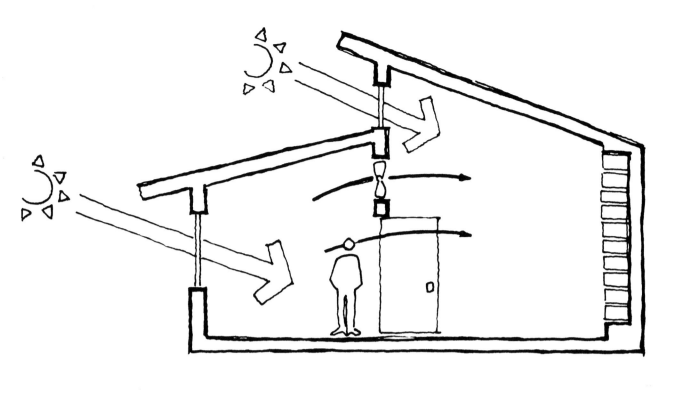

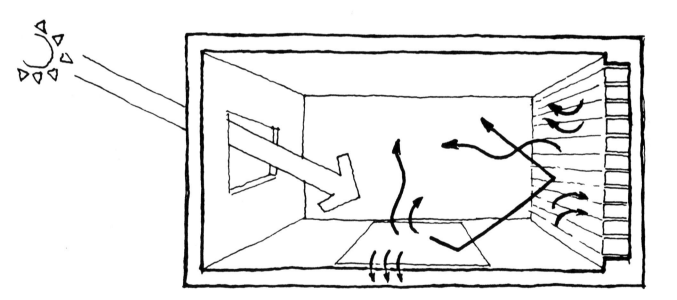

Figure 4-1. *Direct Gain System.*

problems of glare and discomfort arise from direct exposure to the sun, the solar gain has to be prevented by shading the windows or has to be "flushed out" by venting out the excess heat. Also it is not possible, with the present thermal storage capability of conventional materials, to store excess heat from a sequence of sunny days for longer than about two cloudy days.

It is often tempting to make the area of the sun-facing glazing as large as the building design allows, in order to maximize view to an attractive scenery and/or to maximize the penetrating solar energy during the heating season.

An example of a Direct Gain solar building with the whole area of the south wall double-glazed, in Santa Fe, New Mexico, is shown in Figure 4-2. It was designed and first owned by D. Wright. The walls are built of adobe, insulated by 5 cm (2") of Styrofoam, covered by cement/Styrofoam plaster. Interior folding shutters made of Styrofoam plates and canvas provide night insulation in winter and minimize solar overheating in summer.

However, without effective shading, too-large an area of the solar glazing may raise the indoor temperature on sunny days so much that it may exceed comfort conditions in winter. The problem can even be more serious during the spring, summer, and fall seasons, especially in regions with hot summers. There are two other negative effects of too-large glazing areas.

First, ordinary windows, even with double glazing, are usually the weakest thermal point in the building envelope, causing excessive heat loss at night. From the viewpoint of solar energy utilization, the benefits from increasing the size of glazing is of diminishing returns, while the heat loss at night through the glazing is proportional to the glazing area. A point may be reached when the increase in glazing size may cause a net heat loss, unless the glazing is

Figure 4-2. *The Wright Building in Santa Fe, New Mexico. Direct Gain with whole of the south wall glazed and insulated by interior folding insulation.*

equipped with operable night insulation. This issue can be resolved in part by new types of "super-insulating" glazing which have much higher thermal resistance than conventional double glazing. This glazing type was discussed in Chapter 2.

Second, the penalty from summer conductive heat gain through a large area of solar glazing in regions with hot summers, even if the glazing is shaded, may well be greater than the winter benefits. In some cases it may lead to the need to install mechanical air conditioning in places that otherwise do not need mechanical cooling. This penalty can be minimized by *insulated* operable shades which protect the building from daytime overheating while enabling fast cooling in the evenings by large openable windows, as well as by conductive heat loss through the glazing.

Taking into account all the various factors involved and their relative importance to the occupant, there is no single, simple computation method for arriving at the desired glazing size, but from a summary of the experience with occupied residential buildings employing Direct Gain (Givoni 1989), the following "rules of thumb" can give design guidance.

In a region with hot summers the area of "solar" glazing should be about 10–15 percent of the total heated floor area. It may reach 30 percent in the "solar rooms" where it is located, if sufficient thermal storage is available to prevent (a) too-fast a temperature rise and overheating locally and (b) the difficulties of glare, fading of fabrics, etc. Effective convective heat transfer between the "solar" and the "nonsolar" rooms, by natural airflow through internal openings or with forced ventilation, should also be available.

In cold regions a larger solar glazing area (e.g., 20 percent of the total heated floor area) may be acceptable, provided that high thermal resistance glazing (double glazing) is used and, in very cold regions, there is effective additional night insulation.

TYPES OF THE SOLAR GLAZING

In the *Passive Solar Design Handbook* (Jones et al. 1982, Figures G-51 to G-56) a performance sensitivity of the effect of the rating of the glazing on the Solar Saving Fraction (SSF) was presented. The other variables were the climate (six cities in the United States, ranging from mild to very severe), the Load Collector Ratio (LCR—the ratio between the solar glazing area and the net heat loss coefficient of the building), and the availability of night insulation.

In a mild climate the improvement in performance from a single glazing to double and triple glazing was very small, except for the case of a small LCR—either a very large solar glazing area or a building with a very low heat loss coefficient. In regions with cold winters there was a marked improvement in performance with double glazing as compared with single glazing.

Orientation and Location of the Solar Glazing

Solar glazing, by definition, should face the winter sun. However, in reality, as the solar glazing of Direct Gain systems is often determined by the orientation of the building itself, "exact" orientation is not always possible. Deviations of up to about 30 degrees from the true south and north, in the Northern and the Southern Hemispheres, respectively, would not affect greatly the solar radiation impinging on the glazing. Furthermore, in some regions fog is common in the winter mornings and in such places orientation to the south-southwest or the north-northwest (in the Northern and the Southern Hemispheres, respectively) might be preferable.

In many cases, however, several rooms or the building as a whole, do not have a south-facing wall. When such a building is one story high it is possible to utilize clerestories or roof monitors facing the south as solar elements for direct gain. Figure 4-3 shows the Stokebrand house designed by Edward Mazria in Albuquerque, New Mexico, which utilizes such solar elements.

The major advantage of Direct Gain systems is that significant amounts of solar energy may be collected in the heated rooms through elements which would be found in the building in any case—windows, clerestories, and roof monitors (skylights with vertical glazing) facing the sun. Clerestories and roof monitors make it possible to provide Direct Gain also to rooms which do not have the solar exposure of ordinary windows. Thus Direct Gain can be applied to single-story buildings which are elongated south to north and to buildings that do not have any sun-facing exposure.

Sun-facing windows and clerestories can provide solar heat only to the sun-facing section of a building, but without any restrictions on the number of stories. Roof monitors are applicable only to single-story buildings or to the upper story of multistoried buildings. They enable the introduction of solar energy at points far from the sun-facing wall of the building, regardless of the orientation of the building itself. They also are less sensitive than windows to the likelihood of sunlight being blocked by trees or nearby buildings.

However, from the energy aspect, they may be less efficient than windows. The author (see Givoni 1989) compared the measured auxiliary heat in winter and the cooling load in summer, in buildings in the United States, with roof monitors in a DOE monitoring program (Gordon et al. 1986). The auxiliary heat was higher and the cooling load was lower than the values predicted by the DOE-2 simulation model. Better agreement was found in buildings with conventional Direct Gain. This discrepancy could be explained by a lower effective solar heat gain, or a higher heat loss through the roof monitors, when compared with conventional windows.

Thermal Mass in Direct-Gain Buildings

Thermal mass stores energy from sunlit hours, to be given back during the night. From the point of view of the daily cycle, only limited thicknesses of storage elements are useful. Consequently, in the case of thick storage elements, not all the "nominal" mass in a building is effective for storage of solar energy. At present, the most common and cost-effective materials for thermal storage are masonry materials like concrete, bricks, etc., which serve structural purposes as well. Heat capacity is a function of specific heat and mass. Since the specific heat of almost all load-bearing masonry materials (concrete, brick, stone, and so on) is similar—about 0.24 Wh/kg.°C, 860 J/kg.°C (0.24 Btu/lb.F)—the nominal heat capacity is essentially proportional to the total volume and the density of the material. Non-loadbearing materials, such as those made of wood products,

Figure 4-3. *The Stokebrand house designed by Edward Mazria in Albuquerque, New Mexico. Clerestories are utilized as the main Direct Gain solar elements.*

with higher specific heat—about 0.4 Wh/kg.°C, 1440 J/kg.°C (0.4 Btu/lb.F)—but lower density, have usually lower nominal heat capacity.

However, the effectiveness of a thermal storage element depends on the rate at which heat is absorbed in it and is later given back to the indoor air. This rate depends on the surface area of the storage element exposed to the indoor space as well as on the thermal conductivity of the material. The higher the conductivity and the larger the surface area of a storage element the greater is the time constant for thermal storage.

In buildings with lightweight construction, such as the stud-wall buildings common in the United States, interior architectural elements within the area adjacent to the solar wall, with large surface area and built of high-mass materials, can also provide thermal storage. An example of such solution is an interior circular stairwell, designed by Anne Dunning in the Evans house near Santa Fe, New Mexico, and shown in Figure 4-4. The stairs and the thick parapets on both sides, made of adobe, provide a large exposed area of a high-mass material inside a building with a mostly lightweight envelope.

Taking into account the undefined pattern of the radiant and convective flows of the penetrating solar radiation into the storage elements, the minimum surface area of the thermal storage elements is six times the area of the solar glazing, regardless of the thickness.

The overall effective capacity of a "solar" space to store excess solar energy during the daytime and to release it to the indoor space during the night is expressed by its Diurnal Heat Capacity (DHC) (see Chapter 3). For a given size of the solar glazing the performance of the building will improve with the increase in the diurnal heat capacity, up to a given limit. The amount of the required DHC should be related to the amount of the penetrating solar radiation on clear days. In a given location this means that the minimum amount of heat storage should be related to the size of the solar glazing, or vice versa.

SOLAR GLAZING AREA AND THE BUILDING'S HEAT LOSS COEFFICIENT

The actual energy saving from a passive solar system of a given size, "Solar Saving," increases as the building reaches a higher UA value (W/K) or Building Loss Coefficient, BLC (Wh/K.Day), namely with poorer insulation of its envelope. A higher heat capacity, at a given solar glazing area and heat capacity level, increases the Solar Saving. This is illustrated in Figure 4-5 on page 158, where the Solar Saving was computed by the generalized model developed by the author, (see Givoni 1983, 1987), as a function of the area of the solar glazing, in buildings with two levels of the BLC (6000 and 12000 Wh/K.Day) and two levels of DHC (340 and 170 Wh/m².K). The reason for this interaction is that during periods when a highly insulated building would be overheated (i.e.,

Figure 4-4. *An interior circular stairwell in the Evans house near Santa Fe, New Mexico. The thick adobe parapets on both sides of the stairs provide thermal storage in a lightweight Direct Gain building. By permission and courtesy of Anne Dunning.*

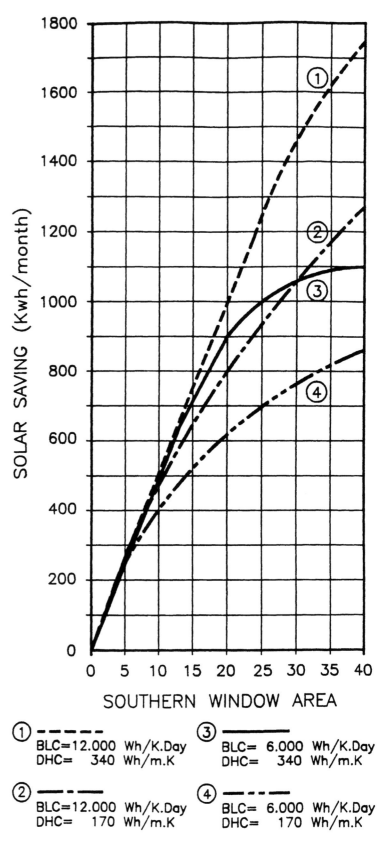

Figure 4-5. *Effect of Solar Glazing Area on Solar Saving Fraction, in Relation to the Heat Loss Coefficient of the Building and the Diurnal Heat Capacity.*

solar energy input has to be stopped or excess heat has to be vented out), a poorly insulated building may still utilize the solar energy.

Calculations based on energy criteria alone may tend to show cost benefits in "solar saving" increases for glazing areas up to about 50 percent of the floor area, especially in poorly insulated buildings. But the excessive solar energy may cause thermal discomfort on clear days, and overheating in summer. It will also aggravate all the functional problems associated with Direct Gain.

THE EFFECTIVENESS OF FLOORS AND OTHER SURFACES FOR THERMAL STORAGE

In buildings with direct solar gain through windows the floors are often considered the obvious building element providing the main thermal storage, as this is the element presumably most exposed to the direct solar radiation. In reality, however, the effective heat capacity of floors may be far less than the postulated capacity assumed in calculations. The reason is that furniture and carpets in inhabited buildings usually cover a large fraction of the floor area. In many houses the area of the floor *exposed* to the penetrating solar radiation is only a small fraction of the total floor area. Consequently, attention should be given to all the other surfaces surrounding the interior space, which may receive the solar energy which is reflected from the irradiated surfaces, for their capacity for thermal storage.

This point should also be considered in evaluating the effect of the interior surface colors on the overall capacity to store solar radiation. When a large fraction of the incoming energy is reflected, reradiated and convected from the furniture and the carpets, the color of the exposed floor areas may be of very limited significance in determining the effective solar absorption capacity of the interior space.

Most of the residential buildings in the United States, as well as in some other countries, are of low-mass wood-frame construction. In the United States buildings with concrete floors are usually carpeted. In such buildings the limited effective heat capacity may be a major factor limiting the utilization of solar energy for space heating by Direct Gain.

COLLECTING STORAGE (TROMBE) WALLS

Collecting storage walls combine in one building element the functions of solar energy collection, heat storage, and heat transfer to the interior. This system was first developed by Felix Trombe and Jacques Michel at Odeillo, France, and is

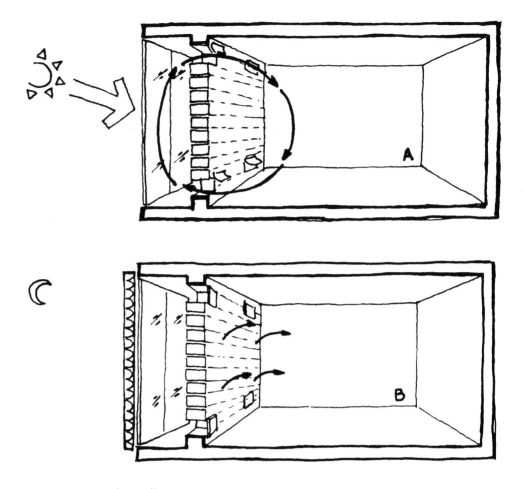

Figure 4-6. *Trombe wall system.*

commonly referred to as a "Trombe (or Trombe-Michel) Wall." In its simplest form it consists of glazing placed in front of a sun-facing massive, conductive wall (e.g., of dense concrete, with an air gap in between). (See Figure 4-6.) The exterior surface of the wall is painted a dark color (or is covered by a "selective surface" (as explained below) to enhance absorption of radiation.

Solar radiation penetrating the glazing is absorbed in the massive wall, raising the external surface temperature and that of the air in contact with it. The fraction of the absorbed heat which is transmitted through the wall to the interior is determined by the thermal conductivity of the material and the wall's thickness, as well as by the combined thermal conductance of the airspace and the glazing. The interior is heated by long-wave radiation and natural convection from the wall's warm internal face.

If vents are provided, both at the bottom and at the top of the wall, then the warm air, in the airspace between the dark surface and the glazing, rises and flows into the building through the upper vents. Room air flows through the bottom vents into the airspace. Thus a thermosyphonic airflow forms, transferring heat to the room by convection, in addition to the conductive heat transfer.

The major advantages of Trombe walls are:

- The indoor temperatures are more stable than in most other passive systems.
- Excessive sunshine, and its associated functional problems, does not penetrate into the inhabited space.
- Installation is relatively inexpensive where construction would normally be masonry, or for retrofitting existing buildings with uninsulated massive external walls.

Some practical shortcomings and disadvantages of this system are:

- Summer overheating problems may outweigh winter benefits in regions with mild winters and hot summers unless effective shading, also from radiation reflected from the ground, is provided.
- In a climate with extended cold cloudy periods, without adequate operable insulation, the wall may become a heat sink. This drawback may be minimized by the use of a selective surface, or prevented by effective use of operable insulation or transparent insulation.
- The effective heating is felt only to a depth of about one and one-half times the wall's height, due to the limited depth of natural convection air currents and the decreasing radiant heat flux from the warmed sun-facing wall.
- In multistory buildings problems with maintenance of the glazing may necessitate the provision of access balconies. Note, however, that such balconies can function as shading overhangs for the glazing below.

If windows are provided alongside or within the wall direct gain can provide light and quick heating of the space in the morning, while the mass is still cold.

A building utilizing a Trombe wall, supplemented by direct gain through southern, eastern, and western windows, is the Bruce Hunn building in Los Alamos, New Mexico, shown in Figure 4-7. The Trombe wall is 3.6 m (11.8') wide and 8 m (26.2') two stories high. It is built of 30 cm (1') filled concrete blocks and is double glazed.

Design Factors Affecting Performance of Trombe Walls

a. *Materials.* As mentioned above, thermal storage walls combine in one element the functions of collection, transfer, and storage of solar energy. For optimal energy transfer through the wall, materials of relatively high thermal conductivity are necessary. In practice, this usually means cast concrete, solid

Figure 4-7. *The Bruce Hunn building in Los Alamos, New Mexico. A double-glazed Trombe wall supplemented by Direct Gain through southern, eastern, and western windows.*

        concrete blocks, or dense bricks. Materials of lower conductivity, like adobe and lightweight concrete, will result in lower efficiency.

b. *Thickness of the Wall.* For each 10 cm (2") of concrete, there is a lag of about 2–2.5 hours between peak solar absorption, and heat delivery at the inside. For total energy saving, the wall thickness will have small effect, but it can be an important factor for the indoor temperature swing and comfort. With wall thickness below about 30 cm (6") the temperature swing of the interior would be excessive. Increasing the thickness above about 40 cm (8") would result in a higher cost while having only a small effect on the indoor swing. From this aspect, and also in considering the time of peak heating, the optimal thickness for concrete in residential buildings is approximately 30–40 cm (6–8").

c. *Color and Surface Properties.* The higher the solar absorption of the external wall surface, the higher the heat gain through the system. Black surfaces are often not acceptable architecturally. The most common choice is therefore a dark paint. The heat lost outward by reradiation from a dark painted surface is, however, also very high due to the high emissivity of common paints for long-wave radiation. The heat loss can be reduced by applying a "selective" surface to the wall, in the form of a metallic film of high solar absorptivity and low emissivity, glued to the wall. Application of a selective film to a concrete wall requires a very smooth surface of the concrete. This point should be taken care of during the casting of the concrete.

Compared with a wall with an ordinary dark surface the one with a selective surface will have a higher heating performance in winter. In regions with hot summers, however, a selective surface may aggravate the problem of overheating (see below). For a given energy need, a smaller area will be required for a wall with a selective surface, facilitating also summer shading and/or insulation.

EFFECT OF VENTS ON PERFORMANCE

Under optimal flow conditions about 30 percent of the total energy flow, in "vented" walls made of concrete about 30 cm (6") thick, is by convection and 70 percent is by conduction. A vented wall exhibits a lower temperature in the airspace and consequently less heat is lost through the glazing. Therefore the overall efficiency is higher by about 10 percent in systems with vented walls as compared with unvented walls. Note, however, that if the vents are not closed effectively at night a reverse airflow is established, which lowers the efficiency of vented walls below the level of unvented ones.

A major problem associated with vents is dust accumulation on the inner surface of the glazing and on the dark absorbing surface. As it is impossible to clean the dust it may eventually reduce the performance, in addition to the aesthetic impact. Experience in buildings where vents have been installed has shown that the need of access to the vents may interfere with possibilities of locating some furniture items in the rooms next to the lower vents. As a result, new buildings which were built in Santa Fe, New Mexico, for example, with collecting storage walls, have mostly unvented walls.

Insulation and Shading of Trombe Walls

The fraction of solar energy absorbed at a Trombe wall which is actually transmitted to the interior of the building (the heating efficiency) is significantly higher in summer than in winter because of the different relative temperature gradients from the absorbing surface to the indoor and the outdoor. While the indoor temperature is not much different in the two seasons the outdoor temperature is of course much higher in summer, so that a larger fraction of the absorbed energy flows inward. This factor increases the likelihood of summer overheating, in spite of the smaller amount of solar radiation impinging on the wall due to the higher altitude of the sun. Even a wall shaded from the direct ra-

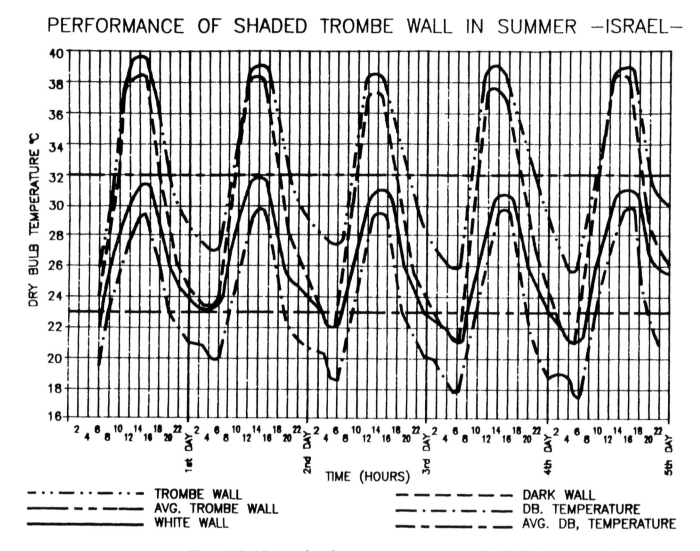

Figure 4-8. *Measured surface temperature patterns of a shaded Trombe wall, an unglazed dark wall, and a white wall.*

diation by an overhang may absorb enough reflected and diffused radiation to cause significant elevation of its surface temperature above the ambient level.

This point was illustrated in a study by a UCLA student in Israel. Moses (1983) demonstrated that the external surface temperature of a collecting storage wall, even when the wall and a sidewalk in front of it were completely shaded from direct radiation by a deep overhang, is elevated above the ambient air by up to 8°C (14.4°F) (see Figure 4-8). This elevation is caused by the diffused, and mainly by the reflected, solar radiation. In summer, and also in spring and fall, glazed solar walls may thus cause severe indoor heat stress.

Therefore it is suggested (Givoni 1989) that *in regions with sunny hot summers* it is desirable to ensure complete shading of the wall, not only from direct sun but also from radiation reflected from the ground. This can be accomplished only by external vertical shading (e.g., by rollable shades). An example

Figure 4-9. *Solar wall shaded by external rollable shutter in Mendoza, Argentina. The wall contains a combination of Trombe walls and Direct Gain. Building designed by Carlos de Rosa.*

of such application is a building designed by Carlos de Rosa in Mendoza, Argentina, which is shown in Figure 4-9. The solar wall contains a combination of Trombe walls and direct gain.

In regions with mild winters (midwinter average temperature about 5°C (41°F) night insulation may not be justified from the solar heating aspect. However, in regions with sunny summers and average midsummer daytime temperature above 27°C (80.6°F), the elevation of the external surface temperature of the glazed dark wall can cause serious overheating of the interior, and operable insulation may then be desirable. Such operable insulation will also improve, of course, the heating performance in winter.

Practically, it is not easy to equip a conventional Trombe wall with operable insulation or even to ventilate the airspace in summer. Ventilation of that space introduces dust on the inner side of the glazing and on the dark surface of the wall, reducing the effective solar transmission and absorption. Operable insulation *outside* the glazing is subjected to wind forces and, in order to be durable, it may be quite expensive.

One way to overcome these problems is to design an accessible space, about 60 cm (12″) wide, between the wall and the glazing. Such a space enables the installation of rollable winter-insulation-summer-shade "curtain" inside the

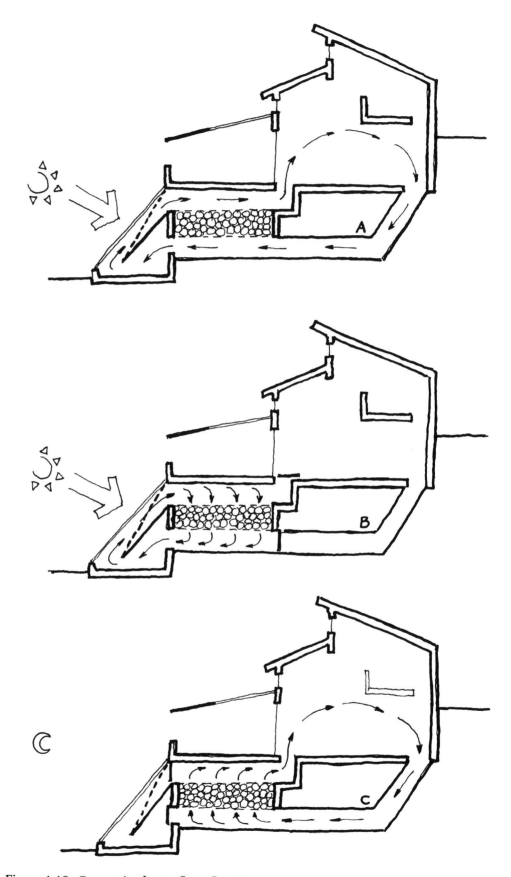

Figure 4-10. *Convective Loop: Steve Baer System.*

protected space, which is accessible for maintenance, dust cleaning, and so forth. The extra cost of this additional space should be taken into account in considering this design detail.

CONVECTIVE LOOPS: THE STEVE BAER SYSTEM

Steve Baer, of Albuquerque, New Mexico, has developed a passive solar heating system specifically designed for buildings located on a steep south-facing slope (see Figure 4-10 a, b, and c on the preceding page). Air heating solar collector and a rock storage bin are located below the level of the building's floor. The airflow can follow three different paths, according to the needs for space heating and the availability of solar radiation. The airflow is driven completely by temperature differences.

During sunny daytime hours warm air rises through the collector and enters a space above the rock storage bin. If the house needs heating during the day the

Figure 4-11. *The house of P. Davis in Albuquerque, New Mexico, utilizing the Steve Baer convective loop system.*

air flows up through floor registers into the house, and returns to the collector through a duct (Figure 4-10a shows the daytime heating mode). If the house does not need heating the air flows down through the rocks, losing heat and heating the rocks, and falls back into the bottom of the collector (Figure 4-10b shows the charging mode). At night, a damper between the collector and the storage bin is closed to prevent back flow. Warm air from the rock bin rises through the floor registers into the house and back to the bottom of the rock bin (Figure 4-10c shows the night heating mode).

Figure 4-11 on page 167 shows the house of P. Davis in Albuquerque, New Mexico, utilizing the Steve Baer convective loop system. A number of passive solar buildings using similar design were built in Santa Fe by architect Mark Jones. One such building is shown in Figure 4-12.

Figure 4-12. *A building in Santa Fe, New Mexico, utilizing the convective loop. Architect Mark Jones.*

THE BARRA SYSTEM: INSULATED, GLAZED, SOLAR WALL, AND STORAGE IN CONCRETE CEILING

This system (Figure 4-13) was developed by Horazio Barra (1987) in Italy. The southern wall is insulated and is detailed as a thermosyphonic air-heating solar collector. The hot air emerging from the insulated collecting wall flows horizontally, within channels imbedded inside a concrete ceiling, which also serves as thermal storage. Part of the heat is stored in the concrete ceiling while the still-warm air exits from the channels at the *northern end* of the building. The air thus warms the distant rooms first before flowing back through the building space to the inlets at the lower part of the sun-facing collecting wall. This assures an even temperature distribution throughout the whole house, which is better than what is achievable with other passive solar systems.

Because the airflow in the solar wall is thermosyphonic the flow rate is approximately proportional to the square root of the temperature elevation of the air in the collector above the indoor level which, in turn, depends on the inten-

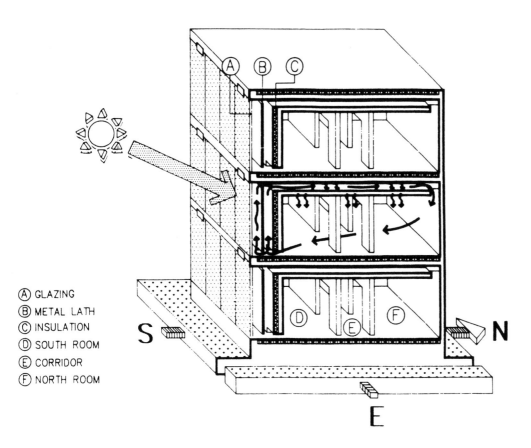

A GLAZING
B METAL LATH
C INSULATION
D SOUTH ROOM
E CORRIDOR
F NORTH ROOM

Figure 4-13. *The Barra System.*

sity of the impinging solar radiation. As a result, the air temperature is relatively high even under low-radiation (and low-flow) conditions. The high temperature of the air flowing within the channels of the concrete ceiling, coupled with the large surface area of the channels, helps in maintaining a high heat transfer from the air to the concrete. The fact that the storage elements are completely interior, within the envelope of the insulated walls, ensures a high-storage efficiency of the concrete ceiling.

With insulated walls surrounding the living space, unwanted heat losses in winter (especially during extended cloudy periods) and heat gains in summer, are minimized in comparison with a thermal storage wall.

The Barra System can be applied to multistory buildings, and even to buildings where the main rooms do not face the sun. When the "front" facade of a building is not facing the sun it is possible to use the rear or side southern facade as the collecting wall because a major part of the solar heat is transferred first by

Figure 4-14. *The house of Eng. Constantini in Italy, utilizing the Barra passive solar system.*

convection to the northern side of the building. Figure 4-14 on the preceding page shows the two-story residence of Eng. Constantini in Italy, utilizing this passive solar system.

Thermal performance of this system depends largely on delicate natural convection currents. The moving air must come into contact with as much surface area as possible of the collecting wall and of the mass in the ceiling, without being slowed too much. These considerations should affect the detailing of the air channels.

Because of its relatively high operating temperatures, higher than in other passive systems, the "collector" wall is subject to large thermal stresses. Polystyrene insulation should not be used, as collector temperatures may well exceed its melting point. Infiltration losses from the airspace can be minimized by good heat-resistant sealing around the glazing, but allowance should be made for substantial thermal movements, especially around the glazing.

If no measures are taken to prevent it, the airflow direction will reverse at night, when the collector is cooler than the indoor space. An automatic backdraft damper is a simple device to prevent such reverse convection. In its simplest form, it may consist of a light flap of plastic film, acting as a one-way valve. Condensation may occur on the inner side of the glazing during cold nights if the dampers are not fully tightened.

SUN SPACES

Sun spaces (also called conservatories in the United Kingdom) are intermediate *usable* spaces between the exterior and interior of the building. Being separated from the main spaces of the building, a much greater temperature swing, resulting from a large glazing area, may be acceptable within sun spaces, more than can be tolerated in direct-gain spaces. Sun spaces contribute to the thermal comfort in the principle spaces and to the options of activities in the dwelling in three ways:

a. They buffer the main spaces from extremes of exposure, thus reducing the potential temperature fluctuation, glare, and fading of fabrics and furniture which may result from excessive indoor sunlight.
b. They increase the heat collection potential of a given facade, by allowing a larger glazing area than is practicable and desirable with Direct Gain.
c. The sun space area itself can constitute an additional living space in the winter and the transitional seasons. With appropriate provision of shading and ventilation in summer, such spaces may be pleasant environments year-round in most climates (Givoni 1989; Mazria 1979).

A well-publicized house with a sun space is the one which was owned by Douglas Balcomb in Santa Fe, New Mexico. Figure 4-15 shows an exterior view of the building. Figure 4-16 shows the interior of the sun space.

Even during overcast winter days, when the sun space temperature would probably be below the indoor comfort level and thus unable to provide "positive" heat to the building behind, the air temperature in the sun space can be appreciably higher than the ambient air temperature. Consequently, the heat loss from the building interior through the common wall would be reduced, leading to energy conservation even when "positive" heating from the sun space is not available.

On the other hand, the overall cost is higher and the energy collection efficiency *per unit area of glazing* of sun spaces is lower as compared with direct gain. Consequently, the payback period of the investment in its construction would be higher for a sun space.

Figure 4-15. *The Balcomb in Santa Fe, New Mexico. Exterior view of the building.*

Figure 4-16. *Interior of the sun space in the Balcomb house.*

Types and Configurations of Sun Spaces

Considering thermal characteristics and building design, two types of sun spaces may be distinguished:

a. *Modified Greenhouses*—with a glazed inclined roof and sometimes also with inclined glazed walls.
b. *Sunporches*—with horizontal opaque and insulated roof, where the glazing is only vertical.

MODIFIED GREENHOUSES

This form, with tilted or curved overhead glazing, shown in the top portion of Figure 4-17, maximizes the transmitted radiation as the roof receives the winter sun rays in late winter at more optimal angle. The glazed roof of a modified

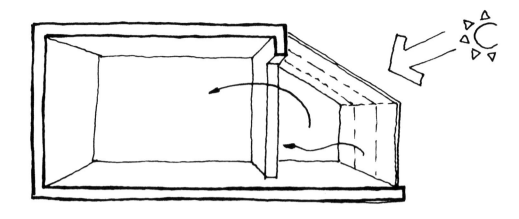

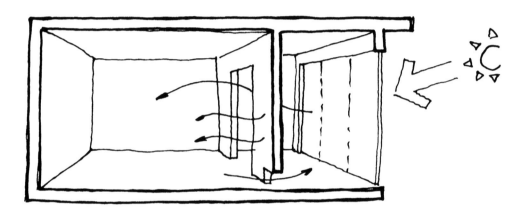

Figure 4-17. *Sun space types: modified greenhouse and a sunporch.*

greenhouse increases the total solar energy collecting area of a sun space of a given height and width. On the other hand, such a form is also subject to higher heat losses in winter during cloudy periods, particularly by long-wave radiation from the horizontal part of the glazing to the night sky. A glazed roof is subjected to very high solar heat gain in summer. Therefore, greenhouses have larger temperature fluctuations, in both winter and summer, than sun porches, and overheating in summer is more likely.

SUNPORCHES

In this type of sun space, shown in the bottom portion of Figure 4-17, the opaque and insulated roof reduces the likelihood of both overheating and the large diurnal temperature swings caused by the overhead glazing. The potential heat gain in winter is lower than in the case of a greenhouse type but the possibilities for control, and for year-round use of the sun space area, especially in hot regions, increases greatly. This type is therefore advisable *in regions with hot summers.* If a sufficient portion of the glazing (e.g., 20 percent) is made openable, such a space becomes, in summer, the equivalent of a shaded outdoor porch, providing shade for the building's wall behind the sun space.

SUN SPACE/BUILDING RELATIONSHIP

Sun spaces can have different relationships to the building "proper," which affect the thermal, functional, and architectural integration of the building proper and the sun space areas, as illustrated in Figure 4-18:

a. Attached: Outside the wall's line.
b. Semienclosed: Surrounded by rooms on two or three sides.
c. Internal: Surrounded by the building on all sides (also called atria).

ATTACHED SUN SPACES

Attached sun spaces share only one wall with the rest of the building. They provide the greatest flexibility, for planning and construction, including solar retrofitting of existing buildings.

In regions with favorable energy balance, they also allow the use of glazed end-walls (eastern and western) for maximum utilization of the morning and/or afternoon sun, although the risk of overheating in summer by solar penetration through the end-walls should not be overlooked.

When the end-walls and part of the southern glazing are openable the sun space area can be effectively cross-ventilated, and thus the likelihood of summer

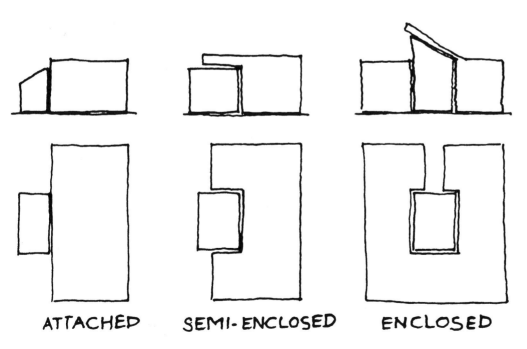

Figure 4-18. *Sun space building relationships.*

overheating is minimized. The protruding end-wall openings can also provide good ventilation potential for the building behind the sun space, especially when the wind direction is very oblique with respect to the sun-facing facades. On the other hand, in cold regions at high latitudes, the end-walls will probably have a negative energy balance in winter, and therefore should be insulated rather than glazed.

Having the largest surface area exposed to the outside, attached sun spaces are subject to both the greatest heat loss in winter and, with fixed glazed (eastern and western) end-walls, the highest solar heat gain in summer.

SEMIENCLOSED SUN SPACES

In this arrangement the sun space is indented into the building. Heat loss through the end-walls is minimized without reducing the solar exposure, thereby increasing the thermal efficiency of the sun space. There is a greater variety of possible architectural connections between the surrounding rooms and the sun space area than in an attached sun space. Thus, for a given size of solar glazing, both the efficiency of collection and of heat transfer to the habitable rooms are enhanced, compared with an attached sun space.

FULLY ENCLOSED SUN SPACES

This sun space type is sometimes referred to as an atrium, patio, or even as a "solar courtyard." As the sun space is surrounded on all sides by rooms, the solar glazing has to be above the level of the roof to the sun-facing side of the sun space. This factor limits the glazing size but this limitation, of lower heat gain potential, is compensated in part by the higher efficiency of heat distribution to the living spaces around the sun space. This type has obvious applications in buildings with deep plan forms. With suitably designed openings and shading, this type may also be used in summer to enhance the ventilation of the main building, by introducing into the building wind flowing above the roof level and serving, in effect, as a wind catcher.

Design Options for the Connecting Wall

The sun space may be connected to the main building by a number of types of walls. Each type has different effects on the amount and rate of heat transfer to the main spaces and on the indoor thermal and lighting conditions, as well as on the thermal environment within the sun space itself. Some of the types of connecting walls include:

a. Thermally conductive, massive wall
b. "Internal" Trombe wall (glazed massive wall)
c. Insulated wall with large connecting openings
d. Glazed and insulated wall

THERMALLY CONDUCTIVE, MASSIVE WALL

This wall type may be built of any one of the conventional masonry materials, and is often an integral part of the building's load-bearing structure. As this wall is not glazed its surface temperature would be significantly lower than that of a Trombe wall under similar ambient conditions and, consequently, the conductive heat transfer to the interior would be lower. Therefore large openings in the wall, leading to the rooms where heat is needed, have to be provided so that during the daytime convective heat transfer can provide most of the required heating to these rooms. Per unit area, the convective heat transfer is much higher than the conductive flow across the wall. The actual amount of the convective flow depends on the size of the door and windows relative to the wall, their shape, and whether the openings actually are kept open during the sunny hours and are closed during the nights. At night most of the heat from an unglazed wall is actually given back to the sun space itself, thereby decreasing its efficiency as a source of useful heat for the interior.

Analysis of the heat flow from the sun space to the rooms in the Balcomb house (Jones et al. 1982) has demonstrated that most of the heat flow to the rooms was provided by convection. The mass wall has served mainly as a heat storage for the sun space itself, moderating its temperature swing.

INTERNAL TROMBE WALL (GLAZED MASSIVE WALL)

By placing a layer of rigid transparent or translucent plastic over a massive conducting wall, an internal Trombe wall is created within the sun space. While the solar energy impinging on the wall surface is lower than in the case of an exposed Trombe wall, other thermal advantages may more than compensate for it. As the sun space temperature is higher than the outdoor's, both day and night, it reduces the characteristic Trombe wall's high heat loss to the outside, thus helping to maintain a higher surface temperature. Also, higher air temperatures than in a Trombe wall are possible in the gap between the glazing and the wall. This increases the efficiency of conductive heat transmission through the wall—the hot air in the gap may be delivered by natural or forced convection to remote rooms in the building. Unfortunately, the performance of this wall type has not yet been studied, either experimentally or by computer simulation.

Insulated Wall with Large Connecting Openings

As the conductive heat transfer across a mass wall is small in comparison with the potential for convective heat transfer, the separating wall may be an insulated one, with large doors connecting the sun space with the rooms behind and providing convective heat transfer to the building. Airflow may be enhanced by the use of ceiling-height door, rather than conventional doors. The temperature swing of the sun space can be moderated by other mass elements within the sun space area, separately from the connecting wall.

At night, when the connecting doors are closed, the insulated wall minimizes the conductive heat flow across the sun space, from the interior to the outdoors. The temperature drop of the sun space can be moderated by thermal storage elements within the sun space area. In summer during daytime, if the connecting doors are closed and shaded, the heat gain to the building is minimized.

Glazed and Insulated Wall

A layer of glazing may be placed in front of an insulated connecting wall. Since an insulated wall itself has no role in transmitting heat by conductance, the principal purpose of this arrangement is to supply air to the interior at a temperature which is higher than that obtained with a glazed conductive mass wall or with an unglazed insulated one.

The hot air may then be used for quick heating of adjacent or remote occupied spaces. Typical applications might be schools and offices, where only daytime occupation need be considered. Alternatively, the warm air may be routed through air channels in the ceiling, to heat remote spaces by convection.

Thermal Mass Inside the Sun Space

If the sun space is to be used for anything other than for heating air, it must contain some thermal mass to moderate its temperature swings. Without thermal storage, diurnal temperature fluctuations of the order of 30°K on clear winter days would not be unusual. The necessary storage mass may be provided in many forms, such as in the floor, connecting walls, or other structural features, or it may be in specialized elements, in the form of large planters, water containers, etc.

Such "additional" nonstructural mass should ideally be located at the base of the glazing. In that location it intercepts sunshine which would not, in any case, irradiate the connecting wall, and where the heat given off serves to set up favorable convection patterns within the sun space.

APPLICABILITY OF THE VARIOUS PASSIVE SOLAR SYSTEMS

The overall performance (in the United States) and the applicability of the various passive solar heating systems, in different climates and building types, are reviewed below.

Overall Energy Saving by Application of Passive Solar Systems in Residential Buildings in the United States

The author (see Givoni 1989) has summarized and analyzed numerous studies in which the performance of solar technologies in residential and nonresidential buildings in the United States was monitored (AIA 1978; Gordon et al. 1986; Haskin and Stromberg 1979; Hill et al. 1987; Jones 1982; Johnson 1978; SERI 1983, 1984; Ternoey et al. 1985). Analysis of the data has demonstrated that the potential contribution of the passive solar systems to the heating energy (at least in the United States) depends mainly on cloudy conditions. In the cold but sunny New Mexico a Solar Heating Fraction (SHF) of up to 0.8 was achieved. (SHF is the fraction of the total heating energy provided by the sun.) In the Denver area the best performance was about 0.6 and in the Midwest and the Northeast about 0.5. These limits can be considered as the "near upper" limits with present thermal storage technologies. However, large variations in performance were noticed in individual buildings, depending on the area of the solar glazing, the specific solar system, the heat loss coefficient of the buildings, etc.

DIRECT GAIN

Direct Gain on a small scale, providing solar energy to sun-facing rooms through conventional windows during clear days, without thermal storage for the nighttime, can be applied in any climate to any building with a sun-facing facade, regardless of the number of stories. Single-story buildings can also have Direct Gain through roof monitors, regardless of the geometry, dimensions, and floor area of the building. Nonresidential buildings which are used primarily during the daytime, such as schools and some offices, are good candidates for Direct Gain, provided that problems of glare and overheating are solved successfully. One possibility of solving the glare problem is to reflect the penetrating radiation, by appropriate details of interior shading, toward the ceiling.

Concerning residential buildings, which are occupied during the nighttime, the building's type applicability is a little more complex. In lightweight buildings, like most of the houses in the United States, it is impractical to store solar heat in the building's structural mass even for one night. Specialized storage elements are needed, which may add substantially to the cost of solar heating. Still, Direct Gain can reduce the consumption of conventional heating energy by providing daytime heating during clear days.

The ability to store solar energy for the nighttime, or even for one cloudy day, however, depends on the availability of substantial thermal storage. In buildings with high-mass walls and partitions, such as concrete or bricks, the ability to store solar heat for the nighttime is an inherent property of the building structure. In lightweight buildings, it seems to the author, wider application of solar heating by Direct Gain depends on the development of new storage elements which can be an integral part of the building structure, such as wall and ceiling panels integrating Phase Change Materials (PCM) within the panel's composition (Salyer et al. 1985; Givoni 1989). PCM are materials which change from solid to liquid when absorbing heat and from liquid to solid when loosing heat. The process is reversible and the phase change takes place while the material's temperature remains relatively constant.

THERMAL STORAGE WALLS

A "Thermal Storage Wall" implies a massive wall made of concrete or bricks, facing the sun. Such a wall is usually part of the structural, load-bearing system of the building and the extra cost of converting it to a solar collecting element is the addition of the glazing, in addition to the cost of the additional material needed to obtain the required thermal storage and suppression of the indoor temperature swing. Therefore, this passive solar heating system is an attractive solution in countries where concrete-and-brick construction is common practice.

A Thermal Storage Wall without provision for external night insulation (a design solution which, to the author, seems an impractical one) is sensitive to cloudiness in cold climate, because during a cloudy period lasting for a few days it becomes a heat sink. Therefore, from the climatic aspect, the main factors affecting the applicability of thermal storage walls *in cold regions* is the duration of cloudy periods.

In regions with sunny hot summers it is desirable to ensure complete shading of the wall, not only from direct sun but also from radiation reflected from the ground.

STEVE BAER'S CONVECTIVE LOOP SYSTEM

Convective loops with the collector located below the building's floor level are applicable only in sites with a steep southern slope (in the Northern Hemisphere).

In summer the collector, with specialized design details for water heating in conjunction with the air heating, can be used for domestic water heating, by disconnecting the passive thermal coupling with the building and thus preventing the likelihood of overheating.

THE BARRA SYSTEM

In contrast with a Thermal Storage Wall, the sun-facing wall in the Barra System is an insulated wall with negligible heat capacity, so it is not sensitive to cloudy periods. During sunny hours solar heat is transferred to the ceiling and then to the indoor space, while at night and during cloudy periods the thermosyphonic flow is stopped and the wall's insulation minimizes heat loss through the sun-facing wall. In summer the wall's insulation minimizes indirect solar heat gain. Consequently, this system is applicable in a wider range of climatic conditions than Thermal Storage Walls.

The storage in the Barra System is in a concrete ceiling, a design detail which in practice is applicable only to buildings with high-mass structural systems. As each floor has its own collecting wall and ceiling storage elements, this system can be applied to buildings with any number of stories. The space heated by this system may be limited, by the horizontal path of the thermosyphonic airflow, to a depth of about 8–10 m (26–33').

APPLICABILITY OF SUN SPACES

Sun spaces may be applied to buildings of almost any type, height, or size, provided they have an unshaded, sun-facing facade. There are some differences, however, among the various types of sun spaces and their applications to different buildings. A sun space in two- or three-story-high dwellings, with an interior stairwell in the back of the building serving as an air shaft, would have a much higher airflow than a sun space in a single-story building.

Sunporches can be applied to the sun-facing facade of any building, regardless of its height, because all the glazing is vertical. Sunporches can thus be placed one on top of the other in multistoried buildings, extending, if so desired, along the whole facade of the building.

On the other hand a greenhouse, by definition, has a sloping glazed roof. If placed one on top of the other, the floor of an upper greenhouse will block the sun from the roof of the lower one. There is, of course, still the possibility to place greenhouses, if they do not extend along the whole width of the building, in a checkerboard pattern. In this way there is a vertical distance of one floor between the floor of the upper greenhouse and the roof of the lower greenhouse at the same vertical "slice" of the facade.

Sunporches can be applied in any climate. In regions with hot summers, however, greenhouses may cause overheating. Provisions for effective cross-ventilation of the sun space are desirable everywhere, and are essential in regions with hot summers.

REFERENCES

AIA Research Corporation. 1978. "Passive Solar Design: A Survey of Monitored Buildings."

Balcomb, J.D. 1983. Heat Storage and Distribution Inside Passive Solar Buildings. Report LA 9694 M.S. Los Alamos National Laboratory, Los Alamos, New Mexico.

Balcomb, J.D., D. Barley, R.D. McFarland, J. Perry, W.O. Wray, and S. Noll. 1980. *Passive Solar Design Handbook, vol. II.* U.S. Department of Energy, NTIS.

Balcomb, J.D., W.R. Jones, R.D. McFarland, and W.O. Wray. 1982. Expanding the SLR Method. *Passive Solar Journal* 1 (2):67–91.

Barra, O.A., G. Artese, L. Franceschi, R.K. Joels, and A. Nicoletti. 1987. The Barra Thermosyphon Air System: Residential and Agricultural Applications in Italy, UK and in the Sahara. International Conference of Building Energy Management. Lausanne, Switzerland.

Givoni, B. 1983. A Generalized Predictive Model for Direct Gain. *Passive Solar Journal* Vol. 2, No. 2, 2 (X):107–115.

Givoni, B. 1987. The Effective Heat Capacity in Direct Gain Buildings. *Passive Solar Journal* Vol. 4, No. 1, 4 (X):25–40.

Givoni, B. 1989. Building Design Guidelines for Solar Energy Technology. Research Report to the AIA/ACSA Council of Architectural Research.

Gordon, H.T., P.R. Rittlemann, J. Estoque, G.K. Hart, and M. Kantrowitz. 1986. Passive Solar Energy for Non-Residential Buildings. In *Advances in Solar Energy, vol. 3.:* Plenum Press.

Haskin, D., and R.P. Stromberg. 1979. "Passive Solar Buildings." Sandia Laboratories.

Hill, B., K. Rittlemann Assoc., and M. Kantrowitz Assoc. 1987. *Commercial Buildings Design: Integrating Climate, Comfort and Cost.* New York: Van Nostrand Reinhold.

Jones, R.W. 1982. Monitored Passive Solar Buildings. Report LA-9098-MS. Los Alamos National Laboratory, Los Alamos, New Mexico.

Jones, R.W., Editor, D. Balcomb, C.E. Kosiewicz, G.S. Lazarus, R.D. McFarland, and W.O. Wray. 1982. *Passive Solar Design Handbook, vol. III.* DOE/CS-0127/3. Los Alamos National Laboratory, Los Alamos, New Mexico.

Mazria, E. 1979. *Passive Solar Energy Book.* Emmaus, Pennsylvania: Rodale Press.

Moses, A. 1983. Experimental Study of Shaded Trombe Wall in Summer. Research Report. Graduate School of Architecture and Urban Planning, UCLA.

Salyer, I.O., A.K. Sircar, R.P. Chartoff, and D.E. Miller: "Advanced Phase Change Materials for Passive Solar Storage Applications." Soc. Automotive Engineering. P-85/164. 3.699-3.709.

Solar Energy Research Institute (SERI). 1983. "Passive Solar Performance: Summary of 1981–1982 Class B Results."

Solar Energy Research Institute (SERI). 1984. "Passive Solar Performance: Summary of 1982–1983 Class B Results."

Ternoey, S., L. Bickle, C. Robbins, R. Busch, and K. McCord. 1985. *The Design of Energy Responsive Commercial Buildings.* New York: John Wiley & Sons.

Chapter 5: PASSIVE COOLING OF BUILDINGS

INTRODUCTION

This chapter is a revised and updated version of Chapter 1, Overview of *Passive and Low Energy Cooling of Buildings* (see Givoni 1994). It is included in the present book because the issue of passive cooling is an integral part of the guidelines for building design in hot climates (Part III of this book), as well as for the benefit of readers who do not have the author's cooling book.

Furthermore, since the manuscript of the cooling book was written, the author has continued to do research on several of the passive cooling systems discussed in that book, as well as on a new cooling system not covered in the first book at all: indirect evaporative cooling by wetted conductive impermeable walls. In addition, a student of the author, Nasser Al-Hemiddi, under the author's supervision, has conducted an extensive experimental evaluation of some new ideas of passive cooling the author had developed, in real-size rooms in the challenging climate of Riyadh, Saudi Arabia. With his consent some of his data are also included in this chapter, for the first time.

Cooling of buildings by passive systems can be provided through the utilization of several natural heat sinks: the ambient air, the upper atmosphere, and the under-surface soil. Such cooling systems include:

- **Comfort Ventilation:** Providing direct human comfort by natural ventilation, mainly during daytime hours.

- **Nocturnal Ventilative Cooling:** Lowering the indoor daytime temperature by ventilating the building at night.
- **Radiant Cooling:** Utilizing the process of nocturnal long-wave radiation to the sky.
- **Direct, Nonmechanical:** Evaporative cooling of the ventilation air, for example, by cooling towers.
- **Indirect:** Evaporative cooling of the building by roof ponds and wetted conductive impermeable walls.
- **Soil Cooling:** Utilizing the soil as a cooling source for buildings.

Some of these systems provide instantaneous cooling effect whenever they are operated, such as comfort ventilation and direct evaporative cooling. In other passive cooling systems, such as ventilative and radiant cooling, cooling energy is collected during the nighttime and the "cold" is stored, in most cases, in the structural mass of the building. The cooled mass serves as a heat sink during the following day, absorbing heat penetrating into and generated inside the building. Cooled soil and roof ponds, in particular, can also "flatten" periodic heat waves, when ambient temperature rises for several days above the normal level for the season.

The applicability of a given cooling system depends on the building type and climate. Some cooling systems may be applied only in specific types of buildings or only under specific climatic conditions. The boundaries of the climatic conditions under which a given cooling system can be applied depend on the comfort expectations of the population and may not be the same in every country. People living in hot regions can tolerate higher temperatures before experiencing distinct discomfort, because of the phenomenon of natural acclimatization, as was discussed in Chapter 1.

A more detailed discussion of the performance characteristics and the climatic boundaries for the application of the various passive and low-energy cooling systems is presented in another book by the author (see Givoni 1994).

COMFORT (DAYTIME) VENTILATION

The flow of outdoor air with a given speed through a building extends the upper limit of the comfort zone, beyond the limit for still-air conditions, and may provide a direct physiological cooling effect. This situation occurs often during the daytime hours. Therefore daytime ventilation can be defined also as direct comfort ventilation, especially in cases when it also lowers the indoor temperatures, such as, when the indoor temperature in unventilated buildings is higher than the outdoor air temperature, due to solar and/or internal heat gain.

With effective daytime cross-ventilation the indoor air temperature tends to follow the outdoor's level, accompanied by a higher indoor airspeed. Therefore the temperature limit of applicability of comfort ventilation is the comfort limit at the enhanced airspeed, at any region or season. Consequently, assuming an indoor airspeed of 1.5–2.0 m/s (300–400 fpm), comfort ventilation is applicable in regions and seasons when the outdoor *maximum* air temperature does not exceed about 28–32°C (82.4–89.6°F), depending on the acclimatization and comfort expectations of the population (see Chapter 1, page 34).

Effect of Mass in Buildings with Continuous Ventilation

An experimental study has demonstrated that even when buildings are cross-ventilated during the daytime hours, the indoor maximum temperatures in a well-insulated high-mass building can be lower by about 2–3°C (3.6–5.4°F) below the outdoor maximum temperatures, while the indoor maximum of a low-mass building is close to the outdoor maximum.

Figure 5-1 shows diurnal temperature patterns of the low-mass and high-mass buildings, when their windows were open day and night, in an experimental study conducted by the author in Pala, California. Exhaust fans were activated during the night hours to ensure an adequate air change rate, in view of the absence of winds at night. The air change rate (ach) at night was about 30 changes per hour.

It can be seen from Figure 5-1 that the maximum temperature of the high-mass building was consistently lower. The cooling of the building's mass at night by the enhanced ventilation enabled it to absorb heat from the ventilation air during the daytime hours, enough to lower the maximum temperature significantly. This means that thermal mass can lower the indoor daytime temperatures and improve the comfort of the occupants even in buildings ventilated day and night, provided that the rate of the night ventilation is sufficient to bring the indoor minimum temperature close to the outdoors' minimum.

On the other hand, in the case of low-mass buildings ventilated naturally during the daytime, fan-assisted night ventilation did not reduce the indoor daytime temperatures significantly.

Analysis of the data has shown that the decrease of the indoor maximum temperature below the outdoor's maximum was correlated with the outdoor's daily temperature swing (maximum minus minimum). A formula calculating the

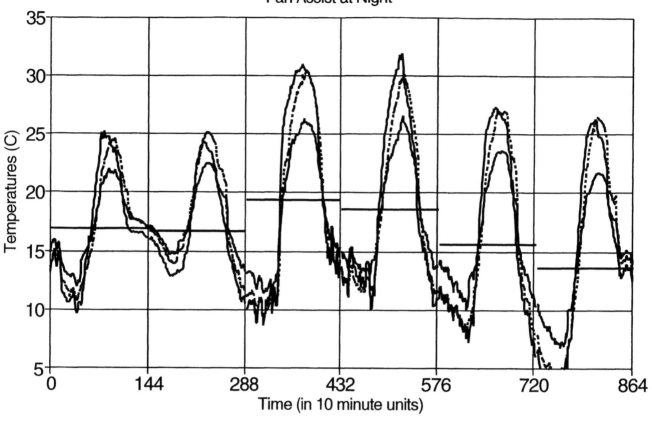

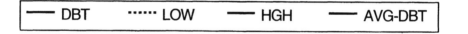

Figure 5-1. *Diurnal temperature patterns of the low-mass and the high-mass buildings, when their windows were open day and night.*

expected indoor maximum in a high-mass building, based on this relationship, has been developed:

$$T_{max-in} = T_{max-out} - 0.31 * (T_{max-out} - T_{min-out}) + 1.6$$

where:

T_{max-in} = Indoor maximum temperature, (°C or °F)
$T_{max-out}$ = Outdoor maximum
$T_{min-out}$ = Outdoor minimum

Applicability of Comfort Ventilation

Assuming that an indoor airspeed of 1–1.5 m/s (200–300 fpm) can be achieved (either by natural ventilation alone, or with the help of an all-house exhaust fan), comfort ventilation is applicable mainly in regions/seasons when the outdoor *maximum* air temperature does not exceed 28–32°C (82.4–89.6°F) even on "hot" days, depending on the acclimatization of the population. It is particularly applicable in regions where the diurnal temperature range is less than about 10°C (18°F). In regions with similar maximum temperatures but with a higher outdoor temperature range ventilation during the night hours only—closing (and shading) the windows during the daytime—may be more effective.

Comfort ventilation can be applied to all types of buildings. In regions with moderate-to-high daytime wind speeds the ventilation can be natural. In places without sufficient wind speeds and/or in buildings where effective cross-ventilation is not possible due to the design of the interior, the indoor air can be exhausted by a fan, with outdoor air entering the building through open windows.

NOCTURNAL VENTILATIVE COOLING

When an insulated high-mass building is ventilated at night its structural mass is cooled by convection from the inside, bypassing the thermal resistance of the envelope. During the daytime, the cooled mass can serve as a heat sink, if the mass is of sufficient amount and surface area and is adequately insulated from the outdoors. It absorbs the heat penetrating into and generated inside the building, by radiation and natural convection, and thus reduces the rate of indoor temperature rise. To this effect, the building should be closed (unventilated) during the daytime to prevent the hotter outdoor air from heating the interior. As a result, the indoor maximum temperature in such buildings can be appreciably lower than either the outdoor maximum or the indoor maximum temperature of a similar building not ventilated at night. This cooling strategy is called nocturnal ventilative cooling.

The effect of night ventilation is shown in Figure 5-2, which shows the different indoor temperature patterns between a low-mass and a high-mass building together with the outdoor temperature, during a period when the buildings were ventilated at night and closed during the daytime hours.

The indoor temperature of the low-mass building was rather close to the outdoor's pattern, except during days with sharp rise of the outdoor maximum.

During the cooler days the indoor maximum was even above the outdoor maximum, in spite of the night ventilation. Thus, in the case of low-mass buildings, nocturnal ventilation is quite ineffective in lowering the daytime temperatures and improving the daytime comfort conditions.

In the case of the high-mass building the night ventilation lowered the indoor daytime temperature consistently below the outdoor temperature.

From the climatic aspect nocturnal ventilative cooling would be preferable to comfort ventilation in regions where the daytime temperatures in summer are above the upper limit of the comfort zone—with indoor airspeed of about 1.5 m/s (300 fpm). This strategy is applicable mainly in regions with a diurnal temperature swing of more than 15°C (27°F), especially arid regions where the day-

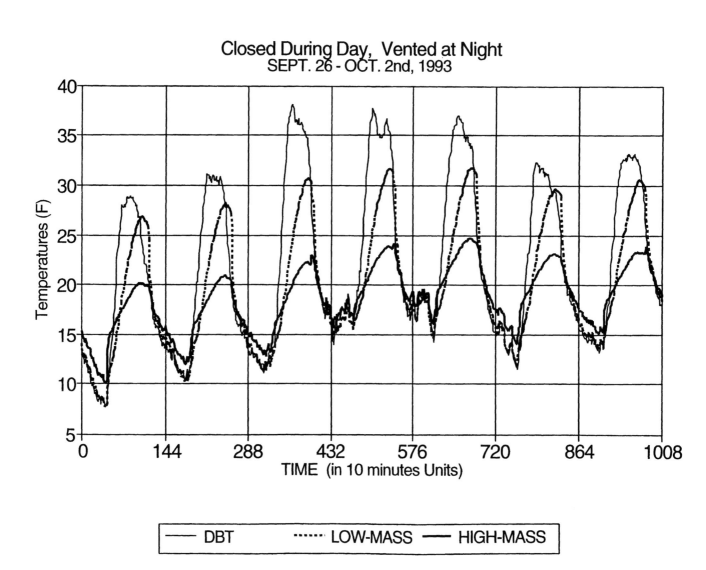

Figure 5-2. *Indoor temperature patterns of the low-mass and the high-mass buildings in California. Windows were closed during the days and shaded. Buildings were ventilated during the nights by fans.*

time temperatures are between 32 and 36°C (89.6–96.8°F) and the night temperatures are about or below 20°C (68°F) (to enable sufficient nocturnal cold storage).

In arid regions with daytime temperatures above 36°C (96.8°F), night ventilation would not maintain the indoor daytime conditions at an acceptable level even in a high-mass building. An exception is the case when the *average* maximum is below 34°C (93.2°F), but during short heat wave periods it is about 38°C (100.4°F). As the rate of change of the indoor temperature of high-mass buildings is smaller than that of the outdoor temperature, a night-ventilated high-mass building may remain comfortable throughout the heat wave period.

Night ventilative cooling is discussed in greater detail in Givoni 1994.

RADIANT COOLING

Any ordinary surface which "sees" the sky loses heat by the emission of long-wave radiation toward the sky, and can be regarded as a heat radiator. Although the radiant heat loss takes place day and night, the radiant balance is negative only during the nights. During the daytime the absorbed solar radiation counteracts the cooling effect of the long-wave emission and produces a net radiant heat gain.

Roofs are usually insulated to minimize heat loss in winter and heat gain in summer. As the radiant loss takes place at the external surface of the roof, the insulation minimizes the actual cooling that a building can utilize from the nocturnal radiation, unless specialized designs (radiant cooling systems) are applied. A detailed discussion of radiant cooling systems is presented in Givoni 1994.

Concrete Roofs with Movable Insulation as Radiators

The simplest concept of radiant cooling is that of a heavy and highly conductive roof (e.g., made of dense concrete) exposed to the sky during the night but highly insulated externally during the daytime (by means of operable insulation). Such roofs, of conventional construction common in many countries, can be very effective in losing heat at night, both by long-wave radiation to the sky and by convection to the outdoor air, which cools down faster than the massive roof. During the daytime the (installed) external insulation minimizes the heat gain from solar radiation and from the hotter ambient air. The cooled mass of the roof can then serve as a heat sink and absorb, through the ceiling, the heat penetrating into and generated inside the building's interior during the daytime hours.

No buildings applying such a system are known to the author, although a number of studies evaluating the performance of this system were conducted with built models. They have demonstrated that concrete roofs, which are very common in many countries, with applied movable insulation, can provide effective radiant cooling and maintain the indoor daytime temperature well below the outdoor level. These studies are described and discussed in another book (Givoni 1994).

However, in the opinion of the author, practical and inexpensive movable insulation is not available at present (see discussion of the "Skytherm" System below). To the extent that simple movable insulation will be developed, concrete roofs could provide simple, inexpensive, and effective radiant cooling in many hot regions of the world.

The "Skytherm" System

Hay (1978) developed a passive solar heating and radiant cooling system, the "Skytherm." In this system the (horizontal) roof is made of structural steel deck plates. Plastic bags filled with water are placed above the metal deck, and an insulation panel above them can be moved by a motor to cover or expose the bags. In winter, the water bags are exposed to the sun during the day and covered by the insulation panels during the nights. In summer, when cooling is needed, the water bags are exposed and cooled during the night and are insulated during the daytime. The cooled water bags are in direct thermal contact with the metal deck and thus the ceiling serves as a cooling element over the whole space below.

Several buildings utilizing various variations of this system have been built in the United States. Some of them were experimental buildings which were subjected to detailed studies, evaluating their physical performance and the operational problems encountered with the movable insulation. They are discussed in details in Givoni 1994.

The main problem encountered with the variations of the "Skytherm" System seems to concern the movable insulation. On the basis of research reports of persons who have tested the system (Marlatt et al. 1984; Clark 1989; Clinton [n.d.]), it is the opinion of the author that the availability of a simple, inexpensive, convenient, and trouble-free system of movable insulation is still in question.

Clark (1989), in summarizing the experience gained with the different buildings which have applied the "Skytherm" System, notes: "As a one-of-a-time kind of installation, the conventional, horizontally rolling panels have also been expensive and mechanically unreliable."

Clinton (n.d.) notes: "Major problems cited with roof pond buildings in the past have been their questionable cost-effectiveness for residential buildings . . . and uncertain reliability of operation of the movable insulation . . ."

Metallic Specialized Radiators

In order to utilize the cooling effect of the nocturnal radiation for buildings with ordinary *insulated* roofs, the cold produced at the external surface, above the insulation, should be transferred into the building's interior. Usually this "cold transfer" is provided by airflow under the radiating element, which transfers the cold generated by the nocturnal radiator to the structural mass of the building.

In practice, a building cooled by such a system would have a horizontal, or slightly inclined, *well-insulated*, roof. The insulation is needed to minimize both heat loss in winter and heat gain in summer. Any roof, either a heavy roof made of concrete or a built-up lightweight roof, would be suitable.

The specialized nocturnal radiator should consist of a metallic layer. The high conductivity of metals ensures that the underside of the radiator approaches the temperature of the emitting surface. Any metallic layer placed over the roof, with an airspace of about 5–10 cm (2–4") beneath it, could serve as a radiator. This "radiator" can serve also as a rainproofing element.

The temperature of a metallic layer over an insulated roof will drop below that of the ambient air level even before sunset. The radiator then gains heat, and this convective heat gain increases with the wind speed next to the surface. The balance between the radiant loss and the convective gain determines the actual drop of the radiator's temperature below that of the ambient air level. The temperature drop attained by the radiator without airflow *underneath* is the "stagnation temperature drop." This temperature drop is the best parameter by which to experimentally evaluate the potential for radiant cooling under given climatic conditions. When the radiant cooling system is utilized the radiator's temperature rises above the stagnation level.

To be of any value as a cooling system the radiator's stagnation temperature should be lower than the ambient air temperature by some minimum temperature drop—e.g., by at least 5°C (9°F)—otherwise, the simpler and less-expensive Nocturnal Ventilative Cooling could be applied. Ambient air drawn under the radiator can be cooled by about one-third to two-thirds of the stagnation depression achieved by the radiator, depending on the flow rate.

The cool air is blown through the interior space to cool the mass of the building, in a similar way to convective cooling discussed previously but with a temperature below the level which can be achieved by ventilation directly with the outdoor air. The cooled mass then serves during the following day as a sink for heat penetrating into and generated inside the building.

Metallic Radiant Roofs for Developing Countries

In many developing countries corrugated metal roofs are very common. During the nights the low-mass roof cools down rather quickly, acting as an effective nocturnal radiator located directly above the living space. The indoor night conditions in such buildings are often more comfortable than in buildings with high-mass roofs. During the daytime hours, however, the indoor climate in buildings with such roofs is often uncomfortably hot, as the uninsulated lightweight roofs are heated to much higher temperatures than a massive concrete roof.

Installing centrally hinged *interior* insulating parallel plates under the roof can greatly reduce the daytime heating without interfering too much with the cooling effect of such roofs during the night. When the plates are in a horizontal position (closed) during the daytime, they form a continuous insulation layer under the roof, minimizing the heat flow into the interior space. During the night the plates should be turned into a vertical position (open), enabling radiant and convective heat flow from the interior space to the ceiling/roof, which is cooled by the long-wave radiation to the sky.

Interior insulation plates are not exposed to the wind and rain and thus can be simpler in construction, lighter, and much less expensive than external insulation panels. The changes in their position, vertical or horizontal, can be controlled from the interior manually by a rope.

A major potential hazard with interior insulation, if made of expanded plastic materials, is the risk of fire. A possible design of noncombustible operable interior insulation is wood frames with linings of aluminum foil. Such panels, when in horizontal (closed) position during the daytime, act as an effective radiant barrier between the hot roof and the interior space. Such simple devices can, with appropriate instructions, be "manufactured" and installed by the inhabitants themselves and also be retrofitted easily in existing buildings.

Research on the actual performance was conducted at University of California at Los Angeles (UCLA) by the author's students Michael Gulich and Carlos Gomez. A test cell of the system was built with internal dimensions of 1 x 1 x 0.95 m (3.1'). In order to evaluate the effectiveness of the operable radiant barrier, and to maximize the relative effect of the roof radiator in a cell with height of about the same dimension as the width, the walls and the floor were

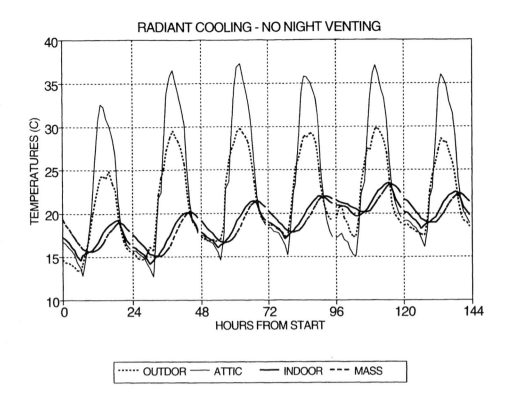

RADIANT COOLING - NO NIGHT VENTING

······ OUTDOR —— ATTIC —— INDOOR - - - MASS

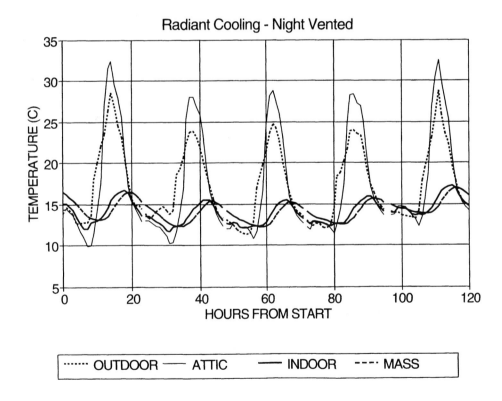

Radiant Cooling - Night Vented

······ OUTDOOR —— ATTIC —— INDOOR - - - - MASS

Figures 5-3 and 5-4. *Performance of radiant cooling by hinged interior insulation panels under a metallic roof. No night venting.*

"super insulated" and consisted of 8-cm-(3.2")thick panels of polyurethane. The roof and the walls were painted white. Thermal mass was provided by 31 water-filled, 2-liter bottles inside the model. The thermal performance of the system was reported by Givoni, Gulich, Gomez, and Gomez (1996).

Figure 5-3 shows outdoor and indoor temperature patterns during a six-day period, when the insulation panels were closed during the day and open at night. For the whole series with this condition (39 days) the average indoor maximum temperature drop below the outdoors' maxima was 5.4°C (9.7°F).

In another series the attic was ventilated by a small fan from midnight till 5 A.M. The open vertical panels diverted part of the incoming air downward and thus ventilated the indoor space and increased the indoor airspeed, thus enhancing heat exchange with the thermal mass. Figure 5-4 shows the temperature patterns during five days of this series. For this whole series with this condition (36 days) the average maximum temperature drop was 6.9°C (12.4°F). The drops of the indoor maximum below the outdoors' were closely correlated with the outdoor daily swings.

EVAPORATIVE COOLING TOWERS

There are two types of cooling passive towers which produce a flow of cooled air. The first is the "Arizona" tower, developed by Cunningham and Thompson at the Research Institute of the University of Arizona in Tucson. The second is the "Shower" cooling tower developed by Givoni.

The Cooling Tower of Cunningham and Thompson

Cunningham and Thompson (1986) developed and tested, for two days, a passive evaporative air cooling tower, attached to a building, in Tucson, Arizona. The system consists of a downdraft tower that has at its top vertical wetted cellulose pads impregnated with antirot salts and rigidifying saturants. Water is distributed at the top of the pads, collected at the bottom by a sump, and recirculated by a pump. The complete system in Tucson also included a solar chimney at the opposite side of the building, to enhance the airflow rate through the cooling tower and the building. Figure 5-5 shows the test building with the evaporative cooling tower and the solar chimney.

The measured performance of the system was very impressive. When the outdoor temperature maximum was 40.6°C (105°F) and the Wet Bulb Temperature (WBT) 21.6°C (71°F) the tower exit air temperature was 23.9°C (75°F). The corresponding speed of the exit air at that time was 0.75 m/s (150 fpm). Analysis of the test results of Cunningham and Thompson, which was performed by Givoni (1994), enabled the development of a mathematical model predicting the performance of the tower and the indoor temperature of a building cooled by it. The model was validated by comparing its predictions with different experimental data on the building's indoor temperatures during three series of five days each in June, July, and August.

Figure 5-6 shows diurnal patterns of the tower's exit and the building's indoor air temperatures, measured during two days by Cunningham and Thompson, together with the temperatures calculated by the model. Details of the mathematical model and its validation are presented in Givoni 1994.

Figure 5-5. *The Arizona test building with the evaporative cooling solar chimney (left) and a tower (right).*

The "Shower" Cooling Tower

This cooling system was originally developed by Givoni while serving as a consultant on cooling outdoor rest areas for the '92 EXPO in Seville, Spain. Figure 5-7 shows the prototype which was built in the Rotunda at the Seville '92 EXPO site: a demonstration facility of the different outdoor cooling systems. This system can also be applied, and has been tested, as a cooling system for buildings.

When fine drops of water (having a very large surface area) are sprayed vertically downward from the top of an open shaft, like a shower, the falling water entrains a large volume of air. The water is collected in a small pond at the bottom of the shaft and is pumped back to the showerhead. The momentum of the

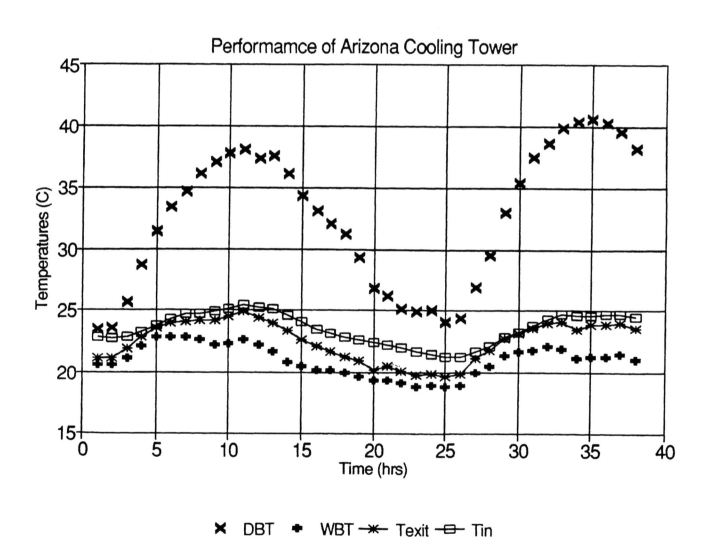

Figure 5-6. *Diurnal patterns of the tower's exit and the building's indoor air temperatures, measured during two days by Cunningham and Thompson (1986).*

falling water is thus transmitted to an airstream, creating an inertial airflow down the shaft. The evaporation from the fine drops cools the water, as well as the air in the shaft, to a level close to the ambient WBT. A wind catcher can be placed above the showerhead, to supplement the inertial airflow by wind effect.

As any evaporation from the droplets takes place in the airstream, any type of water, even brackish or seawater, if available, could be used for this system. In this respect this system can be applied in places where other evaporative cooling systems, which need high-quality water, are not applicable. In fact, no difference was found in the cooling performance of the system when tested with either fresh water or with seawater.

A mathematical model predicting the performance of the tower and the indoor temperature of a building cooled by it has been developed (Givoni 1994).

The performance of this system was tested by the author's graduate student,

Figure 5-7. *A prototype cooling tower for outdoor rest areas, at the Rotunda of the 1992 EXPO in Seville, Spain.*

Nasser Al-hemiddi (1995), first in a model, 4.75 x 1.2 m (15.6 x 3.9'), 2.5 m (8.2') high, in Los Angeles and later with a full-size building, together with other passive cooling systems of the author's design (a new type of walkable roof pond and roof soil cooling, see below) in Riyadh, Saudi Arabia. The building was high mass and well insulated and had four rooms. One room, without any cooling system, served as a control. The other three rooms were cooled by three different systems: a shower tower, a roof pond, and cooled soil layer, respectively. The performance of the "shower tower" is discussed below.

Figure 5-8 shows the measured and computed indoor temperatures of the test model in Los Angeles on October 8, 1992. The outdoor temperature maximum was above 29°C (84.2°F). The indoor temperature maximum was about 33°C (91.4°F). A reasonable agreement exists between the computed and the measured indoor temperatures.

Figure 5-9 (Al-Hemiddi 1995) on page 202 shows measured outdoor and indoor temperatures of a control room and a room with the shower tower cooling system, both of high-mass and insulated walls, measured by Al-Hemiddi in Riyadh, Saudi Arabia, on June 9, 1994. With outdoor air maxima above 44°C (111.2°F), the indoor maxima was about 28°C (82.4°F). It is thus demonstrated that this system can provide effective cooling even in an extreme desert climate.

No quantitative information about the construction details of the building, especially the roof, was available. Therefore it was not possible to calculate the expected indoor temperatures.

INDIRECT EVAPORATIVE COOLING

Instead of cooling by evaporation the air with high-vapor content that is introduced into the building, it is possible to cool by evaporation the roof or a wall of the building, either by having a shaded pond over the roof or by wetting impermeable walls by water circulation over their external surface.

Roof Ponds

Different roof ponds have been constructed and tested with different design schemes. Among them:

a. Ventilated roof pond: A pond with fixed shade over it, with wind flow between the shade and the water.

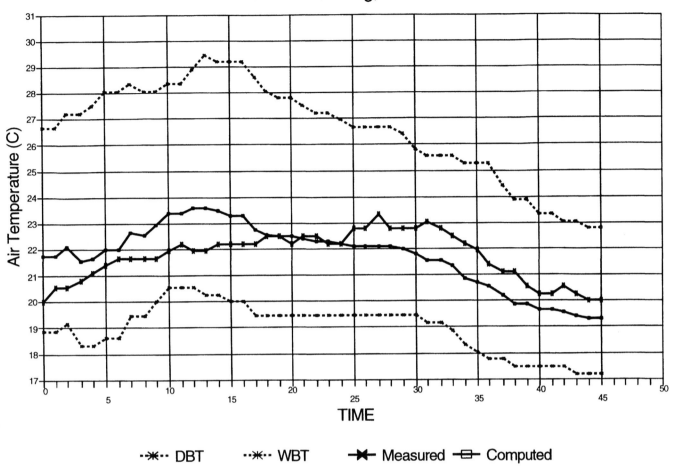

Measured & Computed Room Temperature
Shower Cooling, 10-8-93

TIME

Air Temperature (C)

··✳·· DBT   ··✳·· WBT   ✕ Measured   ⊟ Computed

Figure 5-8. *Measured and computed indoor temperatures of the test model with the "shower" cooling tower in Los Angeles on October 8, 1992.*

b. A pond with floating insulation: Insulation panels floating over the water, with water circulation at night *over* the insulation (invented by Dick Bourne from Davis, California).

c. Tile-covered, pebble-filled insulated pond, with night water circulation: A pond filled with pebbles, with an insulation layer over the pebbles covered by tiles, and with water circulation at night over the tiles.

The performance of the different roof pond cooling was monitored by, or with participation of, the author, in numerous studies in different places: Sede Boqer, Israel; Los Angeles and Sacramento, California; Colima, Mexico; and Riyadh, Saudi Arabia. These experimental studies and their results, except for the one in Riyadh, are described in detail in Givoni 1994.

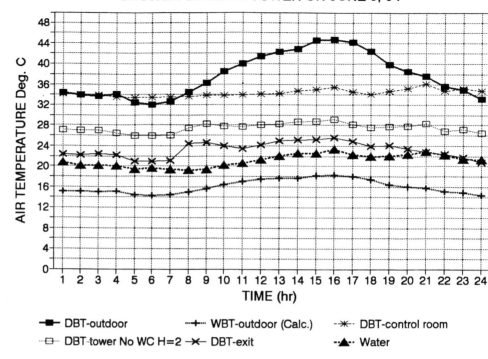

PERFORMANCE OF A ROOM COOLED BY PASSIVE
SHOWER COOLING TOWER ON JUNE 9, 94

Legend:
- ■ DBT-outdoor
- + WBT-outdoor (Calc.)
- ✳ DBT-control room
- ▫ DBT-tower No WC H=2
- ✕ DBT-exit
- ▲ Water

Figure 5-9. *Indoor temperatures in a full-size room with the "shower" cooling tower, measured by Nasser Al-Hemiddi in Riyadh, Saudi Arabia.*

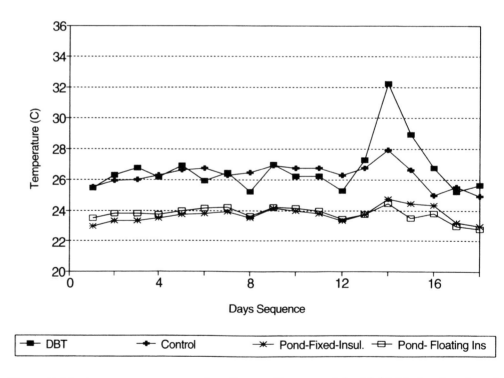

Legend:
- ■ DBT
- ◆ Control
- ✳ Pond-Fixed-Insul.
- ▫ Pond- Floating Ins

Figure 5-10. *Average temperatures in a "control" test model with highly insulated roof and in identical models with two types of roof ponds: a shaded and ventilated pond and a pond with floating insulation.*

a. **Ventilated Pond and Pond with Floating Insulation.** Performance of two test rooms, cooled by two different types of roof ponds, was investigated by the author at the Institute for Desert Research of Ben Gurion University in Sede Boqer, Israel. The ponds were of two different types: a ventilated pond and a pond with floating insulation.

Figure 5-10 shows average temperatures in a "control" model and the two types of roof pond, over a period of 14 days, together with the average outdoor temperature (Givoni 1994).

The indoor temperatures in the two test models with the two types of ponds were very stable and their thermal performance was very similar, in spite of the basic differences in their design details and cooling processes. In the ventilated pond the cooling is produced only by evaporation, which takes place day and night and consumes a large quantity of water. In the pond with floating insulation the cooling effect is produced only at night, mainly by outgoing long-wave radiation, and water consumption by evaporation is very small.

b. **Walkable Pond with Night Water Circulation.** This system has been developed by the author in order to enable utilization of the area above the roof pond. The pond is filled with pebbles and insulation is placed over, and is supported by, the pebbles. Tiles placed over the insulation form the roof's top surface and enable normal use of the roof. Water circulation over the tiles is carried on during the night hours.

This system was installed and its performance was tested by Al-Hemiddi (1995), in a full-scale room in an existing building in Riyadh, Saudi Arabia. It was compared also to a "control" room in the same building which was without any cooling.

Figure 5-11 shows diurnal temperature patterns on August 27, 1994. The outdoor temperature on that day had ranged from 30 to 42°C (86 to 107.6°F), with an average of about 35°C (95°F). The range of the indoor temperature in the control room was from 34 to 35.5°C (93.2 to 96°F). The average indoor temperature of the room cooled by the roof pond was about 28°C (82.4°F), fluctuating between 27 and 29°C (80.6 and 84.2°F). Thus it has been stabilized a little below the outdoor *minimum* temperature.

APPLICABILITY OF COOLING BY ROOF PONDS

A mathematical model calculating the energy balance of a building cooled by a ventilated roof pond, predicting the daily average temperatures of the indoor air, ceiling, and the pond's water under given climatic conditions and building's thermal properties, has been developed (Givoni 1994).

The water temperature in any one of the types of roof ponds described above would be about 1–3°K above the average ambient WBT. When the roof is

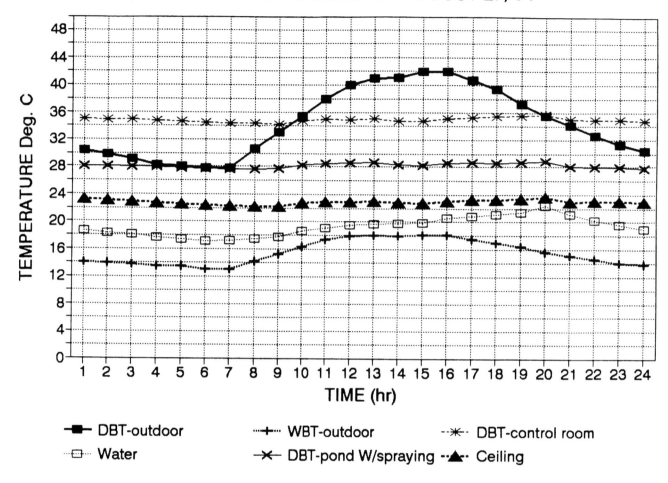

Figure 5-11. *Diurnal temperature patterns of a room cooled by a walkable roof pond in Riyadh, Saudi Arabia.*

made of materials with high thermal conductivity (concrete or a metal deck), the combined water-and-roof structure serve as an integrated "cold" storage. The ceiling temperature, in the case of a concrete roof over a well-insulated building, would be about 2°K above the water temperature.

In this way the soffit of the system, the ceiling, serves as a passive cooling panel for the space below, cooling it by both radiation and by natural convection. Thus the heat exchange between the ceiling and the indoor space is maximized, enabling effective cooling even with a small temperature difference of about 2–3°K between the indoor air and the ceiling. The elevation of the indoor temperature above the WBT level is sensitive, however, to the thermal resistance of the building.

Based on these characteristics it is suggested that indirect evaporative cooling can be applied in places where the daily average WBT is 25°C (77°F) and the maximum Dry Bulb Thermometer (DBT) is 46°C (115°F). Quantitative arguments supporting these suggested limits are presented in Givoni 1994.

Indirect Evaporative Cooling by Wetted Walls

In spite of the impressive performance of passive cooling by roof ponds their application has some practical limitations:

a. The roofs have to be capable of supporting a significant load, a factor affecting their cost.

b. The application of the ponds is limited to single-story buildings, or only to the upper floor of multistory buildings.

c. The waterproofing of the roof has to be perfect. Any crack or a small perforation may cause severe wetting problems and it is very difficult to locate such small cracks or holes.

Considerations of the impressive performance and the practical problems and limitations associated with roof ponds have led to the development of a new indirect evaporative cooling system: the Wetted Impermeable Wall.

The idea was to have any part of the external (vertical) walls of a building made of impermeable material with high thermal conductivity, such as dense concrete or galvanized steel. Water flow over the external surface, in a closed circuit, produces evaporative cooling of that surface. The internal surface of the wall serves as a cooling element for the space behind it. Heat from the interior of the building is transferred, by convection and radiation, to the internal cooled surface and, by conduction, across the wall, to the wetted external surface.

As the wall is vertical, the danger of water leakage is much smaller than it is in the case of a roof pond and the waterproofing layer can easily be renewed. No extra structural load is imposed on the wall. Two versions of the wetted wall concept were tested by a student of the author's, Barbara Ellis, in thermal models: a concrete-blocks wall and a corrugated metal wall.

Testing of the performance of this cooling system at the Energy Laboratory of UCLA included monitoring the performance of two versions of the wetted wall in thermal models: a concrete-blocks wall and a corrugated metal wall. The models were very lightweight and painted white, to minimize the solar gain. A paper describing the system and summarizing its tested performance was presented at the PLEA '94 Conference (Givoni and Ellis 1994).

Figure 5-12 shows diurnal indoor temperatures of the two thermal models cooled by the two types of wetted walls during several days. The performance of the two walls as cooling systems was almost identical. The two cells were of very low mass, resulting in relatively large diurnal swings. Still, the reduction of the indoor maximum temperatures below the outdoors' was significant, especially on hot days. With an outdoor maximum of about 31°C (87.8°F) on March 13, 1994, and of 30.0°C (86°F) on March 14, 1994, the indoor maxima of both models were about 25 and 22.5°C (77 and 72°F), respectively.

In evaluating this performance it should be taken into account that the building's mass does not affect significantly the indoor average temperatures but reduces significantly the indoor swings and the maxima. Consequently, test cells or buildings with a higher mass than those used in this study would have, under the same climatic conditions and external color, lower maximum temperatures.

The potential applications of this cooling system are greater than those of roof ponds, as it can be applied to multistory buildings. As the wall is vertical,

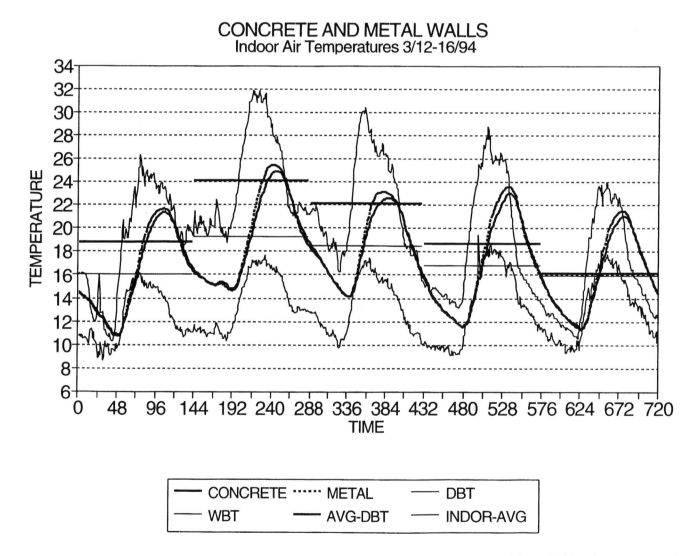

Figure 5-12. *Indoor temperatures of the two thermal models cooled by the two types of wetted walls during January 10–16, 1994.*

the danger of water leakage is much smaller than it is in the case of a roof pond. No extra structural load is imposed on the wall.

THE EARTH AS A COOLING SOURCE

In hot regions, where cooling is of interest, the "natural" temperature of the soil in summer is usually too high for serving as a cooling source. However, using very simple means, it is possible to lower the earth temperature well below the "natural" temperature characteristics of a given location. In order to cool the soil it is necessary to eliminate the heating of the soil by the sun, while enabling cooling by evaporation from the earth surface.

At present two methods have been successfully tried by Givoni (1987b) to lower the earth temperature by shading it while enabling water evaporation from the surface:

1. Covering the soil with a layer of mulch, such as gravel or wood chips, at least 10 cm (4") thick and, in regions with dry summers, irrigating it.
2. Raising the building off the ground and enabling evaporation from the shaded soil surface by water provided either by irrigation or by summer rains.

Once the soil surface temperature in summer is lowered, its annual average temperature, as well as the temperatures of the layers below the surface, are also lowered.

Experimental Data on Soil Cooling

Experiments in Israel and in North Florida have demonstrated that it is possible to lower the earth surface temperature by about 8–10°K below the summer temperature of exposed soil. Figure 5-13 (Givoni 1994) shows diurnal temperature patterns of "natural" and cooled soil in Israel. Figure 5-14 (Givoni 1994) shows seasonal temperature patterns of cooled soil in Tallahassee, Florida. These figures demonstrate that the difference between the outdoor maximum air temperature and the cooled earth temperature in midsummer can be up to about 14–16°K in arid regions and up to 10–12°K in some hot-humid regions. With such a temperature difference the soil can provide a heat sink for a building, especially in cooling the ventilation air.

Figure 5-14 demonstrates also that even in a hot-humid region such as

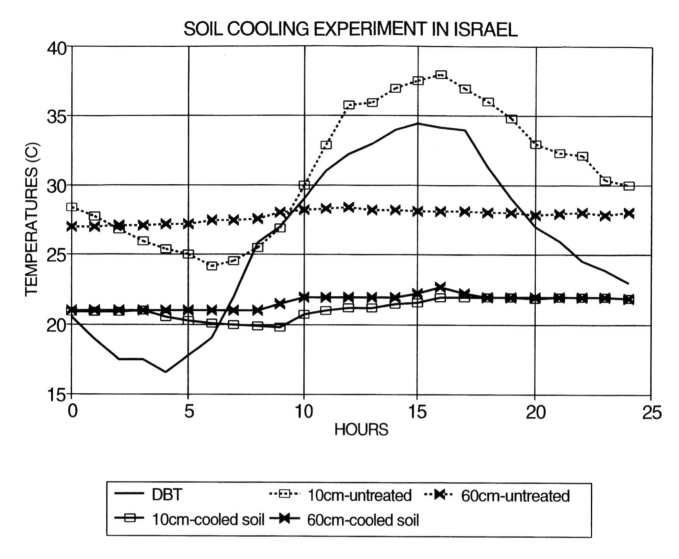

Figure 5-13. *Diurnal temperature patterns of exposed and cooled patches of soil in the desert region of Israel. The soil was shaded by a layer of pebbles and kept moist.*

Florida it is possible to cool the soil in summer to a level below the outdoor minimum temperature. The difference between the outdoor maximum and the cooled soil is largest during periods of ambient heat waves (e.g., June 24–29 and July 17–18).

Measured Performance of a Room with Cooled Soil Over its Roof

The cooling performance of a roof with moist soil shaded by 10 cm (4") of pebbles was tested by Al-Hemiddi (1995), in a full-scale room in an existing

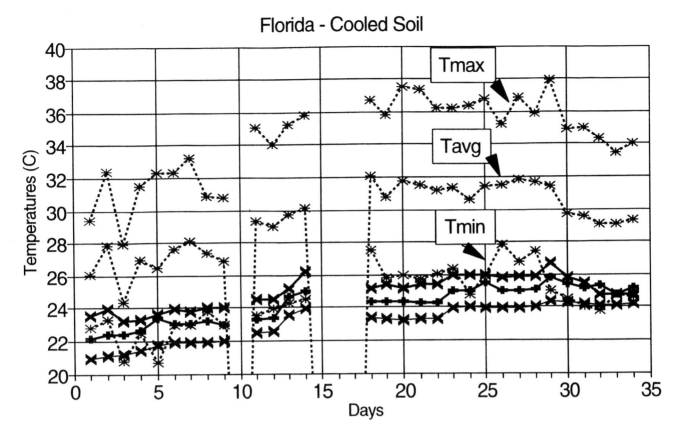

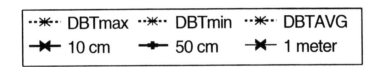

Figure 5-14. *Seasonal (summer) temperature patterns of two soil areas in Tallahassee, Florida, at different depths. Cooled soil shaded by a building raised off the ground.*

building in Riyadh, Saudi Arabia. It was compared also to a "control" room in the same building which was without any cooling (Al-Hemiddi 1995).

Figure 5-15 shows temperature patterns measured on August 28, 1994. The outdoor temperature on that day had ranged from 26 to 43°C (78.8 to 109.4°F), with an average of about 35°C (95°F). The range of the indoor temperature in the control room was from 34 to 35.5°C (96°F). The average indoor temperature of the room cooled by the shaded moist soil was about 30°C (86°F), fluctuating between 29 and 31°C (84.2 and 87.8°F). Thus it has been stabilized a little above the outdoor *minimum* temperature, well below the outdoor average.

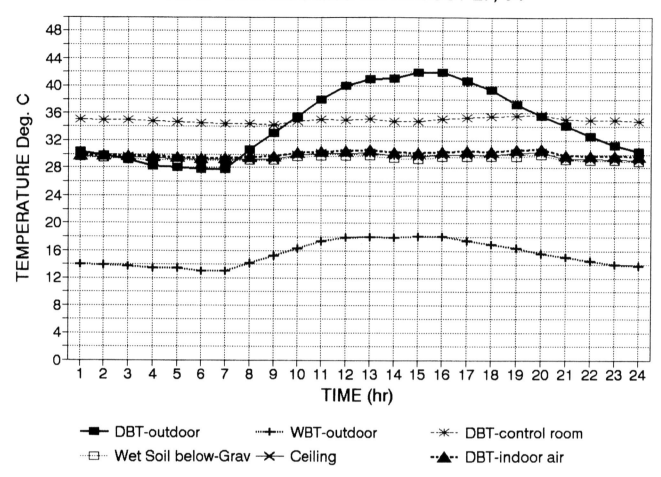

PERFORMANCE OF ROOMS COOLED BY PASSIVE ROOF SOIL COOLING ON AUGUST 27, 94

Legend:
- ■ DBT-outdoor
- + WBT-outdoor
- ※ DBT-control room
- ▭ Wet Soil below-Grav
- ✕ Ceiling
- ▲ DBT-indoor air

Figure 5-15. *Diurnal temperatures of a room cooled by a roof with moist soil shaded by 10 cm (4") of pebbles in Riyadh, Saudi Arabia, on June 26, 1994 (a very hot day).*

Options for Utilizing the Cooling Potential of the Earth

When the soil temperature is cool enough, it is possible to utilize it for cooling buildings by several methods. In the case of earth-integrated buildings, in which the walls are bermed and the roof covered by earth, cooling of the earth mass adjacent to the building provides direct passive conductive cooling for the building. This approach would be most suitable in hot-dry regions with mild winters. In such places this direct conductive cooling of the building will be very effective. Concerning the water availability issue, it should be noted that by effectively shading the soil surface with a layer that is thermally insulating but permeable to vapor (e.g., wood bark mulching), effective soil cooling can be achieved with water consumption much lower than what would be needed to water a lawn, for instance.

If the building is well insulated it is possible to cover only the roof with soil cooled as described previously. The cooled soil then cools the space below by conduction through the roof.

In hot regions with cold winters the direct-conductive coupling of the indoor space with the surrounding soil, through highly conductive walls and roof, although effective in summer, may be undesirable since it will cause a high rate of heat loss in winter.

Another approach, an active one, is to insulate the building and to install air pipes in the soil, circulating through them the air from the building or the ventilation air. The cooler earth mass serves then as a heat sink to cool the air which is reintroduced into the building.

Heat transfer to the cool soil can be by means of an array of pipes, usually of plastics, such as PVC. The air circulation may be through a closed circuit, or it may be outdoor air used for ventilation. Circulating the indoor air through air tubes imbedded in the cool soil can keep the indoor temperature about 10°K below the outdoor average maximum air temperature. During a "heat wave," with abnormal high outdoor temperatures, the cooling effect of the tubes, imbedded in the more-stable earth, can be even greater.

REFERENCES

Al-Hemiddi, N.A. 1995. "Passive Cooling Systems Applicable for Buildings in Hot Dry Climate of Saudi Arabia." Ph.D. Dissertation. Graduate School of Architecture and Urban Planning, UCLA, California: Los Angeles.

Clark, G. 1989. Passive Cooling Systems. In *Passive Cooling*. MIT Press, Massachusetts: Cambridge.

Clinton, J. "Pala Passive Solar Project" Final Report. Solar Energy Analysis Laboratory. San Diego Gas & Electric. California: San Diego.

Cunningham, W.A., and T.L. Thompson. 1986. "Passive Cooling with Natural Draft Cooling Towers in Combination with Solar Chimneys." *Proc. Passive and Low Energy Architecture (PLEA)*. Pecs, Hungary.

Givoni, B. 1987a. The Effective Heat Capacity in Direct Gain Buildings. *Passive Solar Journal* 4 (x):25–40.

Givoni, B. 1994. *Passive and Low Energy Cooling of Buildings.* New York: Van Nostrand Reinhold.

Givoni, B., and B. Ellis. 1994. Wetted Walls as Indirect Evaporative Cooling System. *Proc. Passive and Low Energy Architecture (PLEA '94) Eleventh International Conference.* The Dead Sea, Israel.

Givoni, B., M. Gulich, C. Gomez, and A. Gomez. 1996. Radiant Cooling by Metal Roofs for Developing Countries. *Proc. 21st National Passive Solar Conference (25th ASES Conf.),* 13–18 April at Asheville, N.C.

Hay, H. 1978. A Passive Heating and Cooling System from Concept to Commercialization. *Proc. Annual Meeting American Section of the International Solar Energy Society.*

Marlatt, W., K. Murray, and S. Squier. 1984. "Roof Pond Systems." Report for U.S. Department of Energy by Energy Technology Engineering Center. Rockwell International. NTIS #DE84016401.

Chapter 6: CLIMATIC CHARACTERISTICS OF HOUSING TYPES

INTRODUCTION

The choice of the type of a building for people to be housed depends, of course, on economic factors and on sociocultural preferences, and may differ greatly among different countries and societies with similar climates. This applies also to housing in hot regions, and therefore no attempt will be made to recommend a given type of a house, although some sociocultural aspects of certain housing types may be mentioned. The main subject of this chapter is the impacts of the choice of a given building type on the its climatic performance.

Each type of housing, such as single-family detached, town house/row houses, multistoried apartment buildings, etc., has some specific impact on the thermal comfort and energy expenditure needed to achieve it. In particular, different building types have different potentials for providing effective cross-ventilation, passive solar heating, and application of various passive cooling systems. In discussing the ventilation subject, the main issue to consider is the possibility of providing, in the same residential unit, openings both on the windward sides and leeward sides of the unit.

Consequently there are climatic drawbacks and preferences for different building types in different climatic regions. In addition, some specific psychological factors related to the use-pattern options in different types of houses such as, for example, the frequency of usage of covered or uncovered open areas, may have greater weight in the choice of a given type of housing in arid or in humid regions.

The following housing types are discussed in this chapter:

- Single-family detached houses
- Town houses (row houses)
- Multistoried apartment buildings
- High-rise "Tower" buildings

Most building types can have courtyards as an integral part of their design. The climatic characteristics and impacts on comfort and on energy consumption of courtyards and attached open spaces is discussed in detail on page 232.

SINGLE-FAMILY DETACHED HOUSES

From the energy demand point of view, detached single-family houses, because of their relatively large envelope surface area, and especially their larger relative roof area, are the most energy demanding when they are heated or air conditioned. On the other hand, they may offer the best opportunities for natural ventilation, thus minimizing the need for air conditioning. In addition, they may have the highest potential for utilizing solar energy for heating. Thus, a single-family detached house may minimize the need for cooling, or for heating with conventional fuels.

Such difference in performances is caused in part by the special role of the roof from the energy viewpoint, particularly in low latitudes where the sun's elevation is high, and especially in desert regions. By different design options it is possible to have roofs with very different impacts on the thermal performance of buildings.

The roof is the most exposed surface of the building to the climatic elements, such as solar radiation in summer daytime and radiant loss to the sky at night. As a result, ordinary single-family houses, in which the roof comprises a large part of the building's envelope, experience a larger potential for heat gain in summer and for heat loss in winter, as compared with other types of buildings.

However, the roof is also a building element which, in many types of constructions, can be insulated to a higher level of thermal resistance than the walls can by relatively simple building materials and technologies. Such insulation reduces its relative role in the energy demand of the building as a whole.

Furthermore, when solar heating and/or cooling are contemplated, the roof can be a useful building element for admitting solar energy through roof monitors facing south for winter heating and for summer passive cooling (e.g., by

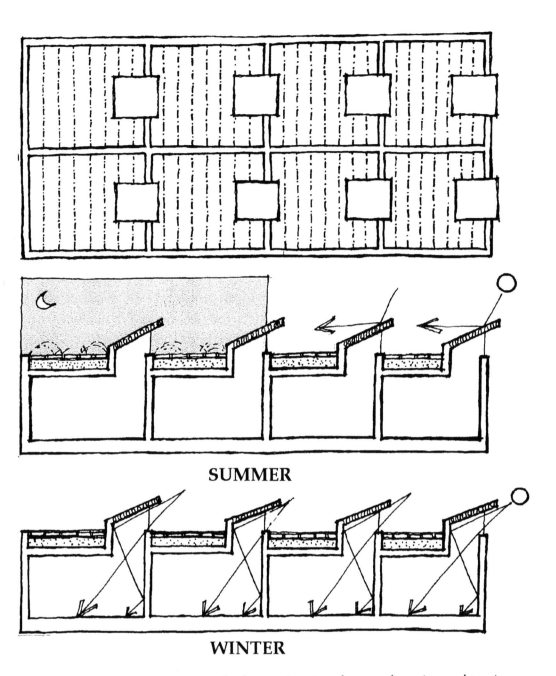

SUMMER

WINTER

Figure 6-1. *A flat roof with direct solar heating in winter by a roof monitor and passive cooling in summer by a roof pond with floating insulation.*

roof ponds with floating insulation extending over the roof area surrounding the monitors (see Chapter 5), as is illustrated in Figure 6-1.

The figure shows a scheme for utilizing part of the roof (about 10 percent of its area) for year-long daylighting and a source of direct solar gain in winter, through roof monitors facing south. The rest of the flat roof area can by covered by a roof pond with floating insulation for summer indirect evaporative cooling.

When such potentials are realized, the roof is transformed from an area of energy load to an energy source.

The good potential of detached houses for natural ventilation results from the possibility of having windows and openable doors on all sides of the building, in at least four directions. To the extent that the internal arrangement of rooms, partitions, and internal doors enables airflow through the various rooms of the building, there is a potential for natural ventilation with any wind direction, as is illustrated in Figure 6-2. Detached houses are therefore the least sensitive to their orientation from the ventilation viewpoint.

Realization of the potential for natural ventilation depends on the availability of wind at the site of the building which, with a given regional wind condition, depends in turn on the details of the urban design, as will be discussed in Chapter 8.

The good potential of detached houses for passive solar heating results from the fact that one external wall faces the winter sun. The realization of this potential also depends on urban design, namely the prevention of shading of the sun-facing wall and windows by the neighbor to the sunny side.

Detached houses enable the occupants to use the land surrounding the dwelling for a variety of outdoor household and functional activities. In all types of hot climates the outdoor climatic conditions are, in some seasons, more comfortable than the indoor conditions. The potential for outdoor activities on the four sides of the building, depending on the available shaded and/or covered areas, adds to the climatic advantages of single-family detached houses. This point is of particular importance for low-income families with many children, who usually can afford very small residences and who cannot afford high utility bills for air conditioning.

Because the external walls of detached single-family houses face at least four directions, these houses are less sensitive to orientation effect, although the

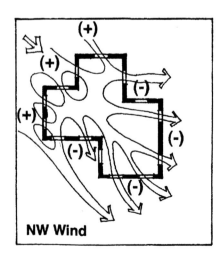
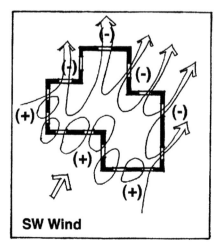
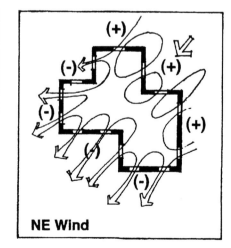

Figure 6-2. *A detached single-family house can have effective cross-ventilation at any wind direction.*

problem of choosing the orientation of the different rooms, and especially the orientation of the large windows, still exists. Thus, detached houses provide more freedom, from the climatic aspect, to an urban designer.

From the viewpoint of natural energies utilization, single-family houses can make good use of the ground area under and around the house as a cooling element (see Chapter 5) or for thermal storage on a larger scale than is possible in multistoried multiunit apartment buildings.

TOWN HOUSES (ROW HOUSES)

Town houses, or row houses as they are called in some countries, are a string of dwelling units, from one to three stories high, attached to one another at their sidewalls. Thus they form a continuous row. Each unit occupies the whole vertical section of the building, from the ground to the roof, inclusive.

The functional integration of the different stories in one dwelling unit under one ownership gives town houses some special properties from the climatic and energy performance aspects. From the ventilation viewpoint the highly effective height facilitates the "chimney effect" in natural thermosyphonic ventilation, especially during windless hours as is shown in Figure 6-3. When a staircase is leading to the roof with an access room, it can also be used as a "wind catcher," as is illustrated in Figure 6-4, to take advantage of the higher wind speeds above the roof's level.

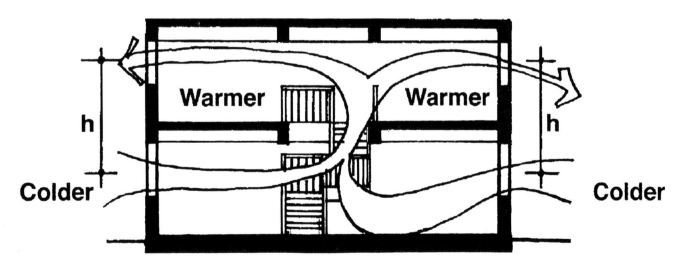

Figure 6-3. *Chimney-effect ventilation of a two-story town house during windless hours, common at night.*

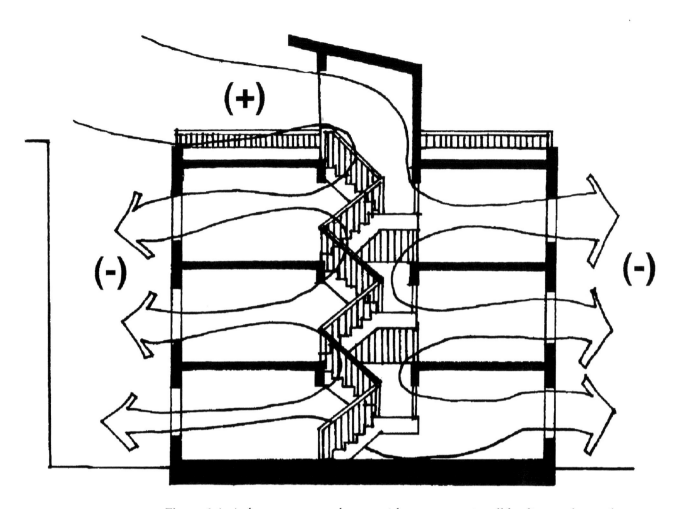

Figure 6-4. *A three-story town house, with an open stairwell leading to the roof serving as a wind catcher.*

Town houses combine some of the advantages, from the energy viewpoint, of both multistoried apartment buildings (smaller external wall area) and of single-family houses (natural ventilation and solar heating options). Considering the envelope surface area, town houses are in between the detached house and the apartment block. Every dwelling unit has its own roof and its own underground area, as well as a piece of land attached to it. When neighboring units share a common wall the total exposed wall area is lower than in single-family houses with the same number of stories.

Except for the end units all dwellings have essentially two external orientations. With architecturally designed projections and setbacks for the different units it is possible to provide four effective exposures to each unit. Such projections increase the envelope surface area but can improve substantially the potential for natural ventilation when the wind direction is nearly parallel to the long facades of the building.

For example, when the prevalent wind is from the west, it usually fluctuates between west-southwest and west-northwest. An elongated building with main facades and windows to the north and south will have poor ventilation potential because of the very small incidence angle of the wind to the wall. However, the projections create pockets of high and low pressure, and if openings are available then the ventilation potential improves appreciably, as is illustrated in Figure 6-5.

With respect to most of the aspects discussed previously, town houses are like single-family houses. One important exception is the sensitivity to orientation. Because the units are lined in a row, orientation with respect to the sun is a much more sensitive issue than in the case of a detached house.

To the extent that solar energy utilization is contemplated, either for space heating and/or for domestic hot water, the solar collecting element of the building should be oriented toward the winter sun, namely towards the equator in latitudes above about 20 degrees. At lower latitudes, in equatorial and tropical regions at high elevation, solar energy can better be utilized by east and west walls and windows, as south and north walls get very little sun in winter. Effective shading in the summer is, of course, essential in this case.

The units in town houses, except for the end units, have land attached to them only in front of the two external walls. Thus the times in which sunny

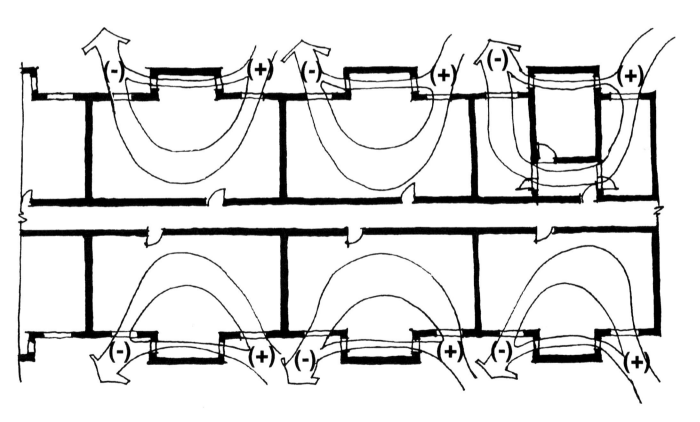

Figure 6-5. *Architectural projections from a flat facade create distinctive zones of high and low pressure when the wind is at very low angle to the walls, providing potential for effective cross-ventilation.*

areas in winter and shaded areas in summer are available for outdoor activities are more limited than in the case of single-family detached houses. Nevertheless, town houses can provide appreciable opportunities for utilizing attached land, compared with all other types of multifamily dwellings.

From the urban design aspect the major feature of town houses is the higher urban densities which they make possible, compared with single-family detached houses, while still keeping most of the functional and social advantages of single-family houses.

In those cases where higher population density is considered desirable—for example, in order to shorten the length of roads, water, sewage lines, and so on, and the walking distance to various services—town houses may be of two or even three stories. With such a design neighborhood densities can be obtained which are close to those obtainable with multistoried apartment houses, when the latter are spaced with adequate distances between them for ventilation and solar utilization.

MULTISTORIED APARTMENT BUILDINGS

With expanded urbanization and increased pressure on, and cost of, urban land multistoried apartment blocks become a more common housing type in most countries, both developed and developing ones.

Multistoried apartment buildings can have various design schemes which, from the comfort and energy use aspects, have quite different properties. Therefore, in this type of dwelling, basic design decisions can render the building to be either appropriate or very inappropriate to the climate.

From the thermal point of view, multistoried apartment buildings have less envelope surface area than other types of residential buildings. In consequence, when the building is heated or air conditioned, the energy demand per dwelling unit of the building, for a given thermal quality of the envelope, is minimized. In particular this applies to the "internal" units, which have adjoining neighbors on each side, above and below.

Therefore, any building form which maximizes the relative number of internal units, such as block buildings in which the length of the block approximately equals its height, will minimize the total thermal energy requirements.

However, all the above applies only to the time in which the building is heated or air conditioned by using *conventional* energy sources. With some types of multistoried apartment buildings the opportunities for natural ventilation, which can eliminate the need for air conditioning or reduce the time in which it is essential, are not available. Furthermore, multistory apartments of some types may have less potential than other building types for the use of solar energy for space heating and domestic hot water.

From the overall urban design considerations it should be pointed out that multistory apartment buildings enable the attainment of higher residential densities. This factor usually reduces the length of infrastructure facilities such as roads, water lines, sewage, etc.

High urban density may present some design challenges both for natural ventilation and for solar energy utilization.

To enable solar heating in winter the multistory buildings have to follow a rather strict orientation. As the roof area of such buildings is relatively small the main building element for solar energy collection is the wall facing the winter sun (the southern wall in the Northern Hemisphere). Any significant deviation from solar orientation will reduce the available solar energy.

With high urban density care should be taken to prevent the shading of a building by another high building to its south. With multistory apartment buildings, more land exists between buildings. This land is "communal" in many respects and remains without individual personal "responsibility." The impact of this factor on the treatment of the land, and the resulting environmental quality, depends on the sociocultural characteristics of the inhabitants.

In some societies, communal care for the land between the buildings may result in better treatment of the land. On the other hand, in some societies communal care of open land may lead to neglect, dust, and wind erosion. Such neglect may be due to lack of personal resources and/or cultural tradition.

In arid and desert regions care of open land is more expensive and difficult because of the high cost and sometimes unavailability of water, a factor which increases the likelihood of neglect.

The issue of maintenance of public open spaces is of particular importance in many developing countries in arid regions, where the low rainfall makes irrigation essential while the population and local governments may lack the financial resources and tradition of care for public space. The desire to imitate the appearance of traditional parks in regions with temperate climates leads in effect to "no man's land."

Types of Multistory Apartment Buildings

Multistory apartment blocks can be divided, from the climatic performance aspect, into two basic types, and each one of them can be further subdivided into two subtypes. The two main types are:

A. Buildings with long corridors providing access to the units along them. Vertical access to the corridors is provided by either staircases or elevators.

B. Buildings with staircases or elevators providing direct access to two, three, or four units.

The two subtypes of the corridor access buildings are:

A1: Building with an internal corridor, providing access to units on both sides. (Double-loaded corridors.)

A2: Buildings with an external corridor located along one wall of the building. (Single-loaded corridors.)

The two subtypes of direct access buildings (from the climatic performance aspect) are:

B1: Multiple staircases or elevators serving two apartments on each floor.

B2: Staircases or elevators serving more than two units at each floor.

DOUBLE-LOADED CORRIDOR BUILDINGS

Long apartment blocks with central double-loaded corridors are common in many multistory housing projects in the United States. Such buildings have the smallest area of external walls of all building types. Therefore, when such buildings are heated and air conditioned mechanically, their energy demand is the lowest. However, the climatic performance of such buildings is quite different when natural ventilation and/or solar energy utilization are contemplated.

In double-loaded corridor buildings the corridors are located at the center of the block, providing access to the dwelling units on both sides. Thus the corridor separates the dwelling units of the building into two groups with completely different exposure conditions. Most units, except the end ones, have only one external wall. As a result almost all the units do not have even the potential for effective cross-ventilation. Such apartments, particularly in regions with hot summers, generally have to use mechanical air conditioning for most of the summer, even in places and during seasons when natural ventilation can provide satisfactory indoor comfort.

From the viewpoint of direct sunlight and solar energy utilization for space heating, one-half of the units in buildings with double-loaded corridors are always at a disadvantage, unless the building is oriented along the north-south axis so that the east wall and windows get the sun in the morning and the west wall and windows get it in the afternoon. A special configuration of the windows, triangular "bay" windows facing southeast and southwest, can maximize the solar gain in winter, for a given window area, and minimize solar overheating in summer, as is illustrated in Figure 6-6.

When the building is oriented along the east-west axis, the southern units

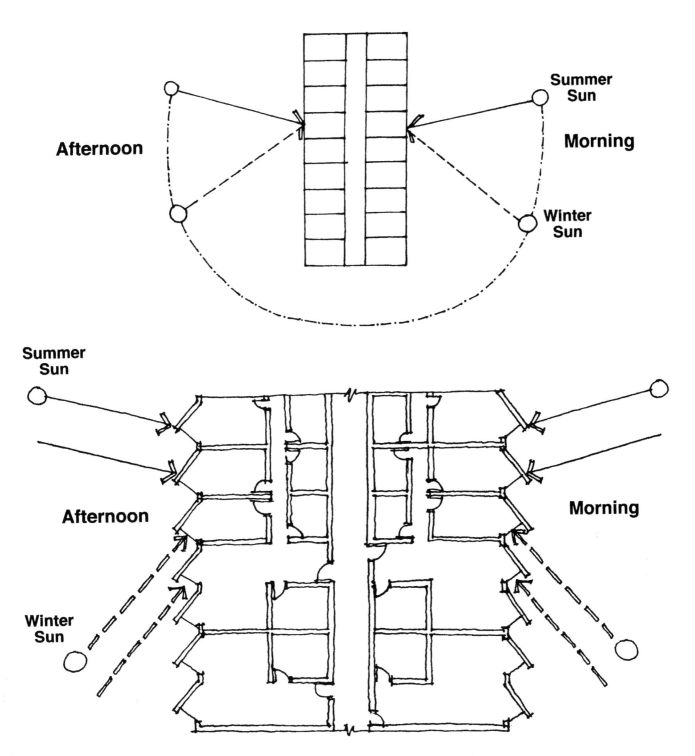

Figure 6-6. *Triangular "bay" windows in eastern and western walls, facing southeast and southwest, respectively, maximize solar gain in winter and minimize solar overheating in summer.*

can benefit from the sun all winter while the northern units do not receive any sun from September through March. This creates very sharp differences between the dwelling units in the two orientations in their thermal performance and the possibilities of the inhabitants to enjoy the sun in winter.

Considering the aforementioned climatic performance characteristics of double-loaded corridor buildings they can be considered as unsuitable from the natural ventilation, comfort, and solar energy utilization points of view, in any hot climate, especially for low-income people who can not afford air conditioning.

An exception is the double-loaded corridor type developed and applied by Le Corbusier in France. In this scheme a central corridor is located every third floor, and every "slice" of it serves two units, each occupying two levels, one at the corridor level and the other one above or below that level. This scheme is illustrated in Figure 6-7. With such a design each unit has direct access to two external walls on the opposite sides of the building, and thus has the potential for cross-ventilation, as well as for solar energy utilization.

It should be pointed out, however, that in cold regions, and for buildings which do not use solar energy, buildings with double-loaded corridors would be the most energy-conserving ones.

SINGLE-LOADED CORRIDOR BUILDINGS

In single-loaded buildings the corridors are located along one wall of the building. Each apartment is thus bound on one side by the corridor and on the other side by an external wall. The corridor may be glazed and closed during the winter and open during the summer, thus providing the option of exposure to the wind on either side of the building.

Theoretically, cross-ventilation is possible in apartments along an open corridor by leaving open windows in the external wall as well as windows and doors in the wall facing the corridor. Practically, however, leaving open doors in the corridor wall reduces greatly the visual and acoustical privacy of the occupants.

The visual privacy issue can be solved by installing shutters in the openings which enable air passage while blocking the view, or by having windowsills just above the sight line. Acoustical privacy, however, cannot be provided with the common types of single-loaded corridor buildings while the building is cross-ventilated. The occupants might be disturbed by noises generated in the corridor and people walking in it can hear what is going on inside.

The subjective severity of this issue depends, to a great extent, on the cultural background of the population and can vary greatly among different societies. Taking into account the potential for cross-ventilation in such buildings, open doors or shutters can be acceptable in hot regions provided that the acoustical privacy conditions are culturally accepted.

A more radical solution of this problem can be provided by special details which enable cross-ventilation without loss of acoustic, as well as visual, privacy. For example, if the rooms have a ceiling height of about 3 meters (10'), but the corridors have a ceiling height of about 2.3 meters (7' 8"), it is possible

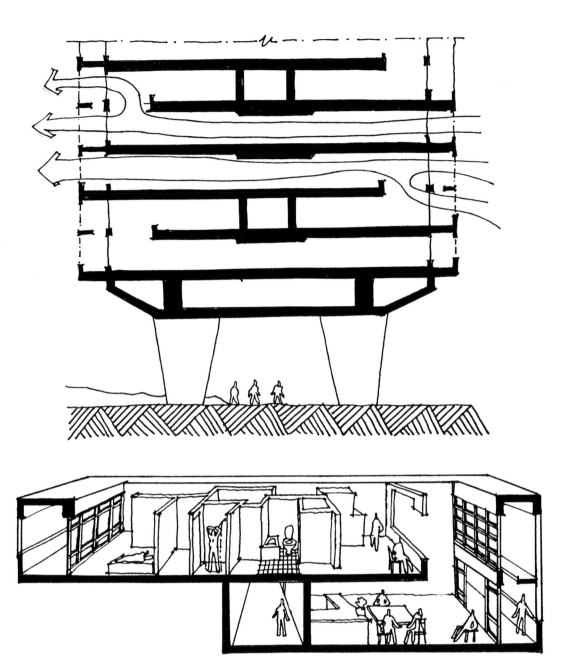

Figure 6-7. *Le Corbusier scheme of double-loaded apartment building: each unit has two external walls, enabling cross-ventilation.*

to provide a breezeway above the corridors by a false ceiling, enabling airflow through the apartments to the other side of the building, as is illustrated in Figure 6-8.

Another design solution for ensuring at least visual privacy to apartment dwellers in buildings with single-loaded corridors is to lower the levels of the corridors about half a meter (1.64') below the levels of the apartments, with stairs leading to the individual dwellings, as is illustrated in Figure 6-9 on page 227. The ventilation of such buildings is sensitive to orientation. The designer

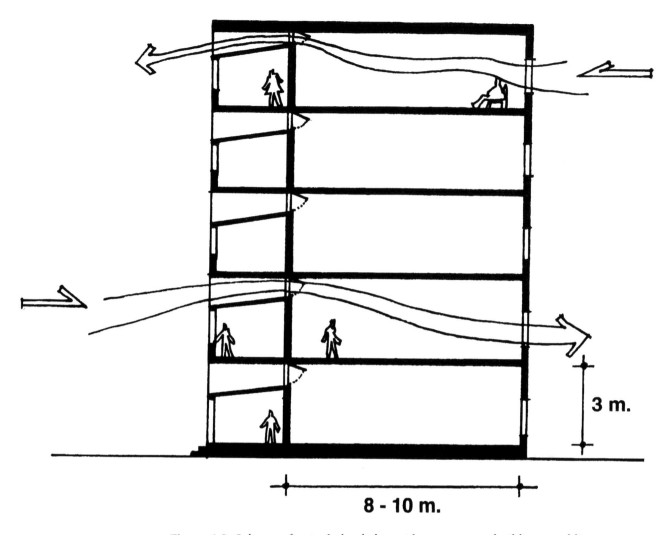

Figure 6-8. *Scheme of a single-loaded corridor apartment building, enabling cross-ventilation while providing acoustic and visual privacy.*

should ensure that one facade (preferably the "front" facade, opposite the corridor) faces the prevailing wind direction at an angle above about 30 degrees.

For passive solar heating of the apartments, only the "true" external wall can be used. Therefore, when solar energy utilization is contemplated, the external wall should face the winter sun. However, when the corridor wall faces the sun, the corridor itself can be solar heated by having it glazed during the winter season. The heated corridor minimizes, or may even eliminate, the heat loss through the apartment's wall facing the corridor, thus contributing to energy conservation.

DIRECT-ACCESS MULTISTORY APARTMENTS WITH TWO UNITS PER STAIRCASE

A much better design scheme than corridor-type buildings, from the climatic viewpoint, is to have low-rise buildings (e.g., up to four floors, with staircases

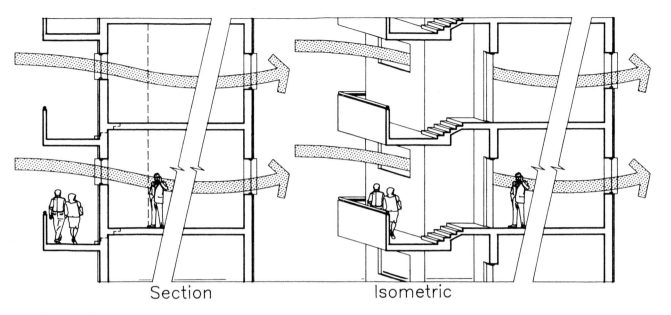

Section   Isometric

Figure 6-9. *Scheme of a single-loaded corridor apartment building, with corridors at lower level, enabling cross-ventilation with visual privacy, but not acoustic privacy.*

directly serving two apartments on each floor). With this scheme each apartment has two opposite external walls and the whole building, a block containing several such staircases, can be oriented optimally.

This building type, in conjunction with appropriate urban (neighborhood) design, provides sufficient exposure of the individual buildings to the sun and the prevailing winds, and can ensure the potential for effective cross-ventilation and solar heating for all the dwelling units.

In contrast with the single-loaded corridor type, such buildings do not compromise the privacy of the inhabitants while the apartments are cross-ventilated. The air flows from inlets in one wall to outlets in the other wall while the apartment is completely isolated from strangers (Figure 6-10). With appropriate partition walls, very effective acoustical insulation between neighboring units can be provided.

With two apartments to a staircase each one of the external walls can serve as a solar heat source. Any one of the various passive solar heating systems discussed in Chapter 4 can be applied to this building type.

The "tolerance" of building orientation, for providing cross-ventilation, is about 60 degrees on either side of the prevailing wind direction. On the other hand, the tolerance of orientation for solar energy utilization is only about 30 degrees on either side of the sun's winter noon position (in latitudes above about 20 degrees north and south). Because of a larger tolerance of the wind orientation, the winter solar considerations should be the main factor in choosing the optimal orientation of the building block.

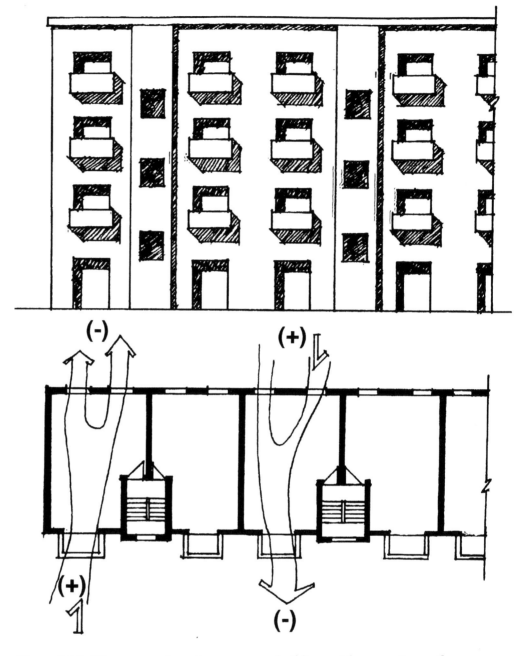

Figure 6-10. *Direct-access low-rise apartment building, with two units per floor, provides cross-ventilation as well as visual and acoustic privacy.*

MULTISTORY BUILDINGS WITH MORE THAN TWO UNITS PER STAIRCASE

When three apartments are accessed directly at each floor from a staircase the orientation issue becomes more sensitive. When the third apartment projects at a right angle to the overall building block, it creates a wind "shadow" when the wind is oblique to the building and blowing toward the projected apartment. While all apartments can still have reasonable ventilation their conditions

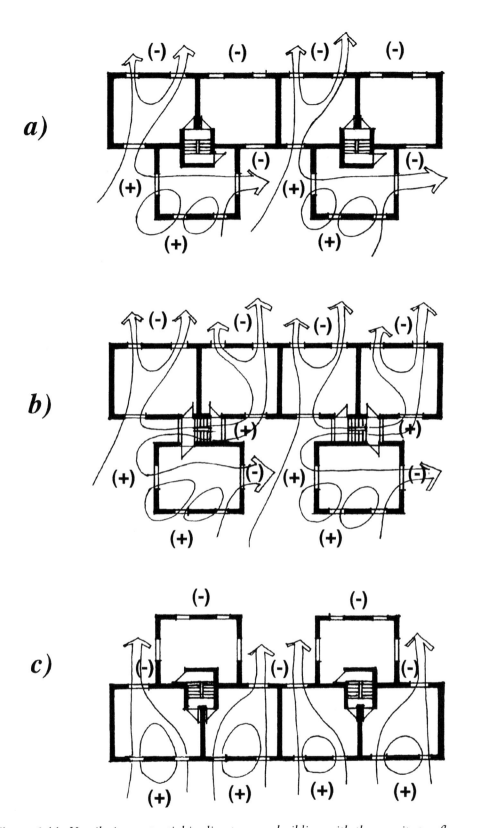

Figure 6-11. *Ventilation potential in direct-access building with three units per floor:*
  a. Internal staircase, third apartment projecting upwind. One unit may be in the wind shadow, with inferior ventilation.
  b. External open staircase improves the ventilation potential.
  c. Internal staircase: Unit projecting downwind has inferior ventilation potential.

are less favorable than in the case of two units to a staircase, as their external walls are all exposed to zones of low pressure (Figure 6-11, Top—see page 229).

A partial solution for improving the ventilation potential of the unit in the wind shadow is when the staircase itself is projecting out of the main block and is open to air flow through it (Figure 6-11, Middle).

When the projection is on the leeward side of the building the third apartment itself is located in the wind shadow. As a result it will always suffer from poor ventilation in this position (Figure 6-11, Bottom).

When the projected apartment is on the sunny side of the building (facing south in the Northern Hemisphere), it creates a solar shadow on one neighbor in the morning and on the other one in the afternoon. If it is projecting on the other side of the building this apartment itself does not receive *any* sun in winter.

Taking into account the problems mentioned above it can be seen that the overall climatic performance of multistory apartments drops when more than two units per floor are accessed from a staircase. When more than three units per floor are accessed from a staircase (or an elevator) some of the units will always suffer from poor ventilation and poor solar exposure conditions. Therefore such design schemes are not recommended for hot climates.

HIGH-RISE BUILDINGS

High-rise buildings depend completely on elevators and other sophisticated mechanical systems for their functioning. Therefore they are suitable only for high-income people. Consequently the applicability of high-rises as a residence type in developing countries is quite limited.

However, from the climatic point of view, they may have distinctive impact on the ground-level urban climate in the area around them, especially on the urban *wind field*. This last point will be discussed in more detail in Chapters 7 and 8.

The inhabitants of the upper floors, located above the roof level of the surrounding lower buildings, enjoy some environmental advantages in hot regions but also are exposed to more severe climatic hazards. Considering all the above factors, high-rise tower buildings deserve some discussion even in a book whose focus is mainly on low-cost housing in developing countries.

Environmental Impacts of High-Rise Buildings

High-rise buildings, placed among lower buildings surrounding them, increase the mixing of the air flowing above the urban canopy with air at ground level. As a major source of urban air pollution is vehicular exhaust at the streets, the upper airstream is usually cleaner than the ground level air. Increased mixing of the air of these two layers reduces the pollution concentration at the ground level, where its impact on the health of the urban population is at a maximum, as is illustrated in Figure 6-12. In this way high-rise buildings tend to *improve* the air quality at the street level around them.

Another impact of such buildings on the ground-level conditions around them is a marked increase in the speed and turbulence of the wind—the wind speed in the streets around high-rise tower buildings can be increased by up to 300 percent, and in specific locations even higher wind speeds could be experienced. The desirability of this effect depends, of course, on the "normal" climatic conditions in the city in question. In cities experiencing insufficient wind this effect will be welcomed. In cities, and during times, with excessive winds this impact of high-rise buildings is a negative one.

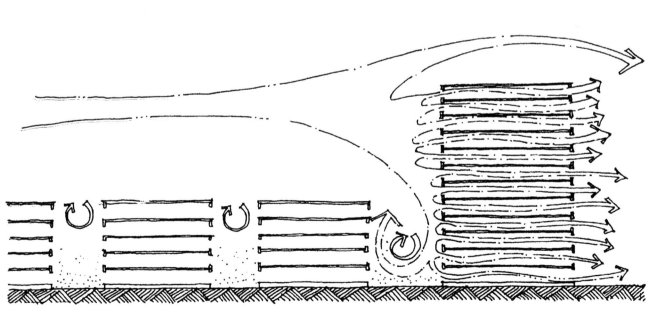

Figure 6-12. *Wind speed near ground level in front of a high-rise building is increased, helping in diluting street-level air pollutants.*

Environmental Conditions in the High-Rise Buildings

The environmental conditions of the inhabitants of the upper floors of high-rise buildings are, to some extent, different from those of the rest of the urban population. The main differences are in the ventilation potential and solar exposure and exposure to storms and wind-driven rain, as well as in the view from the windows.

Because of the generally higher wind speeds above the average height of the urban canopy, and the further increase in the wind speed with height, the upper floors of the high-rise buildings enjoy better ventilation conditions during periods of weak winds but, on the other hand, are exposed to more severe winds during storms.

Penetration of wind-driven rain through openings and joints is also a more serious problem at these floor levels than for the rest of the urban buildings. Consequently more careful details of windows and joints between wall elements are needed there.

High-rise buildings are less likely to be shaded by nearby buildings. Therefore the intensity of solar radiation impinging on them, direct, diffused, and/or reflected from roofs of lower buildings, is higher than that impinging on the "typical" urban buildings. Shading therefore is more important and sometimes more complex to design.

One of the major environmental advantages of the inhabitants of upper floors of high-rise buildings is the better view offered from their windows. While the rest of the city inhabitants may feel their visual environment congested, those living in the upper floors of high-rise buildings often enjoy an expansive view of distant scenes.

The environmental noise level at these upper floors is substantially lower than at the typical urban buildings. Both greater distance from the noise sources and reduced noise reflection contribute to this condition.

CLIMATIC CHARACTERISTICS OF INTERNAL COURTYARDS AND ATTACHED ENCLOSED OPEN SPACES

Internal courtyards and attached open spaces enclosed by walls are very common in many regions, especially in developing hot-dry countries, and can be found both in single-family houses and in town houses. Multistory apartment blocks also are often built around a courtyard.

When analyzed from the thermal comfort and the energy consumption aspects it is found that the performance of courtyards depends greatly on its detailed treatment. With some design details courtyards can provide a pleasant outdoor environment and also improve the *indoor* comfort. With other details courtyards may elevate the indoor temperature and cause poor ventilation in the rooms, or dwelling units, located on the leeward side.

Many household activities can often take place outdoors in a hot climate more comfortably than indoors. Such activities may include washing, cooking, playing, and even sleeping. Therefore, such outdoor spaces could form an integral part of the house.

An integrated open space can have different relationships to the "built" parts of the building:

1. Attached open spaces outside the walls' lines.
2. Semienclosed spaces, e.g., porches, surrounded by rooms on two or three sides but open on at least one side.
3. Internal courtyards, or patios, surrounded on all sides by rooms.

These different types of open spaces can be functionally integrated with the building "proper," providing space for various household activities. But, because of the different levels of integration with the building and separation from the general climatic environment, they can have different climatic characteristics and impacts on the building's indoor climate.

Attached Open Spaces

Attached open spaces can be surrounded by high walls, completely isolated from the "public" outdoors. However, from the thermal aspect, they do not penetrate and indent the envelope of the building and thus do not increase the surface area of its envelope. When adequately treated, such attached open spaces (yards or balconies) can modify the climatic conditions of the ambient environment, next to the "skin" of the building. Such modifications may include:

- Shading the building walls adjacent to the open spaces, either by an overhand or by vegetation.
- Insulation of the walls, e.g., by dense and high shrubs, creating semidead airspace next to the walls.
- Increasing the humidity and lowering the temperature in the semienclosed airspace within the "walled" open space. Such modification of the climate

can be achieved only if the open space is separated from the "general" environment by high walls and is shaded by a roof, or tree canopies, above it.

Semienclosed Open Spaces

Semienclosed open spaces, such as deep porches, do penetrate the periphery of the building, thus increasing its effective surface area. They enhance the interaction between the indoor and the outdoor thermal environments, increasing both the rate of indoor heating during the daytime and rate of cooling at night.

Semienclosed porches can enable adjustment of the building's geometry to changes in the desirable indoor-outdoor relationship. The porches should be equipped with openable insulated panels which could be closed during the hot hours and open during the evening and night hours. The panels may contain small windows, to provide daylight, ventilation, and a view from the porch when the panels are closed.

When the insulating panels are open the porches become semiopen spaces, effectively increasing the surface area of the building's envelope. When the panels are closed the porches form an integral part of the building's interior and their effect on the building's envelope area is minimized. In both cases they are, in effect, an integral part of the building's usable area, as is illustrated in Figure 6-13.

Internal Courtyards

Internal courtyards *maximize* the thermal interaction between the building and the outdoor environment, introducing the outdoors into the heart of the building's core. It is commonly assumed that such internal patios help in maintaining cooled indoor temperatures in hot climates. However, the actual climatic effects of an internal patio depend greatly on its design details and its "treatment."

CLIMATIC CHARACTERISTICS OF COURTYARDS

In comparing the climatic conditions of open spaces and those of a patio or a courtyard the following factors should be considered.

While the total solar radiation penetrating into the space of the open patio is the same as that impinging on an open horizontal earth surface it is *absorbed* in the various vertical surfaces (walls) and the floor of the patio. Wind carries away part of the solar energy absorbed at an open area. The wind speed within a patio is usually much lower than the ambient wind speed and, consequently,

Figure 6-13. *An indented porch with open insulated shutters (top) is part of the outdoor environment, and with closed shutters it becomes part of the interior.*

less solar heat is carried away by the wind and more is absorbed by the surfaces of the patio, elevating both the patio's radiant and air temperatures. Also, the physiological convective and evaporative heat losses are smaller in the patio because of the blockage of the wind and the near-still air conditions existing in it.

Long-wave radiant loss (day and night) is smaller from a patio than from an exposed outdoor horizontal surface, owing to the partial blockage of the sky, and long-wave radiation absorption, by the walls. Ambient air temperature in such "untreated" internal open spaces usually will be higher than in an outdoor open space, especially during the night, because the patio may act as a small-scale enclosed "urban canyon."

Thus, an unshaded internal patio without vegetation or other sources of shade and evaporation is likely to cause higher indoor temperatures in the building surrounding it, as compared with a compact building of the same floor area. During the evening and night hours, of course, the patio itself can provide an area with a more pleasant climate than that of the indoors, in addition to the complete privacy.

The actual climatic conditions within an internal patio depend greatly on its design details and its "treatment." The air and radiant temperatures in an internal patio in some cases are higher, but also can be lower, than the respective ambient temperatures, depending on the design details of the courtyard.

An "untreated" internal patio with bare soil or with a hard floor (concrete, tiles, and so forth) often has higher air and radiant temperatures than the outdoor environment and therefore can *increase* the rate of the indoor temperature elevation. This is due to the blocking of the wind in the patio and to the effective increase in the surface area of the building's envelope.

Consequently, an unshaded internal patio, without vegetation or other sources of shading and evaporative cooling, is likely to cause higher indoor discomfort in hot regions than in a building without a patio with the same floor area. The patio itself can, of course, provide an area with a more pleasant climate than that of the indoors during the evening and night hours, in addition to the complete privacy in the open space.

COOLING TREATMENTS FOR PATIOS

With different treatments a patio can have a much more favorable impact on the indoor climate than the exposed environment in a hot-dry climate, as well as having a more pleasant "outdoor" climate within the confines of the building's envelope. This modification of the patio's climate can be achieved by a combination of minimizing the amount of solar radiation striking the patio's ground in summer and lowering its air temperature by evaporative cooling.

Shading a patio can be accomplished by the design details of the building around it—for instance, by inward-projecting roof and balconies. Shading of the patio's ground can also be by a pergola with vines or by trees with high trunks and wide canopies. To enable light and sun in winter the shading plants within the patio should be preferably of deciduous varieties.

The patio's air temperature near the ground level can be lowered by enhancing evaporative cooling of the air within the space. To enhance evaporative cooling, the "confined" still air within the patio should be in contact with water with as large a surface area as practical. Several design solutions can provide a large surface area of water.

An ordinary pool within a patio has a very limited amount of the surface of the water in contact with air. If it is not shaded, the temperature of the water will be close to that of the ambient air, as the evaporative heat loss is close to the solar heat gain of the water, and will not cause actual lowering of the patio's air temperature. However, a shaded pool with water spray, or other source of sprayed water, can cool the water and the air in contact with it to a lower temperature than that of the ambient "dry bulb" temperature. The surface area of the water can be increased by a fountain with *fine spray* or by having water flow over a vertical wall with a pool in front of it. The larger surface area of the water can significantly increase the "coupling" between the air and water, increasing the evaporation rate and the temperature drop of the water and the air in the patio.

A "shower" cooling tower, or the Arizona-type cooling tower, as described in Chapter 5 (beginning on page 196), can also serve as cooling sources for a patio. The "shower" tower can be integrated architecturally with a pool. In addition to the stream of cool air it produces, it also cools the water to a temperature very close to that of the ambient Wet Bulb Temperature (WBT). A canopy of trees, or a pergola, can effectively reduce the mixing of the cool air within the patio with the warmer air flowing over the building's roof. In this way the patio serves not only as a pleasant protected "outdoor" space but also reduces the heat gain of the building, as compared with an uncooled patio.

RADIANT COOLING OF AN ENCLOSED PATIO

The nighttime temperature within the patio can be lowered somewhat by taking advantage of the radiant heat loss from the roofs surrounding it. In practice this means that the roofs around the patio should slope down toward the patio. The external periphery of the roof should be surrounded by a solid parapet to minimize the wind speed over the roof's surface. An open "transparent" safety parapet (open to airflow) can surround the patio itself. A gutter around the patio should be able to collect and dispose of the rainwater, with any expected intensity, thus preventing flooding of the patio during rain.

In the case of concrete roofs, the roof should be insulated above the concrete, in order to ensure fast cooling of the external surface. Preferably, a corrugated metal layer about 5 cm (2") above the insulation layer may form the external surface. This detail will cool the air at night, both above and below the metallic layer, which may then flow down toward the patio.

These physical concepts can be translated into various architectural design solutions, enhancing the visual quality of the patio as well as improving its comfort conditions. The specialized subject of internal courtyards in hot-dry climates is discussed in Chapter 10.

VENTILATION PROBLEMS IN BUILDINGS WITH INTERNAL COURTYARDS

Internal courtyards in houses, and especially when located at the center of an apartment block, create unequal conditions, from the ventilation aspect, for the rooms or the apartments surrounding it. Wind at any direction creates a low-pressure zone above the open space of the yard. Rooms or apartments on the windward sides of the courtyard have good ventilation potential. However, the ventilation of the rooms on the leeward sides of the courtyard (low-pressure zones) is poorer, as the rooms are surrounded by low pressure on all sides.

When the courtyard is surrounded by an apartment building the unit downwind has poorer ventilation than an apartment in a building without an internal courtyard, when properly placed inlet and outlet openings can direct the airflow across the whole unit.

Part II

Urban Climatology

Chapter **7**: GENERAL CHARACTERISTICS OF THE URBAN CLIMATE

INTRODUCTION

This chapter summarizes the main features by which the urban climate differs from the climatic conditions prevailing in the surrounding rural areas. These differences are affected on one side by meteorological factors, such as cloudiness and wind speed, and, on the other side, by the structure of the city, such as buildings' density and width of streets. Emphasis in this chapter is placed on the urban climate features which are affected by the physical structure of the city and thus can be modified by urban design. Therefore it serves as the basis for the discussion of the role of various urban design features in modifying the regional climate conditions and creating the specific urban climate, to be presented in Chapter 9.

The main differences between the urban and the "rural" climates which affect human comfort are in the air temperatures and wind speeds near street level. These differences are caused by changes in the radiant balance of the urban space; the convective heat exchange between the ground and the buildings, and the air flowing above; and by the heat generation within the city. The chapter starts with discussion of the urban temperature (mainly the "Heat Island" phenomenon) and of the urban wind conditions. The radiant balance of, and sunshine conditions in, a city are discussed later in the chapter.

A very useful distinction can be made between the urban air "canopy" and the boundary layer over the city space (the urban air "dome"), as was suggested by Oke (1976). It is convenient to consider the fabric of the structures in a city as analogous to a "canopy" of a tree, where the impinging solar radiation is gradually absorbed and where specific conditions of air temperature and humidity may exist, distinct from those prevailing in the surrounding space. Therefore the space bounded by the urban buildings up to their roofs is often referred to as the "urban canopy."

However, because of the size of a city, the distinct properties of its air extend above the buildings' roofs and further downwind. This phenomenon can actually be seen in many cities from a distance outside the city, in the form of the layer of turbid air over the city's boundaries. The volume of air affected by the city is the urban boundary layer, also referred to as the "urban air dome."

Oke (1976) emphasizes that the urban canopy is a microscale concept: The specific climatic conditions at any given point within the canopy are determined by the nature of the immediate surroundings. In particular, the materials, geometry, and surface properties of the structures around a given place modify the local ambient climate. Therefore the meteorological conditions within the urban canopy are very localized. Also the upper boundary of the urban canopy varies from one spot to another because of the variable heights of the buildings.

The upper layer, the boundary or air dome layer, is more homogeneous in its properties over the urban area at large. It is defined as "that portion of the planetary boundary layer whose characteristics are affected by the presence of an urban area at its lower boundary" (Oke 1976). The wind speed also affects the boundary of the urban canopy—high winds can penetrate deeper below the roof's level than the effects of light winds, thus lowering the effective height of the canopy.

The distinction between the urban canopy and the air dome is important when mathematical simulation models of the urban climate are dealt with and their application to urban design and human comfort are considered. Such models deal with the overall energy balance of the urban area or its overall characteristics. Therefore they are more relevant to the conditions prevailing within the urban air dome rather than to the local conditions within the urban canopy.

On the other hand, human comfort and energy use of buildings are affected by the local climatic conditions within the urban canopy, which at any given place can be quite different from those existing in other, even nearby, places and from the conditions prevailing above, in the urban air dome.

THE URBAN TEMPERATURE: THE "HEAT ISLAND" PHENOMENON

On the average the diurnal temperature, in a densely built urban area, is warmer than the surrounding open (rural) country. The largest elevations of the urban temperatures occur during clear and still-air nights. During these times temperature elevations of about 3–5°C (5.4–9°F) are common, but elevations of about 8–10°C (14.4–18°F) were also observed. This nocturnal elevation of the urban temperature above the surrounding rural areas is commonly defined as the "Urban Heat Island" and the maximum urban-rural difference is defined as the "Heat Island Intensity." Most of the studies of the urban heat island involve a transverse drive through roads crossing the city during the nighttime and recording the air temperatures along these paths.

During daytime hours the differences in temperatures between city centers and surrounding country are usually much smaller, about 1–2°C (1.8–3.6°F). Often the temperatures in the urban area during daytime are lower than in the surrounding country, as was observed, for example, in Mexico City (Jauregui 1984). During windy periods the urban-rural temperature difference may be insignificant.

As the temperature elevation in the urban centers is largest during the nights, the conventional urban heat island, and especially the heat island intensity, are essentially nocturnal phenomena. Some urban structure features, such as the width of streets and the materials of the buildings (their heat capacity), affect the relationship between the urban and the rural temperatures in opposite ways (see Chapter 8, page 286). Therefore, in considering the implications of studies dealing with the urban climate on urban design the relative importance of the daytime and nighttime climatic conditions, from the comfort and energy use aspect, should be taken into account.

The differences between the urban and the "rural" temperatures are affected by two types of factors. One, they are correlated with meteorological factors such as the cloud cover, humidity, and wind speed. Two, various features of the urban structure, such as the size of cities, the density of the built-up areas, and the ratio of buildings' heights to the distances between them can have strong effect on the magnitude of the urban heat island. Furthermore, to complicate the subject, certain features of a city, such as the width of streets and the buildings materials, may have opposite effects even on the *direction* of the urban-rural temperature difference.

It should be noted that almost all the existing comparisons between the urban centers and the surrounding open spaces, with regard to the daytime temperatures, were done in cities surrounded by cultivated land (rural areas) in temperate climates. The situation may be different in desert cities, which are surrounded by dry land devoid of vegetation cover, as is discussed below.

OVERALL SPATIAL PATTERN OF THE URBAN HEAT ISLAND

The boundaries of the heat island follow the urban air dome. The horizontal temperature gradients, the rise from the periphery to the center, especially during the nights, is largest at the outer boundaries of the urban area and flattens towards the center of a built-up area. During the periods with light winds the heat island is extended downwind beyond the boundary of the urban built-up area. The "height" of the heat island is rather shallow, extending upwards about three to five times the average height of the buildings and coincides approximately with the urban air dome. Above this height the differences between the "urban temperature" and the regional temperature at the same height are very small.

There are several different and independent factors which affect the urban temperature, especially near ground level, and which contribute to the development of the urban heat island:

1. Differences in the overall *net* radiation balance between the urban area and the surrounding open country (as described in the preceding section). While the daytime net radiant gain near ground level in a city may be smaller than in the surrounding open areas, the nocturnal radiation, the lower rate of radiant cooling during the nights, is the major factor contributing to the higher urban temperature.
2. Storage of solar energy in the mass of the buildings in the city during the daytime hours and its release during the night hours.
3. Concentrated heat generation by the activities taking place in the urban area year-round (transportation, industry, and so on), the so-called "anthropogenic heat release."
4. Lower evaporation from soil and vegetation in the urban built-up area, as compared with an "open" rural area.
5. Seasonal heat sources: heating of the buildings in winter and air conditioning in summer. All the heating and air conditioning energy is ultimately released to the urban air.

In cold regions the elevation of the urban temperature is a positive effect, from the viewpoints of the comfort of the residents and the energy consumption for heating. In hot regions, however, the higher temperature increases discomfort and the need for air conditioning.

Some of the factors which affect the urban heat island are meteorological and not subject to human intervention, such as the cloudiness and the regional wind speed. However, from the urban design viewpoint, the factors which can be modified by human action are of interest. Such "manageable" factors include the colors of the buildings (which determine the fraction of the solar radiation reflected away), the amount and distribution of urban vegetation, energy use for heating and air conditioning (as affected by the design of the buildings), density of the built-up areas and types of buildings (which affect the amount of solar radiation reaching the ground level and the nocturnal radiant loss), and orientation of the streets with respect to the wind direction (affecting the wind speed near the ground).

A more-detailed discussion of the effect of the size and density of the built-up area on the urban temperature is presented below.

The relative role of the above-mentioned factors in generating the heat island effect depends upon the climate (dry or humid), season, and type of activities in the city.

Heat generation by heating of the buildings occurs in winter, of course. The magnitude of this factor depends on the climate. In cold regions more energy is used for heating than in cities located in mild regions. But the effect of the climate on energy use for heating may be greatly modified by the thermal quality of the buildings. In fact, a building located in a region with 3,000 degree days (see Chapter 3, page 129 for definition) but super-insulated, with a building heat loss coefficient (BLC) of 2000 wh/C day (3790 Btu/h.F), needs less energy than a poorly insulated building, with a heat loss coefficient of 10,000 wh/C day (18,960 Btu/h.F), located in a mild region with only 1,000 degree days C (1800°F).

Energy consumed by fditioning equipment is converted into heat, is discharged to the outdoors, and ultimately raises the temperature of the urban air. Commercial buildings are usually air conditioned year-round, with peaks during hot summer days. Residential buildings are air conditioned to a much lesser extent. Consequently, the consumption of energy for air conditioning is concentrated mainly in urban commercial centers. All the heating energy, including cooking, washing, and so forth, and energy consumed by air conditioning is eventually released to the environment, elevating the urban temperature.

The quantitative contribution of industrial heat generation to the development of the urban heat island depends on the type of the city. In towns with "hot" industries, such as steel mills, within their boundaries this may be a major factor, while in other towns it may be just a minor component. All the energy consumed by light industry, which may often be located within the urban boundary, is also converted into heat, contributing to the urban heat island.

The contribution of energy use in transportation to the heat island may be related to the size of the city and the relative role of public transportation in it. It can be assumed that larger cities have more overall traffic, but the trips, and the energy they consume, are distributed over a larger area. However, more people and trips are concentrated in the *center* of larger cities, as compared with smaller cities. Thus energy input by transportation at the town's center may be related to the size of the city. This effect may be modified by the type of the urban transportation system. Private cars consume more fuel and generate more heat, per passenger, than buses and electrical subways.

Taking into account the complexity of these factors, the difficulties in developing a realistic mathematical predictive model of the heat island phenomenon can be appreciated. Each one of the individual factors affecting the urban-rural temperature differences has a specific effect and any observed temperature difference reflects the combined effect of all these factors. Understanding the impact of each one of these factors on the urban-rural temperature differences is useful for the analysis of the factors which can be "manipulated" by urban design features.

Localized Distribution of the Urban Heat Island Sources

The diurnal temperature patterns at any specific location in a city depend to a large extent on the local conditions, with respect to the density of the ground cover by buildings and the height of the buildings, the nature of the ground surface (hard surfaces, lawns, trees, shade conditions), the exposure of the site to the regional wind, and so on. Any local place can be either warmer or cooler than the surrounding area.

The intensity of the heat island at night is related more to density of buildings rather than to city size (Chandler 1971). In fact, several detailed studies have demonstrated that heat islands can be developed even on relatively small scale urban areas. Norwine (1972) measured the temperature distribution across a retail shopping center near Chicago. It includes a central trilevel building, several smaller buildings, and a parking space. Temperatures were measured in the late evening hours (10–11 P.M.), during January, February, and March of 1972. During calm weather the complex was warmer by about 3°C (5.4°F) than the surrounding area.

Copra and Pritchart (1972) measured the temperature field in two shopping centers in Norfolk, Virginia. Temperature data were obtained in several field traverses during daytime and night hours in the spring and summer of 1971 and

1972. The centers of the shopping centers' area were warmer by 3–7°C (5.4–12.6°F) than the surrounding area.

The warmer air above such small-scale heat islands mixes eventually with the bulk of the urban air and thus slowly elevates the "ambient air" flowing across the city downwind. Therefore, although the origins of the "urban heat island" may be small pockets, their effect accumulates, to produce the peak of the temperature elevation near the town's center.

Solar Radiation and Urban Geometry Impacts on Urban Temperature

The impact of the impinging solar radiation on the climate near the ground depends to some extent on the ratio of the height (H) of the buildings to the spacing (Width) between them, namely the H/W ratio of the spaces between the buildings.

Ludwig (1970) presents an analysis of the effect of this ratio on the radiation and air temperature near the ground. His analysis is illustrated in Figure 7-1, showing a schematic distribution of the impinging solar radiation in (a) an open-flat country, (b) a built-up area with H/W ratio of about 1, and (c) a high-density urban area with H/W ratio of about 4.

In the flat area, most of the impinging solar radiation is reflected away or emitted, after absorption, as long-wave radiation to the sky. In a medium-density area (H/W ratio of about 1), much of the reflected radiation strikes other buildings or the ground and is eventually absorbed at and near the ground level. In the high-density area (H/W ratio of about 4 or more), most of the absorption takes place high above the ground level. Consequently, the amount of radiation reaching the ground, and heating the air near the ground, is smaller than in the case of medium density.

Oke (1981) introduced the term "Urban Canyon" and presented detailed quantitative analysis of its energy balance and results of measurements dealing with an urban canyon in Vancouver, British Columbia, having a H/W ratio of nearly 0.9. In this study, it was found that about 60 percent of the midday solar gain was transferred as sensible heat to the air contained in the volume of the canyon, about 30 percent was stored in the canyon materials (to be released during the night), and about 10 percent was consumed by evaporation from the canyon surfaces.

The urban canyon concept has been applied by Oke (1981) in developing a predictive formula for the heat island intensity.

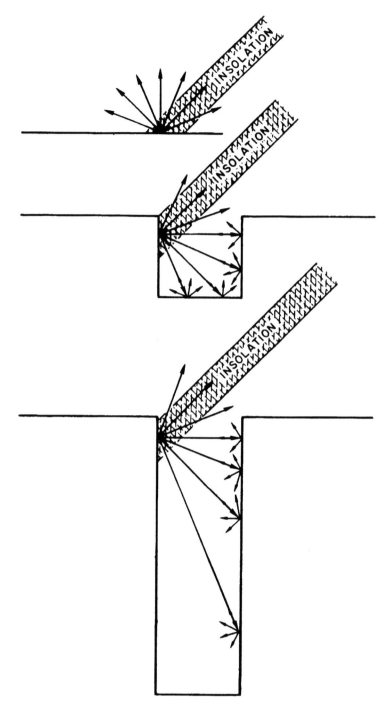

Figure 7-1. *Schematic distribution of the impinging solar radiation in (a) Open-flat country, (b) Built-up area with H/W ratio of about 1, and (c) High-density urban area with H/W ratio of about 4.*

HEAT ISLAND MODELS

A comprehensive description and analysis of various urban climate models is presented in Bornstein 1984. Urban climatic models quantitatively describe the differences which exist with regard to various climatic elements between densely built urban areas and the surrounding rural or open country area. Such differences are observed in air temperature, solar radiation, wind conditions, and air turbidity.

Bornstein, following the suggestion of Oke (1976), distinguishes between canopy-layer models (below roof level) and mesoscale models dealing with conditions in the urban boundary layer above roof level. Boundary-layer models deal with relatively large segments of the city on a mesoscale. They integrate the "inputs" of the smaller, microscale areas to estimate the climatic properties of the air flowing over the city canopy. Because of the relatively large gradients in the properties of the urban atmosphere immediately above roof level, the conditions in the boundary layer may be different from those existing near the street level below.

From the aspects of human comfort and others dealt with in this book, the climate *near the ground* is the relevant one. Therefore, only the canopy-layer models, which can be sensitive to urban microscale features and their effects on the urban climate, are of interest.

Meteorological Nocturnal Urban-Island Models

Most of the existing urban models deal with the nighttime heat island intensity (maximum urban-rural differences) and express the temperature difference as a function of various meteorological factors such as cloud cover, wind speed, and specific humidity.

Thus, for example, Ludwig (1970), on the basis of statistical analysis of measurements of the urban-rural temperature differences (dT) and the corresponding lapse rate (in C/millibar) over the rural area (Y), has suggested a formula predicting the "heat island" as a function of the lapse rate:

$$dT = 1.85 - 7.4 * Y$$

It should be noted that the lapse rate is negative: temperature decreases with height. As the lapse rate is very sensitive to the cloudiness conditions this model expresses indirectly the effect of cloudiness on the heat island.

Another statistical model, cited by Bornstein (1984), is that of Sundborg (1950), which relates the nocturnal heat island of Uppsala, Sweden, with various meteorological elements: cloudiness, N; wind speed, U; temperature, T; and specific humidity, q. The formula found by Sundborg is:

$$dTmax = 2.8 - 0.1 N - 0.38 U - 0.02 T + 0.03 q$$

Such formulae are useful in predicting the variation in the expected heat island intensity under different meteorological conditions unaffected by human action, and are of main interest to meteorologists. However, meteorological-based models do not deal at all with factors which can be influenced by urban design, and therefore are of only limited interest to urban designers aiming at modification of the urban climate by design measures.

As these formulae deal with the *maximum* urban temperature elevation on a given night, such models cannot be applied in estimating, for instance, the effect of the heat island on the energy use for winter heating, which is related to the diurnal temperature *average* rather than to the extreme conditions during the nights. In particular, the heat island intensity information is not useful for estimating the summer cooling energy consumption and peak load, which are related to the daytime average and maximum temperatures, respectively.

The "meteorological" models of the urban heat island concept seem to be mainly of interest in understanding the meteorological mechanisms promoting the heat island. It is of limited application for *urban design*, because the meteorological factors are not under the control of designers. To be of applicable value to urban design the urban effects should be expressed as functions of *urban* design factors. Therefore only models which deal explicitly with urban design factors will be mentioned in the following sections.

The existing models of the heat island phenomenon are based on statistical regression analysis of the relationship between the maximum urban-rural temperature difference, various meteorological factors, and some urban characteristics.

Urban Design-Oriented Nocturnal Heat Island Models

Recently, a number of heat island models were suggested which correlate the maximum urban-rural (nocturnal) temperature difference with a number of features of the urban structure. Only gross urban characteristics were usually included in such statistical models. Thus Oke (1982) has correlated the heat island intensity to the size of the urban population. For cities in North America he suggests the formula:

$$dT = P^{1/4} / (4 * U)^{1/2}$$

where:

dT = heat island intensity (C)
 P = population
 U = regional wind speed (m/s)

The heat island intensity was defined as the maximum difference between the urban center and the open country obtained by automobile traverses, usually during clear calm nights.

Oke has also found that for European cities of a given size the heat island is weaker than in North America and two different regression lines have been developed for the two sets of data. Oke has attributed this discrepancy to the fact that the centers of North American cities have taller buildings and higher densities than typical European cities.

Jauregui (1984) has added to Oke's data on numerous cities located in low latitudes in South America and India. The relationship between population size and the urban heat island intensity for North America, Europe, and South America is shown in Figure 7-2 (from Jauregui 1984). It can be seen from that figure that the heat islands in these cities are weaker than even in the European ones. Jauregui suggests that this phenomenon can be attributed in part to the difference in morphology (physical structure) between the South American and European cities.

Oke (1984) describes some of the main differences between the morphology of tropical cities in developing countries and those in Europe and North America as follows: "In many tropical cities the buildings are arranged in a more compact configuration than in temperate areas . . . It is also common to find a

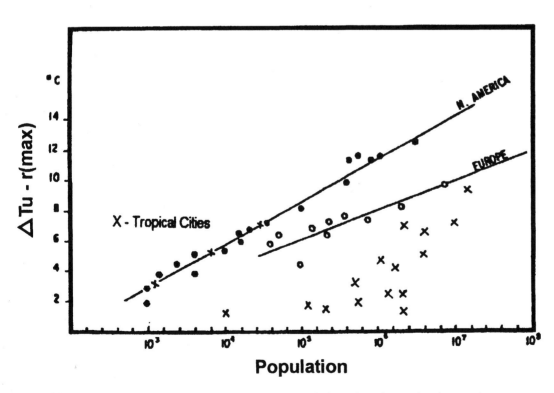

Figure 7-2. *Relationship between population size and the urban heat island intensity for North America, Europe, and South America.*

preponderance of low (single-story) dwellings. Such geometric features, in combination with the prevalence of high solar elevations, make building roofs relatively more important than their walls in term[s] of surface energy and mass exchange. This has implications for the urban surface albedo, surface emissivity, shade and diffuse lighting, day length, screening of outgoing long-wave radiation, aerodynamic roughness, and the interaction between streets and the air above roof level."

Another model of Oke (1981) correlates the heat island intensity with the geometry of the urban canyon, as expressed by the relationship between the building's height (H) and the distance between them (Width), namely the ratio: (H/W). The formula suggested is:

$$dTmax = 7.45 + 3.97 * \ln(H/W)$$

Alternatively, the urban hemispheric height-to-distance ratio, as seen from a given point, can be expressed by the "sky view factor" (SVF). For an unobstructed horizontal area the SVF is equal to 1.0. For a point surrounded by close, very high buildings, or for a very narrow street, it may be about 0.1. Oke has suggested also a formula expressing the urban heat island intensity as a function of the SVF:

$$dTmax = 15.27 - 13.88 * SVF$$

The above formula expresses the hypothesis that the urban heat island is caused mainly by reduced radiant heat loss to the sky from the ground level of densely built urban centers, where the heat island phenomenon is observed and measured, due to the restricted view of the sky. It should be pointed out again that the total long-wave radiant loss from the urban canopy is about the same as from an open rural area. However, at the urban area, most of the radiation is emitted from the roofs and walls of the upper stories of the buildings, with only partial cooling obtained near the ground level. Figure 7-3 shows the relationship between the SVF and the urban heat island nocturnal intensity, for North America, Europe, and Australasia (after Oke 1981).

It should be taken into account that the SVF depends on the specific configuration of the buildings surrounding the point for which the SVF is determined, as well as on the particular climatic conditions during the time of the measurements. When different cities are compared with respect to their SVF and the corresponding heat island intensity, as was done in the examples cited above, with each data point obtained under different climatic conditions, the results indicate a trend rather than an actual relationship between the two factors. A more-accurate evaluation of this relationship can be obtained when the SVF and temperatures are determined for *specific* points under *similar* climatic conditions.

Taha (1988) has measured by car traverse the effect of the SVF on air

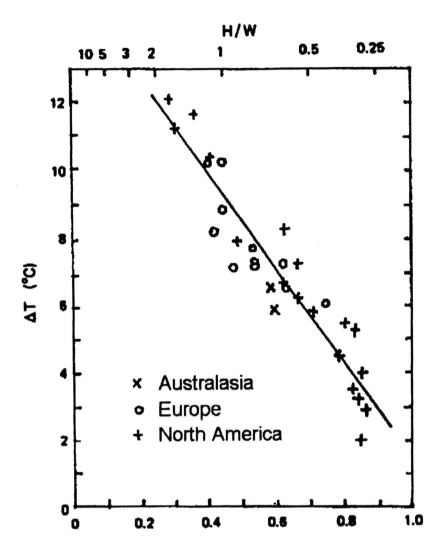

Figure 7-3. *Relationship between the SVF and the urban heat island nocturnal intensity for North America, Europe, and Australasia.*

temperatures at 126 points along nine streets forming a continuous loop in San Francisco during three clear nights. Temperatures were expressed as differences between the different points and a "control" point. At each point the SVF was evaluated from fish-eye lens photography. The range of the SVF was between 0.182 and 0.928. Measurements were taken at 1.5 meters (4.9') above ground between 8 P.M. and 2 A.M.

For each street regression calculations were performed, expressing the temperatures as a function of the SVF. The general form of the formula is:

$$T = A - b * SVF$$

The regression coefficient, b, represents the effect of the SVF on the temperature difference. It is of interest to note that the range of the regression coefficients for the measurements taken during one night, obtained for the different streets, was from 0.010 to 0.110. This ratio of 1:11 of the coefficient indicates that the SVF by itself is not a very strong predictor of the variations in the urban temperatures.

Comments on the Urban Heat Island Design-Oriented Models

The effect of the width to height (W/H) and the SVF on the *nocturnal* urban temperature was established in several experimental studies, as was summarized previously. However, the centers of large cities are characterized not only by higher buildings and relatively narrower streets but also by higher local heat generation from concentration of human activities, mechanical and electrical equipment, and transportation. Therefore the experimental studies, and the models based on them, do not enable one to separate the effects of the geometrical features from the anthropometric factors. The street width and building height are among the main features with which urban design is concerned.

The reader should note that the effect of these urban design features on the urban *daytime* temperatures may be quite different from their effect on the nighttime conditions. Larger W/H ratio and SVF enable more solar radiation to reach the street level and thus may result in higher daytime temperatures. Further elaboration on the subject of the urban heat island and its relation to urban physical features, especially their effect on the urban daytime temperatures, is presented in Chapter 8, page 286.

IMPACT OF THE NOCTURNAL URBAN HEAT ISLAND PHENOMENON ON HUMAN COMFORT, HEALTH, AND ENERGY USE IN DIFFERENT CLIMATES

The impact of the urban heat island on the comfort and health of the inhabitants, as well as on the energy consumption in the urban area for heating or cooling of buildings, may be quite different in different climatic regions and may also be different during the winter and summer seasons in a given region. A higher urban temperature will always be welcomed in winter, except for those regions which are hot or warm year-round. Therefore the heat island should not always be considered as a negative aspect of the climatic modifications occurring in an urban area.

A detailed analysis for the annual pattern of the regional climate, including the diurnal patterns in summer and winter, is needed in order to evaluate the most important effects of the urban heat island on human comfort. Concerning the diurnal patterns, it should be reminded that the temperature elevation in urban areas, as compared with the surrounding countryside, is manifested mainly during the night hours. In hot regions this factor may aggravate the negative aspects of interference with sleep and its effect on fatigue and health.

A distinction should also be made between the impact of the heat island on the comfort of people outdoors in the streets, and its effect on the indoor comfort and energy use in buildings.

The higher urban winter temperature manifested in the heat island also has significant impact on energy consumption for space heating. The energy demands of buildings for heating is roughly proportional to the amounts of degree days (DD) during the heating season. The number of degree days for any given day, $DD_{(i)}$, is customarily given by the formula:

$$DD_{(i)} = (18.3 - T_{av(o)})$$

where $T_{av(o)}$ is the outdoor average diurnal temperature. The total number at DD is the sum of $DD_{(i)}$ over the days of the heating season. Therefore the elevated urban temperature usually reduces the energy demand for heating in proportion to the reduction of the degree days in the urban area relative to the surrounding country.

In regions and seasons where heating is actually provided only in the evening and night hours, a practice common in many developing countries and even in developed countries with mild winters, the reduction in energy usage for heating is actually greater than the amount calculated on the basis of the Degree Days.

As the urban heat island is, in general, beneficial in winter and harmful in summer, its overall effect on comfort, health, and energy consumption needs some evaluation. Such evaluation cannot be exact, but from the viewpoint of urban design guidelines is nevertheless necessary, because certain design decisions will either augment or reduce the heat island effect, in both summer and winter.

The following points are relevant to this overall evaluation:

a. For people outdoors, it is easy to protect oneself from excessive cold by suitable clothing. On the other hand, there is a limit (cultural and legal) to the possibilities to take off clothing when the environment is too hot. In very hot conditions even taking off all clothing will not eliminate the heat stress, especially in hot-dry climates.
b. Heating is much more common, and less expensive, than air conditioning. Therefore the negative effects of the urban heat island in summer, for indoor

comfort and for energy use, are relatively more significant than the beneficial effects in winter. This point has an additional significance in view of the critical importance of a good restful night sleep from the aspect of health. It is particularly important in developing countries, where air conditioning is very rare and limited only to the small well-to-do segment of the population.

The term "heat island" generally has a negative connotation. It seems more appropriate, in cold climates where winters are cold and summers are comfortable, to use the term "warmth island," in order to convey the beneficial effect of the higher urban temperature. In summer, of course, the phenomenon of the urban heat island always aggravates thermal discomfort, both indoors and outdoors. In countries where the use of air conditioning is common, the heat island also increases the duration of operation of the equipment and the rate of energy consumption.

As the main manifestation of the urban heat island is during the night hours, it may have a severe effect on the ability to rest and recuperate from heat stress. This also may have severe health problems and, in extreme cases, cause even higher death rates, mainly of elderly people with cardiovascular problems. Such higher death rates were actually demonstrated in several cases of heat waves recently, in Athens, Greece. In developing countries, where heating in winter and air conditioning in summer are very rare, infant mortality may also be aggravated by thermal stress, either from heat or from cold.

THE URBAN WIND FIELD

From the viewpoint of modifying the urban climate and human comfort by urban design, modifying the urban wind conditions offers the greatest potential. The wind velocities at street level can be suppressed or increased by various urban design elements, according to the different comfort needs in different climatic regions. In particular, such urban elements as the orientation of streets with respect to the wind direction, size, height and density of buildings, distribution of high-rise buildings among low-rise ones, and so on have great impact on the urban wind conditions, as discussed in detail in Chapter 8.

The main climatological factor affecting the urban ventilation conditions is the regional wind (commonly called the gradient wind). In addition, temperature differences between the densely built-up urban core and the surrounding open country can generate centripetal (toward the center) airflow near ground level, especially during calm clear nights.

The urban wind conditions, especially near street level, have direct and pronounced effect on human health and comfort as well as on energy consumption for heating and air conditioning, and on the concentration of air pollutants. The wind conditions in the general urban area also determine the potential for ventilation of buildings as well as the wind exposure of pedestrians outside the buildings. During overheated periods a higher wind velocity can mitigate the physiological heat stress caused by the high temperature. Furthermore, the tendency of the urban temperature to be above the regional level (the heat island) diminishes as the urban wind speed increases.

On the other hand, at specific points (e.g., near high-rise buildings) the local wind speed may be very high, to a degree that it becomes troublesome, even in summer. This phenomenon is greatly affected by the high building's design details and therefore can be controlled by appropriate design.

The ventilation conditions in the urban space as a whole, and in particular in major streets with high vehicular traffic, have significant impact on the concentration of air pollutants at the street level. The higher the velocity and turbulence of the wind at street level, the greater is the mixing of the highly polluted low-level air with cleaner air flowing above the urban canopy. This mixing process and its relation to the wind speed was measured by Georgii (1970) and is shown in Figures 7-4 and 7-5.

Regional Winds

First, the structure of the wind over an open-flat country will be discussed. Then, general characteristics of the urban wind conditions, as distinguishable from the "regional" wind field in the open areas surrounding the city.

The regional "undisturbed" winds are generated by differences in the atmospheric pressure, caused by the uneven distribution of solar radiation and the resulting temperature and air density variations over the globe. The flow from the high- to the low-pressure regions is modified by the Coriolis force, resulting from the rotation of the earth, as well as by the land topography and the global distribution of land and ocean areas.

These undisturbed winds flow at a height of several hundred meters above the ground. The speed of the undisturbed winds increases slightly with height, but at a much lower rate than near the ground. This "undisturbed" flow is called the "gradient wind" and its velocity is called the "gradient velocity."

Near the ground, however, the wind experiences friction. Its speed is retarded more steeply and its turbulence increases. Even over flat open areas, the wind encounters friction by the land surface and the vegetation cover. Shrubs

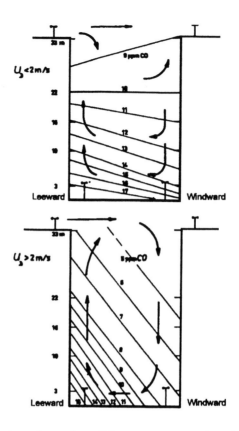

Figure 7-4. *Effect of wind speed on CO concentration (ppm) within streets. (Georgii 1970.)*

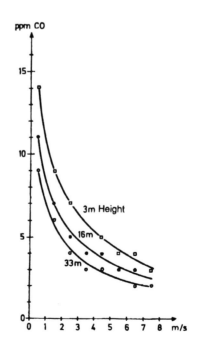

Figure 7-5. *CO concentration as a function of wind speed and height above the street. (Georgii 1970.)*

and trees further increase the friction and the retardation of the wind speed near the ground.

The street-level air velocity and turbulence conditions *depend* on the regional (gradient) wind speed, which is a climatological factor, but they are greatly *affected* by the urban design features. Consequently the street-level concentration of vehicular pollutants can also be modified by urban design.

The wind conditions within the urban area are a major factor affecting the comfort of the occupants, both in cold regions (negative effects of wind) and in warm (especially warm-humid) regions or seasons (beneficial effect of the wind). The wind conditions in the general urban area determine the potential for ventilation of buildings and the wind exposure of pedestrians outside the buildings.

The wind field is characterized by two parameters: the vertical profile of the mean wind speed and the turbulence spectrum. Both are affected and modified by the profile of the terrain and, in an urban setup, by the urban structure. Mathematical models of the wind speed vertical profile (changes with height) are presented on page 262.

General Modifications of the Wind Field by Urbanization

Of all the climatic elements the wind conditions are modified to the greatest extent by urbanization. The urban wind, more than any of the other climate elements, is the one that can be controlled and modified by *urban design*.

When wind flowing over an open area approaches the boundaries of the built-up urban area it encounters a higher "roughness" of the surface, created by the buildings. The increased resistance resulting from the higher roughness reduces the wind flow at the level of the urban canopy.

The reduced wind speeds in a built-up urban area are well documented. Landsberg (1981) mentions several cases where such reductions were measured. The roughness elements in a city are mainly buildings. They are rigid, sharp-angled (bluff) bodies. As Munn (1970) points out, they are not randomly distributed in space but are organized into city blocks, with streets forming corridors in between for the wind flow. The airflow above and around the buildings attains a lower overall airspeed and a higher turbulence, due to the friction by the buildings. Thus the urban wind field is characterized by a lower average speed but higher speed variations and turbulence, as compared with the wind flow over open country. In this way a transitional zone is created between the ground and the undisturbed wind flow above the urban air dome, the so-called "urban boundary layer."

This boundary layer is subdivided into two subzones, especially when the buildings are of the same approximate height. Within the urban canopy the wind speed is much lower than in the open country at the same height, with relatively small speed variations with height (average speed). Above the roof level there is a sharp increase in the wind speed till, at the top of the city's air dome, the wind practically regains the speed it has in the open country at the same height. The specific design details of the buildings and the streets, especially the height of the buildings relative to one another, and the orientation of the individual buildings with respect to the wind, may greatly affect the actual urban wind speed and turbulence at the street level.

In rural areas as well the wind encounters roughness elements, notably trees—but trees are not rigid, so they yield to the wind and their leaves flutter (Munn 1970). Consequently the resistance encountered by the wind near ground level is "soft" and causes less retardation and turbulence than in a densely built-up urban area.

Munn also remarks that the height of the buildings across the urban area is not constant but rises to maximum at the town's center (or even to several scattered maxima when several subcenters exist in the metropolitan area). Munn also mentions the effects of the turbulence generated by vehicles. He notes that in Detroit, at the WJBK television tower, located near an expressway, the nocturnal inversion does not usually form until traffic diminishes (about midnight), while at other comparable locations the inversion develops several hours earlier.

The wind direction in streets and between buildings is modified by their orientation relative to the regional wind direction. Under certain meteorological conditions the average urban wind speed can actually be higher than in the surrounding open country. During periods of calm, especially during clear nights, the heat island of the city generates its own airflow pattern: Warm air is rising over the city's center and flows outward; cooler air from the surrounding country converges near the ground level and flows towards the center.

Jauregui (1984) presents a table which shows urban-rural wind speed differences for Mexico City, during January and July, for several periods of the day. He shows that in the cool season and during daytime hours the urban winds were weaker than over the fringes of the city. The greatest difference was observed in the afternoons (1–7 P.M.). This, he explains, is "a result of the prevailing regional turbulence and greater surface roughness of the city" (see Table 7-1).

During the night hours, and mainly in July, the urban wind in Mexico City was *stronger*. This is explained by the development of rural inversion which reduces the near-surface rural wind speed more than the drop of the urban wind during the night. The phenomenon of higher wind speeds in urban areas during periods of light regional winds and when inversion is formed over rural areas was observed by Chow (1984) in Shanghai. The same phenomenon was also

HOURS:	JANUARY					JULY				
	CITY WIND MORE	MEAN DIFF. m/s	CITY WIND LESS	MEAN DIFF. m/s	CALM %	CITY WIND MORE	MEAN DIFF. m/s	CITY WIND LESS	MEAN DIFF. m/s	CALM %
0-12 :	18	0.7	9	1.2	73	49	0.7	5	0.4	45
13-19 :	19	0.8	74	1.8	6	61	1.0	35	0.8	1
20-23 :	36	1.1	30	1.4	32	58	0.7	23	0.9	11

observed by Lee (1979), as cited by Jauregui (1984). Munn (1970) cites Chandler (1960) who observed that "a pool of cool air accumulates over the countryside, drifting into the city intermittently when the horizontal temperature gradient exceeds some critical limit. The flow of surface air no doubt follows preferred channels such as drainage down modest slopes."

It should be pointed out that specific urban and building details can greatly increase or decrease the urban wind conditions, either intentionally or by design, according to the different human comfort objectives in different climatic regions. The main urban design elements which can modify the wind conditions are:

- The overall density of the urban area.
- Size and height of the individual buildings; existence of high-rise buildings.
- Orientation of the streets.
- Availability, size distribution, and design details of open spaces and green shelter belts.

The Vertical Profile of the Mean Wind Speed

The mean wind speed increases with height above the ground. Actually, it would be more accurate to state that the speed of the "free" wind *decreases* progressively downward as a result of friction with the earth's surface. Several empirical formulae, of different forms, have been developed to describe the variation of the mean wind speed with height (Munn 1970).

In modeling the "urban" effect on the wind speed, use is being made of models describing the vertical profile of the wind, from the "gradient" wind level down to the ground. The urban effect is expressed by modifications of the parameters of the models. A parameter used by some models, which is greatly affected by the urban structure, is the "aerodynamic roughness." The vertical wind profile is described by a logarithmic formula:

$$u(z) = ((t / p^{1/2} / k)\ln (z / z(0))$$

where:

u(z) = airspeed at height z

t = wind shear stress

p = air density

k = von karman's constant, about 0.4

z = height

z(0) = roughness parameter

Landsberg gives the following values of the roughness parameter for urban settings with three types of buildings:

	Building Type (Urban Density)		
Parameter	Low	Medium	High
Height (m)	4	20	100
Silhouette area (m²)	50	560	4000
Built-up area (m²)	2000	8000	20000
Roughness parameter (m)	0.5	0.7	10

The meaning of this model is that, at a height equal to the roughness parameter above the ground level, the wind speed is always zero, regardless of the gradient wind speed above the city. In reality, of course, this is not the case and the wind near the ground surface can be, in many cases, quite high. This point indicates the limitations of the logarithmic mathematical wind models for estimating the urban wind conditions near the ground.

A simple formula developed by Davenport (1960) is:

$$V_z / V_g = (Z / ZG)^\&$$

where:

V_z = wind speed at height Z

V_g = height where the gradient wind starts

Z = the height for which the wind speed V_z is computed.

ZG = the height at which the "gradient velocity," Vg, is first observed

& = an empirical exponent which depends on the surface roughness, stability, and temperature gradient.

Different values for ZG and & are suggested by various authors. The values given by Davenport (1960) were used by Givoni in Table 7-2. Table 7-3 shows

TABLE 7-2. VALUES OF ZG AND & GIVEN BY DAVENPORT (1965)

TERRAIN CONDITIONS	ZG (m)	&
Open country, flat coastal belts, prairie grassland, etc.	270	0.16
Wooded countryside, parkland, small towns, outskirts of large cities, rough coastal belts, etc.	390	0.28
Centers of large cities	510	0.40
Centers of very large cities with (*)	600	0.50

(*) building height over 100 meters
(Extrapolation by Givoni from figure of Davenport).

TABLE 7-3. VALUES OF ZG AND & GIVEN BY POREH AND PACIUK

TERRAIN CONDITIONS	ZG (m)	&
Open fields, desert	300	0.15
Cultivated fields, low vegetation, and scattered trees; low density rural area	400	0.20
Wooded land, urban areas with medium to high density, typical building height 10 meters (3 stories)	400	0.20
City centers, buildings of medium to high density, typical building height 30 meters (10 stories)	400	0.28

TABLE 7-4. SUGGESTED VALUES OF ZG AND & FOR VARIOUS TERRAIN CONDITIONS

TERRAIN CONDITIONS	ZG (m)	&
Open flat country, prairie, grassland	300	0.16
Low wooded land, sparse trees, rural areas, airports, meteorological stations	400	0.2
Wooded land with high trees, small towns, suburbs, urban meteorological stations	400	0.25
Medium size towns, building height up to 5 stories, medium density centers, large cities	400	0.30
Centers of cities, buildings of more than 10 stories	500	0.40
Centers of large cities, buildings of more than 30 stories	600	0.50

the values of ZG and & as determined by Poreh and Paciuk (1980). A "synthetic" table for these parameters, suggested by the author to make them more consistent for different terrain conditions, is presented in Table 7-4.

Chandler (1976) has presented a graphical illustration of the changes in the vertical wind velocity profile over urban/suburban and open rural areas according to this model. His graphic is reproduced in Figure 7-6 on page 265. It should be pointed out that the wind profile described by this "power" law does not represent the realistic wind conditions near the urban ground level—e.g., up to about 5–10 m (16.–33')—because of the high turbulent nature of the urban wind at that layer.

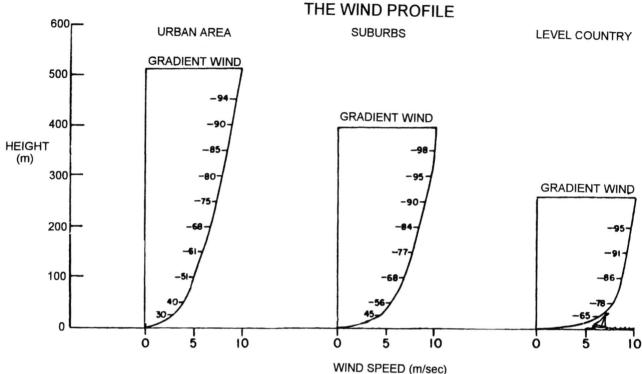

Figure 7-6. *Diagrammatic wind speed profiles above urban, rural, and sea surfaces; percentage of the gradient wind speed.*

The vertical profile of the wind depends also on the temperature profile. During clear nights, when surface radiant heat loss creates an inversion of the normal temperature profile, calms prevail near ground level while the "gradient wind" is still blowing. Above the inversion layer the wind speed increases more sharply with height than in the open country.

Munn (1970) provides data from several experimental studies of the wind profile. In several of these studies it was observed that while the wind near ground level subsided at night the wind at a height of 150 m (490') was even accelerated.

The Wind's Turbulence

The wind speed and direction, mainly near the ground, is not constant but changes constantly in time and between nearby points. The intensity of the wind's turbulence (I_g) is defined by the quadratic value of the wind speed fluctuations around the mean speed (V_{av}). Munn (1970) comments that the instantaneous values depend on the dynamic response of the anemometer used to measure the wind speed, and the averaging time also affects the value of the computed turbulence. Gould (1972) mentions that in urban areas the wind turbulence may reach about 30 percent, while in open rural areas it is about 10 percent.

The wind speed changes at a given point with time, and at the same time it changes between different points. Thus it can be defined by two scales: a length scale and a time scale. The length scale is a measure of the fluctuations of measurements taken at the *same time at different points,* while the time scale is a measure of the fluctuations of measurements at *the same point at different times*. From the urban design viewpoint the length scale is the more relevant one because it is greatly affected by design details of the buildings, the orientation of the streets, the existence of high-rise buildings, and so on.

The wind data for most cities are obtained at standard meteorological stations, which usually are located in open sites. It can be assumed that the wind speed and turbulence in the built-up sections of the cities are different from those measured at the standard stations—the wind speed may be lower and the turbulence higher.

Applicability and Limitations of the Wind Models in Urban Climatology

All the mathematical models of the vertical wind profile assume a smooth curve from the level of the gradient wind down to the ground or to the roughness parameter height. This form represents fairly well the wind speed pattern to the top of the urban canopy. Therefore such models are useful in dealing with problems of air pollution distribution in the urban air dome, as well as for dealing with problems of wind loading on high buildings (protruding above the average height of the neighboring buildings in the city).

In a city near ground level, where the turbulence created by the buildings, both horizontally and vertically, creates a very complex wind field, the situation is different with respect to the wind conditions. From the viewpoint of pedestrian comfort (or discomfort due to excessive wind speed), as well as from the building's ventilation and energy demand aspects, the wind conditions in the airspace of the *urban canopy,* and especially near the ground level, are the relevant ones. However, within the urban canopy the wind field cannot be defined by a simple smooth curve sloping down to the ground. Often the wind speed near the ground may be higher than in the middle of the space between buildings.

As was noted above, the "logarithmic" models predict a zero wind velocity at the height of the roughness parameter under any wind condition, while in reality various wind speeds, sometimes very strong, can be experienced at that level. Therefore such models are not applicable for evaluating the wind conditions within the urban canopy space.

The "power" model of Davenport (1960) does not have this theoretical limitation because it predicts a certain wind speed even very near the ground level. Thus, for example, with gradient speed of 20 m/s (4000 fpm) and gradient height of 510 m (1660') the predicted speed at a height of 0.5 m (1.64') in the center of a large city would be 1.25 m/s (250 fpm). At a height of 10 m (3.28') the predicted speed would be 4.1 m/s (820 fpm). However, quantitatively, the predicted vertical distribution of airspeeds seems to be unrepresentative of the real situation.

In fact, the possibility of defining a representative and meaningful "urban wind speed" by a simple general model is questionable. While in an open area, or at a meteorological station, the measured average speed is representative of the wind conditions in the area, the situation is very different in a city.

In an urban setup the wind speed often changes by a factor three to five times over distances of a few meters, for example between a point in a street parallel to the wind and a nearby point behind the first building along a street perpendicular to the wind. Consequently, the measured wind speed depends to a very large extent on the choice of the specific points where the speed is measured.

Therefore, mathematical models predicting a "general" urban wind speed near the ground level are not very useful as design tools for planning a comfortable urban environment. It is the opinion of the author that a more-useful approach would be to develop mathematical models of the urban wind dealing with the effects of specific urban design features on the urban wind field.

URBAN RADIATION AND SUNSHINE

Any surface on Earth gains heat from solar radiation (short-wave) and loses heat by outgoing (long-wave) radiation. The incoming solar radiation, when absorbed by any "dry" surface during the daytime hours, is converted into heat and elevates the surface's temperature. The solar energy absorbed by plants' leaves and in moist surfaces is partly converted into latent heat by the process of evaporation and thus results in a smaller temperature elevation. The heat loss by outgoing long-wave radiation to the sky is a continuous process, taking place day and night. The solar heat gain takes place, of course, only during the daytime.

The incoming solar radiation is ultimately subdivided into two fractions: the radiation which is absorbed at some point and converted into heat, sensible and/or latent, and the radiation which is reflected away towards the sky, without any effect on the temperature and humidity conditions of the environment. In an open country the absorption of solar radiation takes place near the ground level, but, in a densely built-up urban area with high buildings, a significant portion of the solar radiation impinges and is absorbed at some distance from the ground level.

This vertical distribution of the solar radiation creates, in a densely built-up area and during periods without strong winds, a potential for daytime temperature inversion—the temperature near the ground may be cooler than the air temperature above the buildings, as was observed by the author in Seville, Spain (see Chapter 5, page 288). Daytime winds near the ground reduce this temperature stratification.

The *long-wave* radiant heat loss is a major cooling factor of an area, whether an open country or urban, when the urban canopy is considered as a whole. However, the magnitude of the long-wave radiant heat loss from surfaces near the ground level can be very different in an open country and a densely built-up area. This is one of the major factors which generate the differences between the urban and country areas' climatic conditions. The relative role of the long-wave radiation in the rate of nocturnal cooling of a given area depends on the ambient wind speed. In still-air conditions radiation is the main source of heat loss, while during windy nights convective heat loss may be more important.

The net balance between the solar heat gain and the long-wave heat loss is different in an urban area as compared with an open country.

In a densely built-up area, when the wind subsides at night, natural convection along the walls may become the major component of the heat loss from walls of high buildings in areas where the sky view is restricted.

Radiation Balance in an "Open Country" Area

The solar radiation reaching an open country area, often fully or partly covered by trees and other types of vegetation, is partitioned into several components.

a. Radiation falling on vegetation is absorbed mostly by the leaves, which have a very high absorption coefficient for solar radiation (about 0.8). However, instead of raising the temperature of the leaves the energy is mostly "spent" in the process of evapotranspiration of water from the leaves. Thus an increase in the humidity occurs instead of an elevation of temperature.

b. The radiation which impinges on the soil surface is also partly absorbed and partly reflected, according to the solar absorption coefficient of the soil, which in turn depends on its color. This coefficient may range from about 0.4 for sand to about 0.8 for dark loam soil.

The absorbed radiation raises the temperature of the soil surface. To the extent that free moisture is available in the soil, which is common in rural areas (except in deserts), part of the energy is spent in evaporation of water from the soil, thus reducing the temperature elevation of the surface. Another part of the absorbed radiation is conducted from the soil's surface, down to deeper layers. This heat usually flows back to the surface during the night hours, reducing the rate of cooling caused by the long-wave radiant heat loss. The radiation which is not absorbed either in the vegetation or in the soil is reflected back toward the sky without any effect on the temperatures and humidity near the ground.

The amount of solar radiation impinging on a given area varies in a cyclic pattern, having a maximum value in summer and a minimum value in winter. Quantitatively it depends on the latitude and sky clearness (cloudiness) of the place in question.

Long-wave radiant energy is continuously emitted from the soil surface and the leaves of the vegetation. The amount of the emitted radiation depends on the surface temperature of the soil and the leaves. Therefore it too has a maximum value in summer and a minimum value in winter.

The balance between the impinging solar radiation and the emitted long-wave radiation depends on the season. It is positive in summer (solar radiation is higher than long-wave emission) and is negative in winter.

Radiation Balance in Built-Up Urban Areas

The overall amount of solar radiation reaching the urban dome is essentially the same as that reaching an open field in the country. Sometimes, in the case of very polluted urban air, some of the impinging radiation is reflected from, and absorbed within, the air volume of the urban dome above the urban canopy, so that less solar radiation reaches the built-up canopy, as compared with the radiation reaching the ground in the country. This effect of urban pollution is expressed quantitatively by a parameter termed "the extinction coefficient."

In a densely built-up urban space the path of the solar radiation impinging on the buildings is complex. A significant part of the incoming solar radiation impinges on roofs, high above the ground level. Another significant part hits vertical surfaces—the walls of buildings. Only a relatively small part reaches the ground level. The taller the buildings, and the smaller the distances between them, the less solar radiation hits the ground level in the streets and other open areas between the buildings.

The radiation falling on the vertical walls is partly reflected, mostly towards other walls of nearby buildings, and is partly absorbed at the walls' surfaces. The percentage of solar radiation bouncing off the walls can vary greatly, from about 20 to 80 percent, depending upon the exterior color of these walls. In an urban area, a great part of these bounced-off rays hits walls of adjacent buildings. This begins the process of radiation bouncing back and forth a number of times between the walls of different buildings. At the end of this process, in a densely built-up urban area, only a small part of the solar radiation impinging on walls is reflected upward to the sky, while most of it is absorbed in the walls of the buildings, regardless of the color of the walls, to be released back into the urban dome in the evening and night hours.

The walls and the ground surfaces lose heat via long-wave radiation to the sky. The intensity of this radiant heat loss depends upon the section of the sky toward which the radiation is discharged, or, in other words, the fraction of the sky which the wall, or the street, "sees." Even in the case of a lone building standing in an open area, a wall sees and exchanges radiation with only half of the sky dome. Therefore, the outgoing long-wave radiation from a vertical wall is less than one-half of that emitted from a roof in a similar area. Under urban conditions most of the sky dome seen by a wall is blocked by other buildings. Therefore, the long-wave radiant exchange between walls does not result in a significant radiant heat loss. As a result, the radiant loss by the combination of reflected solar radiation and emitted outgoing long-wave radiation from within the urban canopy is much smaller than the radiant loss from an open space.

It should be pointed out that the overall long-wave radiation emitted from the urban canopy is about the same as that from an open field, but most of the radiation emitted from walls or the ground, in a densely built-up area, is reabsorbed by other walls. The relatively unobstructed long-wave radiation emitted from roofs has very little effect on the conditions at the street level. Consequently, the long-wave radiant loss in a densely built-up urban area results in but little cooling effect of the space near the ground level.

The radiant heat loss is the principal factor in the cooling process of the ground, and the air near the ground, at night, when the winds usually subside. The result of the reduced effective discharge of radiation from the urban space below the roofs' level is expressed primarily in the slower cooling rate of the urban area during the night hours, in comparison with an open country. The higher and more dense the built-up area is, the slower the rate of nighttime cooling. This is one of the major factors causing the urban heat island, as discussed above.

Part of the solar radiation hits the roofs of buildings and thus does not have direct effect on the *local* ground, and the near-ground air, temperatures. The magnitude of the effect of the solar radiation striking the roofs depends, on one hand, on the percentage of the urban area which is covered by buildings and, on the other hand, by the colors (albedo) of the roofs. The amount of solar radiation which is either absorbed in the roofs or reflected off toward the sky depends upon the color of the roofs, and thus varies greatly. The reflected solar radiation can range from 80 percent in the case of white-painted roofs, to only 20 percent in the case of black-tarred roofs.

The absorbed radiation may not affect the temperature near the ground in the immediate proximity to the building where it is absorbed, but it elevates the temperature of the urban air dome and thus the ambient temperature around buildings downwind.

When most of the urban buildings are of about the same height, the emission of long-wave radiation from the roofs is like that from an open area, and the intensity of the radiant loss is maximized. When the buildings are of different heights, however, the walls of the higher buildings absorb part of the reflected and emitted radiation and block part of the sky, thus reducing the amount of solar reflection and long-wave emission from the roofs of the lower buildings. The result is a reduction of the overall radiant heat loss from within the urban canopy.

The differences in the radiation balance between urban and rural areas directly influence the comfort of people in the streets and open areas, especially in summer in hot regions. During the daytime, exposure to solar radiation is often the major heat stress in a rural area. In a city, however, where a person staying outdoors is less exposed to direct solar radiation, the thermal load, with similar air temperatures, is mostly due to the lower wind speed. During the evening hours, a person standing out of doors at ground level in a built-up urban area can discharge less heat by long-wave radiation to the sky and thus is exposed to a higher heat load than a person in an open field.

In summary it should be pointed out that the overall amount of solar energy absorbed within the urban canopy is not higher, and may be even lower, than the amount of solar energy absorbed in a green, vegetation-covered, open country area. The main difference is in the thermal results of the absorbed radiation.

In the open country a significant part of the absorbed solar radiation is transformed into latent heat, in the processes of evapotranspiration from the leaves of trees, shrubs, and grass (except, of course, in desert areas). Only the remaining part is converted into sensible heat and results in temperature elevation.

In an urban area, however, most of the absorbed solar radiation is converted ultimately into sensible heat, which raises the air temperature and, during the night, contributes to the heat island effect.

The reduced long-wave radiant heat loss near the ground in an urban area may be a more significant factor in the development of the nocturnal heat island than the modifications in the solar energy absorption. This explains the occurrence of the maximum urban temperature elevations during clear nights.

Effect of Urban Air Pollution on Sunshine

Urbanization usually leads to an increase in air pollution from various sources such as industry, vehicular traffic, and domestic heating. This last source has a clear annual pattern: maximum in winter and minimum during the summer months, a fact which enabled the identification of the effect of a single pollution source on the urban level of sunshine.

Georgii (1970) cites data of Chandler (1965) on the average sunshine in London for the period 1921–1950. During this period the common fuel for space heating in London was low-cost coal, producing high emission of smoke. This data is reproduced in Table 7-5, showing differences in hours of sunshine per day between inner London, outer suburbs, and the surrounding country.

In July there was practically no difference between the different locations, while in January there was a systematic decrease in sunshine from the surrounding country toward central London, where the duration of sunshine was cut to about 50 percent, compared with the surrounding countryside. The difference between the spatial distribution of sunshine in winter and in summer clearly reflects the effect of smoke emission in winter from domestic heating plants, whose concentration increases with urban density, on the availability of sunshine.

In 1956 the city of London enacted the Clean Air Act. Jenkins (1970) provides data on the annual distribution of sunshine in London's center and two country locations during the period 1958–1967, expressed as a percentage of

TABLE 7-5. AVERAGES OF BRIGHT SUNSHINE, LONDON 1921–1950
(GEORGII, 1970, CHANDLER, 1965)

	HOURS PER DAY		
	JANUARY	JULY	YEAR
Surrounding country	1.7	6.6	4.3
Outer suburbs	1.4	6.5	4.1
Inner high-level suburbs	1.3	6.3	4.1
Inner low-level suburbs	1.3	6.3	4.0
Central London	0.8	6.2	3.6

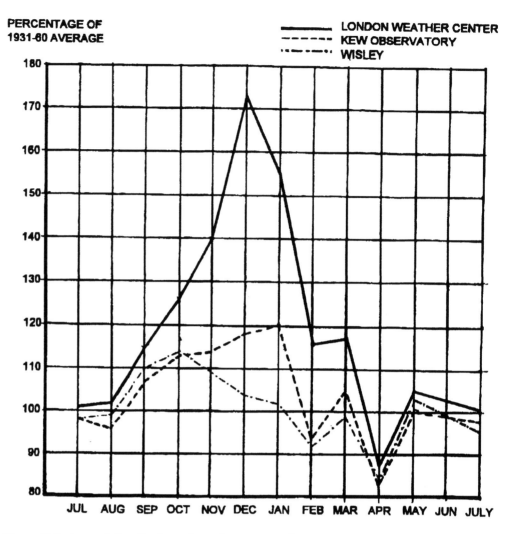

PERCENTAGE OF
1931-60 AVERAGE

LONDON WEATHER CENTER
KEW OBSERVATORY
WISLEY

180
170
160
150
140
130
120
110
100
90
80

JUL AUG SEP OCT NOV DEC JAN FEB MAR APR MAY JUN JULY

Figure 7-7. *Annual distribution of sunshine in London's center and two country locations during the period 1958–1967 (after cleanup), as percent of the 1931–1960 average (before cleanup). (Georgii 1970.)*

the 1931–1960 average. His data are shown in Figure 7-7. It can be seen from Figure 7-7 that during the summer there was very little difference in the available sunshine at the three places. In winter, however, the duration of sunshine in central London increased substantially, by about 50 percent. This increase seems to be a result of the decrease in smoke emission following the Clean Air Act.

The improvement of the sunshine conditions in London also illustrates the potential of public policy to control and improve the urban climate.

REFERENCES

Bornstein, R.D. 1984. Urban Climate Models: Nature, Limitations and Applications. In pp. 237–276. Proc. Technical Conference in Mexico City: Urban Climatology and its Applications with Special Regard to Tropical Areas WMO-No. 652. World Meteorological Organization: Geneva, Switzerland.

Chandler, T.J. 1960. Wind as a Factor of Urban Temperature—A Survey of Northeast London. *Weather* 15 (x):204–213.

Chandler, T.J. 1965. *The Climate of London.* London: Hutchinson & Co.

Chandler, T.J. 1976. Urban Climatology and Its Relevance To Urban Design. Technical Note No. 149. World Meteorological Organization: Geneva, Switzerland.

Chow, Shu Djen. 1984. "Some Aspects of the Urban Climate in Shanghai." *World Meteorological Organization* 1986, 87–109.

Copra, K.P., and W.M. Pritchart. 1972. Urban Shopping Centers as Heat Islands. Proc. Conference on Urban Environment and Second Conference on Bio-Meteorology. October 31–November 2, 1972, Philadelphia. 139–143.

Davenport, A.G. 1960. Wind Loads on Structures. Technical Paper No. 88, National Research Council, Ottawa, Canada.

Georgii, H.W. 1970. "The Effect of Air Pollution on Urban Climates." In Urban Climates, Technical Note No. 108. World Meteorological Organization: Geneva, Switzerland, 214–237.

Givoni, B., and Goldman, R.F. 1973. Predicting Effect of Heat Acclimatization on Heart Rate and Rectal Temperature. *Journal of Applied Physiology* 35 (x):875–879.

Gould, B.J. 1972. Architectural Aerodynamics. *The Architect* (July) 69–71.

Jauregui, E. 1984. The Urban Climate of Mexico City. In Proc. Technical Conference in Mexico City: Urban Climatology and its Applications with Special Regard to Tropical Areas WMO-No. 652, World Meteorological Organization: Geneva, Switzerland. 1986, 63–86.

Jenkins, J. 1970. Increase in Average of Sunshine in Central London. In Urban Climates, Technical Note No. 108. World Meteorological Organization: Geneva, Switzerland. 292–294.

Landsberg, H.E. 1981. "The Urban Climate." *Int. Geophys. Ser., 28,* Academic Press, N.Y.

Lee, D. 1979. "Contrasts in Warming and Cooling Rates at an Urban and Rural Site." *Weather* 24, 60–66.

Ludwig, F.L. 1970. *Urban Temperature Fields in Urban Climates,* (W.M.O.) Technical Note No. 108. 80–107.

Munn, R.E. 1970. Airflow in Urban Areas. In 15–39. Urban Climates, Technical Note No. 108. World Meteorological Organization: Geneva, Switzerland.

Norwine, J.R. 1972. Heat Island Properties of an Enclosed Multi-level Suburban Shopping Center. Proc. Conference on Urban Environment and Second Biometeorology. October 31–November 2, 1972. Philadelphia. 310–317.

Oke, T.R. 1976. The Distance Between Canopy and Boundary-Layer Urban Heat Island. *Atmosphere* 14 (4):268–277.

Oke, T.R. 1981. Canyon Geometry and the Nocturnal Urban Heat Island: Comparison of Scale Model and Field Observations. *Journal of Climatology* 1, 237–254.

Oke, T.R. 1982. Overview of Interactions between Settlements and their Environments. WMO Expert Meeting on Urban and Building Climatology. WCP-37, World Meteorological Organization: Geneva, Switzerland.

Oke, T.R. 1984. "Urban Climatology and the Tropical City." *World Meteorological Organization* 1986. 1–25.

Poreh, M., and Paciuk, M. 1980. "Criteria for Identifying Wind Problems in Initial Planning Stages" (Hebrew) Building Research Station, Technion, Haifa, Israel.

Sundborg, A. 1950. Local Climatological Studies of the Temperature Conditions in an Urban Area. *Tellus* 2 (x):221–231.

Taha, H. 1988. Nighttime Air Temperature and the Sky View Factor: A Case Study in San Francisco, CA. Lawrence Berkeley Laboratory Report No. 24009. Proc. Technical Conference in Mexico City: Urban Climatology and its Applications with Special Regard to Tropical Areas. WMO-No. 652. World Meteorological Organization: Geneva, Switzerland.

World Meteorological Organization (W.M.O.). 1970. Urban Climates, Technical Note No. 108. World Meteorological Organization: Geneva, Switzerland.

World Meteorological Organization (W.M.O.). 1986. Proc. Technical Conference in Mexico City: Urban Climatology and its Applications with Special Regard to Tropical Areas. WMO-No. 652. World Meteorological Organization: Geneva, Switzerland.

Chapter 8: URBAN DESIGN EFFECTS ON THE URBAN CLIMATE

INTRODUCTION

Many features of the physical structure of the city can affect the urban climate. As the structure of a city can be controlled by urban planning and design it is possible to modify the urban climate through urban policies and designs of neighborhoods and whole new cities. With such modifications it is possible to improve the comfort of the inhabitants outdoors and indoors, and to reduce the energy demand of the buildings for heating in winter and for cooling in summer.

The general effects of the following physical features of an urban area on its climate will be discussed in this chapter:

- The location of a town within a region
- Size of towns
- Density of the built-up area
- Land coverage
- Height of buildings
- Orientation and width of the streets
- Subdivision of the building lots
- Special design details of the buildings which affect the outdoor conditions

The effect of parks and other green areas on the urban climate will be discussed in Chapter 9. Recommendations for specific design features in different climates will be presented in the third part of this book: Building and Urban Design Guidelines (Chapters 10–13).

LOCATION OF A TOWN WITHIN A REGION

The location of a town within a given region may have the most permanent effect on the urban climate and the comfort of the inhabitants. Land uses may change with time, buildings and even whole neighborhoods may be demolished and rebuilt, but the *geographical location* of the town may exist for many centuries and millennia. The initial location of a new town also determines the options and direction of its expansion. An unwise locational decision at this stage, even for an initially small town, may subsequently determine the future environmental quality of a very large population.

Therefore the utmost care is advisable in considering locations of new towns. The climatic analysis of the region should form an important aspect in the overall considerations leading to a given choice of a specific location.

Different locations within a given region may vary greatly in their temperature, wind conditions, humidity, precipitation, fog, inversion prevalence, and so on. Such variations may be caused by differences in distance from the sea, altitude, direction of slopes, and the general topography of the area.

EFFECTS OF MOUNTAIN RANGES AND ALTITUDE

When humid air rises over the windward slopes of a mountain it cools down and its moisture condenses into clouds, promoting precipitation. However, as the airstream passes over the top of the mountain range it sinks down and heats up. The water droplets in the clouds evaporate and thus precipitation is prevented. Consequently, there are very sharp differences in the cloudiness, precipitation, and humidity conditions between the windward and the leeward slopes. These differences are manifested primarily in the wind speed, cloudiness, and precipitation, with the windward-facing slopes being more windy and rainy, whereas those of the other side of the ridge are arid and less windy.

Variations in altitude may cause appreciable differences in temperature over short distances, due to the changes in the air pressure. Usually, when a body of air ascends, its temperature falls 1°C (1.8°F) for every 100 m (328') of height, and when the body of air descends, its temperature rises by the same rate, (adiabatic lapse rates of heating and cooling).

The changes in the air temperature near ground level during the daytime are, however, smaller than the adiabatic lapse rate. When an air mass is ascending a terrain slope, the adiabatic cooling is compensated, in part, by heat absorption from the warmer ground. In consequence, the actual cooling rate near the ground is often only about 0.8°C (1.4°F) for each 100 m (328') of elevation in altitude.

The distance from the sea affects the air temperature. Near large bodies of water the diurnal and annual temperature ranges are smaller than in more inland areas. Therefore the summer temperatures and especially the daytime temperatures are lower near a sea. The changes are not linear. Within approximately 20 km (12.4 miles) of the sea there are great differences in the diurnal range within relatively short distances. Beyond this range the moderating effect of the sea becomes smaller. This factor, therefore, has special importance for cities located on coastal plains.

EFFECT OF LOCAL TOPOGRAPHY ON WIND CONDITIONS

Local variations in topography may affect greatly the wind conditions. Windward slopes of a hill experience much higher wind speeds than the leeward slopes. The effect of topography on local wind exposures is illustrated in Figure 8-1 (from Carmona 1984).

A flat valley surrounded by mountains may experience poor ventilation conditions, a high frequency of nightly temperature inversions, and the associated likelihood of air pollution. A narrow valley facing the wind concentrates the airflow and the inhabitants, especially in cold regions, may suffer from excessive

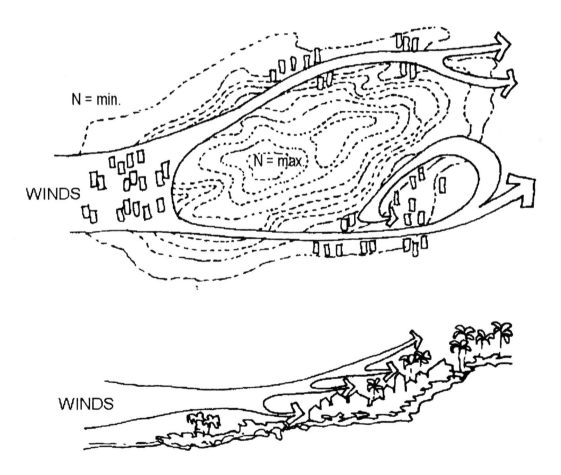

Figure 8-1. *Schematic illustration of the effect of topography on local wind exposures. (Carmona 1984.)*

wind speed. On the other hand, in warm-humid regions, where natural ventilation is essential for comfort and where the general wind speed may be rather low, such windier locations may be the desirable ones.

In long, narrow and steep valleys in mountainous areas, one frequently finds the phenomenon of katabatic winds at night. These winds are created as a result of descending air along the slopes of the mountain, cooling on contact with the earth (cooled by long-wave radiation to the sky), and draining into the valleys. These winds are usually light but, in hot areas without nighttime regional winds, they can prove to be very important for the comfort of the local residents.

COMFORT CRITERIA FOR CHOOSING LOCATIONS

The actual criteria for the choice of a location for a town within a given region depends, of course, on the nature of the climate. Hot and cold regions would have opposite objectives. For example, in a cold region one of the criteria may be protection from the winds, while in a hot region, and especially a hot-humid one, the preference would be for locations with maximum wind exposure.

When considering the location of a new town, a situation frequently arises where a place with natural economic potential, such as mineral deposits or a seashore suitable for a port, has an inhospitable climate. In many cases a town designated for the exploitation of this potential could be located at a higher altitude at some distance, in a location with a more favorable climate, and connected with the workplaces by rapid and convenient public transportation. Such a choice will ensure more comfortable rest at night for persons working in the hotter location and better living conditions for persons staying at home or working in occupations which do not require physical proximity to the natural resource.

The choice of a location with a better natural climate will thus enhance the comfort, health, and productivity of the inhabitants, shorten the length of the seasons when heating or cooling is required, and reduce the energy demand even when heating or cooling *is* being required.

It is important to remember that the natural climatic conditions of a specific site are permanent, and will affect the comfort of the local residents as long as the city exists. The choice of an uncomfortable area, climate-wise, for locating a city, not only lessens its power of attraction, especially with regard to the segment of the population able to choose freely their place of residence, but may also involve higher energy consumption and higher heating and/or cooling costs.

Heavy rainfall, accompanied by windstorms, can create very unpleasant urban climatic conditions. An advantage can be gained in many places, with respect to urban climatic conditions, by exploiting the less-rainy leeward slopes of a mountain range for urban settlement.

AGRICULTURAL LAND USES AND URBAN LOCATION CONSIDERATIONS

In many regions sharp variations in the annual precipitation can be experienced over short distances within a given region. These variations may have decisive impact on the ability to sustain rain-fed agriculture and/or natural pasture, especially in developing countries.

For example, a mountain range of even modest height, perpendicular to the wind direction during the rainy seasons, can cause sharp changes in the precipitation on its windward and leeward slopes. In many regions these sharp variations in precipitation can be observed over distances of only a few kilometers, as across the mountains of Jerusalem in Israel or across the range of hills along the Bay Area (Berkeley) in California.

This spatial distribution of precipitation is of particular relevance to urban location planning in countries which have a national policy to maximize the preservation of agricultural and pasture land. Urban development sharply raises the land value not only in the urban area but also of the rural areas around the area designated for urban development. This process creates powerful pressure from various interest groups for expansion of the urban area and conversion of land from agricultural to urban uses.

Whenever there is a choice for the location of a new town on either the windward or leeward slopes of a mountain range, where sharp differences exist in precipitation over its two sides, a leeward location may be an effective means for preventing future conversion of land suitable for agriculture to, and its use for, urban uses.

Natural Hazards in Urban Location Consideration

Many coastal areas, especially in the tropical and subtropical latitudes, are prone to tropical storms and hurricanes. These storms are accompanied by very heavy precipitation and also, along the coast, by marked elevation of the sea level, resulting from the strong onshore winds. The floods resulting from the heavy precipitation often cause widespread loss of life and property damage. Whenever variations in topography can either minimize or maximize the floods and sea-surge hazards they should be carefully considered in decisions concerning the location of new towns, or expansion of existing towns.

Valley bottoms, even shallow ones, can be reserved for discharge of the runoff water, and land uses allocated to them should be compatible with this function (e.g., grazing or green open spaces) (Davis 1984; Lyons 1984).

Davis (1984) classifies the planning means for dealing with natural hazards into three groups: Prevention, Mitigation, and Preparedness. The *urban design* means should aim, of course, to prevent natural hazards in the first place and to mitigate their impact once they occur.

Lyons (1984) suggests that in flood-prone areas villages could be raised by approximately 1–2 meters above the natural ground level, possibly in combination with digging out fishponds around the villages, which can contribute to the nutritional and economic situation of the inhabitants. A problem to consider with respect to this idea, however, is how to prevent flushing the fish out of the ponds during floods.

The issues of urban design related to hazards from floods and tropical storms are discussed in detail in Chapter 11.

EFFECT OF SIZE OF CITIES ON THE URBAN HEAT ISLAND

In large cities it is common to observe nocturnal air temperatures 3–5°C (5.4–9°F) higher than the surrounding areas and, in extreme cases, higher by up to 8°C (14.4°F). During the daytime hours, however, this difference in air temperature between the city and its surrounding area is smaller—only about 1–2 degrees—and often the daytime temperatures in a densely built-up area are lower than in the open country.

The larger and denser the city, the greater the difference in air temperature which is commonly observed between the center of the city and the surrounding area during the nights. The attempts to describe this effect quantitatively met with difficulties in expressing the size and density of the city in numerical terms. Two of the factors that cause the heat island phenomenon depend upon the size and density of the population, as well as of its standard of living (such as vehicular traffic, intensity of heating in the winter and air conditioning in the summer, and industrial plants). Other factors depend upon the size of the built-up urban area, the building density, and the planning details, such as the rate at which the area heats up by the sun, and cools at night as a result of the emitted long-wave radiation towards the sky.

The diurnal temperature patterns at any specific location in a city depend on the local conditions, with respect to the land cover by buildings and their height around the measurements' site, the nature of the ground surface (hard surfaces, lawns, trees, shade conditions), the exposure of the site to the regional wind, and so on. Depending upon these specific characteristics, any local place can be either warmer or cooler than the surrounding area and several studies have actually demonstrated that local heat islands can be developed even on a relatively small-scale urban area. More detailed discussion of the effect of buildings' density and ground cover is presented in the following section.

The warmer air above such small-scale heat islands mixes eventually with the bulk of the urban air and thus slowly elevates the "ambient air" flowing across the city downwind. Therefore, although the origins of the urban heat island may be small pockets, their effect accumulates, to produce the peak of the temperature elevation near the town's center. In most cases the density of buildings and energy-producing activities in the center of cities also increases with the size of a city. Thus there is a rational relationship between the size of a city and the intensity of the heat island in the town's center. It has been demonstrated that the combined effects of the individual heat pockets, as measured by the maximum difference between the urban center and the open country (dT), can be statistically related to the size of the population (P) of the city. The heat island decreases, however, as the regional wind (U) is stronger. Thus Oke (1982) has derived the formula:

$$dT = P^{1/4} / (4 * U)^{1/2}$$

where:

dT = heat island intensity
P = population
U = regional wind speed (m/s)

The size of a city is a parameter easy to define and to obtain. On the other hand, density of buildings, although having more-direct causal relationship to the urban heat island, is a complex urban feature and, in real cities, very difficult to be defined in a way meaningful to urban climatology. Therefore, it is convenient to substitute the city population size for its density.

CLIMATIC EFFECTS OF DENSITY OF THE BUILT-UP AREA

A given urban density can result from independent design features, which affect the urban climate in different ways such as:

- Fraction of land in a given urban area covered by buildings (land coverage)
- Distances between buildings, including streets' width
- Average height of buildings

The effect of the buildings' average height on the urban ventilation, in turn, depends greatly on the arrangements of buildings with different heights in the urban area. This is especially true of the distribution of high-rise buildings with respect to the wind direction.

The density of the various built-up areas in a city affects the local climate in each one of the discrete urban areas. By its cumulative effect the overall density determines the modification of the regional climate by urbanization. Such modifications occur mainly in the wind conditions, air temperature, radiation balance, and natural lighting, as well as in the prevalence and duration of fog and cloudiness.

Buildings modify the wind, the radiant balance, and the temperature conditions near the ground level. In particular, land covered by buildings cannot be planted. Therefore, the fraction of land covered by buildings in a given area is a relevant factor in evaluating the climatic effect of urbanization. Some architectural details of the buildings, however, especially the color (reflectivity) of their roofs, can change completely the *direction* of the effect of buildings on the urban radiant balance and temperature.

Distances between buildings, either across streets or within an urban block, greatly affect the ventilation conditions, both outdoors and indoors. The distances between buildings along the north-south axis affect the solar exposure of the buildings and the potential for daylighting and for solar energy utilization for space and water heating.

The average height of buildings, with a given density and pattern of land coverage, mainly affects the urban ventilation. With the same pattern of land coverage, higher buildings reduce the ground-level wind speed more than do lower buildings. However, the effect of the average building's height is modified by the *relative height* of the adjacent buildings. In an urban section with buildings of about the same height, the wind conditions near ground level can be quite different from those existing in an area with the same average height but with a combination of low and high buildings in close proximity.

The effect of a given density level depends to a large extent on the details of the urban physical structure. In particular, the color of the roofs and the walls (controlling reflection or absorbance of solar radiation), and the size and shape of the buildings and their relative positions (affecting the urban wind field) can modify the effect of density and even change the direction of the higher-density effect, from a heating to a cooling one. These features can be influenced by urban designers and architects in the stages of urban and building design.

Effect of Land Coverage by Buildings on Air Temperature

As described in the previous section, the temperature modifications by a city are manifested mainly in the "heat island" phenomenon, especially during calm and clear nights, when the urban air temperature is usually higher than the temperature of the surrounding open country. This temperature elevation is caused in part by the lower cooling rate of the building's mass (relative to the cooling rate of open spaces) and the release, during the night, of solar energy which was absorbed in the buildings during the day.

Higher-buildings' density often results in fewer trees and other kinds of vegetation. Plants have a lower rate of heating during the daytime and higher rate of cooling at night, as compared with building materials and other urban hard surfaces. Therefore, less vegetation often means a higher urban temperature. A detailed discussion of the effects of planted areas on the urban climate is presented in Chapter 9.

Another factor contributing to the urban heat island is the heat generated within the urban area by transportation, heating, air conditioning, cooking, and other household and industrial processes generating heat. The density of (commercial) high-rise buildings in city centers results in a concentrated heat generation from interior electrical lighting, heat exhaust by central air conditioning systems, computers, photocopiers, and fax machines, as well as from the high vehicular traffic generated by the high-density land use—factors contributing to the fact that the highest heat island intensity is usually found in the downtown centers of cities.

In the case of heat exhaust (rejection) by central air conditioning systems of high-rise buildings, the location of the rejection (condensers) may have an impact on the urban air temperature near the ground level. Low-level (in relation to the street) condensers reject the heat near the street level, increasing the discomfort of the pedestrians in summer. On the other hand, placing the condensers at roof level rejects the heat high above the streets, with minimum impact on the ground-level air temperature.

Several attempts have been made to express the intensity of the heat island as a function of a specific urban physical feature. Thus Oke (1981) has expressed the intensity of the urban heat island as a function of the Sky View Factor.

The heat island, which is mostly a nocturnal phenomenon, reflects the fact that the urban area is less sensitive than the open country area to the factors promoting a high rate of cooling at night, and therefore is more evident during still, clear nights with strong temperature inversions. Thus, one of the consequences of the heat island is the lower frequency of inversions in urban areas, as compared with the surrounding country. Within the "urban dome" lapse conditions are created at night (temperature decrease with height) below the regional inversion layer.

Regarding the daytime conditions, it is commonly assumed that urban temperatures are higher than rural ones, due to lack of vegetation and a result of the heat generated in the town, although the observed differences are smaller than at night.

However, it is possible to infer from theoretical considerations, as well as from actual measurements in and around buildings, that it might be possible to plan cities, especially in hot-dry regions, so that the ambient *daytime* air temperatures would be significantly lower than in the surrounding country. The main planning factor by which such a modification of the urban temperature seems possible is the average albedo of the whole area of the town.

A densely built area, with a large fraction of the ground covered by buildings with white roofs and walls, would reflect toward the sky most of the solar radiation—all the radiation impinging on the roofs and about one-half of the radiation impinging on the walls. Such an urban configuration can lower the air temperature near the ground below the air temperature of the open country.

The potential for lowering the urban temperature in a hot-dry climate by properly designing high-density neighborhoods is discussed in Chapter 10.

Effect of Urban Density and Building Height on Urban Ventilation

Urban density affects the ventilation conditions in the streets and thus also the potential for natural ventilation of buildings. This effect, however, depends greatly on the details of the urban physical structure. It is possible to obtain a wide range of wind conditions, even in a densely built-up area, by applying different urban design approaches. In fact, it is possible to have an urban area of higher density, obtained by a mixture of high and low buildings, with better ventilation conditions than an area with lower density but with buildings of the same height.

It is usually assumed that an increase in building density reduces the airflow in the urban area, as a result of increased friction near the ground. However, this effect depends mainly on the various physical details of urban space, including the orientation of the streets and the buildings with respect to the wind direction. It is possible therefore to have a wide range of ventilation conditions for a given level of density.

The principle factors which determine the urban density effect on the urban wind speed are the average height of buildings and the distance between them. However, the most important factor with respect to a building's height, from the urban ventilation aspect, is the *differences in the heights* of neighboring buildings. While buildings reduce the speed of the "regional wind" near ground level individual buildings rising above those around them create strong air currents in the area.

The existence of a city creates air currents of different sizes, resulting from the modified temperature in an urban area. The heat island over a city—primarily expressed as a body of hot air in and over the city area—causes a gradual rising of hot air in the center of the city, and a centripetal flow of cooler air, near the ground, from the surrounding areas towards the center. Like the heat island phenomenon itself, this airflow also occurs primarily at night, especially on clear nights without regional winds. The larger and denser the city is, the more intense these phenomena are. Munn (in WMO 1970) mentions several field measurements of airflow patterns in and around cities where this phenomenon has been observed. An example of the airflow directions, as observed around Manhattan (New York City), is reproduced from Munn in Figure 8-2.

In cities where the density pattern is not concentric, and the urban area consists of "patches" of high and low densities and with open spaces interspersed in

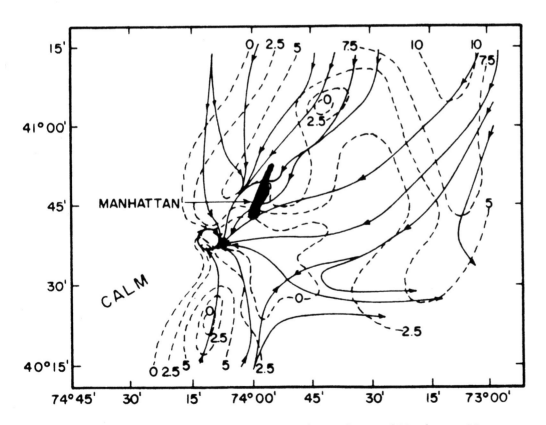

Figure 8-2. *Example of the airflow directions, as observed around Manhattan, New York City (reproduced from Munn 1970).*

between, the pattern of the urban heat island and the associated air currents is rather irregular. The complex temperature field complicates the thermally induced airflow patterns. The patterns of the thermally induced air currents are modified, of course, by the topography and by the variable friction introduced by buildings of different sizes and densities.

During the hours in which there are no regional winds, these air currents, created by the city itself, may create within the urban space nocturnal airspeeds which are stronger than in the surrounding countryside, as was actually observed in Mexico City and is shown in Table 7-1 on page 261. In hot regions it is possible to enhance these nocturnal centripetal air currents by *urban design*, by leaving open strips (e.g., open parks or wide avenues), leading from areas of low densities or outlying green open spaces toward centers of high density.

During the daytime, local wind currents are also created in the city as a result of the differential heating, by solar radiation, of walls of various colors and facing in various directions. The air coming in contact with the irradiated warmer walls (and parts of the roads) heats up and rises, and the air coming in contact with the shaded walls and cooler surfaces sinks downward and flows into the area from which the warmer air has risen. Quantitatively, however, these air currents are rather weak.

CLIMATIC IMPACTS OF STREET WIDTH AND ORIENTATION

The width of the streets determines the distance between the buildings on both sides of the street, with impacts both on the ventilation and solar utilization potential. The layout of the streets also greatly determines the ventilation potential of the buildings, as well as the outdoor ventilation conditions.

Impact of Street Width on Street-Level Daytime Temperatures

The models of the urban heat island discussed in Chapter 7 assume that narrower streets, which result in a smaller height to width (H/W) ratio and Sky View Factors, cause higher intensity of the urban heat island. It was pointed out, however, that the conventional urban heat island concept deals with the night temperatures and that the effect of street width may be quite different on the daytime temperatures. Several experimental studies support this suggestion.

In July 1988 the author took air temperature measurements during two days, at about 1 m (3.28') height, in three streets of very different widths, ranging from a wide avenue (Constitucion) to a very narrow alley (Reinoso) as well as in an urban park (Murillo), and in a large area of bare soil, in Seville, Spain. The measurements were taken with a sling psychrometer between 6 A.M. and 11 P.M. Figure 8-3 shows the patterns in the three streets with the different height-to-width ratios.

It can be seen in Figure 8-3 that in the early morning the temperature in the wide avenue was the lowest (in accordance with the urban heat island models), but during the rest of the day, especially around noon and in the afternoon hours, the temperature patterns were reversed. The highest temperature was measured in the wide modern avenue. The lowest temperature was in the very narrow alley, with a H/W ratio of about 10.

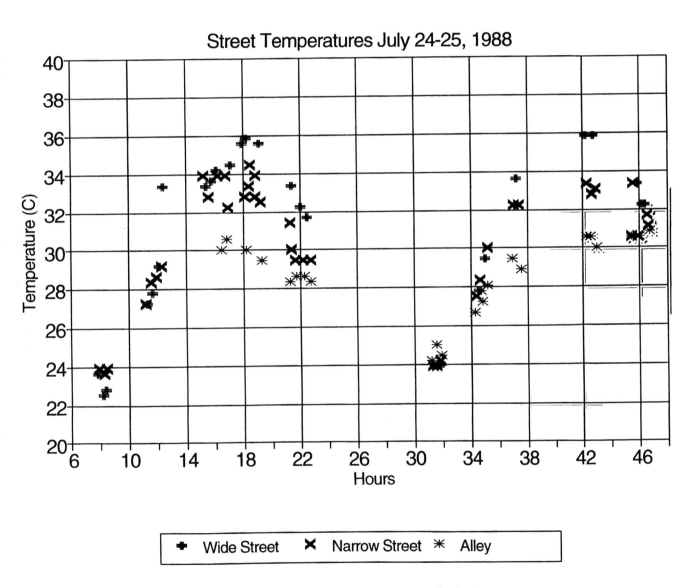

Figure 8-3. *Measurements of air temperature, at about 1 m. (33'), in Seville, Spain.*

An extensive study of the effect of street width, and the resulting solar radiation reaching the ground, was conducted by Sharlin and Hoffman (1984). They took continuous measurements at nine "stations" in the Tel Aviv area of Israel, along two traverses equidistant from the sea, over periods of 21 days in the summer of 1979 and in the winter of 1980. The nine stations were characterized by various numerical indices, each expressed as the ratio of the specific characteristic to the plot area. The most significant were found to be the ratio of the Building's Envelope area to the Site Area (BESA) and the ratio of the Permanently Shaded area around the buildings to the plot Area (PSHA). Other characteristics included the total built and paved area, green area, and estimated population, but their effect was found to be statistically not significant.

In summer both the effects of the BESA and the PSHA were significant in affecting the maximum temperatures and the daily range. In winter the effect of only the BESA was significant. Regression formulae for the mean temperatures and the daily ranges, computed from the data, were:

For the summer:

$$T_{max} = 32.93 - 0.155 * (PSHA) - 0.0061 * (BESA)$$
$$Range = 11.05 - 0.148 * (PSHA) - 0.0011 * (BESA)$$

For the winter:

$$T_{max} = 19.1 - 0.011 * (BESA)$$
$$Range = 10.7 - 0.023 * (BESA)$$

Climatic Impacts of Street Orientation and Width

The orientation of streets affects the urban climate in several ways:

- Wind conditions in the urban area as a whole;
- Sun and shade in the streets and the sidewalks;
- Solar exposure of buildings along the street;
- Ventilation potential of the buildings along the streets.

Streets' orientation determines the annual and diurnal patterns of solar radiation of the buildings along them and of the spaces between them, thus affecting the solar exposure of the buildings and the comfort of persons walking in the streets. Orientation of urban streets often determine the orientation of the buildings along the streets, which in turn affect their solar exposure and daylight conditions.

In a hot-dry climate the main objectives related to the street's layout are to provide maximum shade in summer for pedestrians and minimum solar exposure of the buildings along the streets.

Narrow streets provide better shading by buildings for pedestrians on sidewalks than wide streets. However, shade for sidewalks can be provided even in wide streets by special details of the buildings or by trees.

A north-south orientation of a street may result in an east-west orientation of buildings along and parallel to the street, which will cause unfavorable solar exposure for these buildings. From the solar exposure viewpoint an east-west street orientation is preferable.

In dust-prone areas, common in hot-dry regions, wide streets parallel to the wind direction may aggravate the dust problem in the town as a whole. As the wind direction in many of the hot-dry regions is from the west, there is a conflict between the solar and the dust considerations with respect to street orientation. This conflict can be resolved by design means aimed at suppressing the urban dust level in the *whole* city.

In hot-dry regions the main concern with regard to ventilation is to ensure the potential for ventilating the *buildings* during the evenings. To the extent that such ventilation can be ensured by the design of the buildings themselves (e.g., by use of wind catchers of some type) the street ventilation is of secondary importance, although light winds are desirable in the streets and open spaces, to mitigate the effect of solar heating. In fact, during the hot daytime hours strong winds are *not* desirable, as they promote dust generation. This problem is more common in many developing countries, where many roads may be unpaved.

Combined Impact of Street Width and Orientation on Urban Ventilation

In built-up areas there are great variations in the wind speed in the streets, as well as around and between buildings, depending on the relationship between the wind direction and the orientations of both the streets and buildings. When long rows of buildings in a city block are perpendicular to the wind direction, then shielded zones are established between the buildings, where the wind speed might be just a small fraction of the speed above the buildings' roofs, or in comparison with wind speeds in streets which are approximately parallel to the wind direction.

On the other hand, when the blocks of buildings and the streets are parallel to the wind direction, the wind can blow through spaces between the buildings and along the streets, with a smaller retardation resulting from the friction with the buildings. In this case, much higher wind speeds will be in the streets, sidewalks along the streets, and in the open spaces between the buildings. However, in this case, the buildings are exposed to about the same air pressure on both sides, a factor which reduces the potential for natural ventilation of the buildings.

A special case is when the wind is oblique to the streets and the buildings along it (assumed parallel to the streets). If the buildings are of medium height, up to about two times the width of the street, then the situation will be very different along the two sides of the streets. The wind pressure and speeds will be very different over the two sides of the buildings and along the walkways. Pedestrians on the sidewalk at the downwind side of the street will experience a much higher wind speed than the pedestrians on the sidewalk at the upwind side of the street. The reason is that along the downwind buildings a strong downward airflow will be generated by the winds, especially near junctions with cross-streets. The downwind sidewalk will be directly affected by this downflow of air, while the other sidewalk will be sheltered from the wind.

When the city streets are parallel to the direction of the wind, they create obstacle-free passageways, through which the prevailing winds can penetrate into the heart of the urban area. In this case, as the streets are wider, the airflow encounters less resistance from the buildings on the sides of the streets, thus improving the general urban ventilation. A similar phenomenon occurs when the streets lie at a small angle to the prevailing winds.

When the city streets are perpendicular to the wind direction, and the buildings lining these streets are long row buildings, the principal air current flows above the buildings. The airflow in the streets is mainly the result of a secondary air current, caused by the friction of the wind blowing above the city against the buildings lining the streets. Under these conditions, the ventilation of urban space is hardly affected by the width of the streets, within the range encountered in urban areas.

In regions where higher near-ground wind speeds are desirable this situation can be modified to a great extent by suitable placement of high-rise buildings. Such buildings create zones of high and low pressures above the built-up area, and thus generate vertical currents stirring the urban air mass.

When the streets are angled in an oblique direction of the wind, the wind is distributed between two components. The first flows in the direction of the street, but is concentrated mainly on the downwind side of the street. The second component causes pressure on the upwind side of the buildings. On the upwind side of the *street*, the air flow is gentler and a low-pressure zone surrounds the building. In this case, the widening of the streets improves the ventilation conditions both within the buildings and in the streets.

The desirability of higher or lower wind speeds depends, of course, on the climatic conditions. In general, in hot-dry regions, protection from the sun is more important than ventilation (calling often for narrow streets). In hot-humid regions the opposite may be true. In cold climates, protection from the wind may be one of the main climatic objectives of planning.

IMPACT OF URBAN DENSITY ON ENERGY DEMAND AND POTENTIAL FOR SOLAR ENERGY UTILIZATION

The effects of urban density on the total energy demand of a town are complex and conflicting. On the one hand, higher urban density promotes public transportation and reduces the needs for, and length of, trips by private cars, thereby reducing auto emissions that increases air pollution at the urban air "canopy." It also reduces the length of the streets needed to accommodate a given number of inhabitants. This, in turn, shortens the length of infrastructure facilities, such as water supply and sewage lines, reducing the energy needed for pumping, in addition to the major reduction of energy for "horizontal" transportation.

Higher urban density means also multistory, multiunit buildings, reducing the overall area of the building's envelope and the heat loss from the buildings. This leads to lower demand for heating energy in winter. However, high-rise buildings also involve elevators, thus increasing the need for electricity for the "vertical" transportation.

In cities where local sources of waste heat are available—for example, from industries or from "cogeneration" power stations—district heating and cooling (e.g., by absorption chillers) is more feasible as density is higher.

On the other hand, higher urban density, and higher and larger buildings, may impede the urban ventilation conditions and increase the need for air conditioning in summer, and increase the discomfort of the city inhabitants.

The potential for natural lighting is also generally reduced in high-density areas, increasing the need for electrical lighting and the load on air conditioning to remove the heat resulting from the electrical lighting. However, it should be pointed out that, realistically, at present most office buildings rely almost completely on electric lighting anyway, even when the potential for natural lighting exists. This practice may change in the future due to the increasing cost of electricity.

The direction of the streets in relation to the North, and their width, determines the conditions of shade and sunshine on the facades of the buildings and on the sidewalks lining the streets. This affects the temperature and sun conditions within the buildings as well as the possibilities of protecting the pedestrians from the sun on the sidewalk in summer, or of providing sunlight in the streets in winter. Narrower streets reduce sun penetration to the street level and solar impingement on buildings parallel to the street.

The orientation of the streets with respect to the North also determines in practice the orientation of the subdivision of the land into individual lots and, consequently, it affects greatly the orientation of the buildings. In this way, the street orientation has a major impact on the potential of the individual buildings to utilize solar energy for winter space heating and, to some extent, also for year-round solar heating of domestic water.

In general, streets running in a given direction promote building orientation parallel to the street. This means that the main facades of buildings along a street running from east to west are facing south and north, which of course can help in solar utilization. Therefore, the simplest approach to promoting solar utilization by town planning is to maximize street orientation in the east-west direction.

On an urban microscale density also depends on bylaws concerning minimum distances between buildings and setbacks of the buildable area from the boundaries of the individual property. These regulations can have marked effect on the effective distances between buildings and thus the density of the built-up area.

Higher density usually reduces the potential for solar energy utilization because of mutual shading by adjacent buildings. The impact of street orientation, especially in residential districts, can be modified by the details of the subdivision into individual building lots and by the regulations dealing with setbacks. Such regulatory means can promote the use of solar energy regardless of the orientation of the streets.

In order to maximize solar exposure of buildings, and to minimize shading of one building by its neighbor, the planning objective would be to increase distances between buildings in the north-south direction. For a given urban density to remain constant at a certain level it means reducing the distances between buildings in the east-west direction.

These general objectives can be "translated" into details of a "planned development" of urban areas which eliminate the need for formal subdivision into individual, separate, building lots, or into modifications of the setback regulations concerning individual lots. Following this approach the setbacks will be modified according to the orientation of the boundaries of the lots. Larger setbacks can be required from the northern and southern boundaries and smaller ones from the eastern and western boundaries, regardless of the lot's geometry with respect to the street.

URBAN DENSITY AND THE URBAN WIND FIELD

The "urban canopy," especially near the ground level, in an urban area comprised of closely spaced buildings of about the same height, is relatively sheltered from the winds which flow over the roof's level. This is a desirable situation in cold weather but may produce heat discomfort in a hot climate, particularly in a hot-humid one.

When buildings form long rows of the same height perpendicular to the direction of the wind, the distances between the buildings (within the context of an urban area with medium-to-high densities) have little effect on the speed of the wind currents between the buildings. This is due to the fact that the first row of buildings diverts the approaching wind current upwards, and the rest of the buildings behind are left in the wind "shadow" of the buildings standing in front of them.

In this situation, two separate airflow regimes are created. The regional air currents flow mainly over the tops of the buildings, while in between the buildings a secondary air current is created as a result of the friction between the upper air currents and the building. In this situation neither the distance between the buildings nor the height of the buildings themselves have great effect since most of the buildings are located in the "shadow" of the wind.

In this urban configuration the urban density has a relatively small effect, because even under low urban density conditions (low buildings with large spaces between them) the free wind flow is blocked by the buildings. The wind flow in the street penetrates slightly, in a turbulent pattern, into the spaces between the buildings. However, the width of the area subjected to this flow is quite small. The major source of the airflow in the spaces between the building is the wind flow above the roofs which, by friction, generate some turbulence in these sheltered spaces.

Streets and sidewalks parallel to the building blocks will also be shielded from the wind by the buildings, except at junctions with intersecting streets, running parallel to the wind direction.

Introducing tall buildings, which rise appreciably above the roof level of the neighboring buildings, can modify greatly the wind flow pattern and the wind speed near the streets, at the pedestrian level. The direction and quantitative effect of the high-rise buildings on the urban wind field depends greatly upon their specific locations within the urban fabric.

While addition of high buildings increases the density of the built-up area, their impact can, in effect, be to increase substantially the overall urban wind speed. However, with specific arrangements, the high-rise buildings can block the wind and reduce appreciably the wind speed in the urban area as a whole, if this is desired.

The flow pattern around a high-rise building depends on several factors:

a. The geometrical configuration of the building, expressed in the ratio of its height to its width (the H/W ratio);
b. Whether the upwind facade is flat, concave, or convex;
c. The existence of lower buildings upwind from, and on the sides of, the high-rise;
d. The wind direction with respect to the facades of the building;
e. Specific design details of the high-rise building itself.

Aynsley (1976) has described the flow patterns around a high building standing by itself: A narrow high-rise (the "tower" type) deflects most of the wind sideways. A relatively small amount of air is diverted upwards, above the roof. A turbulent circling flow is generated at the sides and with little uplift at the leeward sides of the building. As the width of the windward wall of the high-rise building increases, turning it into a "slab" type, a larger volume of air is diverted. More air is diverted over the roof, while the air diverted sideward increases only slightly.

The air diverted over the roof creates a stronger upward flow along the leeward facade, while the turbulence along the sides, and near the edges of the back wall, is in a similar pattern as occurs in the case of the "tower" type. Thus, the flow pattern along the side walls is determined mainly by the height of the building, with a secondary effect of its *width*. The flow pattern along the back wall is determined mainly by the width of the building, with only a secondary effect of its *height*.

The shape of the upwind wall can modify the flow pattern. A convex wall diverts more air to the sides and less upward and downward. It smooths the deflection of the flow and therefore reduces the resulting turbulence at the side wall and at the windward wall. On the other hand, a concave windward wall concentrates the flow along this wall, upward and downward. As a result, the turbulence increases.

Existence of lower buildings in front of the high-rise (upwind) can modify greatly the flow patterns, mainly in the space between the high-rise and the lower buildings, as discussed below.

High-Rise Buildings Located Among Lower Buildings

One of the main factors determining the effect of building density on ventilation conditions in a city is the difference in height of buildings. Under a given density condition, high buildings with large open spaces between them will have better ventilation conditions than closely spaced low buildings—approaching in the extreme a pattern similar to a lone building with open space on all sides. However, more than the average building height, it is the *difference between building heights* which affects the ventilation conditions.

Individual buildings rising high above those around them create strong air currents in the area. This phenomenon is due to the fact that the high-rise building is exposed to the main wind currents that flow above the "general" level of the urban canopy, and are stronger than those flowing through the urban canopy itself. Against the facade of the high-rise building which faces the wind, a high-pressure pocket is formed, which causes a strong downward current, and in this way mixes up the air layers near the ground between the lower buildings. In cold countries, and during the winter months in many hot countries, this current is undesirable as far as the comfort of the local residents is concerned, although it is always helpful in dispersing air pollutants which are generated near the ground from traffic.

During the summer, in warm-humid regions which often experience light winds, the stronger air currents may be welcomed for increasing the comfort level of the local residents.

PEDESTRIAN REACTIONS TO EXCESSIVELY WINDY ENVIRONMENTS

The problems which may be caused by excessive wind speeds in front of and around high-rise buildings were studied by several authors, such as Arens (1981), Penwarden (1973), Aynsley (1976), and Isyumov and Davenport (1978). Aynsley mentions three types of problems: those related to the comfort of pedestrians, those related to the high-rise building itself, and those affecting the environment around the high-rise building.

Pedestrians may experience discomfort due to the high speed and turbulent wind in front and on the sides of these buildings. In addition to the chilling effect of the wind, it causes disturbances in walking, by blowing dust and leaves, lifting dresses, blowing off hats, and so on.

The problems in the building itself range from difficulties in opening entrance doors, noises from windows and various attachments, and rain penetration due to the lifting effect of the wind over the windward facade of the upper stories and the whole leeward facade. The problems to the environment include damage to plants, downwash of chimney flues, and erosion of beaches in the case of seafront buildings.

"Historically," the recent interest in wind conditions around buildings started because of negative reactions of shoppers in commercial enterprises near high-rise buildings (Wise et al. 1965). Numerous studies, both field surveys and wind-tunnel model experiments, have been conducted to evaluate the physical airflow conditions and human responses to excessive wind speeds.

Penwarden (1973) reviewed the effects of wind on people and suggested limits to wind speeds which are either acceptable or unacceptable. He reviewed the work of Admiral Beaufort, which has established a scale of wind speed based on its observed effects.

Penwarden stresses the effect of turbulence on the subjective perception of wind discomfort and cites the work of Hunt and Poulton (1972) which suggests that the effect of a turbulent wind is manifested by an increase of the perceptible speed.

Isyumov and Davenport (1978) describe the various changes in the pedestrian level wind environment, brought about by high-rise buildings, such as:

- Accelerated winds near building corners.
- Reverse flow in front of the building.
- Turbulent airflow in the wakes behind, and at the sides of, a tall building.
- Accelerated flow through constricted areas, such as passages, arcades, and spaces under buildings on piles.
- Funnelling and conversion of airflow in spaces between buildings.

Isyumov and Davenport suggest two types of criteria for assessing the acceptability of particular pedestrian wind conditions in a planned project:

a. *Relative criteria:* Comparing the projected wind speed (obtained, for example, in a wind tunnel model testing) with winds at a location considered to have a publicly acceptable wind environment.
b. *Absolute criteria:* When the frequency of occurrence of a certain wind speed is below some acceptable level.

Arens (1981) reviews the "mechanical" effects of wind on pedestrians, ranging from disturbances of clothing and hair to resistance to walking and loss of balance. He cites additional work of Hunt et al. (1976), in which an "equivalent steady wind" (U_s) was defined as a turbulent wind, with turbulence intensity level of ($T I$), giving the same perception or safety effect as a steady wind with average speed of U.

The equivalent steady wind can be estimated by the formula:

$$U_s = U (1 + a * T I)$$

where "a" is an empirically determined coefficient.

The turbulence level ($T I$) is the relative turbulent intensity, defined as the root mean square of instantaneous deviations from the mean speed, divided by the mean speed.

Thus, for example, with an average wind speed of 4 m/s (800 fpm), a turbulence intensity T I of 0.2, and an "a" value assumed at 3.0, the perceptible wind speed, U_s, will be:

$$U_s = 4 \ (1 + 3 \times 0.2) = 6.4 \ \text{m/s} \ (1280 \ \text{fpm})$$

However, it should be noted that different studies came out with different values for the "a" coefficient, ranging from 1.5 (Isyumov and Davenport 1978), up to 4.0 (Penwarden 1973). Thus it seems that the effect of turbulence depends on the specific criterion used in its evaluation, and may depend also on the circumstances and the activities of the pedestrians.

The desirability and relative importance of higher or lower wind speeds depend, of course, on the climatic conditions. In general, in hot-dry regions protection from the sun is more important than ventilation, while in hot-humid regions the opposite may be true. In cold climates protection from the wind may be one of the main climatic objectives of planning.

As discussed earlier, the existence of tall buildings changes the airflow conditions in the streets around them. This is especially important in the case of narrow streets, with long rows of buildings, lying perpendicular to the wind direction. The proper site of tall buildings can improve, in this instance, the ventilation in both the streets and within the buildings.

Arens (1982) suggests the following design ideas for mitigating adverse wind conditions around high-rise buildings:

- Large-slab buildings should not be oriented normally to the prevailing winds.
- Circular and polygonal buildings produce reduced downflow.
- Horizontal projections break and reduce the downward airflow.
- Important pedestrian thoroughfares and entrances should not be planned at the windward corners of tall buildings.
- Vegetation may be used to absorb wind energy in pedestrian areas.

Details of the windward facades of high-rise buildings can greatly control and direct the airflow in front of them. Breaking the facade plane by strong horizontal projections, such as shading overhangs, especially in conjunction with orienting the facade at an angle to the street and the lower "row" buildings, diverts the impinging wind horizontally, reducing the downward flow.

A setback of the tower, with respect to its "base," starting about 6–10 m (20–33') above street level, can eliminate most of the downflow at the street, where it affects the pedestrians. Such a design solution still maintains the positive effect of the high-rise building on the mixing of the street-level polluted air with the clearer air from above.

SPECIAL DESIGN DETAILS OF BUILDINGS AFFECTING THE OUTDOOR CONDITIONS

Some design details of the buildings affect not only the indoor climate but also can have significant impact on the comfort of the pedestrians in the streets.

Sun and Rain Protection

In commercial and recreational centers, where a large number of people are usually found outdoors, protection of pedestrians on the sidewalks from sun and rain, as well as from excessive wind, should be considered a major urban design objective. Such protection can effectively be provided by various special details of the buildings along the streets.

Three basic design approaches can provide sun and rain protection for the pedestrians:

a. An overhang projecting away from the wall of the building along and over the sidewalk.
b. A setback of the ground floor, enlarging the width of the sidewalks with an arcade supporting the upper floors by columns.
c. A setback of the ground floor, with some of the upper floors projecting to-wards the streets.

From the viewpoint of the pedestrian protection and the quality of the street environment the effects of those three design solutions are about the same. However, from the viewpoint of the developers and owners of the buildings along the street there are important differences between them, with different prospects for resistance or acceptance.

The first design solution, an overhang projected beyond the building line, entails a given additional cost for the construction of the overhang but does not reduce the usable area of the building.

The second design solution, a setback of the ground floor to provide the sheltered area and thus also enlarging the width of the sidewalk, reduces the rentable and useable area of the first floor, without compensation to the owner. This solution can be expected to encounter the stiffest resistance and might be the most difficult to implement.

The third design solution, a setback of the ground floor with allowance for projection of some floors beyond the building line, provides economic compensation and incentive to the building's developers and owners to implement and support it.

Design solution "a" and especially "c" reduce also the wind speed at the street level by blocking the downflow of air along the windward walls lining the street. This effect would be usually welcomed in winter but in summer it might increase heat discomfort especially in hot-humid regions. In this case design solution "b," which provides sun and rain protection without reducing the street-level wind speed, might be preferable.

Thus, a comprehensive design solution would be to retract the ground floor and to project over the sidewalks only one or two stories above the ground floor, with the rest set backwards along the original buildings line or even set-back progressively with increasing height. In this way the effective sidewalk area is increased and part of it is protected from sun and rain without adverse effect on the environmental conditions in the streets.

Urban Glare Prevention

The color of the walls of the buildings in the streets affects both the natural lighting in the streets and, in sunny regions, the glare experienced by pedestrians. From the climatic aspect there may be conflicting considerations with respect to the wall's color in hot regions.

From the indoor climate viewpoint, the lighter the external color of the walls the lower the solar heat gain by the buildings. From this aspect white walls are the best. Light wall color also increases the level of the natural light in the streets.

However, white surfaces of large areas may cause glare for the pedestrian, especially in arid regions with high solar radiation. The reflected light also increases the thermal stress experienced by the pedestrians.

"Solving" these problems by having dark-colored walls would cause, of course, higher heating of the buildings thereby elevating the indoor temperature, as well as elevating the ambient air temperature, and therefore is not the proper approach. Fortunately special design details of the walls, as well as the use of vegetation, can reduce the street's glare without imposing higher heating load for the buildings and the pedestrians.

FACADE TREATMENTS TO REDUCE GLARE

Horizontal projections (e.g., overhangs over windows), which extend along the whole length of the walls, create strips of shade and thus reduce the level of the glare for the pedestrians. Also vertical "fins" create strips of vertical shades.

A facade made of small-scale "egg crates" over the wall can effectively shade the wall itself and at the same time reduce the glare in the street.

Rough surfaces, containing microscale projections and indentations, even when white, create micro patches of shade throughout the wall's surface and thus reduce the overall glare at the street level, as the "upper" surfaces of the "projections" reflect the sunlight upwards.

A scheme of the glare caused by white facades, by elements projecting out from the "thermal envelope" of the building and painted with any darker colors, is illustrated in Figure 8-4.

VEGETATION AS GLARE CONTROL

When vines cover the walls they create a surface with low reflection outward while reducing the radiation impinging on the wall itself. Thus they reduce the glare in the street without adding heat load to the buildings. It should be commented that even when the wall is covered by vegetation a white color would be beneficial in hot regions to reflect away the solar radiation which reaches the wall between and through the leaves of the plants.

An exception might be the "solar" wall (the southern wall in the Northern Hemisphere). In this case a dark wall covered by a *deciduous vine* is protected

Figure 8-4. *Facade treatments to reduce glare.*

by the leaves in summer while absorbing the solar radiations in winter, when the plants shed their leaves.

Trees along the sidewalks are also effective in reducing the reflected glare while also protecting the pedestrians from the direct sun.

REFERENCES

Arens, E.A. 1981. Designing for an Acceptable Wind Environment. *Transportation Engineering Journal* 107, 127–141.

Arens, E.A. 1982. On Considering Pedestrian Winds During Building Design. In *Wind Tunnel Modelling for Civil Engineering Applications.* New York: Cambridge University Press.

Aynsley, R.M. 1976. A Study of Airflow Through and Around Buildings. Ph.D. thesis, School of Building, University of New South Wales.

Carmona, L.S. de. 1984. "Human Comfort in the Urban Tropics." *World Meteorological Organization* 1986. 354–404.

Davis, I.R. 1984. "The Planning and Maintenance of Urban Settlements to Resist Extreme Climatic Forces." In WMO (1986). 277–310.

Hunt, J.C.R., and E.C. Poulton. 1972. Some Effects of Wind on People. Symposium on External Flows. University of Bristol, 4–6 July.

Hunt. J.C.R., E.C. Poulton, and J.C. Mumford. 1976. The Effect of Wind on People: New Criteria Based on Wind Tunnel Experiments. *Building and Environment* 11, 15–28.

Isyumov, N., and A.G. Davenport. 1978. Evaluation of the Effects of Tall Buildings on Pedestrian Level Wind Environment. Proc. American Society of Civil Engineering (ASCE) Annual Convention, Chicago, Illinois, October.

Lyons, T.J. 1984. Climatic Factors in the Siting of New Towns and Specialized Urban Facilities. In WMO (1986). 473–486.

Norwine, J.R. 1972. Heat Island Properties of an Enclosed Multi-level Suburban Shopping Center. Proc. Conference on Urban Environment and Second Conference Bio-Meteorology. October 31–November 2, 1972. Philadelphia. 310–317.

Penwarden, A.D. 1973. Acceptable Wind Speeds in Towns. *Building Science* 8 (x):259–267.

Sharlin, N., and M.E. Hoffman. 1984. The Urban Complex as a Factor in the Air-temperature Pattern in a Mediterranean Coastal Region. *Energy and Buildings* 7 (x):149–158.

Wise, A.F.E., D.E. Sexton, and M.S.T. Lillywhite. 1965. Studies of Air Flow Round Buildings. *The Architects Journal* 141, London.

World Meteorological Organization (WMO). 1986. *Urban Climatology and its Applications with Special Regard to Tropical Areas.* Proc. of the Technical Conference. Mexico City, November 1984. World Meteorological Organization: Geneva, Switzerland.

Chapter 9: IMPACT OF GREEN AREAS ON SITE AND URBAN CLIMATES*

INTRODUCTION

Urban "green" areas, both public open spaces like parks and private planted areas around buildings, can have a marked effect on many aspects of the quality of the urban environment and the richness of life in a city. The environmental conditions *within* a public urban open space may have significant impact on the comfort conditions experienced by the persons using them, and consequently on their utilization by the public, especially in places or seasons of stressful climate. The type and details of the plants around a building can affect its exposure to the sun and the wind, its indoor comfort conditions and energy use for heating in winter, and mainly for cooling in summer.

In addition to its effect on the overall urban climate and the microclimate around buildings, urban vegetation affects air pollution, level of nuisance from noise sources, social activities, aesthetic appearance, and so forth. Furthermore, green open spaces can help in shaping the development of the city and in the organization of the urban services.

---

*This chapter was published previously as a paper: Impact of Planted Areas on Urban Environmental Quality in *Atmospheric Environment, Part B: Urban Atmosphere*, vol. 25B, no. 3, 1991. It is reproduced here, in a revised format, by permission of Pergamon Press.

FUNCTIONS AND IMPACTS
OF URBAN GREEN AREAS

Green areas around buildings are effective in modifying the thermal environment to which the buildings are exposed, and hence on the thermal performance of the buildings. Some of these effects, and the design details of planted areas which can help in fulfilling the positive effects, are discussed on page 310. Experimental studies on the climatic effect of plants around buildings are summarized on page 311. The climatic and other environmental impacts of urban green areas are discussed on page 320.

The main design details of *private* planted areas affecting their contribution to the improvement of indoor and outdoor comfort and to the thermal performance of the buildings are:

- Width of the planted area around the building;
- Type of the plants: trees, shrubs, lawn, flowers, vines climbing on walls, pergolas, and so forth;
- Size and shape of trees and shrubs;
- Location of plants of different types with respect to the building.

The principal planning features of *public* urban green areas which determine their contribution to the quality of the urban environment are:

- The total size of open space available to the population;
- Division into individual parcels of the total open space;
- Distribution of the open spaces in the center and in the outskirts of the city;
- The size of the individual areas of open space and their location in relation to residential areas;
- Planning details of the open space: facilities, vegetation cover of the ground, access to the area, internal pathways.

Effects and Utilization of Urban Green Areas' Designs and Locations

Urban green areas fulfill various urban functions, calling for different design details, which may be classified as follows:

IMPROVING THE URBAN CLIMATE
- Improving the urban climate in general;
- Improving urban natural ventilation;

- Providing shade along streets in hot regions;
- Providing open areas with shade and lower temperatures in "hot" cities;
- Providing protection from cold winds in winter.

OTHER URBAN ECOLOGICAL FUNCTIONS

- Reducing air pollution from transportation, industry, heating installations, and natural dust;
- Reducing the impact of noise generated by traffic, neighbors, children at play, and so forth, in and near residential areas;
- Retention and absorption of rainwater;
- Flood control;
- Protection of natural flora and fauna.

SOCIAL/PSYCHOLOGICAL FUNCTIONS

- Providing playground(s) for children of different ages;
- Areas for sport and recreation for the youth, adults, and elderly persons. Each age group may have different needs;
- Meeting places for small groups and offering options for establishing social contacts;
- Meeting places for large gatherings and for social and cultural public activities;
- Providing a chance for isolation and escape from tensions of urban life;
- Providing aesthetic enjoyment from the landscaped areas of the city, both for the residents and for visitors;
- Providing perspectives for viewing public buildings and streets, and creating a feeling of spaciousness.

SHAPING URBAN DEVELOPMENT AND SERVICES

- Determining the direction of future urban expansion;
- Land reserve for future development and public institutions such as schools, museums, and libraries;
- Ground base for urban transportation and service systems (water, sewage, and so on);
- Increasing safety of motor traffic by open-space margins alongside roads;
- Separation between areas of incompatible land uses;
- Territorial separation between individual neighborhoods in the urban system where such separation is desirable;
- Provision of pedestrian and motorized access to various areas within the urban overall area.

DESIGN OF GREEN AREAS IN DIFFERENT CLIMATES

The information presented in this chapter is of general character. Its applications, as design guides of green areas, are presented in the specific chapters dealing with building and urban design in different climates, taking into account the characteristic climatic conditions in each region:

- Chapter 10 (hot-dry climate)
- Chapter 11 (hot-humid climate)
- Chapter 12 (cold climate)

EFFECT OF PLANTS ON THE ENVIRONMENTAL CONDITIONS

A comprehensive discussion of the role of plants in improving the environmental quality of a city is presented in Robinette (1972). It includes also numerous graphical illustrations of the climatic effects of plants. Of special interest in Robinette's book are the chapters dealing with the architectural and the engineering uses of plants (e.g., air pollution and noise control), subjects not dealt with in depth in this chapter, where the emphasis is more on the climatic impact of urban plants.

A distinction should be made between the functions and environmental effects of green areas in general, and of plants in particular, in different types of green urban areas, such as:

- Large public parks
- Small neighborhood parks
- Plants in playgrounds
- Trees along roads
- Plants around buildings

Large urban parks often have an important role in establishing the image of a city and in providing areas for large gatherings and social activities. From the climatic aspect it should be noted, however, that the range of the effect of parks on the climatic conditions within the *surrounding* built-up areas, even in the case of very large parks, is rather limited, even downwind of the parks. Therefore a distinction should be made between the effects of plants on the "overall" climate in the built-up sections of a city as a whole, and their effect, in private areas surrounding buildings, on the microclimate around the building (solar exposure, wind speed, and air and radiant temperatures).

Areas covered by plants have some common properties by which they differ from built-up and hard-surfaced unplanted areas. Leaves of plants absorb most of the solar radiation which impinges upon them. They transform a very small part of the radiant energy by photosynthesis into chemical energy, and in this way reduce somewhat the rate of heating of the urban space. But quantitatively the plants' efficiency in transforming energy is very low (1–2 percent) and therefore the thermal effect of photosynthesis (i.e., in lowering the heating effect of the absorbed radiation) can be practically discounted.

Evaporation of water from the leaves exposed to the sun "consumes" most of the absorbed solar radiation. The evaporation significantly cools the leaves and the air in contact with them and at the same time increases the humidity of the air. The importance and desirability of this factor depends on the local humidity and temperature conditions.

As a result of the evapotranspiration process the air near the ground in green areas is cooler than the air in built-up areas covered by asphalt or concrete. Furthermore, as a result of their lower temperature, the long-wave radiation emitted from leaves is lower than that emitted from the surrounding hard surfaces, and therefore human beings in green areas are subjected to lower radiant heat load.

The effect of vegetation on wind conditions depends to a great extent on the type of the vegetation, and on the details of the planting pattern. Grassy areas pose the least friction (resistance) to airflow and allow for the best possible ventilation conditions. Bushes impede the wind near the ground surface and above them, and this effect will be felt by persons staying in the area. This is desirable in cold regions and seasons, but not in hot, and especially not in hot-humid, regions.

The type and density of trees have a noticeable impact on the airflow near the ground. A densely planted row of trees may obstruct the free airflow. However, trees and shrubs can direct the wind to a desired spot (e.g., an opening serving as an inlet for ventilating a building).

A single isolated tree here and there, especially with a high stem, may concentrate the airflow below the canopy and thus improve ventilation near the ground under the tree. On the other hand, a belt or a grove of densely planted trees lower significantly the wind speed (Taha et al. 1989) and can provide good protection from wind. Therefore in stormy areas, where protection from winds is of importance, such belts can be very important as climatic control features.

CLIMATIC IMPACT OF PLANTS AROUND BUILDINGS

Plants can affect the indoor temperature and the cooling and heating loads of buildings in several ways:

a. Trees with high canopy, and pergolas near walls and windows, provide shade and reduce the solar heat gain with relatively small blockage of the wind (shading effect).

b. Vines climbing over walls, and high shrubs next to the walls, while providing shade, also reduce appreciably the wind speed next to the walls (shading and insulation effects).

c. Dense plants near the building can lower the air temperature next to the skin of the building, thus reducing the conductive and infiltration heat gains. In winter they, of course, reduce the desired solar gain and may increase walls' wetness after rains.

d. Ground cover by plants around a building reduces the reflected solar radiation and the long-wave radiation emitted toward the walls from the surrounding area, thus lowering the solar and long-wave heat gain in summer.

e. If the ambient temperature around the condenser of an air conditioning unit of a building can be lowered by plants the Coefficient of Performance (COP) of the system can be improved.

f. By reducing the wind speed around a building in winter plants can reduce the infiltration rates and the heating energy use of the building (insulation effect).

g. Plants on the southern side of a building can reduce its potential to use solar energy for heating. Plants on the western and eastern sides can provide effective protection from solar gain in summer.

When plants cover the surface of a wall their shading and insulation effects may affect the actual solar load in opposite directions. The sol-air temperature elevation and the solar heat gain are proportional to the *ratio* of the absorbed radiation to the surface coefficient. This ratio depends on the color of the walls. Consequently the effect of plants on the cooling load depends on the walls' color. In fact, it has been demonstrated that the average external surface temperature of white walls, even in a very sunny climate, is lower by about 2°C (3.6°F) than the average ambient air temperature (Givoni 1976). In such a case shading the wall by plants, which may also reduce its long-wave heat loss, may be counterproductive. This interaction between the shading and the insulation effects has not been studied at all in previous investigations.

Quantitatively, the different effects of plants depend on the density and thickness of the foliage layer and the type of the leaves of the plants. These properties change with the age of the plants and with the seasons. The seasonal changes are greatest, of course, in the case of deciduous plants.

As was demonstrated in the experimental studies summarized below, trees and shrubs around buildings can in reality lower the air and radiant temperatures next to the skin of the building and thus lower also the indoor temperature and the cooling load in hot regions or seasons. In cold regions the main advantage from plants around a building is in their ability to lower the wind speed.

Huang et al. (1987) simulated with the DOE-2.1C computer code the effects of plants on the cooling loads of buildings. They estimate that by increasing the general canopy of trees in various cities cooling loads can be reduced significantly.

EXPERIMENTAL STUDIES ON THE THERMAL EFFECT OF PLANTED AREAS

Although a lot has been written on the thermal effect of plants in urban areas, not many experimental studies were done on the subject. Some of the more significant studies which have been conducted are summarized next.

Study of the Author in Haifa, Israel

Givoni (1972) measured the air temperature and humidity in a small urban park, Benjamin Park, about 300 by 300 m (980 by 980') in size and in the east-west streets leading to and out of the park, during four successive days in July 1972, in Haifa, Israel. Five sets of measurements (traverse back and forth) were taken each day at six points, with a sling (dry and wetted) psychrometer, between 5 A.M. and 10 P.M. Points 1 and 2 were in the street west of the park, at distances of 150 and 15 m (490 and 49'), respectively, from the park. Points 3 and 4 were within the park and points 5 and 6 were in the street east of the park, at distances of 15 and 150 m (49 and 490') from the park, respectively. The vegetation of the park consisted of large olive and pine trees and beds of shrubs, with flowers and grass between them. Several small play areas for children and benches along the walkways were available for the park visitors.

During the summer the soil in the park, in the intervals between watering, is rather dry. The wind direction in the early morning is from the east, and from about 10 A.M. it is from the west. So, the street west of the park was upwind and that east of the park was downwind with respect to the park, except for the early morning. The street west of the park is a quiet residential street with some trees. The street east of the park is also residential but it is close to, and leading to, a commercial street serving also as a traffic artery.

The main objective of the study was to see if there is a difference in the temperatures inside the park and in the built-up areas around it and, if so, how far the park's effect is extending. Figure 9-1 shows the temperatures (averages of the two measurements in each traverse) measured during the four days in the different points, with different symbols for each point, and Figure 9-2 shows the averages at each point over the four days. The highest temperatures were measured at point 6, near the traffic street, apparently reflecting the effect of the vehicular traffic and suggesting that at a distance of 150 m (490') downwind there was no noticeable effect of the park. Figure 9-3 on page 314 shows average temperature patterns inside the park and at equal distances—15 and 150 m (49 and

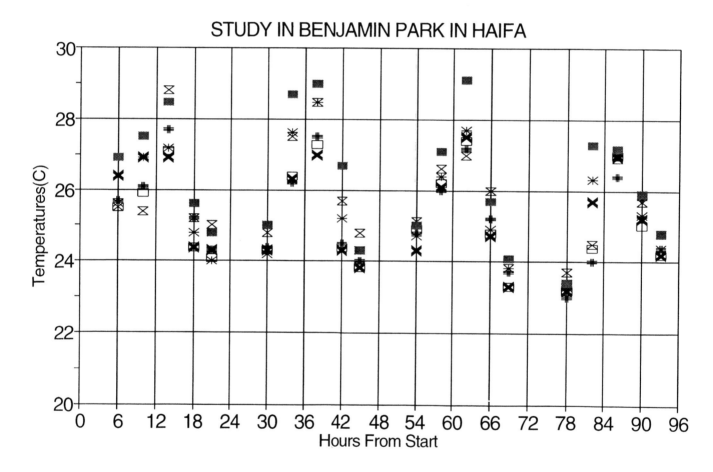

Figure 9-1. *Temperatures (averages of the two measurements in each traverse).*

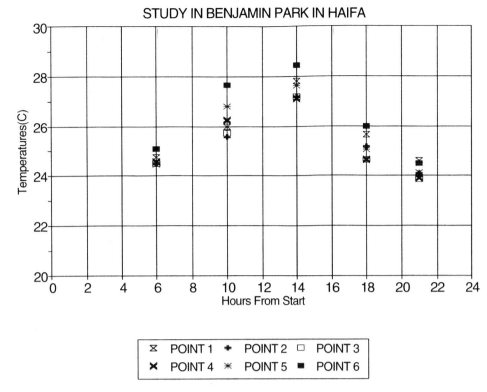

Figure 9-2. *Averages at each point (in Figure 9-1) over the four days.*

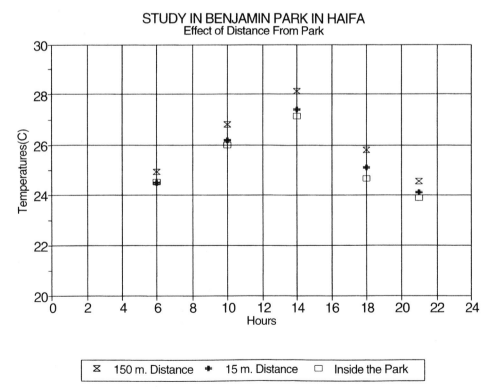

Figure 9-3. *Average temperature patterns inside the park and at equal distances—15 and 150 m (49 and 490'), respectively—from the park in the east-west streets.*

490'), respectively—from the park in the east-west streets. At midday the temperature in the park was about 1.5°C (2.7°F) below the average temperatures in the streets at a distance of 150 m (490'). Near the park, at distances of 15 m (49'), the temperatures were only slightly above the park's temperatures.

Study of Al-Hemiddi

Under the direction of the author, a UCLA graduate student, Nasser Al Hemiddi, measured the effect of surface treatments, including plant cover, on ambient temperatures (Al Hemiddi 1991). In this study the surface and air temperatures at about 1 m (3.3') height, above land areas with different ground treatments, were measured in the UCLA campus around noontime, during different periods over an entire year, for a total of about 70 days. The ground treatments included a shaded sidewalk, unshaded paved plaza, an exposed lawn, a space between a high and dense shrub fence and a building, and a parking lot.

Figure 9-4 shows the measured air temperatures during 57 days spread over the study period with each site marked differently. During clear days, especially in summer, differences in the air temperatures of up to about 3°C (5°F) were often observed between the air above exposed pavement and the space behind the shrubs. Such differences in the air temperature next to the building's skin, in addition to the shading effects of the plants, can reduce significantly the heat gain through walls and the resulting energy consumption for air conditioning. As the air conditioning load contributes to the peak load of the electrical utilities, such effects of the landscape around a building can be of significant economical value to the utilities, in addition to the reduction of the overall energy use.

Figure 9-5 shows the measured surface temperatures, which started sometime after the start of the study. The surface temperatures affect the long-wave radiant gain of persons staying outdoors. During the hottest period of the study the parking lot surface reached about 50°C (about 120°F) while the surface of the lawn was about 29°C (88°F) and that of the shaded sidewalk was about 23°C (73°F).

Studies of Parker

Parker (1983, 1987, 1989) reported on a research in Miami, Florida, in which the effect of landscaping on walls' temperatures was measured. No data were given about the walls' color. On hot sunny late-summer days the average

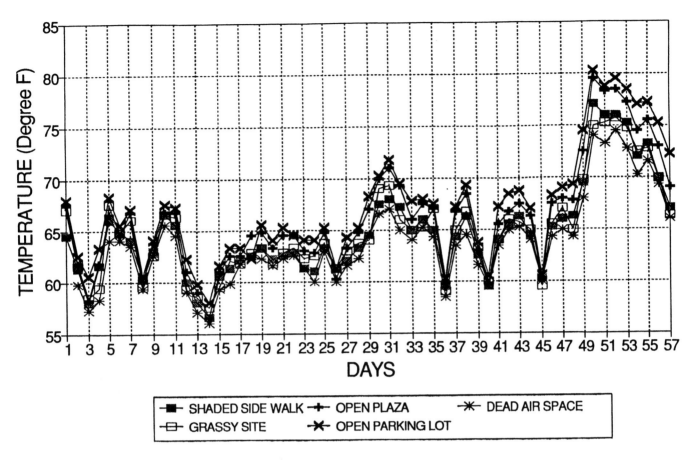

Figure 9-4. *Measured air temperatures at UCLA during 57 days, spread over a year, in sites with different ground cover.*

temperature of walls shaded by trees or by a combination of trees and shrubs was reduced by 13.5–15.5°C (24–27.5°F). Climbing vines reduced the surface temperature by 10–12°C (18–21.6°F).

Parker (1983) has also measured the effect of landscaping on cooling energy consumption. The test building was an insulated double-width mobile home serving as a children's day care center. Energy consumption by the air conditioner was compared during days with similar weather conditions in two periods—before and after landscaping. The landscaping consisted of trees and shrubs around the building. No data on the color of the building were given.

Average daily rate of energy consumption for air conditioning on hot summer days, in the period without plants' shading was 5.56 Kw and after landscaping it was reduced to 2.28 Kw. The effect of planting was even more marked during the afternoon hours (the peak load period): the average peak of energy use was reduced from 8.65 to 3.67 Kw.

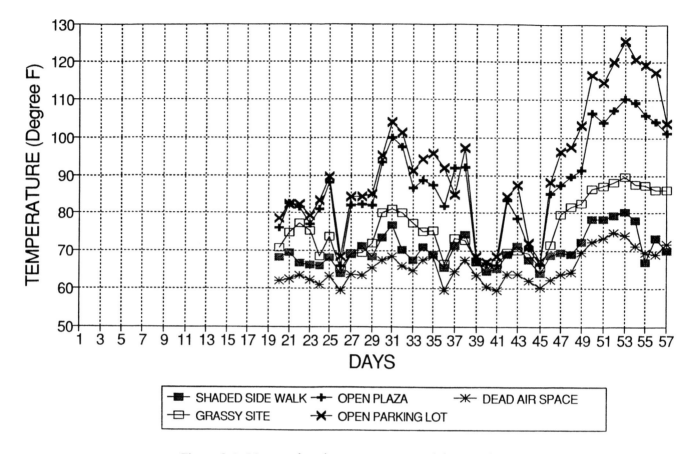

Figure 9-5. *Measured surface temperatures of the sites from Figure 9-4.*

Study of McPherson

McPherson et al. (1989) measured the effect of landscaping on the cooling energy consumption of three one-quarter-scale models of a building. The building's floor size was 3.7 x 3 m (8.4 x 5.4 ft) and the plot's size was 15.3 times 15.3 m (27.5 x 27.5 ft). The landscape treatments consisted of: (a) Bermuda grass turf around the building and no shade; (b) rock mulch around the buildings and the walls shaded by shrubs; and (c) rock mulch with neither grass nor shade. The color of the buildings and the wind conditions was not noted.

The surface temperature of grass turf around noontime was lower by about 15°C (27°F) as compared with that of the rocks. The air temperature, about 0.5 m (1.6') above the turf, was lower by about 2°C (3.6°F) than above the rocks. The model with the rock mulch consumed between 20 to 30 percent more cooling energy than the models with the turf and with the shrub's shade. The turf apparently has reduced the long-wave radiant heat gain and the ambient air temperature next to the building's skin, while the shrubs reduced the solar heat gain.

Study of DeWalle

DeWalle (1983) has measured air infiltration and heating energy use in a small mobile home in central Pennsylvania. The mobile home was first calibrated to evaluate its infiltration rate and then located at different places, either "open" or protected, at various distances from a pine tree windbreak, expressed as multiples of the windbreak height, H. Air infiltration and heating energy use were expressed as a function of the wind speed in the open and of the inside-outside temperature difference. Measured infiltration rates and heating energy were then compared with the "predicted" ones. At distances of 1 to 4H from the windbreak the airspeed was reduced by 40 to 50 percent of the undisturbed wind. The infiltration reductions were from 55 percent (at 1H) to 30 percent (at 4H and 8H). Heating energy reductions were about 20 percent (at 1H) to about 10 percent (at 4H).

Studies of Hoyano

Hoyano (1984, 1988) has conducted several experimental studies in Japan, dealing with use of plants in reducing heat gain of buildings. This section summarizes the results of his studies, mainly those dealing with the effects of plants on surface and air temperatures. The landscape types he has studied, and the observed effects of the planting, are described in more detail in Hoyano 1984 and 1988.

a. **A horizontal Wisteria pergola.** The Wisteria pergola was 15 (east-west) by 4 (north-south) (49 by 13 ft), with a height of 2.5 m (8.2 ft). The leaves produced dense multiple layers. Measurements included solar transmittance, surface temperatures of the leaves, and air temperatures under the pergola and over nearby open ground. The solar transmittance through the pergola was about 0.1–0.2 of the horizontal radiation. The leaf temperature at noon was about the same as the ambient air with solar radiation up to 400 kcal/m²h, (148 Btu/h.ft²) and about 2°C (3.6°F) above the ambient air with solar radiation of 800 kcal/m²h (295 Btu/h.ft²). The air temperature below the pergola was about the same as the air over the open ground, over a wide range of ambient air temperatures, 23 to 35°C (73.4 to 95°F).

b. **A vertical vine sunscreen in front of a veranda.** A vertical vine (Dishcloth Gourd) was installed in front of a southwest veranda of a house and a comparison was made with an unscreened veranda with the same orientation. The screen was effective in providing shade as the insolation inside the screened veranda was significantly lower than in the unscreened veranda. However, the leaf temperature was higher than the ambient air. The air temperature inside the screened veranda was higher than the ambient air but lower than inside the unscreened veranda. Thus, the heating effect caused by the reduced ventilation of the veranda's space was larger than the cooling effect of the shading.

The vertical vine screen has reduced significantly the wind speed through the window in the screened veranda and the cross-ventilation of the room behind it, as compared with the unscreened veranda. Without the screen the airspeed at the center of the window was, on the average, about 45 percent of the outdoor wind, while with the vine screen in the veranda it was about 17 percent. Thus the overall effect of a vertical screen on comfort, in a hot-humid climate, may be negative, due to the reduction of the indoor airspeed.

c. **An ivy screen covering a west wall.** The effect of a Japanese Ivy covering a bare west concrete wall was evaluated by comparing the temperatures across the wall before and after the ivy cover. Temperatures of the ivy leaves, air temperatures, and the temperatures across the wall, were measured in this study. No data on the actual color or absorptivity of the wall were given in the paper.

Without the ivy the exterior surface maximum temperature was about 10°C (18°F) above the ambient air (suggesting a medium-dark color), while with the ivy cover it was about 1°C (1.8°F) below it. The average surface temperature of the exposed wall was about 3°C, (5.4°F) while with the ivy it was only 1°C (1.8°F) above the outdoor average temperature.

d. **A row of trees in front of a wall.** In this experiment grown trees in movable pots were placed in front of a concrete western wall of a building, in different spacing arrangements. The experimental variables were the distances between the trees (45 or 65 cm) (18 or 26") and the distance between the wall and the line of trees (20 or 60 cm) (8 or 24"). All the tree arrangements reduced the heat flow into the building, as compared with an unshaded wall. The solar shading effect was larger when the distance between the wall and the trees was narrower. However, Hoyano has commented that aspects of maintenance should also be taken into account in considering the advisable distance.

e. **Rooftop turf planting.** In Hoyano 1984 models of the surface temperatures of roofs with turf (Zoysia wild) planting were compared with temperature of a roof cover by bare soil. The study was conducted over a period of one year, so that the effect of the turf was observed in summer, with green leaves, and in the winter, with dead turf leaves. In summer the average surface temperatures of both roof types, of the turf and of the bare soil, were above the average ambient air temperature. The maximum temperature of the bare soil was significantly higher than that of the turf. With radiation of about 700 kcal/m²h (260 Btu/h.ft²) the surface temperature of the green leaves was about 8°C (14.4°F) and that of the dead leaves about 12°C (21.6°F) above the coincident air temperature.

Study of Taha et al.

Taha et al. (1989) measured the air temperature and wind speed within the canopy of an isolated orchard and in the upwind and downwind open areas to the south and north of it, in Davis, California. Although the differences between the climatic conditions in an orchard and in open fields may not be the same as the differences between urban green areas and the built-up areas around them, the findings of this study are of interest.

The orchard size was 307 m long (north-south) and 150 m wide (east-west) (1006 by 490'). The canopy had covered about 30 percent of the land area and the soil was wet from irrigation. Empty fields stretched for 2 km (1.24 miles) away from the canopy. To the south of the orchard was a stream lined with a strip of tall trees and shrubs. The daytime wind was mostly from the north and the evening and night winds from the south. Air temperature and wind speed were measured at 1.5 m (4.9') above ground. Measurements were reported for three "stations" within the orchard and for two stations in each, the northern and the southern open fields (behind the strip of trees). The measurements period lasted for two weeks (October 12–25, 1986). The northernmost field station served as a control from which deviations of the temperature and wind speed at the other stations were calculated as "effects."

The average maximum temperature within the orchard was 23.9°C (75°F), while in the upwind field it was 28.3°C (82.9°F). The minimum average temperature in the orchard was higher than in the open field, 2.7 vs. 1.8°C (36.9 vs 35.2°F). The average maximum wind speed in the orchard was much lower than in the open upwind field, 3.75 m/s vs. 8.5 m/s (750 vs 1700 fpm).

The effect of the orchard also extended downwind. The average maximum temperature in the first station in the southern (downwind) field was 25.5°C (78°F) and the average minimum at the first northern station (downwind at night) was 1.8°C (35.2°F). At the furthermost downwind stations the effects of the orchard were much weaker and, in fact, the average maximum there was higher (29°C or 84.2°F) than in the upwind station.

The quantitative differences between the orchard and the open fields were affected by the cloudiness and wind conditions. In clear weather the open fields reached a maximum and minimum temperature of 28.3°C and 5°C (83 and 41°F), respectively, while the corresponding temperatures in the orchard were

26.0°C and 7.5°C (78.8 and 45.5°F). During overcast days, with much higher wind speeds, the open fields' maximum and minimum temperatures were 16 and 10°C (60.8 and 50°F), respectively, while in the orchard the corresponding temperatures were 17 and 11°C (62.6 and 51.8°F). It is not clear, however, why the maximum temperature in the orchard during cloudy days was higher than in the open fields.

Study of Canton, Cortegoso, and de Rosa

Canton, Cortegoso, and de Rosa (1994) have measured the seasonal variability of the solar radiation permeability of large and mature urban trees in Mendoza, Argentina. Measurements were taken during winter, spring, summer, and fall, in the morning and at noontime. The permeability of four species of trees was measured: Platanus acerifolia (London plane), Morus alba (White mulberry), Fraxinius excelsior (European ash), and Melia azedarach (China berry tree). Permeability of global, direct, and diffused solar radiation was evaluated separately.

On the average, summer permeability ranged from 23.1 to 40.6 percent. The winter permeability range was from 42.5 to 79.6 percent.

In discussing their results the authors of that study point out that the criterion they have used in assigning "solar friendliness" to the different tree species is having lowest permeability during the summer and highest permeability in winter. Another consideration was the correspondence between the permeability variations and the variations in monthly heating and cooling degree-days.

For the winter conditions the European ash and the White mulberry were the most "solar friendly." The China berry, even though it defoliates completely in winter, has a tight network of branches that reduces its permeability. The least "solar friendly" was the London plane.

CLIMATIC EFFECTS OF PUBLIC URBAN PARKS AND PLAYGROUNDS

From the human comfort viewpoint public parks and playgrounds in hot climates should provide ample shade in summer, and in hot-dry regions, also protection from dust. In winter, especially in cold regions, protection from the winds is important.

The effects of plants on the climate in the built-up areas depend on the fraction of "green" areas, public as well as private, relative to the whole built-up urban area. The effect of urban plants can be different, under different planting schemes, with respect to the air temperature, solar exposure of pedestrians, and the wind speed in the streets, depending on the particular choice of the plants and the details of the landscaping.

In high-density cities, where most of the land is covered by buildings and roads, and where very limited area is available for plants, the effect of plants on the air temperature may be rather small. Their main contribution to the urban climate may be in providing shade for pedestrians.

In humid regions the specific evaporation is low but vegetation is plentiful and water availability almost unlimited. In such regions the elevated humidity, and especially the reduction of wind speed near the ground are undesirable from the comfort viewpoint. This should be taken into account in the details of the plantings in parks and gardens in hot-humid regions (see Chapter 11).

In hot-dry regions the rate of evaporation from bare soil is small. However, in irrigated urban parks and gardens, water evaporation increases from the plants and soil. Therefore the effect of green areas on the urban climate within and near the "green" areas can be significant, and the effect on comfort desirable.

"Shelter belts" (a dense row of trees perpendicular to the wind main direction) on the windward side of a neighborhood can provide effective protection from high winds (in cold regions) and from dust (in desert regions), especially for low-rise buildings common in many residential areas. Robinette (1972) provides information on several studies in the then Soviet Union and in Germany, in which the effect of shelter belts on the wind speed was measured.

From the viewpoint of urban ventilation, there is no difference between specialized public green open spaces and the regular open spaces between buildings (privately owned). In this respect, even the city streets and open parking lots improve the urban ventilation.

Range and Scope of the Effects of Urban Parks

The influence of city parks and open spaces on the urban climate is limited to the conditions prevailing within these areas themselves, and extends only a short distance into the surrounding, densely built, urban area. For this reason, the contribution of parks is primarily in their function as places providing outdoor areas for rest and recreation with a pleasant climate for people visiting them or living or working near to their borders.

It seems that the size of a park, beyond a given limit, makes little difference in the climatic conditions within its boundaries and in the range of its effect.

Thus the division of the entire space allocated for parks into a large number of small parks, spread over the whole urban area, will have a greater effect on the overall urban climate, than would the creation of a small number of large parks. Likewise, open spaces outside of the city have only small effect on the climate conditions within the built-up urban area.

As the effect of public green areas on the climatic conditions around buildings in the built-up sections of a city, away from the green areas, is rather limited, their effect on ambient conditions around buildings located away from the parks, and the energy demand for heating and air conditioning, is also limited. In this respect, the effect of vegetation in private lots around buildings can be more significant, as was discussed above.

IMPACT OF GREEN SPACES ON AIR POLLUTION

The urban air contains a vast number of microscopic particles which serve as nuclei to which the gaseous discharge from automobiles and incomplete combustion adhere.

Urban green spaces have both a direct and an indirect influence on air pollution. The direct influence is through the filtration of part of the pollutants in the air by the vegetation (i.e., dust, gases, soot). The indirect influence results from the effect of open spaces, regardless of whether they contain vegetation or not, on the ventilation conditions within the city area. The urban ventilation, in turn, affects the dispersal of pollutants, mainly those resulting from motor vehicles which are generated along streets near the ground.

The filtration capacity of the vegetation increases with an increase in the leaf coverage per unit area of land. In this respect, the order of efficiency is as follows: trees, shrubs, grass. In an urban grove of trees, the principal filtration is carried out by the first rows of trees upwind. Therefore, for a given total number of trees, it is more efficient to plant them as narrow and elongated strips of trees over the open area, leaving distances between them, rather than to plant them as a single large grove.

Private gardens and private agricultural plots, within the metropolitan area, are as effective with respect to air purification, as are public parks. However, the possibility of the public to enjoy the cleaner air within the open spaces depends on public ownership of the land or at least free public access to the open spaces.

Hader 1970 summarizes the following conclusions of different studies on the distribution of dust in and out of urban green areas.

- Inside the green area, as well as on wooded land, a diminution of dust is noticeable.
- The quantity of dust content usually decreases from the weather side to the lee side of the plantation and sometimes the minimum is to be found immediately on the lee side, outside of the green area. The dust content then rises rapidly, without attaining the maximum of the weather side.

Particles falling on surfaces with no vegetation, under windless conditions, are soon swept away, while in green areas the grass retains the dust. The grass blades jutting out into the air decelerate the flow of air close to the lawn, causing particles to drop down. This so-called "lattice effect" can be increased substantially by large trees with rich foliage, because a larger volume of air will be caused to drop its dust.

Dense vegetation forming a "wall" perpendicular to the wind leads to an upward deflection of the air, which is swept over the green obstacle, carrying along fine dust and smaller particles, while the larger particles are trapped by the vegetation upon impact. The fine dust sinks down after the air overcomes the obstacle. This reduces the efficiency of green belts as filters, at least in the case of fine dust and particles. Regarding larger dust particles, measurement showed that even the fringes of woods have a notable filtering effect.

From the above observations, it can be inferred that protection from industrial pollution by green belts close to the sources is doubtful, because of the small size of the pollutants and the height of industrial chimneys. On the other hand, green belts can be effective in reducing natural dust, as well as particles generated by motor vehicles on roads and coal burning.

These conclusions are in accordance with research carried out in the Netherlands (HUD International 1973), where it has been found that air pollution is significantly reduced only within the green belt itself and in the area directly behind it. Such effect also applies to trees planted along an avenue, thus helping, to a certain extent, to clean the street air.

Since there is little or no reduction of air pollution outside the immediate vicinity of the trees, it is advisable, from the air pollution aspect, to space trees and public parks throughout the urban area rather than concentrating them in a few spots.

The effect of trees on the concentration of vehicular air pollution in urban streets, however, may sometimes be a mixed blessing. The dispersion of the pollutants depends on the wind speed at the street level and the vertical mixing of the polluted air with less-polluted air at higher levels. Dense canopies of trees along streets can reduce significantly the street-level wind speed and the vertical mixing. This effect should also be considered in planning dense tree lines along streets with a high concentration of vehicular air pollution.

PLANTED AREAS AS NOISE CONTROLS

The effect of open spaces on urban noise is usually one of inserting buffer zones between the source of the noise and the areas sensitive to noise. The buffer area can also serve for various recreational activities. The quantitative effects of such a buffer zone are influenced, however, by the detailed characteristics of the open space, such as its dimension, the type of plants' cover, and so on.

The interposition of distance between a source of noise and a sensitive area results in reductions in the noise level and may be used as an effective planning tool in the acoustical control of an urban area. However, it should be taken into account that this solution has important financial and functional drawbacks, especially in those areas where the cost of land is high. Therefore such barrier areas should also be utilized for other purposes. This is especially important in connection with the space that is to be left open along highways and streets passing through or near cities.

When an open space serves the function of a buffer zone, its potential role as a recreation area is limited due to the noise within the open area itself. Therefore, as an optimal design solution, the buffer zones should be planned so as to both maximize the noise reduction effect they have and at the same time to find additional uses, which are not very sensitive to noise, for these buffer areas. In this way the open spaces, by fulfilling additional functions, may maximize the overall benefit to the urban environment.

A major source of urban noise is from traffic along highways. The noise intensity increases with the traffic density (for a given mix of vehicles) and speed. This is a linear noise source generated at the road level. Its impact on residential areas along the highways (and other sensitive land uses) can be reduced both by distance (linear open spaces along the highways) and by linear solid barriers between the highway and the sensitive areas.

Such solid barriers can be in the form of raised strips of planted soil on both sides of a sunken highway, creating "noise shadows," thus increasing the effectiveness of the buffer zones. The planted slopes of the soil strips reduce the reflection of noise from the highway toward the built areas beyond the buffer zones and along it, as is illustrated in Figure 9-6.

Attenuation of Noise Levels by Vegetation

As summarized in a report by HUD International (1973), the relative effectiveness of plants in controlling sound levels is quite variable. The foliate density varies considerably according to the type of trees and height above the ground.

Figure 9-6. *Planted soil strips as noise protection.*

Deciduous trees will be ineffective during the winter months. In addition, when the air movement is in the direction of the listener, wind gradients caused by the obstruction of the planting may offset the advantage of the screening effect. Even with dense foliage the attenuation of sound appears to be small, especially in the middle and low frequencies, unless the plantation is very deep.

Broban (1967) gives the attenuation effect of vegetation as a function of frequency. His data show that in order to obtain significant reductions in the noise level (in the order of 10 dB), at least a 100-m-deep (328') dense vegetation is required. Robinette (1972) cites results from several studies in which noise attenuation by plants was measured. He is also suggesting design details for using vegetation as noise barriers along highways.

From these studies it may be concluded that the actual sound-reducing effect of vegetation is rather small. However, the plants may have an important psychological effect, by visually hiding the source of noise from the affected person. Trees along urban streets do not reduce the noise level in the buildings but can reduce the reverberation time in the street by sound absorption in the leaves.

SOCIAL FUNCTIONS OF URBAN PARKS

Urban parks and playgrounds fulfill a variety of social and psychological needs of the residents—for example, children's play, social meeting, recreation, and privacy. The mere existence of these parks does not automatically guarantee the creation of social ties, and without other conditions being met, the meetings occurring in these areas can be socially meaningless or even leading to intensified conflicts. However, under favorable circumstances and appropriate physical design details, the parks may help in creating a feeling of a "community" in the neighborhood.

The sociocultural functions of urban parks can be especially important in lower-income neighborhoods. While the living conditions in such areas are much inferior to those of the higher-income areas, the public parks can provide to the low-income residents opportunities for recreation and entertainment within an area with environmental quality equal to those of other urban residents.

The degree to which the parks fulfill this function depends upon the extent to which they are cultivated and contain proper facilities, and especially whether special activities take place within them. It goes without saying that the realization of these possibilities for recreation and entertainment depends upon the existence of proper facilities and involves organizational and financial efforts on the part of the responsible authorities.

The success in fulfilling the social functions by urban parks may be measured by the frequency of the visitation by those sections of the population for whom they were designed. However, the degree of participation depends also upon the existence of proper conditions. It is reasonable to assume that the more interesting and convenient opportunities there are to enjoy in the open spaces, the higher degree of participation will be.

In addition to not fully contributing to the quality of urban life, a park which people do not use attracts criminal elements to the vacuum created by the lack of use. This negative influence is radiated into the neighborhoods surrounding the park, and they in turn become undesirable dangerous areas which people try to keep distant from. Unused parks are also more liable to suffer from destruction and vandalism.

It was argued by Jacobs (1961) that the most efficient way to prevent crime in public parks is the presence of as many people in the park as possible, during all hours of the day and evening. If this point of view is correct, there will be a need for a directed planning policy concerning public parks, which aims to maximize the times and intensity of their use. Such planning should determine location of facilities and roads in the urban network, as well as planning details of the surrounding urban area, such as: land use around the park, institutions to attract persons into the area during various hours of the day, location of public transportation facilities, such as bus stations on the edges of the park, and so forth.

Parks as Social Interaction Areas Between Neighborhoods

Urban parks form areas of separation between neighborhoods adjacent to them. However, the same park may also act as a *link* between the residents of several neighborhoods, providing common services and facilities such as playgrounds, areas for rest, and passageways. As such, the park serves as a meeting place for the residents of the neighborhoods. Two possible outcomes may result from this social interaction between residents of different neighborhoods, often with different sociocultural backgrounds. On the one hand, it can provide for communication and mutual acquaintance, while on the other hand, it can contribute to the development of conflicts and competition for the use of facilities, as well as to quarrels and tensions between the neighborhoods' residents. This problem can be of great social importance when the populations of the adjacent neighborhoods are of different ethnic or socioeconomical background.

The nature of the relationships developing from encounters in the urban public parks can have a far-reaching impact on the process of population integration, especially in cities and countries with a culturally heterogenous population. These relationships are determined by a complex system of factors, which are in part derived from the demographic and socioeconomic characteristics of the population. But the resulting relationships may also be affected by the actual physical planning features of the open spaces, and thus may be affected by the design details of the parks and their facilities.

Among the various factors, which may affect the nature of the social interactions in parks, are:

1. The specific needs of different population groups, with regard to types of activities and facilities in the park.
2. The capacity of the park, from the aspect of its total area and that area given to actual usage, as well as from the aspect of type and size of the population being served.
3. Layout of facilities and types of activities in the park area, and the degree to which this layout causes mutual disturbances between the various activities.
4. In the case of large urban parks, the existence of various special public events, and their organization.

The influence of these and other factors on social interaction is not yet well understood. Research in this field might clarify whether and under what conditions it is possible to use parks as instruments for social and cultural integration.

Size and Character of the Open Spaces

Determination of the optimal size of open spaces, for a given urban area and population, is a complex problem. On the one hand, the allocation and maintenance of a large parcel of land for this purpose is a heavy financial burden even if the municipalities do not have to pay for this land. On the other hand, the size of open spaces can have a great influence on the environmental quality as well as on the quality of life in the city. Urban parks can divide areas with more pleasant climate, relatively quiet, and with cleaner air than the rest of the city. From the sociopsychological point of view they provide areas for play, rest, social meeting, isolation, aesthetic enjoyment, and so on.

Determining the area of parks according to the number of acres required for a specific population size reflects current planning methods, yet it does not deal with the functional needs of the population destined to use the park, and the degree to which the specific planned elements in the park fulfill these needs. In many developing countries, especially in hot-dry regions, this problem is even more complex than in Europe or North America, due to the fact that maintenance costs in these places are much higher, as a result of the need to irrigate in the summer, and because of the limited resources available to the municipalities.

It seems desirable to fundamentally change the basis upon which areas of urban open spaces are allocated. Instead of the "mechanical" planning procedure of determining land area according to the size of the population, it is desirable to establish a method which will enable the evaluation of the need for open spaces, aimed at fulfilling specific functions within the urban network, while striving for intensive usage of the area by the local residents. This functional approach to the determination of standards for open space allocations demands a basic knowledge of the needs of various population groups with relation to the different functions of the open spaces. These needs can express themselves in different habits of recreation, including entertainment, games, and social and family enjoyment. Research in this direction can be very useful.

REFERENCES

Al Hemiddi, N. 1991. Measurements of Surface and Air Temperatures Over Sites with Different Land Treatments. Proc., Passive and Low Energy (PLEA '91) Conference in Seville, Spain.

Broban, H.W. 1967. "Stadebauliche Grundlagen des Schallschutzes." *Deutsche Bauzeitung, 5.*

Canton, M.A., J.L. Cortegoso, and C. de Rosa. 1994. Solar Permeability of Urban Trees of Western Argentina. *Energy and Buildings 20, 219–230.*

DeWalle, D.R. 1983. Windbreak Effects on Air Infiltration and Space Heating in a Mobile House. *Energy and Buildings 5, 279–288.*

Geiger, R. 1950. *The Climate Near the Ground.* Cambridge, Massachusetts: Harvard University Press.

Givoni, B. 1972. Comparison of Temperature and Humidity Conditions in an Urban Park and in the Built-up Area Around It. Research Report (Hebrew). Building Research Station, Technion, Israel Institute of Technology, Haifa, Israel.

Givoni, B. 1976. *Man, Climate and Architecture.* New York: Van Nostrand Reinhold.

Givoni, B. 1989a. Cooling of Outdoor Spaces. Workshop on the Interface Between Physics and Architecture at the International Center of Theoretical Physics, Trieste, Italy.

Givoni, B. 1989b. *Urban Design for Different Climates.* WMO/TD-No. 346. World Meteorological Organization: Geneva, Switzerland.

Givoni, B. 1991. Impact of Planted Areas on Urban Environmental Quality—A Review. *Atmospheric Environment Part B: Urban Atmosphere.* Oxford, United Kingdom: Pergamon Press. Vol. 25B-3, 289–300.

Givoni, B., and M. Paciuk. 1973a. City Planning and the Urban Acoustic Quality. In *Town Planning and Environmental Quality, Part I.* Israeli National Council for Research and Development, Jerusalem.

Givoni, B., and M. Paciuk. 1973b. Effect of Town Planning on Urban Air Pollution. In *Town Planning and Environmental Quality, Part II.* Israeli National Council for Research and Development, Jerusalem.

Hader, F. 1970. The Climatic Influence of Green Areas, Their Properties as Air Filters and Noise Abatement Agents. Climatology and Building Conference paper in Proceedings. Commission International de Batiment, Vienna.

Highway Research Board. 1968. "Can Noise Radiation from Highways Be Reduced by Design?" Highway Research Records, 232. Washington, D.C.

Heisler, G.M. 1989. Effect of Trees on Wind and Solar Radiation in Residential Neighborhoods. Research Report. Illinois: Argonne National Laboratory.

Housing and Urban Development (HUD) International. 1973. Green Belts and Air Pollution. (The Netherlands) Information Series 21.

Hoyano, A. 1984. Effect of Rooftop Planting Layers upon Building Thermal Environment. Memoirs of the Faculty of Engineering, Kyushu University, Fukuoka, Japan. 44 (2): 135–148.

Hoyano, A. 1988. Climatological Uses of Plants for Solar Control and the Effects on the Thermal Environment of a Building. *Energy and Buildings* 11(3): 181–199.

Huang, Y.J., H. Akbary, H. Taha, and A.H. Rosenfeld. 1987. The Potential of Vegetation in Deducing Summer Cooling Loads in Residential Buildings. *J. Climate and Applied Meteorology* 26 (9): 1103–1116.

Jacobs, J. 1964. *The Life and Death of Great American Cities.* New York: Random House.

Laugel, C.H. 1971. Recherchere des Problemes Acoustiques dans la Construction des Villes et Cities Residentialles. Building Research Station, Technion, Israel Institute of Technology, Haifa, Israel.

McPherson, E.G., J.R. Simpson, and M. Livingston. 1989. Effect of Three Landscape Treatments on Residential Energy and Water Use in Tucson, AZ. *Energy and Buildings* 13 (2): 127–138.

Meier, A.K. 1990. Measured Cooling Saving From Vegetative Landscaping. Proc. ACEEE 1990 Summer Study on Energy Efficiency in Buildings—Environment, Washington, D.C. 4.133-4.143.

Parker, J.H. 1983. The Effectiveness of Vegetation on Residential Cooling. *Passive Solar Journal* 2 (2): 123–132.

Parker, J.H. 1987. The Use of Shrubs in Energy Conservation Plantings. *Landscape Journal* 6, 132–139.

Parker, J.H. 1989. The Impact of Vegetation on Air Conditioning Consumption. Proc. Conf. on Controlling the Summer Heat Island. LBL-27872. 46–52.

Robinette, G.O. 1972. *Plants/People/and Environmental Quality.* Washington, D.C.: U.S. Department of the Interior.

Schreiber, L. 1970. Larmschutz in Stadtebau, Bauverlag GMBH, Wiesbaden und Berlin.

Taha, Hader, T., H. Akbari, and A. Rosenfeld. 1989. Vegetation Canopy Micro-Climate: A Field Project in Davis, California. Berkeley, California: Lawrance Berkeley Laboratory, LBL-24593.

White, R.F. 1945. Effects of Landscape Development on the Natural Ventilation of Buildings and Their Adjacent Areas. Research report - 45, Texas Engineering Experiment Station, Austin, Texas.

Part III

Building and Urban Design Guidelines

Chapter **10:** BUILDING AND URBAN DESIGN FOR HOT-DRY REGIONS

INTRODUCTION

Hot dry regions are found in the subtropical latitudes, approximately between 15 and 30 degrees north and south of the equator, in central and western Asia, the Middle East, Africa, North and South America, and in central and northwest Australia. These regions are characterized mainly by their aridity, high summer daytime temperatures, large diurnal temperature range, and high solar radiation.

CHARACTERISTICS OF HOT-DRY REGIONS

The main common characteristic of hot-dry regions, affecting human comfort as well as urban and building design, is the combination of low humidity and high summer daytime temperature. The arid characteristics of many of the hot-dry regions are caused by descending air masses, subsequently dividing and flowing east-and-toward-the-equator, forming the Trade Winds belt, and west-and-Poles-ward, forming the Westerlies belts. In some cases the hot arid climate is caused by winds passing over mountain ranges, precipitating part of their water vapor content while rising over the windward slopes, and being heated while descending on the leeward slopes.

The aridity is accompanied by several other characteristics of importance to human comfort, urban planning, and building design. Direct solar radiation is as intense as the radiation reflected from the light-colored and bare land.

The sky is clear most of the year, promoting solar heating during the days and long-wave radiant loss during the nights. Horizontal global radiation can approach 1000 W/m² (318 Btu/h.ft²) and continuous net long-wave radiation loss can be about 100 W/m² (32 Btu/h.ft²). The result is a large diurnal temperature range, about 15–20°K (27–36°F), and sometimes even more, in summer. Air temperatures can reach in extreme cases up to 50°C (122°F), although in many hot-arid regions the typical maximum air temperature is about 35–40°C (95–104°F). Minimum temperatures in summer are about 25–30°C (77–86°F) in the hotter regions and about 18–22°C (64.4–71.6°F) in the "cooler" hot-dry ones. The ground surface temperature in summer may reach up to 70°C (158°F).

Winds are usually strong during the midday and afternoon hours, subsiding during the evening. However, some hot-dry regions experience strong winds also during the night hours.

A common feature in many hot-dry regions are dust storms, mainly during the afternoons. The dust storms constitute one of the major discomfort and nuisance factors. To a great extent, their severity and the problems they cause can be reduced by appropriate urban and building design features.

Sunlight reflection for the bare, often light-colored ground, may produce intense glare which, together with reflection from building's walls, may cause visual discomfort and significant radiant heat load for windows and walls.

In hot-dry regions the summer is the more stressful season. Therefore the design of buildings and neighborhoods should aim mainly to minimize indoor stress and maximize comfort during the summer period. However, some regions which are hot in summer may experience comfortable winters, while others may have winter temperatures well below freezing (e.g., southern New Mexico in the United States, or the high plateau of Iran). In such regions winter performance should also be considered carefully in the design of buildings and urban open spaces. Because winter temperatures vary from place to place, heating requirements may vary greatly in different hot-dry regions of the world.

These variations in the summer and winter conditions create several types of hot-dry regions. In each one of them different urban and building design principles and details would be appropriate. Therefore, although some common design features would be suitable for all types of hot-dry regions, other features should be designed with consideration of the particular characteristics of the region in question.

Hot deserts exhibit the extreme characteristics of hot-dry regions. Therefore the guidelines will be "geared" toward the hot desert environments.

DESIGN FOR COMFORT AND ENERGY CONSERVATION

While it is possible to greatly reduce energy requirements for maintaining comfortable indoor conditions in desert areas, in most cases there will still be a need for some energy input for winter heating and/or for summer cooling, as well as for the provision of household hot water supply year-round. Fortunately deserts, and hot-dry regions in general, have special characteristics which make it possible to provide most, and sometimes all, of the thermal energy requirements for heating and for cooling from natural renewable sources.

Thus energy conservation could be achieved in deserts by the complementary effects of two lines of action in housing design: minimizing the energy needs by proper building design and maximizing the use of available natural energy sources for heating and especially for cooling.

The first line of action, designing a building to minimize the energy needs for comfort, involves various aspects of housing design: neighborhood planning; type of houses; house layouts; orientation of main facades and windows; size, location, and details of window shading; color of walls and roof; building materials, and so on. All of these architectural features should be considered with a view to their impact on the thermal behavior of the building and its energy requirements.

The second line of action, maximizing the use of natural energy sources available in deserts for heating and cooling, involves analysis of the potential of local energy sources such as solar energy for heating, availability of water for evaporative cooling, cool night air, potential of cooled soil, and nocturnal radiant loss. These natural sources can provide the necessary energy requirements and their utilization can often be accomplished by simple and inexpensive technical solutions. A more comprehensive discussion of passive cooling of buildings, and the performance characteristics of the various passive cooling systems, is presented in Givoni 1994.

Minimizing the environment stress and providing comfortable conditions for the people living in hot-dry regions involve design issues of two scales: the individual buildings and the urban environment. Guidelines for urban design in hot-dry regions are presented in the section Urban Design in Hot-Dry Regions on page 368.

Design Objectives in Hot-Dry Regions

The design of buildings and neighborhoods in hot-dry regions, as well as the design of an entire town, should aim mainly at mitigating the harshness of nature in summer, both indoors and outdoors, and enabling rest and recuperation.

Indoors the main objective is to lower significantly the air and internal surfaces' temperatures, relative to the ambient temperature. Outdoors the objective would be to provide shade and to ameliorate the microclimate around the buildings, in the public open spaces, and in the streets.

The main thermal performance characteristics of a building in a hot-dry region should be:

a. *Slow* rate of indoor heating during summer daytime;
b. *Fast* rate of indoor cooling in summer evenings;
c. Minimizing dust penetration;
d. Good ventilation in the summer evenings;
e. Higher indoor temperatures, relative to the outdoors', in winter.

On the face of it, some of these performance characteristics are conflicting, such as the desire to have indoor temperatures lower than the outdoor average in summer and higher than the outdoors' in winter. The different performance characteristics also may call for conflicting architectural and structural details of the building. Thus, for instance, in order to have a slow rate of heating during the daytime a building should have high thermal inertia, a feature that usually also causes a slow rate of cooling in the evenings. Enhancing ventilation calls for large windows, a factor which usually increases the rate of heating during the daytime hours, and so on.

However, as will be shown below, it is possible by appropriate design details and choice of building materials to "eat the cake and have it too"—namely, to have a building which changes its thermal performance characteristics according to comfort requirements changing hourly, daily, and seasonally. Various architectural and structural design features can contribute to these ends.

Comments on Vernacular Architecture in Hot-Dry Regions

In considering the appropriate design in a hot-dry climate, from the human comfort viewpoint, some lessons can be drawn, of course, from vernacular architecture and town planning. However, it should be noted that any vernacular architecture in any region, including the hot-dry ones, has been developed over many centuries in response to many factors, the climate being only one of them.

In fact, many vernacular buildings in hot deserts have very uncomfortable interiors during the summer night hours, forcing the inhabitants to sleep on the roofs or in open courtyards.

Today, new materials and new knowledge about the interaction between the indoor climate and the outdoor environment, as well as about the impact of urban design features on the urban climate, are available. These new developments provide architectural and urban design solutions which can yield more comfortable indoor and outdoor climates than that experienced in traditional buildings, especially in low-cost houses and in urban open spaces.

COMFORT AND ENERGY CONSERVATION ISSUES IN HOT-DRY REGIONS

Physiological indoor comfort in summer under still-air conditions (rooms with closed windows), for persons acclimatized to hot-dry climate, can be maintained as long as the indoor temperature is kept below 27–28°C (80.6–82.4°F). This seemingly high comfort limit is possible in desert regions because discomfort due to clamminess and wet skin is minimized by the low humidity. The upper limit of the comfort zone can further be extended by increasing the indoor airspeed with the help of ceiling or wall fans. With indoor airspeed of about 1.5 m/s (300 fpm) the upper comfort limit would be about 29–30°C (84.2–86°F).

Elimination of ventilation by outdoor air in the hot hours of the day is necessary in order to minimize the rate of heating of the interior of the house and to keep the mean radiant temperature of the internal surfaces below the level of the indoor air temperature, by taking advantage of the thermophysical properties of the buildings which are recommended for desert regions. This is discussed in more detail in Building Materials in Desert Regions, page 358.

In the late-afternoon hours subjective comfort may be enhanced by opening the windows for ventilation even when the outdoor temperature is higher than indoors, but in this case the ventilation would actually raise the indoor temperature for a few hours. The decision, whether or not to open the windows in those hours, depends on the personal relative preference for a higher airspeed with higher temperatures or lower temperatures at still air. Augmenting the airspeed with interior fans would be preferable from the building's performance aspect.

Afternoon dust storms in many desert regions make it necessary to close the windows during these events, even when ventilation might be welcome for thermal comfort. In areas with frequent afternoon dust storms the rate of rise of the indoor temperature should be kept as low as practicable, by appropriate choice of materials, solar control, and so forth, to postpone opening windows until the winds subside and the outdoor temperature drops sufficiently, when ventilation is desirable both for physiological comfort and to cool the building. At that time the high winds and the dust usually subside in most hot-dry regions.

In winter the objective in arid regions would be to keep the indoor daytime temperature above 20°C (68°F), up to about 25–26°C (77–78.8°F), while nighttime indoor temperatures can be allowed to drop to approximately 18°C (64.4°F). A relatively large interior diurnal temperature swing is actually needed in winter in passive solar buildings utilizing a Direct Gain system in order to store daytime solar energy in the building's mass for the nighttime. Advantage can thus be taken of the winter sunshine which is usually plentiful in desert regions. The performance of various passive solar heating systems, applicability and design details, is discussed in Chapter 4.

Energy Conservation Strategies in Hot-Dry Regions

Energy conservation for summer cooling and winter heating can be achieved in desert regions by combinations of the following strategies:

- Lowering the indoor temperatures;
- Natural ventilation;
- Minimizing heat gain and loss when air conditioning is unavoidable;
- Utilization of natural energies for heating and cooling.

LOWERING THE INDOOR TEMPERATURES

Suitable architectural design and choice of materials (mass and insulation) can keep the indoor maximum temperature about 8–10°C (14.4–18°F) below the outdoor maxima when windows are closed, thus minimizing the need to use mechanical air conditioning in seasons when the outdoor maximum is below about 37°C (98.6°F). Such reduction of the maximum temperature depends on the following conditions:

1. Minimizing the solar heat load on the building through, for example, appropriate orientation, light external colors, and shading of windows.
2. Minimizing the inward heat flow during daytime hours by adequate insulation and minimal air infiltration.
3. Slowing down the rate of indoor temperature rise by minimizing the surface area of the building's envelope during the daytime hours, adequate insulation, and the provision of high heat capacity.
4. Enabling rapid heat loss from the interior during the evening and night hours by natural (or fan-assisted) ventilation, and enlarging of the building's effective envelope area.

There seems to be a conflict between the shape of buildings which promote a slow response of the building to rising temperature during the daytime (compact buildings) and the shape promoting fast response to falling temperatures in the evenings (spread-out buildings). This conflict can be resolved by a specific building shape (see page 342).

NATURAL VENTILATION

Minimizing the need to use mechanical air conditioning in summer can be accomplished by window location and design that provide effective natural ventilation whenever outdoor temperatures are favorable.

Effective natural ventilation means that the indoor average airspeed is about 35–50 percent of the outdoor wind speed. Assuming an outdoor wind speed of 2–3 m/s (400–600 fpm) outside the house, which is common in the evenings in desert regions, it means the indoor airspeed would be about 1.0–2.0 m/s (200–400 fpm). This indoor airspeed should be realized at the level of occupation in the house—i.e., at a height of about 1 m (3.3') above the floor. It calls for appropriate design of the openings: their location, size, and details.

MINIMIZING SUMMER HEAT GAIN AND WINTER HEAT LOSS

Minimizing cooling and heating loads and the resulting energy consumption, *where and when air conditioning is unavoidable,* is possible by suitable choice of materials, solar control, and so on. By proper design of the house the size of the air conditioning system can be reduced, bringing down the initial investment, as well as reducing the operating cost and energy consumption of the system over its lifetime.

NATURAL ENERGIES UTILIZATION

Utilizing the natural energies available in desert regions for heating and cooling can minimize or even eliminate the use of mechanical air conditioning and conventional fuels. The different options for passive solar heating are discussed in Chapter 4. The passive cooling systems are discussed in Chapter 5.

COMMENTS

In some cases realization of one comfort option reduces or eliminates the possibility of applying another one. Thus, for example, daytime ventilation may provide comfort when the outdoor temperature is up to about 32°C (89.6°F), but the possibility to reduce the indoor temperature below the outdoor level is lost. Furthermore, in the evening when the wind subsides, a house which was ventilated during the hot hours would be hotter and less comfortable than a house which was kept closed in the daytime, due to the extra heat absorbed in the structural mass from the ventilation air. The relative efficacy of ventilation versus temperature reduction, from the human comfort viewpoint, depends on both the type of climate and the details of the house design and its occupancy. Sometimes special requirements of building usage, such as natural illumination in offices and classrooms, may render some approaches impractical or undesirable.

ARCHITECTURAL GUIDELINES FOR HOT-DRY REGIONS

The building design details appropriate in hot-dry regions, mainly deserts, are:

- The layout of the building's plan
- Internal and attached open spaces
- Orientation of main rooms and windows
- Window size, location, and details
- Shading devices
- The color of the building's envelope
- Vegetation near the house

The choice of thermal properties of building materials in hot-dry regions is discussed in Building Materials in Desert Regions on page 360.

Building's Shape in Hot-Dry Climates

In a hot-dry climate in summer it is desirable to lower the rate of temperature elevation of the interior during the daytime hours. To this end the building should preferably be compact: the surface area of its external envelope should be as small as possible, to minimize the heat flow into the building. Also, the ventilation rate should be kept to the minimum required for health (about 0.5 air change per hour), in order to minimize heating of the interior by the hotter outdoor air. A small surface area of the walls and the roof, when the construction is not completely airtight (as is the case with the stud-wall construction common in the United States), also helps in reducing daytime infiltration.

However, during summer evenings the outdoor temperature in many hot-dry regions (and in almost all hot regions during some months) drops down rapidly and reaches a level below the indoors, within or even below the comfort zone. This situation changes the desired climatic performance of the building. The objective in the summer evenings would then be to speed up as much as possible the cooling rate of the interior. This calls for a spread-out building with greater exposure to the outdoor air. The need to enhance the rate of cooling in the evenings is of special importance in the case of high-mass buildings, which "naturally" have a very slow response to changes in the outdoor temperature.

As was discussed in Chapter 2, it is possible to change the effective surface area of the building's envelope by indented porches equipped with closeable *insulated* shutters along the lines of the external walls. When these shutters are closed the porches become an integral part of the building's envelope and the envelope area is minimized, as is illustrated in Figure 10-1. With the shutters

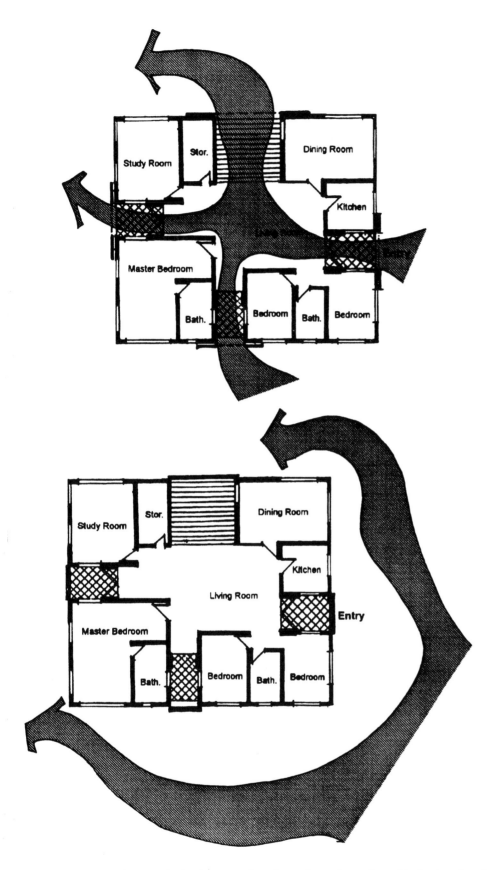

Figure 10-1. *A scheme of a building with indented porches, closeable by insulated shutters.*

open the envelope area increases and the porches' area actually becomes part of the outdoors. These shutters could be in the form of insulated doors, for example. Small windows can be incorporated in the shutters to provide daylight and view when the shutters are closed.

In addition to the modification of the surface area of the envelope these deep porches also modify the exposure conditions of the openings which connect them to the adjoining rooms. When the insulated shutters are closed the openings of the adjoining rooms are then within an interior, or semiinterior, space. Thus they are not only protected completely from solar radiation and dust but are also exposed to still air, at temperatures closer to the indoor than to the outdoor level. Thus the heat gain through the doors and windows' glazing, the most sensitive part of the building's envelope, is greatly reduced, helping to minimize the rate of daytime heating of the interior.

During the evening and night hours, however, the insulated shutters should be opened. The airspace of the porches immediately becomes part of the outdoor environment. The high-mass walls between the rooms and the porches are now exposed directly to the outdoor air and thus can more easily get rid of the heat stored in them during the daytime hours. The large openings, when open, may provide effective cross-ventilation even when the outdoor wind speed decreases during the evening hours.

To the extent that such porches face south, southeast, or southwest, they can serve in winter as passive solar heating elements. To this end they should be equipped also with openable glazing, in addition to the insulated shutters. In winter the glazing elements can be kept closed all the time, thus transforming the porches into sunspaces. The openings leading to the adjoining rooms should be kept open during the sunny hours and could be closed afterwards. Also the insulated shutters could be closed in the evenings.

With such geometrical configuration and operating (management) procedures the building is "compact" during the summer daytime hours and during the winter and is "wide-spread" during the summer nights. The changeable surface area of the effective envelope minimizes the rate of heating of the interior during summer daytime and maximizes the rate of cooling in the evenings.

The area of the porches can be usable year-round and thus forms an integral part of the effective floor area of the dwelling.

Climatological Aspects of Internal and Attached Open Spaces in Hot-Dry Regions

A configuration that has a special role in hot-dry regions is an internal courtyard or patio. It is often suggested that such internal patios and courtyards help in maintaining cooled indoor temperatures. This notion is based on the fact that such buildings are very common in such regions and have been for centuries and millennia. It should be realized, however, that courtyard houses were developed in response to different needs and limitations, and climate was only *one* of these factors.

The general climatic characteristics of the different types of "enclosed" open spaces was discussed in Chapter 6. This chapter will focus on the special aspects of "enclosed" open spaces in hot-dry climate.

The outdoor environment in a hot-dry climate, especially in desert areas, is barren and hostile. Any open land which is not taken care of by a private owner or by the public becomes a potential source of dust. Care of open land in hot-dry climates is difficult because most plants, except specific desert plants like cacti, need plenty of water, which often is scarce and expensive.

Private care of open land is more likely in protected areas, demarcated by walls and/or fences. In an enclosed open space such as in a fenced yard or in an internal courtyard or patio, it is also possible to modify, to some extent, the outdoor microclimate. The potential for climatic modification depends on the level of separation of the open space from the general environment. Thus, with relatively small expenditure of water, it is possible, by landscaping of courtyards, to maximize the benefits.

Many household activities in hot-dry regions can often take place outdoors more comfortably than indoors. Such activities may include washing, cooking, playing, and even sleeping. Therefore, from the design viewpoint, such outdoor spaces should form an integral part of the house.

Vernacular buildings in hot-dry regions traditionally have incorporated different forms of open spaces as integral elements of the habitat. An internal patio provides completely private open space, visually and acoustically separated from the external public environment. This factor is of special importance in societies and cultures which require a high degree of privacy, especially for women.

TEMPERATURE CHARACTERISTICS OF COURTYARD HOUSES

The actual climatic conditions within an internal patio depend greatly on its design details and its "treatment." In some cases the air and radiant temperatures in an internal patio are higher, but also can be lower, than the respective ambient temperatures, depending on the design details of the courtyard.

In a hot-dry region an unshaded internal patio with bare soil or with a hard concrete or tile floor often has higher air and radiant temperatures than the outdoor environment, especially in the case of low-rise buildings, where the width of the patio is large relative to the building height. This is due to the blocking of the wind in the patio while solar radiation can reach most of the patio's area. As the ratio of the height of the building surrounding the patio to its width at the roof's level increases, less sun penetrates into the ground level of the patio. This increases the shaded area and reduces the daytime air and radiant temperatures at the occupied space of the patio.

In many "traditional" neighborhoods in hot-dry regions, where patios are common, they are unshaded, with bare, hard floors. Figures 10-2 and 10-3, photographed in Tunisia by Professor Patrick Quinn of Rensselaer Polytechnic Institute (R.P.I.), illustrate this point. Unshaded courtyards with hard floors are also common in more affluent houses, as is illustrated in Figure 10-4 on page 348, also taken in Tunisia by Professor Quinn. The expected temperatures in such courtyards would be higher than in an open street.

Shading a patio can be accomplished by the design details of the building around it—for instance, by inward-projecting roof and balconies and/or by specific shading elements, as is illustrated in Figure 10-5 on page 349. Such shading

Figure 10-2. *A "traditional" neighborhood in Wamamey, Tunisia. Unvegetated courtyards. Photographed by, and with permission of, Professor Patrick Quinn of R.P.I.*

Figure 10-3. *A courtyard of a house in Wamamey, Tunisia. Photographed by, and with permission of, Professor Patrick Quinn of R.P.I.*

elements can be, for example, trees with high trunks and wide canopies, retractable canvas screen at the roof opening, and a pergola with vines. A shaded patio is a pleasant and inviting place, as is illustrated in Figure 10-6 on page 350, photographed in Barcelona, Spain, by Professor John S. Reynolds AIA, from the University of Oregon. A courtyard shaded by a tree, like the one shown in Figure 10-7 on page 349, taken by Professor Quinn in Tunisia, provides a much more comfortable climate than the unplanted courtyards shown above. To enable light and sun in winter the shading plants within the patio should preferably be of deciduous varieties.

An enclosed, landscaped courtyard full of trees, as shown in Figure 10-8 on page 352, taken by Professor Quinn in Istanbul, Turkey, would have an air temperature lower than that of the ambient. When located upwind of the building it enables ventilation of the building with air cooler than the ambient air.

A dry climate offers several possibilities of lowering the patio's temperature by various evaporative cooling systems, as is discussed in Chapter 5. The combination of shading and evaporative cooling can lower the daytime air temperature at the ground level of the patio by several degrees below that of the outdoor temperature. An interesting cooling element is a wetted wall, with water running over it down to a pond. The water is then recirculated, as is illustrated in Figure

Figure 10-4. *A courtyard in an affluent house in Kairovan, Tunisia. Photographed by, and with permission of, Professor Patrick Quinn of R.P.I.*

10-9 on page 351. Such a wall could be built of concrete and waterproofed. It provides cooling not only to the patio space but also to the room behind it.

Building Orientation and Solar Exposure

The main objective in deciding upon a given orientation in hot-dry regions is to minimize the impact of the sun on the building in summer. In regions with cold winters a second objective is to maximize solar utilization in winter. Ventilation in the evening hours is also very important in hot-dry regions but, as ventilation is less sensitive to orientation, this factor is secondary in the choice of orientation.

Most of the world's hot-dry areas are located in subtropical latitudes, where the highest intensities of the impinging solar radiation in summer, except for the roof, occur on the eastern and western walls. In winter this occurs on the southern wall.

This pattern of solar irradiation on the different walls results in a clear preference for north-south orientations of the main facades, and especially of the windows. Such orientation enables easy and inexpensive shading of the south-

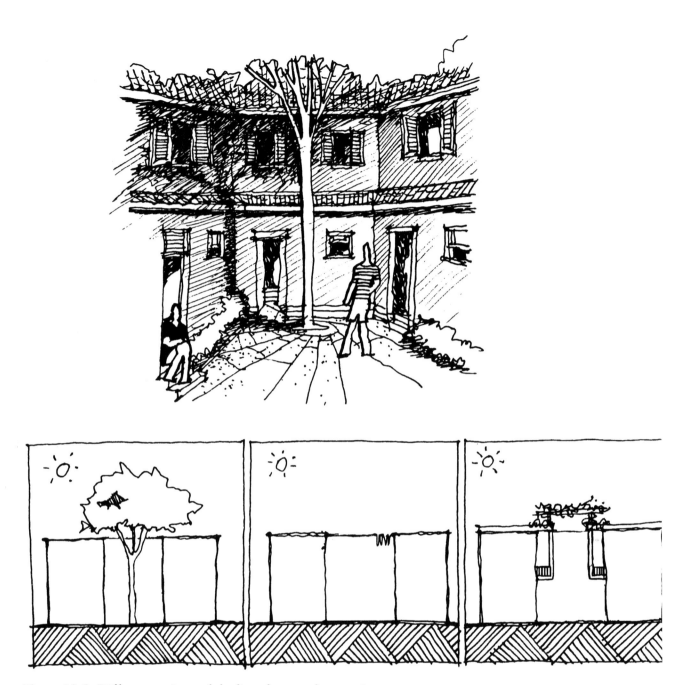

Figure 10-5. *Different options of shading elements for a patio.*

ern windows (in the Northern Hemisphere) in summer, and the southern-facing wall in general by horizontal overhangs. Southern overhangs can effectively block the rays of the summer sun high in the sky (solar noon altitude of 70–80 degrees) while enabling irradiation of the southern wall in winter.

However, it should be emphasized that the intensity of the solar radiation reflected from bare ground is quite significant in many hot-dry regions. With a horizontal radiation of 1000 W/m² (320 Btu/h.ft²) and ground albedo (reflectivity) of 0.6, both features common in midsummer in many hot-dry regions, the

Figure 10-6. *A shaded patio in Barcelona, Spain. Photographed by, and with permission of, Professor John S. Reynolds of the University of Oregon.*

Figure 10-7. *A courtyard shaded by a tree in Tunisia. Photographed by, and with permission of, Professor Patrick Quinn of R.P.I.*

reflected radiation, I_r, reaching a wall at any orientation (recalling that the reflected radiation is diffused equally in all directions and assuming that the ground extends to the horizon), would be :

$$I_r = (0.6 * 1000) / 2 = 300 \text{ W/m}^2 \ (95 \text{ Btu/h.ft}^2)$$

The amount of radiation transmitted through a window with conventional glazing (transmissivity of 0.7) would be 210 W/m² (67 Btu/h.ft²). The amount of absorbed radiation depends, of course, on the absorptivity (a) of the wall's surface. A dark wall (a = 0.7) would absorb 210 W/m² (67 Btu/h.ft²) while a white wall (a = 0.25) would absorb only 75 W/m² (24 Btu/h.ft²).

Overhangs do not block the radiation reflected from the ground, and protection of windows from reflected radiation in summer by shading devices such as shutters would also be desirable.

The issue of orientation in hot-dry regions concerns mainly the windows and other glazed areas. The heating effect of solar radiation impinging on walls can easily be minimized by choosing reflective (very light) colors for the walls. In fact, a white western wall exposed to the sun in summer, in a hot-dry location with wide-open light-colored soil, can have about the same temperature as a dark southern wall fully protected from direct radiation by an overhang.

Figure 10-8. *A landscaped courtyard full of trees in Istanbul, Turkey. Photographed by, and with permission of, Professor Patrick Quinn of R.P.I.*

Calculating the sol-air temperature in these two cases can illustrate this point. Assuming an air temperature of 35°C (95°F), horizontal radiation (Ih) of 1000 W/m² (320 Btu/h.ft²), direct solar radiation striking a western wall (Iw) of 600 W/m² (190 Btu/h.ft²), soil reflectance (r) of 0.6 (typical to many desert regions), convective coefficient of 20 W/m².C (3.5 Btu/h.ft².F), and wall surface absorptivities (a) of 0.7 and 0.25 for a dark southern wall and for a white western wall, respectively, the sol-air temperature (Tsa) for the two cases can be computed. It is also assumed that the temperature drop of an exposed wall, due to long-wave radiation to the sky, is 2°C (3.6°F) (Givoni 1976).

For a dark southern wall protected from direct radiation:

$$Tsa = 35 + (0.7 * 0.5 * 0.6 * 1000) / 20 = 45.5°C (116°F)$$

For an exposed white western wall:

$$Tsa = 35 + 0.25 * (300 + 600) / 20 - 2 = 44.25°C (111.5°F)$$

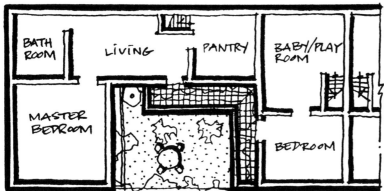

Figure 10-9. *A scheme of a patio cooled by a wetted wall.*

The effect of wall and roof color in desert regions is further discussed in Colors of Buildings on page 355.

Window Size, Location, and Details in Hot-Dry Regions

This section deals with specific issues of window design in hot-dry regions, and especially hot deserts. In such a climate, where the outdoor daytime temperature is much higher than the indoor temperature, conventional windows tend to raise the indoor temperature. Also, the larger the window area the greater the heating effect, especially when sun penetration is not effectively prevented by shading or orientation. Sunlight in hot-dry regions is very intense, and large windows may cause glare discomfort, reinforcing the notion that small windows are more suitable than larger ones for deserts. This view is supported by the observation that vernacular buildings in desert regions, built mainly from compacted mud, adobe blocks, or stone, usually have very small windows.

However, it should be pointed out that the traditional way of life of inhabitants in vernacular houses in hot-dry regions was to sleep on the roof or in a courtyard, testifying to the uncomfortable indoor conditions which prevailed during the nights. In fact, effective night ventilation is of primary importance for the cooling of the building's structural mass. Without effective cross-ventilation at night, the building's interior may be unbearably hot during the nights, when comfort is essential for restful sleep. As will be discussed later, it is possible by proper design (with large windows!) to provide acceptable indoor comfort in hot-dry regions both during the daytime and night hours. From the physiological viewpoint, night comfort is more important than during the daytime.

With special design details, large windows can be provided in these regions with advantages from the thermal point of view. When highly insulated shutters are added to large openable windows, their thermal effect can be adjusted to varying needs, both diurnally and annually. In summer, the shutters can be closed during the hot hours, admitting light into the house only through small, shaded windows. In the evening, the shutters and the windows can be opened, increasing the rate of cooling of the interior.

In winter, large southern-facing windows can provide significant direct solar heating of the interior. Closing the insulated shutters during the night traps the heat indoors, reduces the rate of cooling, and thus helps maintain comfortable indoor night temperatures.

In regions where dust is a significant nuisance, design details of windows and shutters should enable tight closure.

In some hot-dry areas insects may be abundant in certain periods. Screens should then be included as an integral part of the window system. It should be possible to keep the screens closed when the windows and shutters are open.

To facilitate cross-ventilation when desired, windows should be placed on both the windward and leeward facades. If such a location is provided, effective ventilation can be achieved even through relatively small windows (e.g., with a total openable area of about five to ten percent of the floor area).

Shading of Windows in Hot-Dry Regions

Because of the high intensity of solar radiation in desert regions, the problem of overheating by solar energy, penetrating through windows or absorbed at the external surfaces of the wall, is of particular importance. The intense direct radiation, and that diffused from the sky, is augmented by solar radiation reflection and by long-wave emission from the surrounding ground, which often is of relatively light color and without vegetation cover. These points emphasize the importance of providing protection not only from the direct sun but also from the radiation reflected and emitted from the ground. The possibilities to reduce the direct and the indirect solar load by shading is therefore of particular interest in hot-dry regions. This section deals with "architectural" shading devices, fixed or operable, in a hot-dry climate. The subject of shading by landscaping of the site, around the building, is discussed in Chapter 9.

In hot-dry regions, where both the direct and the reflected radiation are higher than in other climate types, the effect of the differences in thermal efficiency among various shading types is more pronounced.

FIXED SHADING DEVICES

Most fixed devices do not intercept solar radiation reflected from and emitted by the ground or nearby buildings. In desert regions, where the amount of the reflected radiation can be quite significant, such devices have inherently limited efficiency.

The following three types of fixed shading devices for windows will be discussed in terms of their relative effectiveness in different orientations, in the framework of a desert environment:

a.   Horizontal overhang extending on both sides of the window;
b.   Vertical fins extending above the window;
c.   A "frame" made of a horizontal projection and vertical fins, often referred to as "egg crate."

A horizontal overhang above a southern window, extending sufficiently in front and on both sides, can provide complete shading from the direct sun during midsummer, and still enable solar penetration in winter. However, an overhang does not provide any protection from the radiation reflected from the ground in front of the window. Furthermore, in the late-summer and early-fall months (mid-August to mid-October in the Northern Hemisphere), the ambient air temperature in hot-dry regions may still be quite high while the sun is already low enough in the sky to strike most of the window area. In this situation the shading by an overhang may not be enough to prevent significant solar penetration and overheating.

In the case of eastern and western orientations, vertical shading devices (fins) are more effective than horizontal overhangs of the same depth. However, neither can provide complete shading in these orientations.

The only way by which an eastern or a western window can be shaded effectively by fixed devices is by a "frame" consisting of a horizontal overhang and a vertical "fin" oblique at 45 degrees towards the south.

For northern windows, vertical fins, especially on the western side and extending above the window's height, can provide protection from the late afternoon sun.

The different efficiencies of the fixed shading devices also influences how the shape of a window shaded by such devices affects its thermal performance.

Horizontal elongated windows on southern, eastern, and western walls can be protected more effectively by fixed shading than square or vertical windows. Vertically elongated windows with these orientations cannot be effectively shaded by fixed devices, unless the shading is extended to a very large depth, even in the case of southern windows. Vertical eastern and western windows cannot be shaded effectively at all by fixed devices perpendicular to the wall.

EXTERNAL OPERABLE SHADING DEVICES

The common feature to all operable devices is that they can be adjusted at will, to either exclude or admit solar radiation. As with fixed devices, they intercept the sun's rays before they hit the glazing. Many of the operable types can intercept solar radiation reflected from the ground, in addition to intercepting the direct and most of the diffused radiation from the sky.

On the other hand, operable shading devices can admit solar radiation when this is desirable, in winter. Therefore, operable devices are inherently more effective than the fixed shading. Most of the operable shading devices can be applied with about the same effectiveness to all orientations and to any shape of window.

Operable shutters can also be opaque and insulated, with only a small glazed area for daylighting. When open they fully enable solar radiation to impinge on the glazing or, with open windows, enable natural ventilation. When closed, they can provide high thermal resistance to the windows.

In desert regions, such insulated shutters are of special interest. They minimize the heating rate during summer days, enable convective cooling during summer evenings and nights, admit solar heating during winter days, and minimize heat loss during winter nights. In this way the special climatic characteristics of deserts—namely a large diurnal temperature range, pleasant or cool nights in summer, and plentiful solar radiation in winter—can be turned into assets by the application of insulated shading panels.

Operable external shading devices can reduce solar heat gain through windows and other glazed areas down to about ten to 15 percent of the radiation impinging on the wall while enabling daylighting to enter. With insulated shutters the solar heat gain can even be reduced to about five percent of the impinging radiation.

The color of external operable shading devices may have little effect on their thermal performance unless they are completely closed.

INTERNAL OPERABLE SHADING

Internal shading devices can be in many forms, such as venetian blinds, roller blinds, and curtains. All of them intercept the sun's rays after transmission through the glazing, i.e., indoors. In consequence, all the different types of internal shading have low efficiency from the thermal point of view, although they can effectively control indoor lighting conditions. Therefore, they are generally not suitable in desert regions, especially when applied to large windows and other glazed areas.

The only exception is insulated internal shutters. When closed they can reduce greatly the solar heat gain even when they intercept the radiation after transmission through the glazing. In winter they are most effective in reducing heat loss through the windows.

Colors of Buildings

The color of the walls and the roof has a tremendous effect on the solar impact on the building and its indoor climate, particularly in desert regions where solar intensity is higher than in other regions.

Because of the different patterns of solar incidence on the roof and on walls with different orientations, the importance of color as a controller of the indoor climate is variable. For the roof, the influence of color is at a maximum. The difference in the maximum surface temperature in summer between a white roof and a black one in a desert can be about 40°K. The resulting heat gain to the building interior depends on the thermophysical properties of the roof, but in general it is quite significant.

The effect of the external color of the walls and the roof on the surface temperature, the heat load, and indoor temperatures is so great that it has a profound impact on the required thermal resistance of the envelope and the heat capacity of the building. This point is elaborated on below.

Eastern and southern walls are also very sensitive to their external color, while the northern wall is the least sensitive. The southern wall presents a special case because it receives most radiation in winter, when heating may be desirable.

The problem of external colors in the desert becomes more complicated because of glare. Most deserts exhibit too much glare because of the light color of the terrain and the lack of vegetation. All-white buildings, while being better from the thermal viewpoint, may intensify the environmental glare. Therefore, a solution should be sought which will minimize the heat load on the building in summer without causing too much glare. Such a solution can be provided by careful design of some building elements and a selective choice of colors for different parts of the building.

A great potential is offered by a variety of building elements projecting from the enclosed space, such as overhangs, wall extensions, and open balconies, as was discussed in Chapter 8. The thermal contact between such elements and the interior of the building is much less than that of the walls and the roof directly enclosing the indoor space. Therefore, they can have darker colors without increasing greatly the heat load. As such elements are the most exposed to the outside, their darker colors can significantly reduce the glare. The building surfaces behind them, which are in direct contact with the interior, can be kept white. Such treatment can also contribute to the visual variety of the environment. Such projections also cast shade on the walls behind them, at some hours thus reducing the glare when the walls are white.

To fully utilize these possibilities in desert regions, it is desirable to plan such projections specifically, so as to create areas of sufficient visual dimension, where darker colors can be applied without causing excessive heat load. In addition, it is possible to have medium-light colors applied to the northern and southern walls and thus add further to the variety of the environment, if such variety is considered desirable.

Plants as Climatic Control in Hot-Dry Climates

In many desert regions, the amount of vegetation which can be afforded on private lots is limited by the availability and cost of water for irrigation. Therefore, it would be desirable to use the vegetation in such a way that the contribution of a small green area to the comfort of the inhabitants is maximized.

PLANTS AROUND THE BUILDING

Plants near the house in desert regions can affect and improve the microclimate inside and around the house in several ways and also fulfill several objectives. For each one of the various objectives, different plants and different landscape design details may be the most effective. The climatic objectives of plants in hot-dry climate may include:

- Shading of the roof, walls, and windows of the building;
- Shading of play and rest areas outside the house;
- Reducing and filtering dust in and around the house;
- Elevating the humidity level in too-dry climates (practical only in confined spaces);
- Reducing the temperature in the vicinity of the house;
- Reducing the wind speed where this is desired;
- Concentrating airflow and increasing airspeed where this is desired.

Considering all these effects, it should be emphasized that the areas over which the influences of the plants are of quantitative significance are limited to the planted areas themselves. Only a narrow margin of peripheral area around the green area (on its leeward side) is affected by the vegetation. The only exception is the effect of high and dense windbreaks on the wind speed, which extends to a larger distance than the other effects.

PUBLIC PARKS IN HOT-DRY REGIONS

The climatic characteristics of hot-dry regions, from the viewpoint of public park design for maximum utilization, are the intense solar radiation (leading to the need for ample shade in summer), the prevalence of dust, and in many cases scarcity of water. Because of the ambient low humidity, lowering the wind speed by the vegetation is not likely to cause discomfort, and a higher humidity in the planted areas brought about by the evaporation from the plants is actually welcome.

Urban public and private planted areas, to the extent that they can be properly maintained (mainly irrigated), are a great asset in a hot-dry region, because of the scarcity of natural vegetation.

As a result of the lower temperature of the leaves and the air passing by them, the temperatures in green areas are significantly lower than above bare-ground, hard surfaces such as along roads, or in a hard-surfaced open area, such as a parking area. In addition, the surface temperature of soil shaded by vegetation in a hot-dry area is substantially lower than the surface of unshaded soil. As a result of the above factors the radiant component of the thermal load on persons staying in "green" areas is greatly reduced, in addition to the lower air temperature.

Because of the intense solar radiation and the prevalence of dust, parks and playgrounds should provide ample shade and protection from dust in summer. Large lawns and flower beds without shade around or within them contribute little to the recreation possibilities of the inhabitants: adults, elderly, and children alike, to rest, relax, or play on a hot sunny day. Thus, plenty of places to sit in the shade should be provided along roads and trails in public parks and in playgrounds. Shaded spaces for play and rest thus minimize the danger of overstress and heat strokes.

Large groves of trees, preferably deciduous, can provide attractive locations for children's play facilities, rest areas for elderly people, and so on.

Provisions for wind protection in winter in urban parks is of particular importance in arid regions with cold winters. The availability of sunshine and the absence of much rain in winter can enhance greatly the attractiveness of settlements in these regions as winter resorts. This factor may be of significant economic value to the community. Protection from cold winds will help greatly in enjoying these winter climatic qualities in the public urban parks.

Public areas within the neighborhood borders should also be limited in size to areas which can be well kept. Large public bare land is frequently the source of dust nuisance for the built-up area around it. In land reserved for future development the natural vegetation cover should be kept and protected.

Low hedges are effective in reducing wind speed and filtering dust near the ground, while not blocking the wind at higher elevations. Their use, together with other types of vegetation, should be considered as means for controlling dust in the neighborhood.

A more detailed discussion of the impact of green spaces on the quality of the urban environment is presented in Chapter 9.

BUILDING MATERIALS IN DESERT REGIONS

Traditional buildings in hot desert areas are built of high-mass, thick walls made of heavy materials, such as stone, bricks, adobe, and mud. Vaulted roofs, with flat impervious external finish covered with earth, also provide high mass to the building. Windows are usually small and protected from the sun by the thickness of the wall in which they are placed and in many cases are also provided with wooden shutters. The thick and heavy structure of the walls and the roof suppress the swing of the external temperature and stabilize the indoor temperature at a level close to the *average* sol-air temperature of the external surfaces of the building's envelope.

The actual suppression of the indoor daytime (and especially the maximum) temperatures depends on the color of the envelope which, in turn, determines the sol-air temperature. With very light colors of the walls and the roof, the indoor average temperature is close to that of the outdoor average so that the small indoor diurnal swing can result in a maximum significantly lower than the outdoors' maximum. However, with dark colors of walls and the roof, the indoor average may be about 4–5°C (7.5–9.5°F) above the outdoors' average. In this case the indoor daytime temperatures may be close to the outdoor maximum, even with a very small diurnal swing.

The indoor maximum is usually reached in the late evening and the rate of cooling is usually quite low. This fact may cause severe indoor discomfort during the nights. Traditional solutions in many desert regions to such indoor nocturnal heat stress is to sleep outdoors, on the roof, or in a courtyard. In some areas, even the daytime summer indoor temperature is too high and comfort can be provided only by air conditioning or other means of cooling, such as evaporative cooling.

Today, the availability of modern insulating materials, together with application of passive cooling systems, makes it possible to maintain indoor temperatures significantly below the average of the outdoor air temperature. With such design details it is possible to provide natural comfort through longer periods of the year and to use much less energy for summer cooling and winter heating.

From the climatic applicability aspect, the ability to keep the indoor conditions within the comfort level without mechanical cooling, by designing light-colored, high-mass, well-insulated buildings, depends mainly on the outdoor *average* temperature. The reason is that in such buildings the indoor temperatures are stabilized about 1–2°C (1.8–3.6°F) above the outdoor average with a diurnal range of about ten to 20 percent of the outdoor's swing, or about 2–4°C (3.6–7.2°F). Thus, in regions and seasons where the average outdoor temperature in summer is at the lower part of the comfort zone, about 20–25°C (68–77°F), indoor conditions can be maintained at the comfort level throughout the day even without intensive night ventilation. With intensive night ventilation (e.g., air changes of about or above 20 per hour), the indoor maximum temperature can be reduced to a level close to the outdoor average temperature. Consequently, such buildings can still be comfortable during periods when the outdoor average is up to about 29–30°C (84.2–86°F), by increasing the indoor airspeed during the day with interior fans (not by natural ventilation with the hot outdoor air).

However, in places and seasons when the average outdoor temperature during the summer months exceeds about 29°C (84.2°F), indoor temperatures, both air and radiant, would be too hot during the daytime and may prevent restful sleep at night, causing accumulating fatigue. In this case some additional passive or low-energy cooling system, such as evaporative cooling, is needed to ensure indoor comfort.

Recommended Thermal Resistance in Hot-Dry Regions

In hot deserts, high thermal resistance of the envelope elements is necessary in order to minimize the conductive heat flow into the building's mass during the daytime hours. As different desert regions have different daytime (maximum) temperatures in summer the required thermal resistance may be related to a "design" summer temperature of the region in question, for example, to the average maximum temperature experienced in the hottest month (e.g., usually July or August in the Northern Hemisphere).

A high thermal resistance of the envelope would of course also reduce the rate of cooling during the evening. But the cooling rate can be enhanced by ample ventilation of the interior in the evening and night hours, thus bypassing the thermal resistance of the envelope.

The conductive heat flow, from the external surface inward, depends on the external surface temperature. The surface temperature, in turn, depends not only on the outdoor air temperature but also on the solar energy *absorbed* at the surface, namely on the sol-air temperature.

Consequently the required thermal resistance of the external walls and the roof can be specified for a given region as function of the "design" maximum outdoor air temperature ($T_{(o)max}$ in °C), the peak intensity of solar radiation (Global radiation, I_{max}, in w/m^2) and the absorptivity of the surface (a). As the roof is exposed in summer to higher solar radiation than the walls it should have a higher thermal resistance.

The following recommendations for thermal resistance (R_{req}) of walls and roofs in hot regions (in m^{2}C/w) were suggested by Givoni (1979) for regions with mild winters and hot summers, where the summer considerations should determine the properties of the building materials:

For walls:

$$R_{req} = 0.05(T_{(o)max} - 25) + 0.002(a * I_{max})$$

For roofs:

$$R_{req} = 0.05(T_{(o)max} - 25) + 0.003(a * I_{max})$$

$T_{(o)max}$ is the average maximum air temperature, and I_{max} is the Global (horizontal) solar radiation, for the hottest month (usually July or August in the Northern Hemisphere).

Recommended Heat Capacity

A high heat capacity (Q) is desirable in desert regions in order to take advantage of the large diurnal range and to lower the indoor maximum, by closing the building during daytime hours and ventilating it in the evening and night hours. To be effective in stabilizing the indoor temperature the mass of the building should be within an "envelope" of insulating materials.

"RULES OF THUMB" FOR THE EFFECTIVE HEAT CAPACITY OF A BUILDING

Accurate evaluation of the effective heat capacity of a building, affecting its response both to the temperature wave of its envelope and to interior heat gains and losses such as penetrating solar radiation and ventilation, involves the calculations of its Thermal Time Constant (TTC) and its Diurnal Heat Capacity (DHC), as discussed in Chapter 3. However, such calculations require very detailed description of the building and the use of sophisticated computer codes. Furthermore, beyond a given level of thermal resistance and heat capacity, the indoor temperature changes very little with higher levels of these two variables, so that accurate calculations are not actually essential.

In the opinion of the author the "exact" calculations are too complicated for suggesting "rules of thumb" for design of buildings appropriate for a given climate. Approximate calculations and recommended standards for the building's heat capacity are presented in the following section.

The approximate heat capacity of a building element, Q_i, is defined as the product of the area (A) and thickness (L) of the element multiplied by the density (ρ) and the specific heat (c) of its materials:

$$Q_i = (A * L * \rho * c)_i$$

The specific heat (c) of common building materials, such as concrete or bricks, is about: 0.25 (wh/kg.C) (0.25 Btu/lb.F).

In dealing with the heat capacity of the building, the interior mass (partitions, intermediate floors, and so on) is also effective in suppressing the indoor temperature swing, in addition to the mass in the envelope elements. Therefore, the total mass of the building should be taken into account. The heat capacity of the building as a whole, Q_b, is thus the sum of the heat capacities of the envelope and the interior elements:

$$Q_b = Q_i$$

The simple approximate evaluation of the building's heat capacity is applicable when most of the mass of the building is inside an envelope of insulation and its surface area is at least equal to the building's envelope area.

These simple calculations can be done at the various stages of the design of a building and thus apply the recommended standards of heat capacity in hot-dry regions.

The needed heat capacity depends not only on the outdoor air temperature range. As the building's envelope absorbs more solar radiation, the building's external surface experiences a larger diurnal temperature range, increasing the effective temperature range affecting the indoor temperatures.

Therefore, the required heat capacity (Q_{req}) should be related not only to the outdoor temperature range ($T_{(o)max} - T_{(o)min}$) but also to the solar energy absorbed at the envelope's surfaces ($a * I_{max}$).

Givoni (1979) has suggested the following requirements for the building's heat capacity (in Wh/m^2C).

For walls:

$$Q_{req} = 2.5 * (T_{(o)max} - T_{(o)min}) + 0.1(a * I_{max})$$

For roofs (flat structural roofs):

$$Q_{req} = 2.5 * (T_{(o)max} - T_{(o)min}) + 0.15(a * I_{max})$$

The heat capacity of a building can be approximated in terms of the total mass of the building (M, in kg) per unit area of the envelope (M_{req}/m^2 of envelope). In these terms, the recommended heat capacity of the building as a whole can be specified by the following approximate formula (averaging the heat capacity of the walls and the roof):

$$M_{req}/m^2 = 10(T_{(o)max} - T_{(o)min}) + 0.5(a * I_{max})$$

For a "typical" desert, with a diurnal range of 15°C (27°F), and maximum solar intensity, I_{max}, of 1000 W/m^2 (320 $Btu/h.ft^2$), and for a building having nearly white external color (a = 0.2), the required mass becomes:

$$M_{req}/m^2 = 10 * 15 + 0.5 * 0.2 * 1000 = 250 \ (kg/m^2) \ (50 \ lb/ft^2)$$

and for a building with an "average" color (a = 0.5):

$$M_{req}/m^2 = 10 * 15 + 0.5 * 0.5 * 1000 = 400 \ (kg/m^2) \ (80 \ lb/ft^2)$$

The above values of the recommended heat capacity are applicable *only* if the required thermal resistance of the envelope is ensured and when the mass is distributed at least along most of the building's envelope area. High thermal resistance can reduce the required mass to levels well below those encountered in "traditional" buildings in deserts.

BUILDING TYPES CONSIDERATIONS IN HOT-DRY CLIMATES

Different building types exhibit different thermal performance characteristics in a hot-dry climate. A more detailed discussion of these characteristics was presented in Chapter 7. Here, their impact on comfort and energy demand in hot-dry climate is discussed.

Single-Family Detached Houses

Single-family detached houses have the highest envelope surface area among the various building types. When they are built around an internal courtyard the envelope surface area is further enlarged. Consequently, in hot-dry regions, the rate of temperature rise during the daytime hours in single-family houses is the fastest, for a given thermal conductance and mass of the walls and the roof. From this viewpoint this building type may exhibit the highest indoor discomfort and cooling requirement in summer and the highest heating load in winter, as compared to buildings of other types, *properly oriented and ventilated.*

On the other hand, single-family houses are less sensitive to orientation with respect to the sun and the wind direction. They also can best utilize surrounding vegetation for climatic control. Therefore, when the topography or other factors do not enable optimal orientation of the buildings, both with respect to the sun and the wind direction, detached single-family houses may be the most appropriate type in hot-dry regions in spite of their larger envelope surface area. This point is of special interest with regard to housing for low-income people with large families, for which single-family houses often are the most suitable for various social and other reasons.

Relatively high thermal resistance of walls can be achieved in inexpensive "self-help" buildings by double-layered walls, built of sun-dried adobe blocks with internal airspace. Adobe is a common material in many hot-dry regions. Urban planning of community organization for building individual buildings, with organized technical guidance, can also be instrumental in alleviating a housing shortage.

Town Houses (Row Houses)

Town houses are more sensitive than detached houses to their design details and orientation, both with respect to the sun and the wind direction. As a result town houses, if properly designed and oriented, are better thermally adapted to the climate in hot-dry regions than single-family detached houses. However, with inappropriate design, they may be less comfortable and need more cooling.

In a hot-dry climate a north-south orientation for the external walls will minimize the exposure of the town house to the sun in summer and maximize its potential for solar heating in winter. The situation may be more complex with respect to orientation for ventilation, as in many hot-dry regions the dominant wind direction is from the west. In this case an orientation of the long walls to north-northwest and south-southeast, with design details which "catch" the western wind by inlets in the north-northwest wall and with outlets in the south-southeast wall, as discussed in Chapter 3, can be a good optimal solution for town houses.

Multistory Apartment Buildings

The discussion of the performance of the various types of multistory apartments in hot-dry climates will follow the classification which was presented in Chapter 6—namely double-loaded and single-loaded corridor buildings.

DOUBLE-LOADED CORRIDOR APARTMENT BUILDINGS

Double-loaded corridor buildings minimize the heat gain during the daytime but have poor ventilation characteristics and poor solar exposure of at least one-half of the apartments. Therefore, from the summer comfort aspect, they are not suitable at all in hot climates unless high ventilation, especially during the night hours, can be ensured by some mechanical device, for example, a whole-house or apartment exhaust fan.

SINGLE-LOADED CORRIDOR APARTMENT BUILDINGS

Single-loaded corridor buildings may be appropriate in hot-dry climates if they are so oriented that the corridor is open in summer and is located on the leeward side of the building. This orientation enables cross-ventilation of the apartments when door and windows in the corridor wall are left open.

It should be taken into account, however, that the privacy of the occupants is compromised when the dwelling is ventilated. In societies that value privacy to the extent that comfort will be sacrificed for the sake of privacy, this building type should be avoided. A design solution for this problem is suggested in Chapter 6.

DIRECT-ACCESS MULTISTORY APARTMENT BUILDING

This type of multistory apartment building provides direct access to several dwellings at each floor, usually from two to four units, from a staircase or an elevator. The ventilation conditions and the potential for solar energy utilization of the individual dwellings depend on the number of units accessed directly from the staircase.

TWO UNITS PER STAIRCASE

When only two apartments are accessed at each floor from the staircase, all the dwelling units can have, with appropriate orientation, cross-ventilation in summer and potential for solar heating in winter. At the same time the envelope of each unit consists of only two external walls, except the top floor and the end (gable) units. Consequently, this subtype has reduced heat gain in summer and heat loss in winter. However, such buildings are very sensitive to orientation in their thermal performance.

Consequently, with appropriate orientation, this building type has the lowest rate of daytime heating in summer, combined with good ventilation and convective cooling in the evenings, compared with all the other building types. In winter the units have the lowest demand for heat combined with good potential for solar heating.

In hot-dry regions the appropriate orientation of the long facades would be to south and north, to minimize solar exposure in summer and to maximize it in winter. However, in many hot-dry regions the dominant wind direction in the evenings, when the buildings should be ventilated, is from the west. In such cases the optimal orientation would be north-northwest and south-southeast.

With a "wrong" orientation, e.g., to east and west, the building will have high solar load in summer and low potential for solar heating in winter.

In summary, with proper orientation, this building type is climatically the most suitable in a hot-dry climate. It should be noted, however, that limiting the number of dwelling units directly accessed from a staircase to two units involves higher cost.

THREE OR MORE UNITS PER STAIRCASE

With more than two direct-access dwelling units the ventilation and/or solar access conditions of at least one-third of the apartments is compromised. In hot-dry regions where the wind direction is from the north, the ventilation issue can be "solved" when the building as a whole faces north and south and the third unit "projects" northward of the building block and the staircase. All units would then have good ventilation in the evenings although the northern units would not have access to the winter sun.

With more than three dwelling units per staircase a significant number of apartments would have poor ventilation and solar exposure conditions. Therefore, such buildings are not recommended for hot-dry regions.

URBAN DESIGN IN HOT-DRY REGIONS

The main objective of urban design in hot-dry regions, from the climatic aspect, is to mitigate the stresses imposed by the climate on people staying outdoors (working, shopping, playing, or strolling). An additional objective is to improve the chances of the individual buildings to provide a comfortable indoor environment with minimum usage of energy.

The outdoor environmental stresses in the desert are mainly of four types:

a. High heat stress on summer days, resulting from the high ambient air temperature and the intense solar radiation.
b. High glare from direct and reflected sunlight.
c. Prevalence of dust storms, mainly in the afternoons.
d. (In regions with cold winters) cold winds in the winter season.

To ameliorate the heat stress on summer days, neighborhoods should be planned so that distances for walking people and playing children are short. Sidewalks should be shaded as much as possible, either by trees or by the buildings along them. Shade is particularly desirable in places where people (and mainly children) congregate outdoors during daytime hours.

Distribution of shopping places, schools, and urban services depends, of course, on the organization of such services in the society and may differ greatly between different countries and societies. In any case, it is desirable to ensure close-by basic services even in societies which rely mostly on individual and organized motorized transport, such as private car trips to central shopping centers, bussing to schools, and so forth.

From the point of view of the urban climate, the design details in hot-dry regions should aim at providing shade over sidewalks, playing grounds, and other public areas, securing adequate ventilation, minimizing dust, and reducing glare.

The urban design features discussed in this chapter are:

- Location of the town in a region.
- Density of the built-up area.
- Orientation and width of streets.
- Design details of "green" areas.
- Special details of the buildings affecting outdoor comfort.

The details of urban design with respect to each one of these issues can modify several of the elements of the urban climate. These effects, and guidelines for the appropriate design decisions in hot-dry climates, are discussed in the following sections.

Location Within a Region

In choosing a location for a town or a neighborhood in a hot-dry region one should look for places with lower summer temperatures and good ventilation conditions, mainly in the evenings and at night. Different locations within a given region may differ in their temperature and wind conditions. Variations in altitude, in particular, may cause appreciable differences in temperature over short distances.

Thus, for example, locations can be found in close proximity but at different elevations with daytime temperatures around 35°C (95°F) at higher elevations and 40°C (104°F) and more at lower elevations, with elevation differences of about 600 meters (1970'). These temperature variations are very significant from the human comfort viewpoint, and may also affect greatly the appropriate building design. (Bitan, 1974, 1982).

Local variations in topography may affect greatly the wind conditions. Thus windward slopes of a hill experience much higher wind speeds than the leeward slopes. Similarly, windward slopes of mountains may be more moist and experience higher precipitation than the leeward slopes.

A common opinion is that wind is not important, or is even undesirable, in hot-dry regions because the outdoor air temperature is above skin temperature and the wind increases the convective heat gain of the body. However, it is the personal experience of the author that, even with air temperature of about 40°C (104°F), a light wind actually reduces discomfort by reducing the wetness of the skin, especially when one stays outdoors and is exposed to the sun.

Good building ventilation, which depends on the availability of wind in the area, is essential in a hot-dry region in the evenings, both for indoor physiological comfort and for enhancing the cooling rate of the building's interior.

When considering the location of a new town, a situation frequently arises where a place with natural economic potential, such as mineral deposits or seashore suitable for a port, has a hot, inhospitable climate. Traditionally, cities were established near these resources. However, it is possible to locate a town designated for the exploitation of a potential at a higher altitude at some distance, or on the other slope of a mountain range, in a location with a more favorable climate. This location can be connected with the workplaces by a rapid and convenient transportation system. Such a choice will ensure more comfortable living conditions for persons staying at home, or working in occupations which do not require physical proximity to natural resources, and can lead to significant savings of energy for provision of thermal comfort.

Urban Density Considerations in Hot-Dry Regions

A high density of the built-up area (land coverage by buildings) in a hot-dry climate may have both positive and negative effects on human comfort outdoors and on the indoor climate of the buildings.

With buildings' heights increasing, urban density means smaller open spaces between and around the buildings. The effect of the reduced distances in hot-dry regions depends to a large extent on the orientation of the walls in question.

When the distance between the buildings is decreased along the east-west axis the mutual shading of the east-west walls of a given building by its neighbor's increases. As long as adequate natural ventilation of the building can be achieved, either without openings in the eastern or western walls or if the natural ventilation through openings in these walls is not greatly affected by the reduced distances, the effect on the indoor climate can be beneficial because the solar impact on the walls in summer is reduced.

With proper design of the individual dwelling units a building can be cross-ventilated even when openings are provided only in the northern and southern walls. In this case, the distance between the buildings along the east-west axis can be eliminated altogether. This creates "row houses" or "town houses" instead of individual, detached houses.

Consequently, when the main orientation of the building's long facades is to the north and the south it is possible to increase the density of the built-up area by reducing the side distance between neighboring buildings without causing deterioration in the thermal quality of the urban environment.

The effect of distance between buildings along the north-south axis is quite different. In winter it may reduce the possibilities of utilizing solar energy for heating, which has great potential in hot-dry regions, because of the low altitude of the sun in the sky. Solar radiation on a southern wall (in the Northern Hemisphere) of one building may be blocked by another building in front of it. The geometrical relationships between building's height, distances, and shape, as affecting the "solar access" of a building, are discussed in details in Knowles 1981.

Untreated urban land in a hot-dry region is often a source of dust, while land covered by plants helps in filtering out the dust from the air. The lack of rain in hot-dry regions and the high cost of "imported" water limit the capability of cities to landscape open land.

In developing countries most of the population cannot afford the expenses of planting and maintaining the open areas between buildings. Therefore, an appropriate urban design policy in hot-dry regions would be to limit the distances between buildings (setbacks by regulations) to the sizes which can be expected to be landscaped by the individual inhabitants. This consideration leads to higher urban densities than in other types of climate, such as hot-humid ones.

Density and Urban Air Temperature in Hot-Dry Regions

The temperature modifications by a city are expressed mainly in the "heat island" phenomenon, especially during calm and clear nights, when the urban air temperature is usually higher than the temperature of the surrounding open country.

Regarding the daytime conditions, it is commonly assumed that urban temperatures are higher than rural ones, due to lack of vegetation and excess heat generated in the town, although the differences observed are smaller than at night. During daytime hours part of the incoming solar radiation is absorbed in the mass of the buildings, in part in the walls of high floors, far above the street level. These factors may reduce daytime temperatures at the street level where "urban temperatures" are measured, although they may, on the average, still be higher than in the country.

It is possible to infer from theoretical considerations, as well as from actual measurements in and around buildings, that in hot-dry regions it might be possible to plan cities so that the ambient daytime air temperatures would be lower than in the surrounding countryside. The main planning approach by which such a modification of the urban temperature seems possible is a combination of urban density, building heights, and an average albedo of the built elements in the city, which will reduce significantly the amount of solar radiation absorbed in the urban fabric. The average urban albedo depends on the color of the roofs, walls, roads, parking areas, and so forth. The land fraction covered by vegetation affects the urban temperature but this effect is not due to the albedo of the plant, as the solar absorptivity of leaves is rather high.

The urban albedo is the main factor determining the amount of solar radiation absorbed in the urban area, and the color of the built urban elements, especially the buildings' roofs, is controllable by urban design. Because the roofs comprise a large fraction of the urban area in a densely built town the radiation balance in such case can be controlled and thus may have a pronounced effect on urban air temperature in hot-dry regions.

"High land coverage by buildings" means that a large part of the radiation exchange will take place at the roof surfaces and not at the ground level and at the walls. By assuring that all the roofs are colored white—by yearly repainting, for example—it is possible to achieve a negative radiation balance: the longwave radiant loss can substantially exceed the absorbed solar radiation even on a clear day in midsummer. Under these conditions, the average temperature of the roof surfaces will be lower than the average regional air temperature. As cool air is heavier than warm air, it will sink into the city's streets if suitable details of the roof are provided. If the city is large enough, and built densely enough, it can be assumed that it will be possible to achieve a daytime air temperature at the street level that is a great deal lower in the "controllable city" than in the arid surrounding areas.

Dense buildings slow down the rate of nighttime cooling of cities near the ground. However, if the nocturnal radiant cooling at the roof's level can be utilized to "drain" cooled air downward, the cooling rate near the ground will be accelerated. Specific design details of the buildings can either augment or hinder the drainage of cooled air from the rooftops to the ground level, where it can be utilized to lower the "urban temperature."

In the open areas between buildings, on public as well as on private land, planting trees should be encouraged as much as water availability and financial resources enable. Solar radiation absorbed in leaves of vegetation *increases* the evaporation rate instead of raising the temperature. The resulting elevated humidity, in an arid region, can be welcomed from the comfort viewpoint. Thus, large coverage of the land surface by a combination of white roof and trees can result in significant lowering of the urban temperatures in hot-dry regions.

Density and the Ventilation Potential in Hot-Dry Regions

Hot-dry regions commonly have strong winds during daytime that usually subside in the evenings. Furthermore, during the daytime hours building ventilation is not desirable, while in the evening it is essential for indoor comfort. Therefore, as related to urban density and building design, the main concern in hot-dry regions is how to provide the potential for evening and night ventilation for the buildings.

In high-density neighborhoods, where streets are narrow, distances between buildings small, and buildings are of about the same height, there is a sharp drop in the wind speed below the roofs' level. Below the roofs the wind is very light, while above the roofs it is much stronger. Under these conditions it is difficult to provide good indoor ventilation, especially when the ambient wind speed is very low. This point is of particular importance for the rooms where the inhabitants sleep.

To the extent that the same family occupies the whole vertical "chunk" of a building, from the ground to the roof, it is possible to improve the ventilation potential by special building design details. If the bedrooms are located at an upper floor, and if this floor covers a smaller area than the lower floors, surrounded by open "roof balcony" and thus more exposed, the ventilation potential of the bedrooms will improve. Air introduced at the upper floor can also flow downward and ventilate the lower floors.

When the same family occupies the whole vertical section of the building, it is also possible to make use of "wind catchers" to catch the wind blowing above the roofs' level and to direct it downward. Such devices can be an integral part of the functional design of the building, such as stairwells leading to the (flat) roof, or to an upper story extending only over part of the roof. The open part of the roof can be used as a private open space.

With such building design the land-coverage density at the ground floor can be quite high without impairing seriously the potential for natural ventilation, especially of the bedrooms. On the other hand, it should be realized the too-high density of the built-up area can lead to unsatisfactory ventilation and cause severe heat stress.

In neighborhoods with high-rise apartment buildings, higher overall urban densities (total Floor Area Ratio) can be maintained with adequate potential for natural ventilation. Reasonable distances between the building blocks should be ensured, and long buildings should not form "walls" perpendicular to the wind direction. The wind can then "negotiate" between the buildings so that the *potential* for natural ventilation exists. The extent to which an individual apartment will actually have adequate ventilation depends on its design details.

SETBACKS AND DISTANCES BETWEEN BUILDINGS

With a given size and height of buildings the distance between buildings determines the overall density of the built-up urban area and the fraction of land coverage by buildings. In a planned neighborhood the distances between buildings are often controlled by setback regulations. Such regulations are tools for preventing harmful consequences of the economic pressure to increase urban density beyond certain limits. From the viewpoint of climate, the distances between buildings affect the solar and wind exposures of the walls. The actual effect depends on the direction (orientation) of the space between the buildings. However, the setback regulations often do not take into account the orientation of the buildings.

In a hot-dry region setback regulations should take into consideration the possibilities of minimizing solar heating of buildings and shading of pedestrians walking between buildings, while at the same time ensuring the potential for natural ventilation. From these aspects there is special importance in hot-dry regions to the distance between buildings in the east-west direction.

Around the latitudes of 20 to 30 degrees (north and south), where the hot-arid regions are mostly found, a *small* distance between buildings in the east-west direction, relative to their height, can be very helpful in providing mutual shading for the walls. Assuming a typical height of urban residential buildings (e.g., walk-up apartments, four stories high) to be about 12 m (39'), a distance of 4 m (13') between buildings would give a 3:1 ratio of height to distance. It means that the sun's altitude should be more than 70 degrees before the ground between the building will be exposed to it, namely only between about 11 A.M. and 1 P.M.

From the ventilation potential viewpoint, on the other hand, even a narrow distance of about 2 m (7') enables utilizing the wind flowing through the gap between the buildings. Consequently there is an advantage in a hot-dry region in reducing the distances between buildings, in the east-west direction, to about one-fifth of their height, with the minimum determined by functional and land-use considerations. The shaded ground area and the walls of the buildings would benefit from the natural shading by the walls.

The situation is clearly different with regard to the distances between buildings in the north-south direction, mainly from the viewpoint of solar utilization for heating in winter. Because of the lower altitude of the sun in winter larger distances between buildings are needed to prevent mutual shading. The actual distance depends on the latitude, but generally a distance of 1.5–2 times the height of the buildings would be needed to provide solar access in winter.

Impact of Street Layout on Urban Ventilation

In hot-dry regions the main concern with regard to ventilation is to ensure the potential for ventilating the *buildings* during the evenings. To the extent that such ventilation can be ensured by the design of the buildings themselves (e.g., by use of wind catchers of some type), the street ventilation is of secondary importance, although light winds are desirable in the streets and open spaces, to mitigate the effect of solar heating. In fact, during the hot daytime hours strong winds are not desirable, as they promote dust generation. This problem is more common in many developing countries, where many roads may be unpaved.

The orientation of streets affects the urban climate in several ways:

- Wind conditions in the urban area as a whole;
- Sun and shade in the streets and the sidewalks;
- Solar exposure of buildings along the street;
- Ventilation potential of the buildings along the streets.

The width of the streets determines the distance between the buildings on both sides of the street, with impacts both on the ventilation and solar utilization potential. In a hot-dry climate the main objectives related to the street's layout are to provide maximum shade in summer for pedestrians and minimum solar exposure of the buildings along the streets.

The urban ventilation aspect, as related to street layout in a hot-dry climate, is secondary because during daytime hours high airspeed is not needed outdoors and not desired indoors. In the evenings people can be comfortable outdoors even with light winds, as temperatures are lower than indoors. Narrow streets provide better shading by buildings for pedestrians on sidewalks than wide streets. However, shade for sidewalks can be provided even in wide streets by special details of the buildings or by trees.

A north-south orientation of a street may result in an east-west orientation of buildings along, and parallel to, the street, which will cause unfavorable solar exposure for these buildings. From the solar exposure viewpoint an east-west street orientation is preferable. On the other hand, in dust-prone areas, which are common in hot-dry regions, wide streets parallel to the wind direction may aggravate the dust problem in the town as a whole. As the wind direction in many of the hot-dry regions is from the west, there is a conflict between the solar and the dust considerations with respect to street orientation. This conflict can be resolved by design means aimed at suppressing the urban dust level in the whole city, a subject to be discussed later.

STREET ORIENTATION AND SHADE OVER SIDEWALKS

In a hot-dry region the provision of shade in the streets in summer is one of the major design means for minimizing the heat stress of people walking in the street. Different orientations of the streets will result in different annual and diurnal patterns of the shading in the streets and along the sidewalks. These patterns depend on the latitude of the city in question, and most hot-dry regions are around the 30 degrees north and south latitudes.

Knowles (1981) has compared the street shade patterns in different street orientations. He has concluded that streets running north-south have better shading conditions in summer and better light conditions in winter than east-west streets. A street grid in "diagonal" orientation: northeast-southwest and northwest-southeast was found to be a preferable pattern from the solar exposure aspect. It provides more shade in summer and more sun exposure in winter.

STREET ORIENTATION AND THE POTENTIAL FOR SOLAR ENERGY UTILIZATION

In hot-dry regions there is great potential for solar heating of the buildings in winter and for water heating year-round. Street orientation may affect significantly the possibility of achieving these objectives. The direction of the streets in relation to the north determines the conditions of shade and sunshine on the face of buildings that are parallel to the street and on the sidewalks lining the streets. This affects the temperature and conditions within the buildings as well as the possibilities of protecting the pedestrians on the sidewalk from the sun in summer or of providing sunlight in the streets in winter.

The orientation of the streets also determines (in practice) the orientation of the individual lots into which the area is subdivided, and consequently it greatly affects the orientation of the buildings. In this way the street orientation has a major impact on the potential of the individual buildings to utilize solar energy for winter space heating, and to some extent also for year-round solar heating of domestic water.

In general, streets running in a given direction promote building orientation parallel to the street. This means that the main facades of buildings along a street running from east to west are facing south and north, which of course can help in providing solar utilization. Therefore, the simplest approach to promotion of solar utilization in buildings by urban design is to maximize street orientation in the east-west direction.

However, with such street orientation in midlatitudes, and with continuous row housing, a considerable proportion of the space *between* buildings may be in permanent shadow. An inclination of the facade towards the east may slightly reduce the solar radiation on the facade but the afternoon sun can penetrate in the space between buildings, avoiding the cold damp areas in permanent shade during the winter months.

In case of streets running north to south it would be advisable in hot-dry regions to encourage subdivision into narrow and deep land lots. This pattern will enable locating long buildings perpendicular to the streets and facing north and south. Planning regulations should enable and even encourage this type of building.

Special Details of Buildings Affecting Outdoor Conditions

Protection against sun for pedestrians on the sidewalks is very desirable in hot-dry regions. It can be provided by buildings with overhanging roofs, or colonnades in which the ground floor is set back from the edge of the road, with the upper stories jutting out, supported by pillars (or other means).

The color of the building walls not only affects the interior climate conditions, but also the lighting and glare in the streets. In this respect, in many instances, contradiction may exist between the requirements for comfortable indoor climate and those necessary to reduce the glare in the streets. In a hot-dry climate a white color of the walls will reduce indoor heat load but will increase outdoor glare. These conflicting requirements can be often resolved by horizontal overhangs projecting from the walls that not only protect the windows from solar radiation but also extend over the entire length of the wall. Such overhangs cast shade on the section of the wall below them and also block from pedestrian view part of the sunlighted section above them. In this way they can greatly reduce the glare for the pedestrians.

In hot-dry regions solar protection for pedestrians is much more important than rain protection. Built overhangs and colonnades provide, of course, protection from both sun and rain. When such built features are not available, solar protection can be provided by trees planted along sidewalks. Although they do not protect from the rain, their contribution to pedestrians' comfort is sufficient to justify their introduction as a climatic control feature.

When shading by trees is planned the design details of the sidewalks should take into account the need for irrigation of the trees and their protection (e.g., by fencing them).

Reducing Dust by Town Planning

Dust storms in desert regions are of two types:

1. Regional storms, in which dust extends to great heights (hundreds of meters) and covers very large areas (hundreds or thousands of kilometers). Such dust storms occur from time to time but are not a daily phenomenon.
2. Local dust "waves," originating in the local area and extending in height to several meters and in distance to several hundred meters. Such "storms" are a daily phenomenon in many places.

Nothing can be done on the neighborhood scale to stop or even minimize the impact of regional dust storms outdoors, although it is possible to minimize the penetration of dust indoors. On the other hand, much can be done in neighborhood planning to reduce the occurrence and minimize the impact of local, more frequent, dust "waves." The main factors affecting the frequency, intensity, and range of local dust storms are ground cover and the wind speed near ground level. Both these factors can be affected by neighborhood design features.

While in humid regions open, extended spaces can be assumed as being covered by natural vegetation, the situation is different in hot-dry regions, especially within an urban area. Without irrigation the soil is practically exposed and provides a source of dust. In many cities, especially in developing countries, the individual citizen and the municipalities cannot landscape private open spaces between buildings or even large public open spaces. Therefore, as a planning policy, the density of the built-up area (land coverage) should avoid unbuilt areas that the private citizen and the municipality cannot realistically keep up as landscaped areas.

Treatment and upkeep of ground cover should be analyzed separately for privately owned and public areas. But any bare ground not planted, irrigated, or paved may constitute a source of local dust storms. The extent of such bare land should not, therefore, be overlooked in planning outdoor space on either a neighborhood or private scale. In view of the fact that water is scarce and expensive in most arid areas, private plot sizes should be such that the owners can easily plant and cultivate, or take care in other ways, of all the area belonging to them. This calls for, in the case of individual houses, rather small lot areas for low-cost housing, which are sufficient for small gardens and can be kept efficiently well by the inhabitants. An exception, from this point of view, is the case of the well-to-do, who can afford the expenses involved in the upkeep of large gardens.

In the development of new neighborhoods in desert regions, special attention should be paid to the treatment of the windward borders. The land should be kept in its natural condition as far as possible, so that the natural ground cover of desert plants will limit the generation of dust.

REFERENCES

Bitan, A. 1974. Climatological Aspects In Locating Settlements In Arid Regions. *Geoforum* 20, 39–48.

Bitan, A. 1982. The Jordan Valley Project—A Case Study in Climate and Regional Planning. *Energy and Buildings* 4, 1–9.

Givoni, B., 1979. *Man, Climate and Architecture* 2d ed. New York: Van Nostrand Reinhold.

Knowles, R. 1981. *Sun, Rhythm, Form.* Cambridge, Massachusetts: MIT Press.

Chapter **11:** BUILDING AND URBAN DESIGN FOR HOT-HUMID REGIONS

INTRODUCTION

This chapter deals with the objectives and design principles in hot-humid regions, both on the building and urban scales, from the aspects of human comfort and energy conservation.

Hot-humid regions are distinguished, from the urban and building design viewpoint, by the following features:

- The summer climate is uncomfortable, and the most difficult to ameliorate by design.
- The people living in many of the hot-humid regions are mostly poor.
- Less-systematic research has been done on climatically appropriate urban and building design for this climate in comparison with research on other climates.
- Some of the hot-humid areas are subjected to strong and destructive storms (hurricanes, typhoons) and floods.

The fact that most of the countries in the hot-humid areas are developing countries has direct impact on the practicality of some "modern" concepts of urban and building design from the climatic viewpoint. The vast majority of people cannot afford air conditioning. Therefore, thermal stress (and its impact on health and productivity) should be minimized primarily by appropriate urban and building design details which do not involve high cost. Landsberg

(1984) notes that about 40 percent of the world population is living in the zone between the Tropics, and this proportion is expected to increase to about 50 percent at the end of the century. These population figures demonstrate the importance of improving the comfort conditions in the hot-humid regions by adapting the buildings, and the cities at large, to the climate.

Many of the hot-humid regions, especially on the eastern sides of the continents, are also subjected to tropical storms: hurricanes in the Caribbean Islands and in southeastern United States and typhoons in Southeast Asia and Northeast Australia. This factor calls for heavy and sturdy construction systems, often based on reinforced concrete, resulting in a high-mass building. This seems to be in contradiction with the low-mass building types traditionally considered as the appropriate building type in hot-humid regions. New structural solutions, incorporating both safety during the storms and thermal performance characteristic of low-mass buildings, are explained in Structural Considerations Concerning Hurricanes on page 400.

CLIMATIC CHARACTERISTICS OF HOT-HUMID REGIONS RELEVANT TO BUILDING AND URBAN DESIGN

All regions with hot-humid summers have some common characteristics. Therefore, they can be subdivided into several climate types. A division which would be meaningful from the building design aspect is between, on the one hand, equatorial and tropical-marine regions, which are warm year-round and, on the other hand, regions with hot-humid summers but with cool to cold winters. Equatorial and tropical-marine regions have similar temperature, humidity, and rainfall conditions but are different in their wind conditions, a factor which should have an impact on the design of buildings.

The equatorial climate type extends along a "strip" of up to ten to 15 degrees on either side of the equator: in Southeast Asia, northeast Australia, Micronesia, Africa, and Central and South America. The tropical-marine climate is found along the *eastern* margins of southern Africa and South America. Regions with hot-humid summers but with cool winters are found, for example, in Southeastern China and in the southeast United States along the Gulf of Mexico (Florida, Georgia, Alabama, Louisiana, and Texas). Even more northern areas in the Northern Hemisphere, such as Tennessee, the Carolinas, and Virginia, in the United States and east China, and central and southern Japan, which have cold winters, are quite hot-humid during the summers.

The main climatic features characterizing the equatorial and the tropical-marine climates are the relative constancy of the annual *average* temperature and humidity. While day-to-day variations may be significant, the monthly averages are almost constant. The annual mean temperature is about 27°C (80°F), and the range of the average monthly temperature is about 1–3°C (2–5.5°F). The diurnal temperature swing, on the other hand, is about 8°C (15°F). Average maximum temperatures are about 30°C (86°F), but on clear days may reach about 38°C (100°F).

Humidity and rainfall are high most of the year. The specific humidity (amount of water vapor in a unit mass of dry air) is about 20 gr/kg, sometimes rising to about 25gr/kg (0.02–0.025 lb/lb), with relative humidity often around and above 90 percent.

The wind conditions depend on the distance from the sea and may vary during the year, depending on the annual shifting of the trade wind belt northward or southward. In coastal regions, the constant heating and cooling patterns of the sea and land areas create regular sea breezes, providing regular air motion and mitigating the heat stress, mainly during the afternoon hours. Nights are often windless. In inland regions, calms are frequent even during the daytime, intensifying the thermal stress caused by the combination of high temperature and humidity.

The tropical-marine zones more regularly enjoy the trade winds, blowing westward and converging toward the equator. The path of the trade winds moves north and south with the annual shift of the sun's declination.

Hot-humid areas subjected to frequent hurricanes and typhoons are found in the Caribbean Islands, southeast United States, southeast China and Japan, the Philippines, and northeast Australia.

The combination of high humidity and temperature, in addition to its impact on human comfort, enhances mold and fungi growth, rusting of metals, and rotting of wood and other organic materials. Building materials may decay rapidly. Various insects, flies, and mosquitoes are plentiful.

As an example of a hot-humid climate Nieuwolt (1984) gives climatic data for Singapore: the diurnal temperature patterns depend mainly on the cloudiness conditions. On clear days the diurnal range can be nearly 8°C (14.4°F), with minima and maxima of about 24° and 32°C (75.2 and 89.6°F), respectively. On cloudy days the diurnal range is only about 4°C (7.2°F) with minima and maxima of about 23° and 27°C (73 and 80°F), respectively. On the other hand, the monthly averages of the hourly means are almost constant year-round, indicating the absence of any seasonal variations.

From the viewpoint of urban and building design, the average climatic conditions cannot be used without direct reference to the day-to-day variations in the climate. Thus, for example, the *average* intensity of solar radiation is lower in the equatorial regions than in some other climates and the *average* maximum temperature does not exceed about 30°C (86°F), but on clear days solar intensity can be much higher and temperatures may reach about 38°C (100°F), coupled with the very high humidity. However, most of the time the sky may be partially cloudy and the diffused radiation from the sky comprises a significant component of the total solar heat gain. Consequently, shading devices which intercept only the direct solar radiation would be less effective in hot-humid regions than in places with mostly clear sky in summer.

A typical characteristic in many hot-humid locations is the significant diurnal elevation of the ambient vapor content with the rising temperature. This can be seen in Figure 1-5 (page 24) which shows maximum and minimum Dry and Wet-Bulb Thermometer temperatures in a hot-humid city, Colima in Mexico (Givoni 1994). The reason is the increased evaporation from the leaves of the ample vegetation and from the moist soil, resulting from the higher temperature and the solar radiation. This feature adds, of course, to the discomfort of the inhabitants. It affects also the applicability of some passive cooling systems.

In the equatorial regions precipitation is caused mainly by rising convection currents of moist air, resulting from the convergence of the trade winds at the equatorial zone, after passing over extensive ocean areas. This flow pattern leads in many areas to a regular pattern of afternoon rains, often accompanied by violent thunderstorms.

From the building design viewpoint the conditions prevailing during the sunny days (mainly at midday hours) are the important ones, as the design details should aim at alleviating thermal stress precisely at these times. From the safety aspect, in regions subjected to tropical storms, it is important to construct buildings which can withstand the hurricane and typhoon forces. The buildings should, of course, also minimize the thermal discomfort and the need for mechanical air conditioning.

ARCHITECTURAL GUIDELINES FOR HOT-HUMID REGIONS

Many architectural and structural features of buildings in a hot-humid climate can affect the indoor climatic conditions, occupants' comfort, and energy consumption for air conditioning. In regions subjected to violent tropical storms and floods the basic design of buildings can affect also the safety of the occupants. Thus, the design objective should be to *modify* the indoor climate in order to improve the comfort of the inhabitants, reduce the energy consumption of the buildings for heating in winter and for cooling in summer, and minimize the dangers to life and property damage from tropical storms.

The main design objectives in hot-humid regions (some of them apparently conflicting from the building design aspect) can thus be summarized as follows:

- Minimizing solar heating of the buildings;
- Maximizing the rate of cooling in the evenings;
- Providing effective natural ventilation, even during rain;
- Preventing rain penetration, even during rainstorms;
- Preventing entry of insects while the windows are open for ventilation;
- Providing spaces for semioutdoor activities as integral part of the "living space."

In regions subjected to hurricanes or typhoons a major design objective should be to *minimize the risks from tropical storms.*

The main building design details which affect the attainment of these objectives are:

- Building layout;
- Orientation of the main rooms and the openings;
- Size and details of windows and doors;
- Organization and subdivision of the indoor space;
- Shading of openings and walls;
- Provision of verandas and balconies;
- Roof type and details;
- Thermal and structural properties of walls and roof;
- Site landscaping.

Building Layout

The appropriate layout of buildings in hot-humid regions depends on whether the building is planned to be air conditioned most of the time or if it is intended to rely on natural ventilation as much as possible. In the first case, to minimize the load on the air conditioning, the building should be compact to minimize the surface area of its envelope, relative to the occupied space, and, in particular to minimize the area of the windows, and thus to reduce the heat gain through the envelope and the load on the cooling equipment. This solution is applicable, of course, only to people who can afford the installation and operation of air conditioning and will not be elaborated on in this book.

In the second case, a spread-out building with large openable windows enables better natural cross-ventilation than a compact one. Once the building is cross-ventilated during the daytime hours its indoor temperature tends to follow the outdoor pattern. In this case, the heat flow through the envelope is small and the larger surface area of a spread-out building does not significantly affect the daytime indoor temperature. On the other hand, during the evening and night hours, when winds usually subside, a larger area of the envelope and larger open windows enable faster cooling and better ventilation, thus minimizing disturbances to restful sleep.

Figure 11-1 shows a design exercise by a Ph.D. candidate at UCLA, Sukanya Nutalaya, comparing the ventilation potential (optional locations for windows) of two design solutions for two houses with the same floor area and a given program: a compact and a spread-out one.

Deep porches, between surrounding rooms, can also help in promoting the ventilation potential and the cooling rate during the evening and night hours. They can also provide a protected semioutdoor space for family use, with some degree of privacy.

As air conditioning cannot be afforded by the vast majority of people in the developing countries, which cover most of the hot-humid regions, a building layout which provides good potential for cross-ventilation is more suitable for public housing.

The most effective design feature, combining natural ventilation and rain

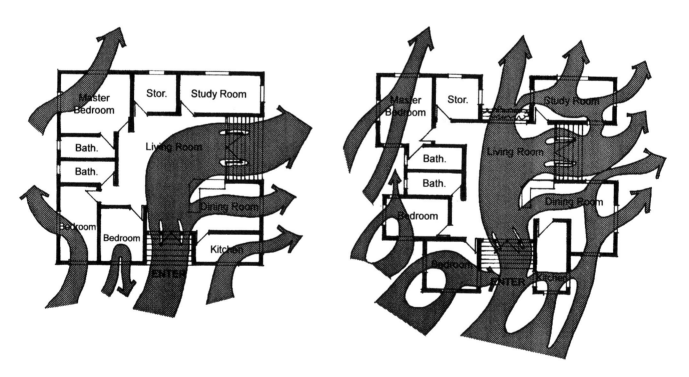

Figure 11-1. *A comparison of the ventilation potential (optional locations for windows) of two design solutions: one compact and one spread-out, with the same floor area and program.*

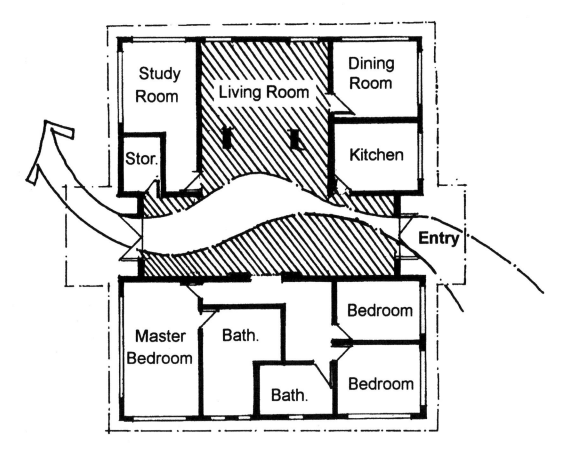

Figure 11-2. *Schematic design illustrating a breezeway.*

protection, is the breezeway. It is a passage "cutting" across or extending along-side the whole width of the house, wide enough for accommodating seating or eating, about 2–3 meters (7–10 feet) wide. Such a breezeway can concentrate the wind and thus enhance comfort during very humid or even rainy periods with very light winds. The breezeway could be equipped with operable shutters of a type which can prevent rain penetration while allowing airflow during light winds, but able to block the wind during storms, as illustrated in Figure 11-2.

A breezeway can also be designed with details which enable good ventilation conditions even when the wind is almost parallel to the long axis of the building. For example, in a place with predominant winds from the east, a building oriented with its long axis east-west will have poor ventilation potential for the rooms in the western part of the building (see Chapter 3). In fact, only the rooms along the eastern wall will have good ventilation potential. A breezeway "cutting" across the middle of the building, with details as shown in a schematic design as illustrated in Figure 11-3, can provide a comfortable area for various family activities.

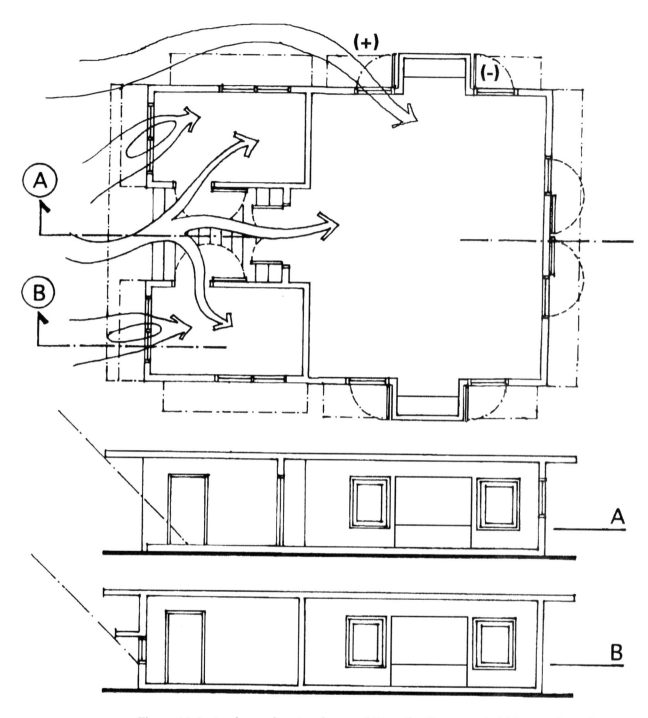

Figure 11-3. *A scheme showing the possibility of utilizing a wind blowing from the east through openings facing north and south and protected from the sun.*

Orientation of Main Rooms

In view of the primary importance of natural ventilation in hot-humid climates the relationship of the building to the wind direction should be a major consideration in determining the location of the main rooms—living and sleeping rooms—during the design stage.

Because of the low latitude of the hot-humid regions the annual pattern of the sun's motion results in a very large difference, more than at higher latitudes, between the radiation striking the eastern and western walls, on one hand, and, on the other hand, the radiation striking the northern and southern walls. The eastern and western walls and windows receive, year-round, much more radiation than the northern and the southern walls.

Many hot-humid regions at low latitudes have winds mainly from the east (the trade winds belt), changing in a given location between east-southeast and east-northeast direction with the annual north-south shift of the trade winds belt. In this case there seems to be a conflict between the best orientation from the solar aspect (south-north) and that optimal for ventilation. This apparent conflict can be resolved by suitable design details.

As is discussed in detail in Chapter 3, orientation of the buildings for ventilation does not imply having the building perpendicular to the wind direction. Oblique wind at angles between 30 and 120 degrees, and especially between 45 and 105 degrees to the wall in which the (inlet) window is placed, can provide effective cross-ventilation if openings are provided in the windward and the leeward walls, respectively.

The constancy of the eastern winds facilitates design details enhancing the ventilation by winds from that direction. But at the same time, the problem of undesirable direct solar radiation penetration through eastern windows, and of indirect solar heat gain through the eastern walls has to be, and can be, solved by architectural means.

The solar radiation load on a building can be controlled by effective shading of the openings and by the color of the opaque walls. A white wall, or a wall shaded by vegetation, effectively absorbs a low level of radiation, even when facing east or west. Similarly, an eastern or western window equipped with an appropriate operable shutter can practically be protected from the sun while taking advantage of an easterly (or westerly) wind for ventilation.

Porches can be designed to be interspaced between rooms, especially those facing east and west. The main openings of the rooms (doors and large windows, for example) can be located in the wall sections leading to the porches with only small and shaded windows in the main eastern and western walls. The porches, if large enough, can also serve as semiopen space, providing protection from sun and rain for many family activities. With this design detail the building can have cross-ventilation by the easterly winds while the main openings face north and south, and are effectively protected and shaded by the porches. It should be ensured that the air can flow inside the building from the inlet to the outlet openings with as little impediment as practical.

A scheme of a building aimed at achieving these objectives is illustrated in Figure 11-4. It shows the possibility of utilizing a wind blowing from the east through openings facing north and south and protected from the sun.

Organization and Subdivision of the Indoor Space

A building plan which is considered as "ideal" for a hot-humid climate is a detached elongated building with a single row of rooms with openings (windows and/or doors) in two opposite walls. Such an arrangement enables cross-ventilation of each individual room independently of the others. The rooms should have direct access to open balconies or verandas on one or two sides of the building. The balconies provide protection to the walls and the windows from rain and sun, and also can serve as an area for outdoor activities. Such design is common in vernacular architecture and also in some modern buildings in hot-humid regions.

However, with urbanization and the rising cost of land, it may be impractical to design such narrow and elongated buildings for public housing. Often the building depth has to be increased to accommodate at least two rooms between

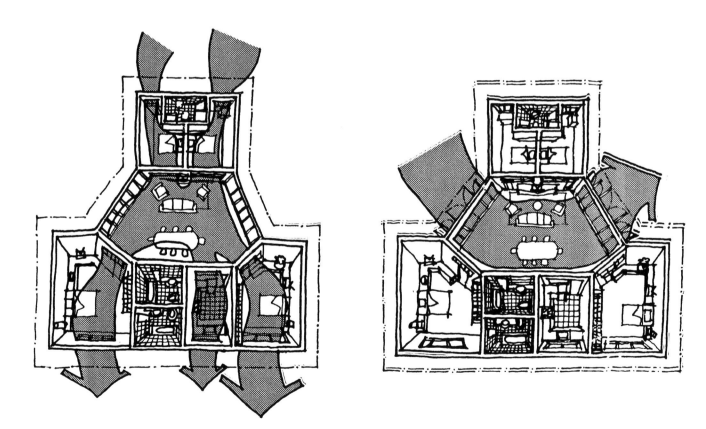

Figure 11-4. *A breezeway cutting across a house.*

the external walls. This is particularly the case in multistory apartment buildings, which become more common in dense urban areas. The ability to have cross-ventilation then depends on the organization of the indoor space: The air entering the building through an opening (window or door) in one room has to be able to flow with minimum restriction through another room (or a series of rooms) before it can exit through the outlet opening in another room.

It should be realized, however, that in such a case the acoustic privacy between these two rooms is compromised. Therefore, the ventilative "coupling" of various rooms should take into account the sensitivity of the uses of the rooms to acoustic privacy. Thus, a master bedroom may be coupled with a study room but it may be a problem to couple it with a child's room, even with a corridor in between.

Internal "Open" Planning

The optimal interior design in hot-humid regions is to have an open plan for the dwelling unit. An "open plan" implies locating various functions within an undivided space. Separation between the various functions is accomplished by "symbolic" barriers, such as furniture, changes in level, or open grids. Many functions which traditionally were located in separate rooms, such as living room, dining room, kitchen, study, and so on, can be located within a single space, or interconnected spaces, which enables free flow of air through it.

To the extent that it is socially acceptable in a given culture of a population group, the open plan is preferable to the isolation of the various functions of family life in separate "closed" rooms, from the ventilation aspect. However, the problem of providing privacy exists in dwellings using the open plan design. This problem is more serious in bedrooms, because cross-ventilation is important in hot-humid regions throughout the night.

Visual privacy can be provided by designing doors made like shutters blocking the view but giving passage to airflow. Another solution is to have the upper section of a room-height door, above the eye level, openable with hinges at the top. When the upper section is opened, it directs the air flowing through it downwards to the lower, habitable part of the room.

Acoustic privacy is much more difficult to provide in rooms which are ventilated by airflow passing through other spaces of the building. Therefore, where such privacy is important, the room should be able to be cross-ventilated independently by having both inlet and outlet windows in it.

Relationship of the Building to the Ground

Hot-humid regions often experience floods. Raising the buildings on stilts reduces the likelihood that floods will reach the floor level. A scheme common in Thailand of a raised whole platform, accommodating both the rooms and outdoor living spaces, is shown in Figure 11-5 (drawn by Sukanya Nutalaya, a Ph.D. student from Thailand).

In addition to the flood problem, raising the building off the ground can improve greatly the potential of ventilation. Due to the high precipitation, the land in hot-humid regions is often covered by vegetation, such as trees, high shrubs, and grass. Together with the buildings, the vegetation reduces the wind speed near the ground. The windows of single-story buildings at the ground level are often located in the zone of restricted wind speed, a factor which reduces the potential for cross-ventilation of the indoor space.

Figure 11-5. *A scheme common in Thailand of a building complex raised over a platform, accommodating both the rooms and outdoor living spaces (by Sukanya Nutalaya, a UCLA Ph.D. student from Thailand).*

Above the level of the shrub canopies the wind speed increases rapidly. Thus there is a sharp separation in the environmental wind speed between two levels above the ground: the level of the dense vegetation and that above it. When the building is raised on stilts to a height of about 2.5–3 m (8–10')—clear space—above the ground level, several advantages can be gained:

a. The windows of the rooms are at an average height of about 4 m (13') above the ground. The prospect for cross-ventilation is better than for rooms located at the ground level because of less interference from the vegetation on the wind flow.
b. The area under the building is effectively shaded and protected from the rain. It can be used during both rainy hours, and hot sunny hours, by family members for many activities, such as a children's playing area.
c. If floods occur, the risk of damage will be greatly reduced. Only with a flood level of 2.5–3 m (8–10') above ground will water penetrate the building.

Size and Details of Openings

Openings in a hot-humid climate play a major role in determining the thermal comfort of the occupants. Their location and size determine the ventilation conditions of the building. In this respect, large openings in all the walls can provide the design solution for effective cross-ventilation. However, solar radiation can penetrate directly through unshaded openings into the interior of the building and elevate the indoor temperature above that of the outdoor. Therefore, utmost care should be taken in ensuring that the openings in the envelope of the building are effectively shaded.

To enable independent cross-ventilation to every individual room in the building, each room should have at least two openings, in different walls, preferably one of them in a wall facing the wind direction. In practice it is difficult in many cases to have independent cross-ventilation of every individual room in the building, especially in large apartment blocks or even in a row town house. In such cases it is important to make sure that air can flow in and out of every room, passing through a series of rooms in the building.

When the wind direction is at a very small angle (nearly parallel) to the wall, as in the case of an elongated building facing north and south in a region with winds from southeast to northeast, it is possible to create effective cross-ventilation in a given room by having at least two windows in the windward wall, each one with a *single* "wing wall" or vertical projection (see discussion in Chapter 2). In each one of these windows the projection should be installed on alternative (left and right) sides. The windows should preferably be vertical, that is, narrow and high. With any direction of the wind, across an angle of down to about 15 degrees from the wall, one window will be in a wind pressure zone, acting as inlet, and the other window will be in the suction zone, acting as outlet. Architectural elements projecting in front of the main wall, such as alcoves or bookcases, with windows in front and behind them, can be as effective in enhancing ventilation.

Figure 2-18 (page 104) illustrates the enhancement of ventilation by architectural projections.

Shading of Openings and Walls

Together with the ventilation issue, effective prevention of solar heating of the building is critical for providing indoor comfort in hot-humid regions. The issue of shading may be even more complicated in hot-humid climates than in hot-dry climates for two reasons: (a) the windows may be much larger for the sake of ventilation, and (b) protection from the diffused radiation of a cloudy sky is more difficult than protection from the direct sunbeam.

Concerning the walls, the need for shading depends mainly on their color. There is no intrinsic need for high thermal insulation nor for a high heat capacity in ventilated buildings in hot-humid climates. However, if the walls and the roof have dark external color, and have relatively low thermal insulation, they will cause a high rate of heat flow from the solar-heated external surfaces to the interior. In this case, even if the building is effectively cross-ventilated and its daytime indoor *air* temperature is close to the outdoor level, solar heat flow across the walls will elevate the indoor surface's temperature, causing *radiant* heating and thermal discomfort for the occupants, especially during windless night hours.

It is not simple and easy in a hot-humid climate to secure a white color for walls, especially walls "permanently" shaded by vegetation, because of fungi growth. Two approaches to deal with this issue: (a) to increase significantly the insulation to counteract the solar gain, or (b) to maintain, by repeated painting, a white color of unshaded walls so that the sun will help in drying the walls and reducing the growth of fungi.

In single-story buildings it is possible to shade the walls and the windows by wide verandas, designed as roof extensions, or overhangs, above the walls. Such overhangs form, in effect, a covered outdoor open area, shaded and protected from the rain, which can serve for semioutdoor family activities. Shading by vegetation can also be provided relatively easily to low-rise buildings in hot-humid climates, as is illustrated in Figure 11-6.

In low-latitude regions it is possible to provide effective shading for walls

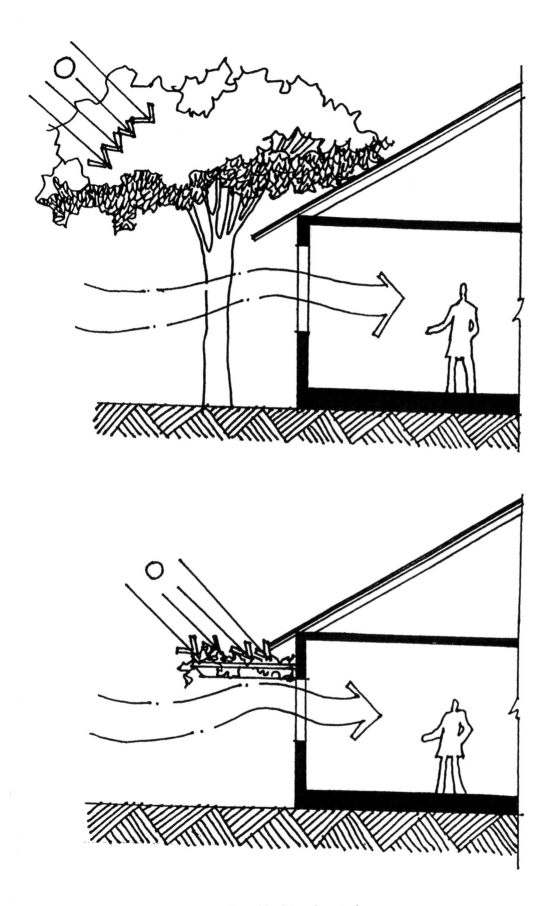

Figure 11-6. *Shading by plants without blocking the wind.*

and openings facing north and south; in multistory buildings, by wide balconies extending along the whole facade.

Eastern and western walls are subjected to the impact of the low sun. Fixed shading for the windows should therefore be capable of blocking the low sun rays in order to be effective. If the windows are in the form of horizontal narrow strips, it is possible to effectively shade them by inclined overhangs, reaching down near the sill level of the window. This detail enables ventilation while blocking sun rays and preventing rain penetration. It should be noted, however, that it also blocks part of the view.

Role and Details of Verandas and Porches

Often the outdoor climate in hot-humid regions is more pleasant than the indoors. Furthermore, the house size in low-cost housing is usually too small to accommodate all household activities, and many functions have to be carried out outdoors. In this respect, outdoor areas protected from rain and sun can be very useful. Trees and pergolas can provide, of course, protection from the sun but not from rains which are frequent in many hot-humid regions.

A common feature in some vernacular buildings in these regions is a veranda surrounding the whole building. Often, the veranda is formed by structurally extending sloping roofs beyond the walls, but they can also have a structural system separated from that of the roof.

Such verandas can provide effective shading and reasonable rain protection for the entire periphery of single- or even two-storied buildings. The shaded area can be used for outdoor activities even during hot, sunny or rainy periods, when the outdoor protected area may be much more comfortable than the indoor space. This is so in particular during windless periods.

In regions subjected to cyclonic storms, the high winds may blow out the veranda. If the veranda is structurally an extension of the roof of the building proper, the storm also can destroy the roof itself. It is possible to separate the structure of the veranda from that of the roof proper, so that even if it is destroyed by the wind the roof may remain unaffected.

Some contemporary multistory apartment buildings are using balconies as a major architectural element, as is illustrated in Figure 11-7—a photograph of a building in Boca Raton, Florida (courtesy of Professor Patrick Quinn). Such balconies provide some comfortable outdoor area in high-rise buildings.

Figure 11-7. *A multistory apartment building in Boca Raton, Florida, with balconies as a major architectural element. Courtesy of Professor Patrick Quinn.*

Landscaping Around Buildings and in Public Parks

Because of the high humidity characterizing hot-humid places, adequate wind speed *around* the building and in the public parks and play areas is very important for comfort. Therefore, in designing landscape, minimizing wind blockage should be one of the major considerations.

Climatic objectives in landscaping in hot-humid regions should be:

- To minimize blockage of the wind on the building site, especially in front of the windows.
- To provide shade around buildings and for the users of the public parks.
- In planning urban open green areas an additional objective could be to minimize flood hazards in the more-sensitive urban areas.

Because of the high precipitation in hot-humid regions, local plants do not need irrigation most of the year. Therefore, it is possible to maintain the vegetation with less maintenance work and expenses than in arid regions.

The impact of plants on human comfort in hot-humid areas can be a mixed blessing. The shading provided by trees is always welcomed. However, the blockage of the wind and the contribution to the humidity level by evaporation from the leaves may increase human discomfort, especially during hours with very light winds.

Trees with a high trunk and wide canopy are the most effective plants in providing usable shade, especially if they also can shade parts of the roof. If densely placed on the windward side of the house they, of course, block the wind. Therefore, the best strategy with such trees is to have them only at the spots where their shade will be utilized without blocking the wind, such as near the walls but not in front of windows. Pergolas of vines in front and above windows can also provide effective shading without wind blocking (Figure 11-8). If the trees and the vines are deciduous they enable daylight and solar gain in winter. However, one should be careful to prevent low-growing trees and high shrubs in front of windows *on the windward* sides of the building. Such plants can act, in effect, as wind breakers and reduce greatly the ventilation potential.

High shrubs block the wind and "contribute" to the humidity level without providing useful shade, except when they are placed alongside walls. Therefore, their introduction should be minimal, especially at the windward parts of the site.

A combination of grasses, low flower beds, and shade trees with high trunks is thus the most appropriate plant combination in landscaping in hot-humid climates.

Low-lying areas prone to floods can be grassed and planted with trees which can withstand flooding. If the vegetation can withstand a given height of water for a few days, then such areas can be utilized as flood controls during, and immediately after, rainstorms. In the periods between storms such areas can again be useful public green spaces for recreation, grazing, and so forth.

STRUCTURAL DESIGN AND CHOICE OF MATERIALS IN HOT-HUMID REGIONS

The climatic role of materials, in un-air conditioned, naturally ventilated buildings in hot-humid regions, is to minimize solar heating of the interior during daytime and to maximize the rate of cooling during the evening and night hours. Significant reduction of the indoor air temperature below the outdoor level is not practical in hot-humid regions because of the need for daytime ventilation of the buildings and the small diurnal temperature range. This situation suggests medium thermal resistance of the envelope, mainly in proportion to the expected impact of solar radiation on the walls and the roof of the building.

Lightweight materials such as wood construction (a low heat capacity) is typical in vernacular buildings in hot-humid climates. Such low heat capacity can enhance the rate of cooling of the building during the evening and night hours, when the winds usually subside. However, recent research has demonstrated that if effective night ventilation can be ensured by the provision of exhaust fans, high-mass buildings can be more comfortable, especially during the daytime hours, than lightweight buildings. This point is further elaborated on in Thermal Mass Considerations on page 400.

Furthermore, in many hot-humid regions where hurricanes occur, low-mass buildings are vulnerable to severe damage and even destruction during the storms. This vulnerability presents an apparent conflict between the climatic and the safety considerations. This issue is covered in the discussion on Special Problems of Roofs in Developing Countries on page 405.

Thermal Resistance of the Building's Envelope

When a building is cross-ventilated, the indoor air temperature follows closely the outdoor level, especially when the wind speed is above about 2 meters per second (2 m/s) (about 7 km/h) (400 fpm), which is a rather mild wind. However, the temperatures of the internal surfaces of the building's envelope can be much higher, as a result of solar energy absorption at the walls' and roof's external surfaces and heat flow inward. The elevated indoor radiant temperature increases the physiological heat stress and the thermal discomfort of the inhabitants. During windless hours the indoor air temperature is also elevated, even if windows remain open, by heat flow inward from the warm mass of the walls. The indoor air then practically follows closely the average surface (the radiant) temperature.

The need for thermal resistance in a building which is ventilated continuously, from the summer aspect, is determined therefore by the desire to minimize the elevation of the indoor radiant temperature, namely the temperatures of the interior surfaces of the roof and the external walls, above the indoor air temperature.

The solar heating of the external envelope of the building depends on the intensity of the impinging solar radiation and on the absorptivity (color) of the external surfaces, which to some extent is a design factor.

In a hot-humid climate it is impractical to assume a white color to the walls and the roof because of the abundant fungi growth. Therefore, even if dark colors are avoided by painting, the actual absorptivity of the external surfaces can be assumed to reach, in time, a value around 0.6, unless the building is periodically repainted white.

The intensity of the impinging solar radiation depends, of course, on the shading conditions of the walls. When walls are shaded by a veranda or a balcony, the impinging radiation is mainly that reflected from the ground and nearby buildings. As vegetation cover of the soil is common in hot-humid regions, the reflected radiation would not be very high.

As discussed above, shading of northern and southern walls in low-latitude regions is easy, by, for example, extended balconies. But shading of eastern and western walls from the sun is not easy and is limited in practice to the use of vegetation, by climbing vines or by trees.

By "allowing" a given elevation of the indoor *surface* temperature of a wall or a ceiling above the indoor *air* temperature during the outdoor's peak temperature hours, assuming very light winds, and assuming also a certain intensity of solar radiation striking the external surface, and given external and internal surface coefficients, it is possible to suggest a required level of thermal resistance as a function of the external color and the shading conditions. The suggested procedure is based on some approximating assumptions.

ASSUMPTIONS (METRIC UNITS)

(Computation results are also given in British units.)

- The indoor air temperature is the same as the outdoors'. This assumption is closer to reality during the daytime, in buildings with open but shaded windows, more than at night.
- With very light winds the external surface coefficient, h_o, is about 15 (W/m².C) (2.64 Btu/h.ft².F) for the roof and for the walls. With very light indoor airflow the internal surface coefficient, h_i, is about 7 (W/m².C) (1.2 Btu/h.ft².F). The surface resistances, r_o and r_i, are the reciprocals of the corresponding surface coefficients: 0.067 and 0.14 (0.38 and 0.8), respectively.
- Solar radiation intensity on the roof is 1000 and on the walls 500 (W/m²) (320 and 160 Btu/h.ft²).
- The "allowable" elevation of the internal surface temperatures above the air temperature, dT_i, is 2°K (3.6°F). This limit would depend in practice on the economic conditions of the inhabitants.

The sol-air temperature elevation, of a roof under clear sky, dT_{s-a}, can then be estimated by the equation:

$$dT_{s-a} = (a.I/h_o) - 5$$

and of a wall:

$$dT_{s-a} = (a\ I/h_o) - 2$$

when "a" is the absorptivity (color) of the surface, assumed as 0.6 for surfaces which are not painted periodically (medium color). For painted surfaces absorptivity is assumed as 0.3 (light color).

With the above assumptions the sol-air temperature elevation will be:

for medium-colored roof: $dT_{s-a} = 0.6 * 1000 / 15 - 5 = 35°K$ (63°F)
for light-colored roof: $dT_{s-a} = 0.3 * 1000 / 15 - 5 = 15°K$ (27°F)
for medium-colored wall: $dT_{s-a} = 0.6 * 600 / 15 - 2 = 22°K$ (39.6°F)
for light-colored wall: $dT_{s-a} = 0.3 * 600 / 15 - 2 = 10°K$ (18°F)

The required thermal resistance of the medium-colored roof would then be:

$$R = (0.14 * 35) / 2 - 0.14 = 2.3\ (m².C/W)\ (13ft².F.h/Btu)$$

and for a light-colored roof:

$$R = (0.14 * 15) / 2 - 0.14 = 0.9\ (m².C/W)\ (5ft².F.h/Btu)$$

for the medium-colored wall:

$$R = (0.14 * 22) / 2 - 0.14 = 1.4\ (m².C/W)\ (8ft².F.h/Btu)$$

and for the light-colored wall:

$$R = (0.14 * 10) / 2 - 0.14 = 0.6 \ (m^2.C/W) \ (3.4ft^2.F.h/Btu)$$

It can be seen that with naturally ventilated buildings the required thermal resistance (and the corresponding insulation level) of the envelope elements is greatly affected by the color or shading conditions of the envelope. Painting the roofs and the walls in hot-humid regions white can reduce greatly the need for insulation for a given level of comfort, as well as enhancing energy conservation for air conditioned buildings.

This procedure can be used to calculate the required thermal resistance with any assumptions concerning the colors, impinging solar radiation (or shading effect on it), and the acceptable elevation of the indoor radiant temperature above the indoor air level.

Thermal Mass Considerations

Vernacular buildings in hot-humid regions are built mostly of low-mass materials, mainly of wood construction. Such buildings are considered appropriate for this climate as their indoor temperature drops rapidly in the evenings, when the winds usually subside. High-mass buildings cool down more slowly during the evening hours, a feature which may cause discomfort and restless sleep. Another reason for the prevalence of wood-construction building type is the availability of plentiful plant materials in hot-humid regions.

However, as has been demonstrated in an experimental study of the author in Pala, California, ventilated high-mass buildings have *lower* indoor maximum temperature than low-mass buildings. If nighttime ventilation is assisted by an exhaust fan (a very low-cost, low-energy device!) the indoor night temperatures in high-mass buildings are very close to those in low-mass buildings, as can be seen in Figure 11-8. The conclusion drawn from this study was that, when fan-assisted night ventilation is provided, high-mass buildings can be more comfortable during most of the time than low-mass ones.

Structural Considerations Concerning Hurricanes

Many of the hot-humid regions, especially on the eastern sides of the continents, are also subject to tropical storms: hurricanes in southeast United States, typhoons in Southeast Asia and in northeast Australia, and so forth. A major characteristic of these storms, from the building design aspect, is

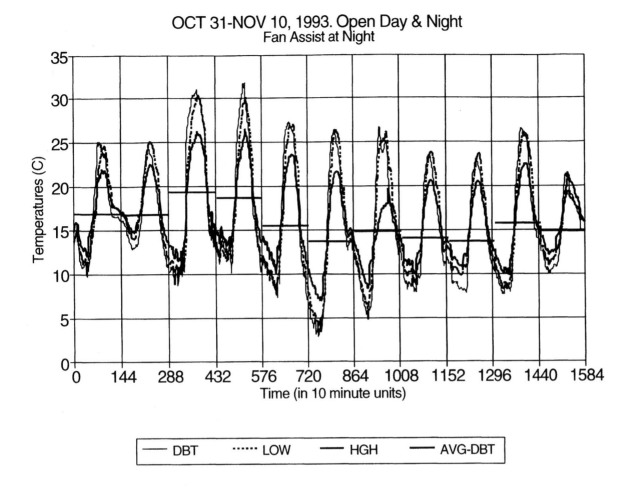

Figure 11-8. *With effective day and night continuous ventilation, the daytime temperatures of a high-mass building are lower than those of a low-mass one.*

their strong lifting power, literally blowing away roofs and sometimes whole buildings.

For a building to withstand the forces of such storms it should preferably have a heavy and strong structural system, often based on reinforced concrete, which would result in a high-mass stable building, able to resist the lifting and pulling power of the storm. However, a high-mass building seems to be in contradiction with the low-mass building type, which is traditional in hot-humid regions. A new structural solution, which ensures safety during the storms and at the same time maximizes comfort in the high-humidity environment, is suggested here.

As mentioned above, the main climatic performance problem of high-mass buildings in hot-humid regions is their slow rate of cooling and their high interior surface temperatures in the evenings, when the wind subsides, even when the windows are open for ventilation. Two design solutions are possible to overcome these difficulties.

One is to equip the building with an exhaust fan, to enhance the ventilation rate during the night hours.

The second solution is structural: lining concrete walls and roofs with an *internal* insulation layer; for example, one made of polystyrene and plastered with a fire-retardant plaster (e.g., gypsum plaster). Such wall detail ensures good coupling between the interior surface temperatures of the envelope elements and the indoor air when the building is ventilated, even with a small air change rate. Such interior insulation will provide the required resistance for minimizing the impact of solar energy absorbed at the envelope. From the viewpoint of thermal characteristics, such a building, when ventilated, behaves similarly to a light-weight building.

It should be noted, however, that the internal insulation precludes the potential for storing daytime solar energy for night utilization in winter. Therefore, this design is suggested only for hot-humid regions with *mild* winters, where solar daytime heating without storage may be acceptable.

Tropical storms are accompanied by heavy rains and floods, and, in coastal areas, also by a sea surge. Raising heavy concrete buildings on stilts about 3 m (10') above ground level may reduce the frequency of, and in many cases even eliminate, flood damage in the buildings without compromising the ability of the buildings to withstand the storm. A fringe benefit resulting from raising the building above the ground level is the improved potential for natural ventilation.

A high-mass, heavy-concrete building, insulated internally, thus combine the thermal performance characteristics of a low-mass building with superior protection from tropical storms. It seems to the author that this structural design can be the ideal solution in hot-humid regions susceptible to hurricanes or typhoons.

HURRICANE PROTECTION FOR WINDOWS

While the heavy structural construction of the walls and the roof discussed above may provide protection from the tropical storms, the windows remain the weak point of the building. The large windows recommended for enhancing natural ventilation may constitute a hazard during a hurricane. Adequate protection from the high winds can be provided by strong external opaque shutters. Such shutters, if designed in such a way that their lower half can be hinged outward at an angle of about 45 degrees, provide very effective shading without impeding the potential for natural ventilation, especially for eastern and western windows. When closed and secured to the high-mass walls, they can provide effective protection for the glazing during the storms.

Special Problems of Roofs in Developing Countries

Common roof types in hot-humid regions are asbestos-cement or galvanized-iron corrugated sheets, and clay or cement tiles. To the extent that such roofs can be kept white the problem of solar overheating can be minimized. But it is usually assumed that in a hot-humid climate it is impractical to maintain white colors for roofs, due to fungi growth. The experience in Bermuda refutes this assumption.

On the Island of Bermuda the coral-based ground cannot retain the ample rainwater. Consequently, every house has to collect and store the rainwater, as no public water distribution exists there. For hygienic reasons, all the roofs in Bermuda (which are made of cement tiles) are painted white with a mixture of lime and machine oil. The white color keeps up for about five years before repainting of the roofs is required.

The experience in Bermuda demonstrates that even in a humid climate it is possible to maintain a white color for roofs. Such white painting can have a very significant role in reducing the heat stress in low-cost housing. Shading the roof, where practical, can also minimize solar overheating.

In many developing countries, a very common "modern" roof type is that made of galvanized-steel corrugated sheets. Such roofs are highly conductive and cause severe thermal stress and discomfort during the *daytime* hours. However, during the night hours, such roofs cool down very fast, often below the ambient air temperature level, owing to long-wave radiation to the sky. Therefore, they are favorable in summer from the night comfort viewpoint.

Shading would be very helpful in reducing the daytime temperature of such roofs. Trees with high trunks and wide canopies, planted near and around the walls, can provide effective shade over the roof. Vines climbing over the roof may not be practical, because of the need for repeated painting to minimize corrosion of the metal sheets.

A passive radiant cooling system "tailored" to buildings with bricks or concrete walls and metal roofs has been described in Chapter 5 (page 194).

A model of such a system was built and tested at UCLA. The model was built of insulated plywood panels walls and floor and a metallic gable roof. The hinged panels in the model were made of aluminum foil wrapped around a wood frame. Interior mass was in the form of water filled bottles. The model was closed day and night to eliminate ventilation and convective heat exchange, so that the cooling occurred at night through the roof, mainly by the long-wave radiant loss to the sky.

Figures 5-3 and 5-4 (pages 195) show outdoor, indoor, and attic temperatures which were measured in a physical model of this system. The metallic roof acted as an effective radiant cooling system during the night while the hinged ceiling panels minimized the heat gain from the much-hotter attic during the daytime.

CLIMATIC CHARACTERISTICS OF DIFFERENT BUILDING TYPES IN HOT-HUMID REGIONS

Different building types have specific climatic performance characteristics in hot-humid regions. As most countries in the hot-humid areas are developing countries, the special social problems and needs of the population should be a critical factor in choosing a given housing type. However, as this book is limited to dealing with the climatic aspects, the social impacts of the different building types will not be discussed here, except for some comments when seemed appropriate. The climatic characteristics of different building types in the context of the developing countries in the hot-humid climate are discussed below.

Detached Single-Family Houses

By definition, detached houses are exposed to the outdoor air on all sides. This feature provides good potential for natural ventilation and is advantageous in a hot-humid climate. For a given thermal resistance of the envelope, the expected indoor temperatures and human comfort during the daytime hours, if the building is ventilated, would not be worse than in a more-compact building type. Furthermore, during the evening and night hours, when the outdoor wind usually weakens or subsides, a detached house will cool down faster than other types of buildings, thus providing better comfort.

This building type is the least sensitive to the orientation of the building from the ventilation aspect. In many cases homeowners like, or planning regulations require, that the buildings are aligned with the streets. Detached houses thus can be designed with any street layout without compromising ventilation. This feature is especially advantageous in a hot-humid climate.

With a given urban density (Floor-to-Area Ratio—FAR) and a given overall floor area of a house, a double- or even triple-story detached building provides better potential for natural ventilation than a single-story building. This is due to two reasons: First, with the same floor area, a single-story building covers a larger fraction of the building's lot and thus leaves smaller distances between buildings, a factor which reduces the ventilation potential. Second, the ventilation of the ground floor is often inhibited by trees and nearby shrubs, which may be plentiful in many hot-humid regions, while the higher floors are more exposed to the wind.

In summary, from the climatic aspect a detached house is the most suitable in a hot-humid climate. This feature should be taken into account by urban planners, especially since this type is also more suitable socially and functionally to the needs of large, low-income, families. However, detached houses lead to a low urban density, with its accompanied problems of urban sprawl, traffic congestion in the downtown areas, and so on.

Town Houses (Row Houses)

Town houses are comprised of a set of several single-family units, attached to each other at their sidewalls, thus forming a "row" of dwelling units. The units can range in height from a single story up to three stories, all occupied by the same household. In hot-humid regions town houses provide, from the climatic aspect, the next-best building type for mass housing after detached houses, while enabling higher urban densities. However, town houses are much more sensitive than single-family houses, from the ventilation aspect, to their orientation with respect to the wind direction.

In multistoried town houses, internal staircases can form natural shafts for vertical airflow. When these shafts are large enough, they transform the whole space of the house into an integrated space from the airflow aspect. Consequently, during windless periods, multistory town houses can utilize the indoor-outdoor temperature differences for thermosyphonic ventilation more effectively than single-story houses, especially during the night, when the wind usually subsides.

Multistory Apartment Buildings

This building type is the least-expensive for mass housing, especially for buildings with elevators, and therefore many public housing authorities tend to prefer it over other building types. However, multistoried apartment buildings may present difficulties in providing cross-ventilation, unless they are planned with staircases (or elevators in buildings with too many stories for walk-up) serving only two units per floor, as is discussed in Chapter 6.

Such buildings are much more sensitive than single-family houses, from the ventilation aspect, to their orientation with respect to the wind direction. The worst conditions would be in buildings with internal, double-loaded corridors.

Therefore, such apartment buildings should be avoided in hot-humid regions unless each apartment can be provided with a whole-house exhaust fan or such fans are provided for each room in the apartment.

When the corridor is external and open (like a balcony), it is possible to have cross-ventilation in the apartments along it only by having open windows also on the corridor side of the apartments. This, of course, severely interferes with the visual and the acoustic privacy of the occupants.

An effective design solution to the visual privacy issue in apartment buildings with an external corridor is to plan the corridor at a lower level, about 50–70 cm (20–28") below the main floor's level, with stairs leading individually to each unit from the corridor. Windows in the corridor wall of the apartment, with a sill height of about 1.20 m, would then be just under the ceiling in the corridor, above the eye's level of persons walking in the corridor, as is illustrated in Figure 2-14. This design detail enables cross-ventilation of the dwelling unit while providing visual privacy.

When a staircase in an apartment building serves only two units per floor, each apartment is exposed to at least two external walls. With adequate internal organization of the indoor space it is then possible to ensure good ventilation conditions to all the dwelling units. To achieve this goal, the building should be so oriented that one of its long facades is either perpendicular to the prevailing wind or oblique to the wind direction with an angle of not more than 60 degrees from the perpendicular position.

When multistory apartment blocks are built around a courtyard the downwind blocks have inferior conditions from the ventilation aspect. Both the courtyard "interior" side of the building block and the "exterior" side are under low pressure. One design solution to this problem is to lower the number of stories of part of the upwind block, as is illustrated in Figure 11-5.

High-Rise "Tower" Buildings

This type of building, which requires sophisticated structure, elevators, and other mechanical systems, is suitable mainly for relatively high-income people and therefore cannot solve the mass housing problems in most countries, especially the developing countries. However, this building type has some interesting features from the climatic aspect in hot-humid regions and therefore deserves attention.

When high, narrow buildings are placed relatively far apart, they do not reduce the airspeed near the ground level, as was discussed in Chapter 9. In fact, such buildings can increase appreciably the ground level airspeed around them, thus improving the ventilation potential for lower buildings between them, as well as in the streets. The occupants of the high stories enjoy lower temperature, as well as lower humidity (as vapor is generated by evaporation from vegetation and moist soil at, or near, the ground level). This is in addition to the better ventilation potential and the view offered from the high stories.

Providing high-standard, although expensive, housing in a city can also increase its attractiveness for professionals and high-income population groups, an attraction which may be an asset for towns in developing countries.

URBAN DESIGN GUIDELINES FOR HOT-HUMID REGIONS

The main urban design objectives in hot-humid regions involve two types of issues:

- Minimizing the hazards from tropical storms and floods.
- Minimizing thermal discomfort and cooling energy consumption.

These general objectives can be further elaborated upon:

MINIMIZING THE HAZARDS FROM TROPICAL STORMS AND FLOODS

- Minimizing the hazards of floods by water flowing in from areas beyond the city limits (mainly a location problem).
- Rapid disposal of excess rainwater resulting from urbanization.
- Providing rain protection for pedestrians in "commercial" streets.

MINIMIZING THERMAL DISCOMFORT AND COOLING ENERGY CONSUMPTION

- Providing shade for pedestrians (on sidewalks).
- Providing shade for outdoor activities, such as children's playing areas.
- Enabling good natural ventilation of the urban space (streets, open spaces between buildings, public open spaces, and so forth).
- Providing good ventilation potential for the buildings (airflow conditions around them).
- Minimizing the "heat island" effect in densely built areas.

The main urban design features which can contribute to the achievement of these objectives are:

- Location Considerations within Hot-Humid Regions.
- Minimizing Flood Hazards by Specialized Urban Design Features.
- Layout of the Streets' Network.
- Urban Density and Building Heights in Hot-Humid Regions.

Discussion of the impact of these urban design features on the climate of inhabitants' comfort in hot-humid regions and suggestions for the relevant design strategies is presented next.

Location Considerations within Hot-Humid Regions

When a new town is planned in a given region having a hot-humid and "wet" climate, or when a new neighborhood is being planned or reconstructed in an existing city, the following considerations should guide the planners:

- Avoidance of flood-prone areas for dense residential or commercial land uses. Such floodwater may originate in areas far away from the town itself (e.g., mountains around it).
- Preference for areas with good natural wind conditions and also, if available, lower temperatures. This factor is important mainly for residential areas. However, even in the streets of commercial areas, assuming that the buildings are mostly air conditioned, good ventilation is important for the comfort of the pedestrians.
- Availability of natural drainage in the small-scale topographical features of the area, mainly for excess rainwater accumulated within the urban area itself.

FLOOD-RISK CONSIDERATIONS

Flat areas along rivers or near outlets of rivers may be subjected to severe floods when heavy rain, often in far away catchment areas, raises the water level above the "normal" flood level.

Many hot-humid coastal regions are in areas prone to hurricanes (or cyclones as they are called in Southeast Asia). The storms are accompanied by very high rainfall. Along the coastal areas, the rise of the sea level and the high waves caused by the very high onshore winds may cause severe damage and loss of life to people living in the flooded areas.

Some protection from hurricane winds can be achieved by taking advantage of certain topographical features which provide shelter from high winds in choosing a location for a settlement. Also dense groves and forests of high and strong trees can provide some protection from the hurricane winds. (after de Carmona 1984).

Davis (1984) states that the main areas vulnerable to high winds and floods are river valleys, estuaries, and the coastal belts in areas subject to cyclonic storms. Often such areas are attractive for naturally irrigated agriculture because of the fertility of the land, or for providing opportunities for fishing and coastal trade. This economic attractiveness should be weighted against the risks of life and property losses during cyclonic floods.

NATURAL VENTILATION CONSIDERATIONS

A major factor determining the level of thermal stress in a hot-humid region is the potential for natural ventilation. Topographical features of the land may exhibit very different characteristics of the wind conditions in nearby places, especially during periods of light winds.

Windward slopes are preferable to leeward slopes from the ventilation viewpoint. Valley slopes may experience downslope air currents during windless nights, thus providing more comfortable conditions as compared with the valley floor area (Lyons 1984).

Seashore and large lakeshore areas may benefit from the daytime sea and nighttime land breezes. Of particular importance is the daytime sea breeze which usually reaches its maximum speed in the afternoon, when the temperature difference between the cooler sea and the warmer land is largest. In this case, the sea breeze provides comfort to the affected areas by the combination of higher velocity and lower temperatures, as compared with more "sheltered" nearby areas.

Minimizing Flood Hazards by Specialized Urban Design Features

Floods in urban areas can be caused either by water, originating in far away areas, flowing through the city or by excess rainwater generated over the area of the city, which cannot be absorbed in the soil or discharged away fast enough. During rains, the city itself increases the excess of water runoff: the ability of the ground in an urban area to absorb water is reduced, as a result of the coverage of the land by buildings, roads, parking areas, and so forth. This factor increases the risks from floods in low-lying flat urban areas.

The concentrated flow of rainwater from far away areas, very much greater than the town's area itself, can raise the water level several yards above the "normal" and cause major destruction. No urban design details can prevent such floods except simply avoiding locations prone to them. Therefore, the prevention of such hazards, often also involving loss of life, is by *avoiding* urban development in areas where such floods are common.

In practice, other considerations, mainly economical, may put pressure for urban development in flood-prone areas, such as along riverbanks, low-lying flat areas, and so on. The probability of a given flood level occurring within a given period (number of years) is often used as a basis for cost/benefit considerations for urban development in a given area prone to floods by water originating far away. Careful consideration of this aspect at the stage of initial location of a town can later save lives and reduce the property damage resulting from severe floods in densely inhabited areas.

On the other hand, the risk of floods from excess rainwater within the boundary of the city itself can be minimized by details of urban design. The following design details can be applied to achieve this goal:

- Increasing rain absorption in soil in the urban area, thus reducing runoff.
- Preserving land features of natural drainage such as interconnected valley systems.
- Collecting excess runoff in urban reservoirs, such as minilakes, which can also be incorporated in the urban landscape design.

The network of valleys which naturally drain off the rainwater from the town's area can serve as urban parks and other open spaces. With proper planting they can be reused for such functions after the rainwater subsides. In this way, they serve the sociofunctional needs of the people together with this climate-related function.

From the above it is obvious that minimizing flood hazards has to start with location and land-use planning, the initial stages of urban design.

Dunne (1984) has presented two types of design strategies which can reduce the hazards of flooding in urban areas, aiming at the following objectives:

- Reducing storm runoff volumes.
- Delaying runoff and extending the period of draining into the drainage channels.

REDUCING RUNOFF VOLUMES

Dunne notes that the "most obvious method of reducing runoff is to maintain as much of the natural vegetation and permeable topsoil as possible." He also recommends "planting of covers that are effective in maintaining high infiltration capacities and in protecting against soil erosion . . . Trees, like many eucalypti, which render the soil beneath them bare and erodible, are not very useful for runoff control."

It should be noted that a significant portion of the urban surfaced area is not subjected to heavy vehicular traffic, such as parking lots, pedestrian areas, and the like. These areas can be surfaced with permeable pavement, such as open-grated concrete blocks or special bricks. Soil can be laid and seeded with suitable grass to promote infiltration. A layer consisting of a mixture of sand and gravel under the blocks can increase the area of effective infiltration below the semihard surface, thus increasing the rate of water absorption in the ground.

An interesting planning policy for increasing absorption of rainwater in the ground was implemented in the city of Davis, California. All public parking areas are surfaced with perforated blocks. Instead of underground drainage pipes, the runoff discharge is through an interconnected series of wide, shallow, grassy minivalleys, functioning as natural drainage features of the area. These shallow "valleys" form an integral part of the urban open-spaces system. The natural exposed drainage channels proved to be more effective than the conventional underground drainage pipes during extreme rainstorms.

DELAYING RUNOFF

Delaying the peak and spreading the duration of the runoff water involves temporary storage of a given amount of water over a land surface, or within a gravel layer over the soil.

Many new institutional, commercial, and industrial urban buildings have flat roofs which structurally can hold a layer of water. Dunne (1984) suggests that such roofs can be used to retain water during the rain and release it slowly afterwards.

It should be noted that if these "roof ponds" keep a given level of water also after the rain, to be evaporated during the sunny periods between rains, they can significantly reduce the heat load on the building.

Temporary shallow ponding of rainwater is possible also in parking lots, provided that the height of the pond does not prevent the functional use of that area. If the parking area is filled with a layer of gravel of a given depth below the functional surface, it temporarily can hold a given amount of water without interfering with its use.

Dunne suggests also that it is possible to utilize natural depressions or excavations within the urban area as temporary storage of rainwater. Another suggestion of Dunne is to construct small dams where topography is suitable to create detention basins. Such basins can be used as grazing or recreation areas between storms.

However, care should be taken to avoid pools with long-term standing water where insects may breed.

Layout of the Streets' Network

The main climatic objectives in a hot-humid climate, concerning the street layout within the urban area, are to provide good ventilation conditions for pedestrians in the streets and good potential for ventilation of the buildings along the streets. The "ideal" design solutions for these two objectives are not the same (see Chapter 8, Street's Width and Orientation, page 288) and a compromise may be called for.

Another objective is to provide shade over sidewalks in streets with large concentrations of pedestrians. Such shade can be provided by trees along sidewalks, as well as by special details of the buildings. When conflicts exist between a street layout aimed at provision of ventilation and that aimed at shading of the sidewalks, the ventilation aspects may be more important in a hot-humid climate.

The issue of street orientation and width is of importance mainly in densely built urban sections, such as commercial sections and high-density residential areas with large apartment blocks. In low-density residential areas, where detached single-family houses with private open spaces around them are common, the problem is of minor significance. In such urban areas, the wind can flow between and around the buildings. Consequently, the role of the streets for wind passage is rather small. Therefore, the following discussion is relevant mainly to high-density urban sections.

The best ventilation *within the streets* and the sidewalks is achieved when the street is parallel to the direction of the prevailing winds during the afternoon hours (when the urban temperature reaches its maximum). However, when streets are parallel to the wind direction and the buildings along them face the street, the *ventilation potential of the buildings* is compromised. The reason is that with this orientation, all the walls of the building are in "suction" zones. Effective indoor cross-ventilation can occur in a building only when at least one of its walls (and windows) is in a "pressure" zone.

Streets perpendicular to the wind direction, with closely spaced, long buildings along them, may block the wind in the whole urban area; therefore, such long uninterrupted streets actually *impede* the urban ventilation in hot-humid regions.

A good street layout from the urban ventilation aspect in a hot-humid region is when wide main avenues are oriented at an oblique angle to the prevailing winds (e.g., at about 30 degrees). This orientation still enables penetration of the wind into the heart of the town. The buildings along such avenues are exposed to different air pressures on their front and back facades—the upwind wall is at the pressure zone while the downwind wall is at the suction zone.

This street orientation thus provides a good potential for natural ventilation of the buildings, while at the same time provides also good ventilation within the streets. It is desirable mainly in high-density residential urban zones.

Urban Density and Building Heights in Hot-Humid Regions

Urban density is among the major factors which determines the urban ventilation conditions, as well as the urban temperature. Under given circumstances, an urban area with a high density of buildings can experience poor ventilation and strong "heat island" effect. In hot-humid regions these features would lead to a high level of thermal stress of the inhabitants and, in air conditioned buildings, to increased use of energy.

de Carmona (1984) has commented that although "the natural arrangement of buildings in the wet tropics would seem to tend towards a certain amount of scattering . . . economic and social imperatives dictate that cities must become more concentrated, making it necessary to increase the density to reduce the cost of public services and achieve required social cohesiveness."

Thus the reality of modern urbanization leads to higher densities than were in traditional settlements. However, with suitable urban and building design details, this should and could be accomplished with minimum worsening of the environmental quality.

Generally speaking, the higher the density of the buildings in a given area, the poorer will be its ventilation conditions. However, for a given density level, there can be quite different urban ventilation conditions, depending on the particular configuration of buildings by which this density is obtained.

An urban configuration to be avoided as much as possible in hot-humid regions is that of high, long buildings, of the same height, perpendicular to the prevailing wind direction. This configuration blocks the wind and creates poor ventilation conditions both in the streets and for the buildings, as the first row of buildings acts as a wind barrier.

An urban profile of variable heights, where buildings of different heights are placed next to each other, and when the long facades of the buildings are oblique to the wind, actually enhances the urban ventilation (see Effect of Urban Density and Building Height on Urban Ventilation, in Chapter 8, page 284).

At a given density level, the theoretically best urban climate conditions exist in a hot-humid climate when that density is obtained with high, narrow buildings ("towers"), placed as far apart from each other as is consistent with the given density. Such configuration provides the best ventilation conditions for the given urban section as a whole, and especially for the occupants of the buildings. Several factors contribute to this effect:

a. Narrow, "towerlike" buildings located far apart cause mixing of the airstream at higher elevations with the air near ground. Part of the wind momentum at the higher level is thus transferred to the lower level, increasing the wind speed near the ground. This effect improves the ventilation conditions for the lower floors, as well as for the pedestrians in the streets and the open spaces between the buildings.

b. With this configuration a greater proportion of the population lives and works at higher elevation above the ground. Both the temperature and the vapor pressure decrease with height, especially in a densely built-up urban area. Therefore, the comfort conditions for the people living in the upper floors are improved.

c. As the air temperature at a height of 30–40 m (98–130') is lower than the air near the ground, (which is heated by the warmer ground) the mixing of the layers from different heights lowers, generated by the high buildings, and *lowers* the air temperature at the "pedestrian level."

It should be noted, however, that high buildings involve "high" technology, both in their construction process and in their occupation patterns. In particular, high buildings need elevators and regular maintenance. Consequently, they are suitable mainly for high-income people. It should also be noted that high buildings are not suitable for families with small children, especially the large, low-income families forming the vast majority of the population in developing countries.

In summary, it seems that high-rise buildings, designated for high-income families with few or no children, can contribute to the urban climate in hot-humid regions when dispersed among lower buildings. Encouraging urban development with buildings of different heights next to each other, thus improves the urban ventilation.

REFERENCES

Davis, I.R. 1984. The Planning and Maintenance of Urban Settlements to Resist Extreme Climatic Forces. In W.M.O. (1986) 277–312.

de Carmona, L.S. 1984. Human Comfort in the Urban Tropics. In W.M.O. (1986) 354–404.

Dunne, T. 1984. Urban Hydrology in the Tropics: Problems, Solutions, Data Collection and Analysis. In W.M.O. (1986) 405–434.

Givoni, B. 1994. *Passive and Low Energy Cooling of Buildings*. New York: Van Nostrand Reinhold.

Givoni, B., M. Gulich, C. Gomez, and A. Gomez. 1996. Radiant Cooling by Metal Roofs for Developing Countries. *Proc. Twenty-first National Passive Solar Conference (25th American Solar Energy Society Conf.)*, Asheville, N.C., 13–18 April.

Landsberg. 1984. Problems of Design for Cities in the Tropics. In W.M.O. (1986) 461–472.

Lyons, T.J. 1984. Climatic Factors in the Siting of New Towns and Specialized Urban Facilities. In W.M.O. (1986) 473–486.

Nieuwolt, S. 1984. Design for Climate in Hot-Humid Cities. In W.M.O. (1986) 514–534.

World Meteorological Organization (W.M.O.). 1986. Urban Climatology and its Applications with Special Reference to Tropical Areas. Proceedings of Technical Conference held in Mexico City. November 1984.

Chapter **12:** BUILDING AND URBAN DESIGN IN COLD CLIMATES

INTRODUCTION

Cold regions are defined here as regions with average temperatures during the winter months (November through March) below freezing zero °C (32°F) and with cool-to-comfortable summer conditions. In such regions the main climatic design concerns are to minimize heating energy in the buildings, prevent discomfort from drafts, and minimize cold discomfort outdoors. Summer comfort issues in these regions are minor in comparison with the winter problems and it is assumed that just good ventilation can ensure indoor comfort.

The minor importance of the summer comfort aspects of urban and building design is the main difference between the "cold" regions, discussed in this chapter, and the regions with a cold winter but in which people experience also significant heat discomfort in summer, regions which are discussed in Chapter 13. Consequently this chapter will deal only with the winter problems and their impacts on building and on urban design.

Outdoor cold discomfort is strongly affected by the wind speed which, together with the air temperature, determines the so-called windchill. Hence the importance of wind protection in open public spaces such as streets, winter playgrounds, and parks with winter activities.

Improving the urban microclimate in cold cities can have a significant economic value as well. Pressman (1988) notes that in Canada some cities suffered from the flight of the well-to-do segments of the inhabitants, to which the harsh climate has presumably contributed, and thus reducing the tax-base of the cities.

In this respect, the possibilities of outdoor recreation and sport activities for children, adults, and the elderly, as well as minimizing the discomfort, inconvenience, and dangers involved in urban mobility in winter, may have an impact on the attractiveness of the city, especially for the population segments which have more options of employment elsewhere.

In cold cities and villages it is essential to enable the inhabitants to make easy and economical daily journeys to work, shops, schools, and so on. The attainment of these objectives requires access and affects the design of housing, employment, urban services (e.g., snow removal) and recreation. Pressman suggests the following "catalogue" of urban design ("physical realm") objectives in cold cities:

a. *Pedestrian protection* through the design of colonnades, covered arcades and galleries, through-block passages, connected atriums, and underground walkways.

b. *Optimized accessibility* by reducing outdoor walking distances to transit facilities, parking lots, major retail centers, schools, and recreation centers.

c. *Integrated development* through guidelines and policies promoting improved microclimate through appropriate urban forms and solar access, higher-density mixed-land uses, transportation corridors, and so forth.

d. *Conceptions of public spaces in relation to seasonal use:* Design and management of civic spaces and neighborhood parks to maximize year-round use. This can be achieved by multifunctional use of the major elements in the area.

The issues of cold cities are discussed at two scales: (a) the building itself and the site around it, and (b) the urban scale.

BUILDING AND EXTENDED SITE DESIGN IN COLD CLIMATES

In cold regions, as defined above, buildings are heated continuously for months during the winter. The heating season is long and the temperature difference between the heated buildings and the outdoors is large. Consequently, at the building scale, the main concern is to minimize the heat loss from the building. It means the provision of high levels of insulation to the walls, roof, and windows of the building. Heat capacity, or thermal mass, has minor impact on the heating energy use, except in buildings heated by passive solar systems.